LATENESS AND BRAHMS

AMS Studies in Music

Mary Hunter, *General Editor*

Editorial Board

Joseph H. Auner
J. Peter Burkholder
Scott Burnham
Richard Crawford
Suzanne Cusick
Louise Litterick
Ruth A. Solie
Judith Tick
Gary Tomlinson
Gretchen Wheelock

Conceptualizing Music:
Cognitive Structure, Theory, and Analysis
Lawrence Zbikowski

Inventing the Business of Opera:
The Impresario and His World in
    Seventeenth-Century Venice
Beth L. Glixon and Jonathan E. Glixon

Lateness and Brahms:
Music and Culture in the Twilight
    of Viennese Liberalism
Margaret Notley

LATENESS AND BRAHMS

Music and Culture in the
Twilight of Viennese Liberalism

Margaret Notley

OXFORD
UNIVERSITY PRESS

2007

OXFORD
UNIVERSITY PRESS

Oxford University Press, Inc., publishes works that further
Oxford University's objective of excellence
in research, scholarship, and education.

Oxford   New York
Auckland   Cape Town   Dar es Salaam   Hong Kong   Karachi
Kuala Lumpur   Madrid   Melbourne   Mexico City   Nairobi
New Delhi   Shanghai   Taipei   Toronto

With offices in
Argentina   Austria   Brazil   Chile   Czech Republic   France   Greece
Guatemala   Hungary   Italy   Japan   Poland   Portugal   Singapore
South Korea   Switzerland   Thailand   Turkey   Ukraine   Vietnam

Published by Oxford University Press, Inc.
198 Madison Avenue, New York, New York 10016

www.oup.com

Oxford is a registered trademark of Oxford University Press

Library of Congress Cataloging-in-Publication Data
Notley, Margaret Anne.
Lateness and Brahms : music and culture in the twilight of Viennese
liberalism / Margaret Notley.
p. cm.—(AMS studies in music)
Includes bibliographical references and index.
ISBN-13 978-0-19-530547-0
ISBN 0-19-530547-7
1. Brahms, Johannes, 1833–1897—Criticism and interpretation.
2. Vienna (Austria)—Intellectual life—19th century.   I. Title.   II. Series.
ML410.B8N67 2006
780.92—dc22   2006008848

ACKNOWLEDGMENTS

I thank a number of institutions and individuals for assistance of various kinds. The National Endowment for the Humanities supported my work for a year with a Fellowship for College Teachers and Independent Scholars. At different stages in the book's gestation, a Research Grant from the American Philosophical Society and a Fulbright Scholar Grant from the Austrian-American Educational Commission and J. William Fulbright Foreign Scholarship Board allowed me to conduct research in Vienna. I greatly appreciate the fact that Walter Frisch, James Hepokoski, Leon Plantinga, and the late John Daverio wrote letters on my behalf when I applied for those grants.

As a Fulbright Scholar, I was resident at the Gesellschaft der Musikfreunde in Vienna. I am grateful to Otto Biba, Director of the Archive, for allowing me extended access to Brahms's manuscripts and personal library and to George Bozarth for helping arrange my residency. Professor Doctor Biba very kindly provided, free of charge, the photographs that appear as the frontispiece and figures 3.1 and 3.2. I also wish to thank the staff of the Wiener Stadt- und Landesbibliothek for graciously honoring my requests for heavy volumes of old newspapers over many years of research and for making my research there both pleasant and efficient.

More recently I received financial assistance from the University of North Texas. This supported my work on the book for two summers, two short research trips to Vienna, acquisition of the illustration that appears as figure 1.1, and permission to use the Klimt painting as cover art. Funds from my university also paid for production of the musical examples by one of our fine graduate students, William McGinney. Except where noted, we used the collected works issued by Breitkopf & Härtel in the 1920s as the basis for the examples from Brahms's music.

Several of the chapters draw on previously published articles. I based chapter 1 on "Brahms as Liberal: Genre, Style, and Politics in Late Nineteenth-Century Vienna," *19th-Century Music* 17 (1993): 107–123. The beginning and the end are almost unchanged, but I have largely rewritten the middle of the original article. I have taken several sections of chapter 5 from "*Volksconcerte* in Vienna and Late Nineteenth-Century Ideology of the Symphony," *Journal of the American Musicological Society* 50 (1997): 421–454. (Copyright © 1997, American Musicological Society, Inc.

All rights reserved. Used by permission.) I have likewise based much of chapter 6 on "Late-Nineteenth-Century Chamber Music and the Cult of the Classical Adagio," *19th-Century Music* 23 (1999): 33–61. While other parts of chapter 6 are newly written, one section includes several paragraphs from "Brahms's Cello Sonata in F Major and Its Genesis: A Study in Half-Step Relations," in *Brahms Studies,* ed. David Brodbeck (Lincoln: University of Nebraska Press, 1994), 1:139–160. The editors of the original four articles, David Brodbeck, James Hepokoski, and Paula Higgins, gave me valuable advice, and I have incorporated many of their editorial suggestions in the revised versions that appear here.

I am grateful to Mary Hunter, Editor of the American Musicological Society Studies in Music, for having read several drafts of this manuscript. Her wise, unsparing comments were immensely helpful to someone new to the special demands of writing a book. I wish also to thank Norman Hirschy, Assistant Editor at Oxford University Press, for providing various kinds of assistance, always promptly, expertly, and cheerfully.

Daniel Beller-McKenna and I have shared an intense interest in Brahms and late nineteenth-century Austro-German politics for over a decade now. I am honored to have him as a friend and colleague. At the University of North Texas, my fellow musicologist Deanna Bush has done everything in her power to make it possible for me to finish this book, while providing a model of grace under pressure. I would also like to thank Morten Solvik, a wonderful musicologist and host, for having made my research trips to Vienna, where he resides with his family, even more pleasant than they otherwise would have been. Recently his student assistant, Amanda Fuerst, helped me by inquiring at Viennese libraries about possible illustrations.

I dedicate this book to the people to whom I feel the deepest gratitude: my mother, Beulah Notley, my husband, Fred Yackulic, and our sons, Will, Charles, and Ethan. I could work on this book only because of their loving and patient support.

CONTENTS

15. Juni 1896. Letzte Aufnahme

MARIA FELLINGER

Brahms on the lawn in front of the Fellinger family's house. Photograph by Maria Fellinger with a handwritten note, "15 June 1896. Final photo." Reproduced by kind permission of the Archive of the Gesellschaft der Musikfreunde, Vienna.

LATENESS AND BRAHMS

LATENESS AND BRAHMS

One of the most celebrated moments in Brahms's music comes near the end of the F Major String Quintet's middle movement, completed in 1882.[1] The movement has combined the typically contrasting keys, affects, and tempos of a slow movement and scherzo, three Grave sections in C-sharp minor/major alternating with two interludes in A major, an Allegretto vivace and a Presto. Remarkably, though the two types are contained within one movement, the contrast between them is more striking than usual in Brahms, the keys and types seemingly irreconcilable. The coda of the final Grave, like the two that preceded it, consists of a bare, circular chord progression. (See ex. I.1a and b for the first and third codas.)

In each of the previous codas, the progression moved twice, relentlessly, from a C-sharp minor triad through an altered A major triad and a Neapolitan chord to a full cadence in C-sharp minor. The coda of the third Grave begins with a C-sharp *major* tonic followed by an unaltered A major triad, but it appears as if the concluding tonic will still be C-sharp. After two statements of the chord progression, however, Brahms rhythmically augments the first two chords and proceeds no further, repeating the chords as if considering which to settle on as tonic: the sense of subjective presence is strong. In an extraordinary plagal cadence, C-sharp major cedes to A major, a D minor triad, the minor Neapolitan in C-sharp major/minor, reinterpreted as the minor subdominant in A major.[2] In suggesting conscious thought and human agency, the ending conveys a psychological drama unprecedented in instrumental music, a thinking subject seeming to choose a key and the associations it has accumulated in the course of a movement.[3]

---

1. See the appendix for a list of Brahms's multimovement instrumental works.

2. In a type of enharmonic reinterpretation motivated by organicist impulses and therefore beloved by nineteenth-century composers, the E-sharp in the altered (augmented) A major triad of the first and second codas becomes F-natural in the plagal cadence of the final coda.

3. The Viennese critic Theodor Helm called the ending "Beethovenian, moving," but no comparable moment occurs in Beethoven. *Beethoven's Streichquartette: Versuch einer technischen Analyse dieser Werke im Zusammenhange mit ihrem geistigen Gehalt* (Leipzig: C. F. W. Siegel, 1885), 318. As Donald Tovey observed, "nothing else like this is to be found in music." "Brahms's Chamber Music," in *The Main Stream of Music and Other Essays* (Cleveland: Meridian Books, 1959), 259.

EXAMPLE I.1a.   Brahms, F Major String Quintet, Op. 88 / II, mm. 26–31

This moment has a bearing on several overlapping themes of this book. One theme concerns concepts of genre and especially various kinds of cultural significance assigned to chamber music and slow movements. In this instance, not only does the movement's conclusion depend on Brahms's manipulation of meanings embedded in the genres of slow movement and scherzo but also it is a quintessential chamber-music moment. Critics have often observed that Brahms always composed in chamber style; in doing so, they usually single out the extreme refinement and complexity of the technical details in his music. But inwardness and expressive subtleties are also characteristic of both chamber music and slow movements.

EXAMPLE I.1.b.   Brahms, F Major String Quintet, Op. 88 / II, mm. 196–208

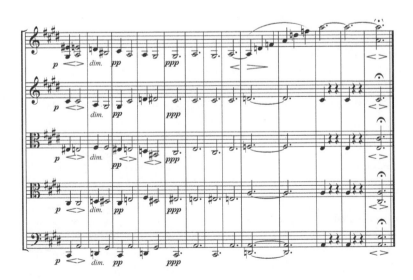

The quality of the inwardness in Brahms's conclusion, with its clearly implied reflecting subject, places the Quintet near the turn of the twentieth century: the moment sounds of its time. Interest in the human mind had been strong throughout the nineteenth century, as new frameworks for understanding the psyche were developed, and would culminate toward the century's end in Sigmund Freud's epoch-making work. While the immediate Viennese milieu in the final decade and a half of Brahms's life was a center for innovative ideas about psychology, this particular musical moment resonates more with lingering "premodern"—that is, Liberal—concepts of human reason and agency. Like earlier forms of Liberalism, nineteenth-century variants privileged the rational will of individuals, a position problematized by Freud's discoveries and other aspects of an emerging modernist outlook. A second theme of this book is the specific historicity of Brahms's music.

In certain respects, Brahms's movement can be compared to the "Heiliger Dank-gesang" from Beethoven's late A Minor String Quartet (Op. 132, completed in 1825). The "Heiliger Dankgesang" resembles Brahms's movement in that it alternates slow and fast sections, and it conveys a more explicit drama through detailed expressive markings for each: "Holy Song of Thanks to the Godhead from a Convalescent, in the Lydian Mode" and "Feeling New Strength." Stark contrast between the F faux-Lydian of the slow sections and the D major of the faster interludes is also essential to Beethoven's movement, but the tonal center is never in question: an earlier composer would not have applied tonality in instrumental music as Brahms did. Although the F Major String Quintet is usually placed slightly before Brahms's personal "late period," he composed it during the late period of common-practice tonality and the genres, forms, and other conventions associated with it. Other themes of this book are lateness within Brahms's oeuvre and in broad historical and music-historical narratives that encompass him and his time.

LATE STYLE AND MUSIC-HISTORIC LATENESS

Motivating my selection of these themes is a wish to counter the common tendency to regard Brahms in neutralized, ahistorical terms. This tendency, which makes the composer and his music seem considerably less interesting than they are, became apparent soon after he died in 1897. In 1912 the Viennese critic Richard Specht observed: "Scarcely any other master of his art has become a 'classic' so quickly after his death as Johannes Brahms," adding that his music was already seen as "timeless." Specht found it problematic that a mere fifteen years after his death Brahms had turned into a canonic figure admired from a distance.[4] The early metamorphosis of the composer into a transhistorical figure continued in much subsequent scholarship, which has often positioned him only among his friends and family and considered his compositions within those restricted circles.[5]

---

4. "Zum Brahms-Problem," *Der Merker* 3 (1912): 41 and 46. Here, as elsewhere in this book, the translations are my own, unless otherwise indicated.

5. See, for example, the admirable life-and-works treatment by Karl Geiringer, *Brahms: His Life and Work,* 3rd ed. (New York: Da Capo Press, 1981). For some new directions in English-language scholarship on Brahms, see work by Daniel Beller-McKenna, Kevin Karnes, and Sandra McColl listed in the bibliography.

Western Marxism, with its utter commitment to historical perspectives, offers one vital alternative. Especially in the years between the two world wars, accounts informed by Western Marxist ideas tried to bring order to the musical heritage of the eighteenth and nineteenth centuries, the middle-class era, when Liberalism and the free-market capitalism associated with that worldview had been ascendant in Europe. The authors, who include such significant figures as Theodor Adorno, Ernst Křenek, and Paul Bekker, regarded the *bürgerlich* culture of tonal music as having come to an end and, consequently, that music as a closed repertory they could contemplate in its entirety. Hence Bekker wrote a highly influential brief survey of the symphony from Beethoven to Mahler.[6] Writers concerned with music and social history, and especially those working within Marxist critical traditions, recognize Brahms's importance as a crucial representative of that culture in its late phase.

Lateness is indeed a central concept in this vein of criticism: Brahms composed during a late historical period, using conventions of common-practice tonality that had grown old and at the same time become so customary as to seem rooted in nature. Georg Lukács, a seminal Western Marxist literary critic, made a related point about the social milieu that gave rise to the novel, using the term "second nature" to signify "the world of convention."[7] Adorno latched onto this idea in his philosophical and sociological writings, as well as in his work on music, where he repeatedly invokes second nature in reference to tonality and its semblance of naturalness. Thus in *Philosophie der neuen Musik* he writes: "The second nature of the tonal system is historically formed appearance." And he connects the structure of tonality directly to that of capitalism, "whose own dynamic strives toward totality and with whose fungibility that of all tonal elements corresponds most profoundly."[8] Adorno's reinterpretations of Lukács's evocative concept have wide applicability to the late nineteenth century, when the putative naturalness of the Liberal worldview came under growing critical scrutiny, and more particularly to Brahms, who in his late works had to force meaning back into the second nature of tonality's conventions. No one thus far appears to have given sustained attention to implications for Brahms studies of ideas sketched by Lukács, Adorno, Bekker, and others.

Adorno's own neglect of Brahms is most surprising. In many references, usually short and fragmentary, he revealed how important Brahms was for his understanding of music history. To be sure, he did develop his ideas about the composer at some length in three books: *Philosophie der neuen Musik, Einleitung in der Musiksoziologie,* and a manuscript on Beethoven unfinished at his death and published much later. But he devoted no extended work exclusively to Brahms, merely a short, posthumously published essay that dates from 1934 and a peripherally important review, published in 1932, of an edition of the piano music.[9]

---

6. *Die Sinfonie von Beethoven bis Mahler* (Berlin: Schuster und Loeffler, 1918). Many writers, including Adorno, place the beginning of the middle-class era earlier.

7. *The Theory of the Novel: A Historico-Philosophical Essay on the Forms of Great Epic Literature,* trans. Anna Bostock (Cambridge, Mass.: MIT Press, 1971), 63. Lukács completed the book in 1916; it was first published in 1920.

8. *Philosophie der neuen Musik* (Frankfurt am Main: Suhrkamp Verlag, 1976), 20.

9. The essay, "Brahms aktuell," and the review, "Eduard Steuermanns Brahms-Ausgabe," both appear in vol. 18 of *Gesammelte Schriften: Musikalische Schriften V,* ed. Rolf Tiedemann and Klaus Schultz

For the most part, Adorno left only a number of frustratingly brief but suggestive allusions to the composer. Beyond a few vague references to "the later Brahms," moreover, he never addressed late style in Brahms, although he made substantial contributions to late-style theories in essays on Goethe, Wagner, and Beethoven.[10] Late-style criticism, as represented in these essays, focuses on stylistic development within an artist's lifework. In this portion of his oeuvre, Adorno was working within a tradition, largely German-language, that had no necessary ties to Marxism. While late style and music-historic lateness are based on different assumptions, both concepts offer valid frameworks for considering Brahms's later music and can be brought into illuminating alignment, each conditioning the other. They stand in a dialectical relationship.

When Adorno wrote about Brahms's music, he usually focused on matters of themes, motives, and form as part of a broad historical narrative that presents the composer as a link between Beethoven and Schoenberg. An artist's style, however, transcends single types of technical features such as these. It appears that Adorno could not closely consider Brahms's style in all its complexity, much less the possibility of stylistic change, because the idea of music-historic lateness so strongly colored his perspective. Consequently, the composer's oeuvre emerges as a more or less undifferentiated group of works. Still, Adorno's late-style criticism and his few scattered comments about Brahms have unexplored potential for understanding the composer's late music.

More recent German writers have brought other valuable perspectives to bear on Brahms studies. Tibor Kneif, for example, emphasizes that he was a middle-class composer: in Kneif's words, "middle-class in the nineteenth-century sense," that being the only century "truly dominated by the middle class."[11] Christian Martin Schmidt likewise notes that his habits as artist and as private individual exemplified middle-class virtues, and he observes three topoi in Brahms reception: chamber-music composer, Classical or last Classical composer, academic composer.[12] While neither Schmidt nor Kneif connects these personal traits of Brahms and themes in the reception of his music to an immediate context, they took on charged, local significance in late nineteenth-century Vienna.

(Frankfurt am Main: Suhrkamp Verlag, 1984). The unfinished manuscript was published as *Beethoven: The Philosophy of Music,* ed. Rolf Tiedemann and trans. Edmund Jephcott (Stanford: Stanford University Press, 1998).

10. "On the Final Scene of *Faust,*" in *Notes to Literature,* ed. Rolf Tiedemann and trans. Shierry Weber Nicholsen (New York: Columbia University Press, 1991), 1:111–120; "On the Score of *Parsifal,*" trans. Anthony Barone, *Music and Letters* 76 (1995): 384–397. "Alienated Masterpiece: The *Missa Solemnis,*" trans. Duncan Smith and Richard Leppert, and "Late Style in Beethoven," trans. Susan H. Gillespie, are both reprinted in *Essays on Music,* ed. Richard Leppert (Berkeley: University of California Press, 2002), 564–583. "Ludwig van Beethoven: Six Bagatelles for Piano, Op. 126" is reprinted in *Beethoven,* 130–132. This posthumously published book offers many additional insights into Beethoven's late style.

11. "Brahms—Ein bürgerlicher Künstler," in *Johannes Brahms: Leben und Werk,* ed. Christiane Jacobsen (Wiesbaden: Breitkopf und Härtel, 1983), 9–13.

12. *Johannes Brahms und seine Zeit,* 2nd ed. (Laaber: Laaber-Verlag, 1998), 56–64 and 163.

BRAHMS IN THE TWILIGHT YEARS
OF VIENNESE LIBERALISM

Until the 1990s, commentary on the older Brahms rarely situated him in *fin-de-siècle* Vienna, the city of Gustav Mahler and Freud, among others.[13] Brahms's position within this turbulent milieu must account for the oversight. In Vienna, as elsewhere in Europe, the advent of the first wave of modernism in about 1890 virtually coincided with the movement toward mass democracy and the decline of classic middle-class—Liberal—culture. To both supporters and critics of Liberalism in the city's music circles at the time, Brahms had little to do with the new; rather, he embodied the waning culture.

A number of scholars have explored the paradoxical confluence of coarse-grained politics and extraordinary intellectual and artistic vitality in Vienna at the turn of the twentieth century.[14] Several closely spaced events suggest the rapid pace of change in the city. Shortly before Brahms died in the spring of 1897, Karl Lueger took office as mayor after having ousted the Liberal incumbent through a strategic blend of politicized, anti-Semitic Catholicism and rabble-rousing, at times German-nationalist populism. During that same spring, forty members of the Künstlerhaus (Artists' House) resigned and formed the Secession to promote innovation in the visual arts; half a year later, Mahler, though Jewish, assumed leadership of the city's preeminent cultural institution, the Hofoper (Court Opera). Two facts in themselves situate Brahms squarely in *fin-de-siècle* Vienna: Dr. Josef Breuer, who had collaborated with Freud on *Studies on Hysteria* in 1895, served as Brahms's physician in his final illness; and Lueger, whom Brahms had despised, attended the composer's funeral in his official capacity as the city's mayor.[15]

In the decade and a half before the watershed of 1897, longstanding antagonism between so-called progressive and conservative musical factions had taken an intensely politicized turn in Vienna. Progressivism in music was associated above all with Richard Wagner, whose death in 1883 happened to coincide with the formation of a viable anti-Liberal movement in Vienna. Wagnerism went on to play a critical role in that movement and the attendant transformation of political conduct, the emphasis on theatricality and appeals to emotion that enabled Lueger's rise to power. Many of the Wagnerites challenging the Liberal worldview in the final decades of the nineteenth century were young people in revolt against a society that privileged middle age over youth and reason over instinct and emotion.[16] As a matter of course, they disdained Brahms as much as they revered Wagner and other progressive composers.

---

13. Leon Botstein, "Brahms and Nineteenth-Century Painting," *19th-Century Music* 14 (1990): 154–168; and Margaret Notley, "Brahms as Liberal: Genre, Style, and Politics in Late Nineteenth-Century Vienna," *19th-Century Music* 17 (1993): 107–123.

14. See, especially, two collections of essays by Carl E. Schorske, *Fin-de-Siècle Vienna: Politics and Culture* (New York: Vintage Books, 1981), and *Thinking with History: Explorations in the Passage to Modernism* (Princeton, N.J.: Princeton University Press, 1998).

15. Max Kalbeck, *Johannes Brahms,* 4 vols. (Tutzing: Hans Schneider, 1976), 4:498–499 for Breuer and 4:521 for Lueger.

16. See Schorske, "Generational Tension and Cultural Change," in *Thinking with History,* 141–156.

Brahms's very status as, in Schmidt's words, "chamber-music composer" acquired political meaning in late nineteenth-century Vienna. Critics who favor a broad view of music history, such as Adorno and Bekker, as well as Schmidt, often oppose symphonies to chamber music: the one aimed at a wider audience and thus supposedly more direct in its appeal, the other reserved for an elite few. Within the narrower context of late nineteenth-century Vienna, ideas about genre became overtly political for activist musicians who took the implications of those ideas seriously. Thus the populist sentiments of the time tended to give the allegedly more accessible genre of the symphony even greater stature than it already possessed. Yet the symphony, like the other genres that had developed with tonality, had itself gone into a widely recognized decline. In a recent book about Brahms's Second Symphony, Reinhold Brinkmann writes about the aging of the symphonic genre and writes eloquently, as well, about contemporary artists' perceptions that their time was a late period.[17] General themes of historical lateness and a perceived decline in music but also of historical aspects of Brahms's music more specific to the time and place likewise converge in my consideration of him and his milieu.

A sense that an era had ended emerges clearly in writing from the early twentieth century. After the death of Brahms and the almost simultaneous dissolution of Liberal hegemony, some former rebels came to regard him with greater sympathy, without, however, tempering their emphatic rejection of the culture in which he had played a central role. Such selective rewriting of history no doubt fostered the transformation of Brahms into a "timeless" classic. Passages in essays by the Austrian writer Hermann Bahr illustrate the bifurcated view of Brahms and the Liberal milieu I am referring to. In 1911, Bahr described Austrian Liberals as "people living only from the brain, possessing nothing other than a fine little collection of ideas, ideas imported from the West with which they now intended to take care of everything."[18] Bahr continued to look down on his father's ideology of reason, part of the "religion" of blind assumptions that had supported the interests of the Liberal middle class. But in a 1912 essay about Brahms, he made it clear he had changed his mind about the composer, with whom he had earlier found similar fault.

A remark by Hugo Wolf that Bahr quoted in his 1912 essay demonstrates the extreme antipathy both had felt toward Brahms in the late 1880s. In conversation with Bahr, Wolf voiced an opinion many young people in Vienna seem to have held at the time: he dismissed the older composer's works as "brain music" (*Gehirn-musik*).[19] In 1912, however, Bahr probed subtleties of expression he and his contemporaries had ignored when the composer was still alive; like other members of his generation, he retrospectively corrected his earlier exaggeration of Brahms's reliance on intellect. Viewing a recently completed statue of the composer displayed in the Berlin Secession had reminded Bahr of the deep affinity its forward-looking

17. *Late Idyll: The Second Symphony of Johannes Brahms,* trans. Peter Palmer (Cambridge, Mass.: Harvard University Press, 1995).

18. *Austriaca* (Berlin: S. Fischer Verlag, 1911), 9.

19. Bahr, "Brahms," in *Essays* (Leipzig: Insel-Verlag, 1912), 41.

sculptor, Max Klinger, felt for Brahms's music.[20] More fundamentally, Bahr could revise his attitude toward Brahms because new forces and ideas had successfully confronted the hegemonic culture with which the composer had been so closely linked in Vienna.

In a number of respects, an era can be said to have come to a close around the turn of the twentieth century.[21] Some recent historians of course suggest that the "long nineteenth century," which began with events leading up to the French Revolution, concluded only with the dissolution of the German, Ottoman, and Austro-Hungarian empires after the First World War.[22] No doubt more profound changes did occur in the wake of the First World War than at the close of the nineteenth century. Even the supposed end of tonality, the "first step on a new path" Arnold Schoenberg took in 1908 or 1909, did not occur until more than a decade after the political eclipse of Viennese Liberalism.[23] Yet Brahms rightly considered himself to be the last in a line of composers, as the final distinguished product of pedagogical traditions he had had to reconstruct for his own purposes.[24] Bahr's revisionism in 1912 notwithstanding, the tradition that ended with Brahms had in fact placed high value on a kind of intellect in music. And the types of coherence his own conception of "musical logic" encompassed were for the most part not only particular to tonal music but also linked temporally and ideologically with the ascendancy of the Liberal worldview in eighteenth- and nineteenth-century Europe. Brahms thus wrote his late music during the twilight years of Liberal politics and musical culture in Vienna.

While cultural historians have given the Viennese *fin de siècle* a great deal of attention, the decades before the turn of the century have received less notice, as has the more conservative art that continued to be produced even as modernism increasingly overshadowed it.[25] The irredeemable dreariness of much establishment art from the late nineteenth century, especially in comparison with the new art's excitement, goes far toward explaining the disproportion. Still, Brahms's compositions, many of which have long been staples of the concert repertory, derived from, indeed helped create, the culture that went into decline around the turn of the century. The very

20. On Klinger, see Botstein, "Brahms and Nineteenth-Century Painting," 165–168; and Thomas K. Nelson, "Brahms's Fantasies: In Accorde with Max Klinger," *American Brahms Society Newsletter* 18/1 (spring 2000): 1–5, and 18/2 (fall 2000): 4–7.

21. Carl Dahlhaus argues for considering the years between 1889 and 1914 a period in musical as well as social and political history. *Nineteenth-Century Music,* trans. J. Bradford Robinson (Berkeley: University of California Press, 1989), 330–332. As Mary Hunter pointed out to me, the long nineteenth century comes into conflict with a potential long twentieth century in these attempts at periodization.

22. David Blackbourn, *The Long Nineteenth Century: A History of Germany, 1780–1918* (New York: Oxford University Press, 1998).

23. "How One Becomes Lonely," in *Style and Idea: Selected Writings of Arnold Schoenberg,* ed. Leonard Stein and trans. Leo Black (Berkeley: University of California Press, 1984), 49.

24. See chapter 4.

25. An exception is *Pre-modern Art of Vienna 1848–1898,* ed. Leon Botstein and Linda Weintraub (Annandale-on-Hudson, N.Y.: Edith C. Blum Art Institute, 1987). William J. McGrath explored an earlier period but focused on the developing anti-Liberal movement in *Dionysian Art and Populist Politics in Austria* (New Haven: Yale University Press, 1974).

sense of being outdated, the tension between Brahms and the changing times, may have given rise to a body of compositions in his oeuvre that have the peculiar, ambivalent qualities of "late works."

OTHER SOURCES, METHODOLOGY, AND OVERVIEW

The historical perspectives in this book, then, are of two kinds. On the one hand, throughout most of this book I attempt to understand Brahms and his music in the context of late nineteenth-century Vienna by exploring both what I conjecture to be his positions and what I interpret as prevailing "climates of opinion." Many of the attitudes in question concern musical genres and aspects of musical logic. On the other hand, I also develop the theme of lateness in its various manifestations. At certain points the two perspectives come together. As I discovered in the course of reading a great deal of journalistic criticism, ideas about music formulated most fully in the twentieth century by Bekker, Adorno, and others have traceable origins in the late nineteenth century. This is not surprising, since Marxism developed out of Liberalism, in response to both its strong points and its shortcomings. Because Brahms composed his late works at the end of an era, furthermore, historical lateness as explored in Marxist writing converges at times with the separate tradition of late-style criticism. Both perceptions of lateness warrant further elaboration and, even more important, offer a hermeneutic point of entry into compositions by the older Brahms. For my abiding love of that music was the fundamental impetus for writing this book.

During more than a decade of research, I read countless reviews and articles from contemporary newspapers and music journals. These have a value like that of music dictionaries, treatises, textbooks, and so on, in that they provide firsthand glimpses of musical and general cultural life in Vienna and elsewhere. While I do not consider contemporary reception necessarily to have a privileged position over other criticism, it helped me understand the origins of the twentieth-century interpretive traditions that interest me. Contemporary reception, moreover, sometimes suggests an unforeseen angle on the music, allows one to uncover fresh critical categories that otherwise would not have come to mind. For me this is the greatest reward these sources have to offer. In the beginning, Brahms's absence in, for example, Carl Schorske's accounts of Viennese culture perplexed me. By working with neglected contemporary sources, including passages in Max Kalbeck's biography of Brahms, I came to understand why scholars had overlooked his role in the culture.

I did not start out with a methodology; if I had, it would have predetermined what I found. Rather, I developed a methodological framework as I began to see possible patterns in the reception, which I tested against other ideas and scholarship using basic procedures of critical thinking. Through lengthy immersion in the journalistic sources, I became acquainted with the various writers' strengths and limitations, as well as with the overall tone of the periodicals they wrote for. Then, as now, certain critics are unilluminating, even incompetent; I have therefore rarely included their work. In those instances when I have chosen, say, to cite an anonymous review, I do so because the journalist best expresses a view that appears in other reviews, as well. The critics whose work I use most extensively wrote for papers or journals significant for one reason or another, or had important careers, usually not confined to journalism.

Thus a number of the critics played several roles in the city's music worlds, which tends to make their reviews more valuable than most music criticism, by definition an ephemeral kind of writing. They include the authors of the first substantial biographies of Brahms and Anton Bruckner: Kalbeck, who also translated opera librettos, and August Göllerich, a former student of Liszt who was active as a pianist.[26] Kalbeck's work as a critic is relatively well known, especially in the Bruckner literature, where his reviews are cited as evidence of the abuse Bruckner endured in Vienna. Göllerich, who briefly wrote reviews for a significant anti-Semitic newspaper in the city, oddly enough has received almost no attention.[27] Knowing the journalistic work of both writers and their place in Viennese music life makes it easier to understand blind spots in their biographies, both of which contain documentary evidence of the time, all the more interesting because of the authors' clear biases.

The sheer bulk of the information in these biographies and other sources causes problems. Although Brahms's famous self-protective reticence makes it difficult for scholars to conduct certain kinds of research, the wealth of other types of documents means that potentially enlightening passages sometimes go unnoticed.[28] At least several volumes of Brahms's letters, for instance, contain material of unrecognized importance, as does perhaps the most useful source of all, a diary kept by the Viennese musician and journalist Richard Heuberger, in which he recorded conversations with the composer.[29] Working with these printed sources, as with the journalism of the time, usually entails additional research to reconstruct and elucidate obscure events and attitudes the authors allude to.

Brahms's personal library, most of which he left to the archive of the Gesellschaft der Musikfreunde in Vienna, provides other insights because of his habit of marking in books and journals as he read them. The Gesellschaft der Musikfreunde also owns valuable manuscripts of Brahms: the autographs of much of the music discussed here, as well as an unusual extant sketch, which I discuss in chapter 3, and his so-called collection of octaves and fifths, the topic of chapter 4.

---

26. Göllerich, *Anton Bruckner: Ein Lebens- und Schaffens-bild,* 4 vols. in 9, vols. 2–4, ed. Max Auer (Regensburg: Gustav Bosse Verlag, 1974).

27. Other anti-Semitic critics who supported Bruckner come up in recent literature on him, but Göllerich is oddly absent. I discuss this in "Bruckner and Viennese Wagnerism," in *Bruckner Studies,* ed. Paul Hawkshaw and Timothy L. Jackson (Cambridge: Cambridge University Press, 1997), 54–71.

28. Brahms burned most of his compositional sketches and drafts, as well as much of his early correspondence with Clara Schumann, and he became guarded about personal matters in his later correspondence.

29. See the published correspondence listed in the bibliography. I shall refer to volumes published by the Deutsche Brahms-Gesellschaft as *Brahms Briefwechsel.* Heuberger's diary appeared as *Erinnerungen an Johannes Brahms: Tagebuchnotizen aus den Jahren 1875 bis 1897,* ed. Kurt Hofmann, 2nd ed. (Tutzing: Hans Schneider, 1976).

The chapters move between detailed treatment of certain musical pieces—and critical traditions relevant to them—and consideration of the contexts in which Brahms's late style developed. After lengthy examination of the available sources, I concluded that a person of his acuity was capable of modifying his political outlook and that he seems in fact to have done so; for me, this conclusion was crucial for understanding his late works. I explore his political views in chapter 1 and the epilogue, with emphasis in the former on the 1880s and in the latter on the 1890s. Beyond beginning a discussion of Brahms's politics, chapter 1 places the composer in the Vienna of his later years by focusing on the politicized conflicts between the factions around Bruckner and Brahms and suggesting that genres and musical logic had significance beyond that attributed to the concepts today. In chapter 2, I introduce the topic of late style, still working with contemporary reception but also with twentieth-century criticism devoted to the topic.

Chapters 3 and 4 have to do with both music-historic lateness and Brahms's late style. Chapter 3 moves away from the immediate context to address the more general tradition of regarding Brahms as a middle-class composer, a tradition represented in the work of Kneif and Schmidt, as well as Adorno and other Marxist critics. My musical commentary concentrates on questions concerning thematic style in a late form and in Brahms's own late period. In chapter 4, I connect the manuscript collection, which he worked on in his final years, to the new field of musicology, arguing that together they served as one source of renewal for his final chamber compositions, the F Minor and E-flat Clarinet Sonatas.

Chapter 5 demonstrates connections between concepts of genre in Brahms's time and later formulations by Bekker and others and asserts the relevance of Jürgen Habermas's well-known monograph on the public sphere to ideas about the symphony. In chapter 6, I reconstruct a critical tradition of viewing the adagio as a genre. This perspective, an example of the fresh critical category I mentioned earlier, now seems self-evident to me because of the centrality of adagios in late nineteenth- and early twentieth-century music. Yet I arrived at it empirically by reading many reviews and other documents from that period in which I noted recurrent idealizing references to adagios and the occasional transformation of the adagio into a metaphor. Chapters 5 and 6 both discuss the role of genre concepts in narratives of decline, which became prominent in late nineteenth-century public discourse. In these chapters and elsewhere, I take for granted that choices of language often matter a great deal, a premise that comes into play in several ways, for example, in analyzing imagery linked with particular genres. More broadly, uses of language had become vital in Brahms's Vienna in transforming the sociopolitical status quo.

When I write about his music, I assume the validity of concepts of structural levels, and thus of structural dominants and tonics, ideas associated most closely with the writings of Heinrich Schenker, a younger contemporary of Brahms. But I have used other theoretical approaches when they had something to offer for understanding a particular piece or passage. Again, I did not want to predetermine what I would hear in the music by limiting myself to one methodology. Within this eclectic theoretical framework, I attempt to answer a number of questions. In what respects does Brahms's late music sound different from his earlier music? How has he addressed the problems caused by the aging tonal conventions he worked with?

Where did he find renewal, both within and outside traditions of common-practice classical music? Ideas of late style and historical and music-historical lateness provide an illuminating foundation for understanding, in context, music that has too often been separated from the culture it helped create and the music-historical approaches it partially inspired. The music of a historical Brahms takes on rich and nuanced meaning not possible when it is considered in isolation.

CHAPTER I

BRAHMS AS LIBERAL,
BRUCKNER AS OTHER

In an account of Brahms's dissatisfactions with Vienna, Kalbeck recalled that after Wagner's death, "music got mixed up with politics, and obscurantists from various parties had their hands in the matter." His biographer was referring to Brahms's anger in the 1880s at the "anti-German" policies of the Conservative Czech-Polish-Clerical coalition then in power in the Austrian government: the composer believed that priestly machinations lay behind the unsatisfactory state of affairs. Kalbeck added that "musical conditions in the imperial city also did not please him." Using the religious theme of *Parsifal* as a tenuous connective to the previous topic of suspected Catholic intrigues, he seized the opportunity to lash out at "sanctimonious demagogues" who had found Wagner's music useful because it "suppresses the intellect and unleashes the senses."[1] This remarkable account, which mingles the perspectives of Brahms and Kalbeck, displays a complex of attitudes that students of nineteenth-century Austrian cultural history will recognize as basic aspects of the Liberal worldview: pro-German sentiment, antagonism toward the Catholic Church, and profound distrust of anti-intellectual trends.

Kalbeck's treatment of the opposition, Bruckner, within the Brahms biography is no less telling. According to Kalbeck, part of Bruckner's appeal after Wagner's death lay in a politically motivated reaction against Brahms: "The troops called up to arms against Brahms received fortification from extremists of various reactionary religious, political, and social congregations."[2] While Kalbeck acknowledged the unwarranted harshness of Brahms's own stance toward Bruckner, he carefully avoided mentioning the vicious journalistic assaults on Bruckner in the 1880s that Carl Dahlhaus later deemed "one of the sorriest chapters in the history of music criticism."[3] Ample evidence supports Dahlhaus's view. The attacks on Bruckner by the critics Eduard Hanslick, Gustav Dömpke, and Kalbeck himself were both brutal and personal: in one well-known, scurrilous review, Dömpke called the com-

---

1. *Brahms,* 3:402–403.
2. *Brahms,* 3:404.
3. *Nineteenth-Century Music,* 271.

poser an "Untermensch" and said that he composed "like a drunk."[4] But Dahlhaus's further judgment that these attacks "struck a man who, unlike Wagner, was largely unable to defend himself" requires some qualification. Bruckner received ardent support in the conflict from an unexpected journalistic source: the press of the Pan-Germans and the Christian Socials, the most important of the right-wing anti-Liberal parties formed during that decade.

In a curious twist of fate, some of the broader cultural dimensions of the Bruckner–Brahms controversy survived in Bruckner scholarship but, despite the tantalizing leads in Kalbeck, disappeared in the literature on Brahms.[5] Indeed, when I began dissertation research, I discovered I could find out more about Brahms's Viennese milieu by reading work on Bruckner than on Brahms himself. An array of factors, including smoldering resentment about the mistreatment of Bruckner, no doubt caused the disparity in the reception histories of the two composers; one result, an ahistorical Brahms, fits into a familiar pattern.

What ostensibly lay at the center of the Bruckner–Brahms dispute was an artistic disagreement concerning the relative merits of melodic inspiration and logical elaboration, stereotypically opposed musical desiderata that were linked to the contrasting connotations of the symphonic and chamber genres.[6] The argument, though, was not solely aesthetic. As Kalbeck claimed, it acquired political overtones and is best understood within the context of late nineteenth-century Vienna.

Both composers lived permanently in Vienna from the late 1860s until their deaths in 1896 (Bruckner) and 1897 (Brahms). Their residence thus corresponds closely with the brief period of dominance of political Liberalism in the city: 1867–97. Austrian Liberals resembled other nineteenth-century European Liberals in their general belief in progress and each individual's right to self-fulfillment and in their espousal of scientific methods and laissez-faire economics. And like other European Liberals, many Liberals in Austria overlooked the fact that most of the population neither benefited from the economic system nor enjoyed the privilege of self-realization, a shortsightedness that would contribute greatly to Liberalism's undoing.

What distinguished the Austrian variant from Liberalism in other parts of Europe was its short ascendancy and its circumscribed constituency within the multicultural empire. Despite the strong presence of the Catholic Church, Austrian Liberals tended to be resolutely anticlerical, and the party drew its members from an

---

4. Dömpke wrote in the same review, of Bruckner's Seventh Symphony, "explanations for abnormalities must be sought," *Wiener Allgemeine Zeitung,* 30 March 1886, quoted in Manfred Wagner, *Bruckner: Leben-Werke-Dokumente* (Mainz: Schott, 1983), 174.

5. In addition to Wagner, *Bruckner,* see his "Bruckner in Wien: Ein Beitrag zur Apperzeption und Rezeption des oberösterreichischen Komponisten in der Hauptstadt der k. k. Monarchie"; and Johannes-Leopold Mayer, "Musik als gesellschaftliches Ärgernis—Oder: Anton Bruckner, der Anti-Bürger: Das Phänomen Bruckner als historisches Problem." Both essays are in *Anton Bruckner in Wien: Eine kritische Studie zu seiner Persönlichkeit,* ed. Franz Grasberger (Graz: Akademischer Druck- u. Verlagsanstalt, 1980).

6. Constantin Floros calls the aesthetic issue "Einfallsapologetik gegen Verherrlichung der Ausarbeitung," in *Brahms und Bruckner: Studien zur musikalischen Exegetik* (Wiesbaden: Breitkopf und Härtel, 1980), 30–34. See also Bryan Gilliam, "The Two Versions of Bruckner's Eighth Symphony," *19th-Century Music* 16 (1992): 60–61.

intellectual elite: the educated, culturally formed German and Jewish-German middle and upper middle classes, the so-called *Bildungsbürgertum*.[7] In 1867, Austria had ratified a constitution that implemented Liberal ideas of religious freedom and equality before the law. Viennese Jews felt an especially strong allegiance to the Liberal party, often referred to as the *Verfassungspartei* (Constitution Party), for the "1867 Constitution was from the standpoint of Austrian Jewry the culmination of the long struggle for emancipation."[8]

Still, the Liberals maintained a majority in the central government only until 1879, and they were increasingly under attack in Vienna thereafter. The 1880s witnessed a growing cleft in Viennese society, with the rise of political leaders representing various dissatisfied constituencies—the lower middle and working classes, Slavic nationalists, Pan-German extremists, and discontented Catholics from every social stratum, including the aristocracy—who eventually broke the Liberals' hold on the city. Rebellious university students figured especially in the Pan-Germans, the group on the outermost part of the right-wing fringe. Of the leaders to emerge during that decade, however, the most successful proved to be Lueger, who received much of his initial support from the lower Catholic clergy and the newly enfranchised lower middle class. When Lueger took office as mayor in 1897, it marked the end of political Liberalism in Vienna.

The Bruckner–Brahms conflict played out against the backdrop of this sociopolitical upheaval. Like the political situation, the musical controversy grew more and more heated during the 1880s, as political matters increasingly spilled over into the city's musical life and Bruckner finally gained a voice through his supporters' efforts. Articles in contemporary anti-Liberal newspapers and books about Bruckner written soon after his death drew an analogy between anti-Liberal political activity and the struggle to gain a hearing for his compositions, adding that the two causes shared the same enemy: the Liberal establishment and in particular the Liberal press. One article, for example, protested an obituary by Brahms's colleague Heuberger, which had suggested that advocacy of Bruckner's music was politically motivated, arguing, to the contrary, that opposition to Bruckner "was and is a factional matter." The author, Heinrich Schuster, attributed the antagonism toward Bruckner to "the camp that represents in the musical sphere what the old Liberal does in the political" and linked the circle around Brahms with waning Liberal hegemony. Writing that the Liberal musical and political factions "use the same press organs, in fact often consist of the same people," Schuster added that these camps were "at last in the process of dying out."[9]

Each side thus accused the other of factionalism; extramusical motives were at work on both sides. On the one hand, Liberal critics of Bruckner belittled his close

7. For two commentaries on Austrian Liberal culture, see Schorske, "Politics and the Psyche: Schnitzler and Hofmannsthal," in *Fin-de-Siècle Vienna*, 5–10; and Albert Fuchs, *Geistige Strömungen in Österreich: 1867–1918* (Vienna: Globus-Verlag, 1949), 10–12.

8. Robert S. Wistrich, *The Jews of Vienna in the Age of Franz Joseph* (New York: Oxford University Press, 1989), 145.

9. Both the *Neue Freie Presse* and the *Wiener Tagblatt* had printed Heuberger's obituary. Most of Schuster's article (*Deutsche Zeitung*, 5 November 1896) is reprinted in Wagner, *Bruckner*, 221–223.

ties to the Catholic Church and his manifest *Unbildung*—Brahms himself described his rival as "a poor crazy person whom the priests of St. Florian have on their conscience."[10] On the other hand, critics in sympathy with the anti-Liberal movement saw Brahms as not merely an insider to the Viennese establishment but also a quintessential Liberal. There is a good deal of truth in that assessment: his Liberal identity extended beyond the prejudice against Catholicism he voiced more than once, beyond even his pride in being both a German and a self-made man. Indeed, values he held in common with the besieged Viennese *Bildungsbürgertum* were also fundamental to his artistic creed. As we shall see, criticism of Brahms in the 1880s culminated in overt anti-Liberal critiques at the decade's end, which focused either on his connections to the city's elite cultural institutions or on traits considered specifically Liberal—or Jewish.

POLITICAL VIEWS HELD BY BRAHMS
AND HIS VIENNESE CIRCLE

Despite his guardedness, aspects of Brahms's political outlook can be reconstructed from comments and anecdotes scattered throughout Kalbeck's biography and other sources. Brahms's German chauvinism comes through clearly in a number of stories from the 1880s. For instance, Kalbeck ascribed his decision to spend the summers of 1886–88 in Switzerland to his love of the *Oberland* climate and landscape and, perhaps, an inclination to be near a friend, the journalist and poet Josef Viktor Widmann. But Kalbeck believed Brahms's sense of outrage about the Conservative coalition that had replaced the (German) Liberals in the Austrian central government in 1879 had also motivated the composer's choice of summer residence. In Kalbeck's words, Brahms "fancied himself in the romantic role of 'political refugee'—that is to say, a Liberal German man in a depressed emotional state who turned his back, for the time being, on Minister Taaffe and his Czech-Polish-Clerical majority."[11] Brahms's pride in being a German at times veered into jingoism, and in the third of these summers it caused a temporary rupture of his relationship with Widmann. In August 1888, Widmann wrote an article critical of the new kaiser, the young Wilhelm II, to which Brahms reacted with predictable indignation, offering a defense not only of the kaiser but also, gratuitously, of Wagner and Bayreuth.[12]

Kalbeck noted that the composer's sense of German superiority had been especially strong in 1883, as well. Although it would become an untenable position by 1890, in 1883 a belief in the supremacy of German culture still had an unquestioned central place in Austrian Liberal ideology. In the spring of that year, Friedrich Maaßen, the rector at Vienna University, publicly advocated establishing a Czech elementary school in Vienna. Toward the end of June, this touched off not only demonstrations by radically pro-German students at the university but also protests by mainstream Liberals. Most notably, a large number of professors at the univer-

---

10. Kalbeck, *Brahms*, 3:408, n. 1.
11. Kalbeck, *Brahms*, 4:1.
12. Kalbeck, *Brahms*, 4:151–153.

sity signed an open address to Maaßen, published in the powerful Liberal newspaper *Neue Freie Presse,* which denounced his proposal. Among them were the celebrated surgeon Hermann Nothnagel, the geologist and political leader Eduard Sueß, and two friends of Brahms, Hanslick and the surgeon Theodor Billroth.[13] In a letter of 27 June 1883 to Billroth from his vacation place in Wiesbaden, Brahms wrote: "After reading about Vienna and Austria with increasing distress throughout the summer, I took the greatest pleasure in your letter to Rector Maaßen."[14] He made similar remarks in a letter to Hanslick:"I must shout my hurrah to someone, my happy, strong hurrah to the professors for their letter to Rector Maaßen."[15] Kalbeck connected the incident to the composer's secular outlook as well as his German identity, observing that "the free-thinking German in Brahms was angry about the increasing strength of Czech-Clerical interests in Austrian politics."[16] Writing from the perspective of 1935, Billroth's son-in-law Otto Gottlieb-Billroth, editor of the Billroth–Brahms correspondence, implicitly doubted the wisdom of their position, which he observed had been the party line of Austrian Liberals at the time. Gottlieb-Billroth characterized Brahms's views on this matter and on everything else having to do with national conflicts in the empire as those of a "learned Austrian."[17]

In this incident, as in many others, the students merely presented the Liberal older generation with a circus-mirror image of its own attitudes. Billroth had already experienced this in 1875 with the publication of his book *Über das Lehren und Lernen der medicinischen Wissenschaften an den Universitäten der deutschen Nation* (On the Teaching and Study of Medical Sciences in the German Nation's Universities).[18] Since Billroth taught in Vienna, the title of this massive tome tacitly—and significantly—grouped the city's university with others "in the German nation." The book included an excursus on the topic of poorly educated Jewish students from poverty-stricken backgrounds who came from the empire's outer provinces to study medicine in Vienna. Both the content and tone of this part of the book seem utterly unacceptable today, as they also did to many Viennese citizens then. While members of the Liberal press reproved Billroth, the university's Leseverein der deutschen Studenten (Reading Group of German Students) eagerly endorsed the unthinking anti-Semitism evident in those pages. Offering Billroth an unsolicited defense against the outcry that had followed the book's publication, the students wrote that this "was to be expected from certain organs of 'public opinion.'"[19] In

13. *Neue Freie Presse,* 24 June 1883.

14. *Billroth und Brahms im Briefwechsel,* ed. Otto Gottlieb-Billroth (Berlin: Urban und Schwarzenberg, 1935), 348.

15. Eduard Hanslick, *Am Ende des Jahrhunderts* (Berlin: Allgemeiner Verein für Deutsche Litteratur, 1899), 395–396.

16. *Brahms,* 3:382.

17. *Billroth-Brahms Briefwechsel,* 350.

18. The full title is *Über das Lehren und Lernen der medicinischen Wissenschaften an den Universitäten der deutschen Nation nebst allgemeinen Bemerkungen über Universitäten: Eine culturhistorische Studie* (Vienna: Carl Gerold's Sohn, 1876).

19. This speech was printed as "Adresse des Lesevereins der deutschen Studenten Wien's an den Professor Dr. Th. Billroth, überreicht am 15. December 1875," in a pamphlet, *Prof. Dr. Th. Billroth's Antwort auf die Adresse des Lesevereins der deutschen Studenten Wien's* (Vienna: Carl Gerold's Sohn, 1875),

his response, Billroth protested that the students had misunderstood his remarks in construing them as "an incitement to conflicts among those studying at our university, to racial hatred and similar brutalities."[20]

Shortly before the Maaßen incident, Billroth founded an organization—later called the Rudolfiner-Verein in honor of Crown Prince Rudolf, who was sympathetic to Viennese Liberals regarding many questions—to raise funds for a hospital.[21] In a reversal of the usual practice, this institution would not be associated with the Catholic Church and would be open to the wounded and ailing of all faiths. Despite Billroth's ecumenical stance in this matter and despite his experience with the university students in 1875, he failed to recognize the consequences of German nationalism and of the attendant casual anti-Semitism, paradoxical because of the ties between Jews and Liberalism. That awakening would happen later.

In a less public manner, Brahms was likewise guilty of occasional conduct that we would consider to be in poor taste, if not downright anti-Semitic, although those relating the anecdotes distanced him from that charge. Thus Daniel Spitzer, a Jewish journalist resident in Vienna, focused one of his *Neue Freie Presse* columns on his conversations with Brahms in Ischl during the summer of 1889. On the negative side, Spitzer wrote about Brahms's love of "humor and wit" and especially of the "splendid anecdotes in which Jews aptly made fun of their own weaknesses" but which they no longer felt free to tell because the stories would provide the anti-Semites with their "sharpest weapons." Yet he also referred to Brahms as someone "who earlier frequented Jewish circles only now and then, but this time has decided to spend a summer exclusively in Ischl." Spitzer's remark indicates that Ischl, a favorite summer retreat for Vienna's upper middle class and Brahms's choice for the final eight summers of his life (1889–96), had become associated with the city's Jews. (Not only the *Neue Freie Presse* but also other Viennese Liberal newspapers included reports from Ischl in summer issues, and Liberals were increasingly equated with Jews, as we shall see.) Spitzer noted: "perhaps Brahms himself will soon become the hero of a Jewish anecdote," since he had recently become familiar with Sabbath delicacies from the kitchen of a local Jew, David Sonnenschein. In his playful conclusion to this story, Spitzer speculated that Brahms might be moved to honor his host in a "Sunlight" (Sonnenschein) Sonata.[22]

An account by the composer Karl Goldmark of an unpleasant incident, which seems to have taken place in 1893, is far more damning.[23] At a dinner party, Brahms

5–7. The controversy had thus begun before the official publication of Billroth's book in 1876. A copy of the pamphlet was tipped inside Brahms's copy of the book, held by Vienna's Gesellschaft der Musikfreunde. Brahms made no marks on either the book or the pamphlet.

20. *Billroth's Antwort,* 8.

21. Letters between Billroth and the crown prince appear as an appendix to Oskar von Mitis, *Das Leben des Kronprinzen Rudolf mit Briefen und Schriften aus dessen Nachlass,* ed. Adam Wandruszka (Vienna: Herold, 1971).

22. Quoted in Kalbeck, *Brahms,* 4:175–176. In a letter of 7 August 1884, Brahms had asked Billroth to write down the stories that Adolf Exner told about Jewish students at the University. *Billroth-Brahms Briefwechsel,* 366.

23. Goldmark's piece was performed on 3 December 1893. See Richard von Perger and Robert Hirschfeld, *Geschichte der k. k. Gesellschaft der Wien,* 2 vols. (Vienna: Adolf Holzhausen, 1912), 1:312.

remarked loudly of Goldmark, "Don't you think it strange that a Jew should set a text of Martin Luther's to music?" For his part, Goldmark attributed the other composer's rage to his having overlooked the "exquisite" text for his own use. Brahms had, in fact, originally refused to believe that the work was by Luther but then discovered the truth of the matter. Goldmark also thought that Brahms might have felt guilty afterward for having lost his temper. From our present perspective, the story's most surprising aspect is the equanimity with which Goldmark told it, focusing on the intensity of Brahms's wrath rather than the offensiveness of his behavior. Goldmark prefaced his account by remarking that Brahms "was as great a man as he was an artist," adding that "there was not a blot on his superb character" but that "he was never accustomed to restraining himself nor to holding his tongue."[24] In a separate account, Richard Specht emphasized the permanent damage done to the relationship between the two men and the deep hurt that Goldmark had suffered. Yet Specht also avowed that Brahms "despised" anti-Semitism, that "he was a stranger to intolerance of any sort and held it in abhorrence."[25] As the impetus for his outburst, a text by Luther, implies, German pride and careless anti-Semitism were intertwined as late as, apparently, 1893, even for the Liberal Brahms, despite his vehement rejection of the dangerous extremes to which both had been taken by then.[26]

LIBERAL CULTURE AND MUSICAL
LOGIC AS SECOND NATURE

Liberalism was more than a political and economic philosophy. In 1905, the music critic and theorist Rudolf Louis, who had been a student in Vienna during the years around 1890, called it a "Weltanschauungskomplex," an all-encompassing way of viewing the world. Both supporters and critics acknowledged the paradoxical conservatism of the Liberals' cultural practices, Louis by voicing the repugnance he still felt for their artistic tastes. "In peculiar contrast to its name and the political and economic views it represented, Liberalism constantly professed its allegiance in aesthetic matters to a small-minded, repressive conservatism. The artistic expression of the 'Liberal' spirit was the academic-epigonous classicism that seems so thoroughly finished to us today."[27]

Looking back on the period from the perspective of 1932, the musicologist Arnold Schering showed considerably more tolerance for late nineteenth-century Liberals and their predilection for classicist as well as Classical art. According to Schering, who had grown up in the social stratum he was describing, "these circles were the true guardians of all things classical, but devoted as well to the new as long as it promised to develop the inner person. It was these for whom Spohr, Mendelssohn, Loewe, Schumann had composed." Along the same lines, he noted that after the middle of the century, "at a time when politically radical currents had

24. Carl Goldmark, *Notes from the Life of a Viennese Composer,* trans. Alice Goldmark Brandeis (New York: Boni, 1927), 154–155.

25. *Johannes Brahms,* trans. Eric Blom (New York: Dutton, 1930), 185.

26. See the epilogue.

27. *Anton Bruckner* (Munich: Georg Müller, 1905), 97–98.

arisen everywhere, [these circles] feared the collapse of their old ideals in music." Consequently, in upper middle-class homes such as his own, "for all the devotion to the Romantic world of emotion, the greatness of the Classical era was seen as unsurpassable," and he added that "the center of their musical life was chamber music," a genre especially associated with Brahms.[28]

Brahms's tradition-oriented approach to composition clearly suited the tastes of many within the prevailing culture. Beyond that, the substance of his music projected values that his contemporaries, whether positively or negatively, perceived as "Liberal." Noting that Brahms stressed the artistic and "logical" working out of musical ideas—themes and motives—a number of writers have connected this to middle-class attitudes, in particular the Protestant work ethic that Max Weber described. In one of several similar anecdotes, the composer told George Henschel in 1876, invention "is simply an inspiration from above, for which I am not responsible, which is no merit of mine . . . which I ought even to despise until I have made it my own by right of hard work."[29] And Schering asserted that the composer's audience responded to his music in part because it manifested "self-restraint and rigorousness."[30]

What has been insufficiently underscored is the great value Brahms placed on musical intellect and the broader significance of this. While a high regard for reason has characterized Western civilization throughout most of its history, a politicized ideology of reason is a particular hallmark of European culture from the seventeenth century through the nineteenth century, when the middle class had gained ascendancy. This period was also marked by the rise of a supposedly autonomous or "absolute" instrumental music whose existence came to be justified by the tonal system and appeals to techniques of musical logic linked to that system. The full flowering of tonal and thematic logic in Classical music explains in part late nineteenth-century Liberals' preference for that repertory over the Romantic music of the more recent past.

The first, minimal allusions to "musical logic" had indeed appeared at the peak of the Classical era, in a 1787 composition manual by Heinrich Koch and a seminal history of music by Johann Forkel published the following year. Here, as in later sources, the concept's meaning fluctuated. Whereas Koch invoked "the language of logic" to explain phrase-structure, Forkel applied "musical logic" to harmony: the proper use of harmony assured clarity and correctness for melodic expressions as logic (grammar) did for verbal expressions.[31] By the late nineteenth century, references to music as a language and to musical logic had become more frequent and, in keeping with the time, mingled with both organic metaphors and natural theories of music. Writing in 1853, Moritz Hauptmann went so far as to call music "the universally understandable language," while simultaneously thinking of music as

28. "Brahms und seine Stellung in der Musikgeschichte des 19. Jahrhunderts," *Jahrbuch der Musikbibliothek Peters für 1932* (Leipzig: C. F. Peters, 1933), 10 and 12.

29. *Personal Recollections of Johannes Brahms: Some of His Letters to and Pages from a Journal Kept by George Henschel* (Boston: Richard G. Badget, 1907), 22.

30. "Brahms und seine Stellung," 12.

31. *Versuch einer Anleitung zur Composition* (Leipzig: Adam Friedrich Böhme, 1787), 2:356; and *Allgemeine Geschichte der Musik* (Leipzig: Schwickert, 1788), 1:25.

literally a matter of nature: triads are consonant, and dissonance demands resolution in the ears of every person.[32] One might say that he construed laws of music, a matter of second nature, as laws of first nature.

Hanslick likewise mixed linguistic and organic models in his celebrated polemic *Vom Musikalisch-Schönen,* the first edition of which appeared in 1854 and eighth in 1891. He called music a language that "we speak and understand and yet are not able to translate."[33] In one of the most frequently quoted passages, Hanslick asserted that every *trained* ear "through mere intuition perceives that a group of tones is organic, reasonable or unintelligible, unnatural" (80). Later he described a musical composition as evolving "in organically distinct phases, like abundant blossoms from one bud," this germinal source being the main theme, "the actual material and content (subject matter) of the entire tonal structure." Despite the theme's immediate appeal, we "want to see it challenged and amplified, which then takes place in musical development, analogously to a logical unfolding" (216).

The site in which musical logic was understood to operate thus moved between the harmonic syntax that supports the tonal system and the working with themes and motives, between the particular composition and an immanent logic in absolute music itself. In 1895, the young Schenker challenged the view that music had an innate logic and made it clear that he saw coherence in complex instrumental music as a phenomenon not of nature but rather of culture, of history. As he explained, "through the habit of possibly many centuries, the art of music eventually imagined itself to possess by its nature a logic similar to that of language."[34] Like many of his contemporaries, Schenker appears to have conceived melody as a kind of first nature.[35] And he noted that although composers had come up with many purely musical devices, such as modulation and patterns of repetition and contrast, to extend their structures well beyond simple melodies, they hid the artifice so listeners could hear the music as inevitable, natural:

> The feeling of completeness, of self-enclosure simulated always through associative means conceptual thought. . . . And thus semblance of the logic of thought shimmered deceptively above all the expanded shapes [born] of a marvelously artificial arbitrariness, and soon one began to believe even that the same sort of necessity rests in an artificial shape as in a natural organism.[36]

Among recent writers, no one has explored the concept of musical logic more extensively than Dahlhaus. In his work on Brahms, he focused on the aspect of mu-

---

32. *Die Natur der Harmonik und der Metrik: Zur Theorie der Musik* (Leipzig: Breitkopf und Härtel, 1853), 6 and 7.

33. *Vom Musikalisch-Schönen: Ein Beitrag zur Revision der Ästhetik der Tonkunst,* 8th ed. (Leipzig: Johann Ambrosius Barth, 1891), 79. Here Hanslick did not go so far as Hauptmann and deem music a "universal" language, but see the epilogue.

34. "Der Geist der musikalischen Technik," reprinted in *Heinrich Schenker als Essayist und Kritiker: Gesammelte Aufsätze, Rezensionen und kleinere Berichte aus den Jahren 1891–1901,* ed. Hellmut Federhofer (Hildesheim: Olms, 1990), 136.

35. "Der Geist der musikalischen Technik," 147. On this passage, see Allan Keiler, "Melody and Motive in Schenker's Earliest Writings," in *Critica musica: Essays in Honor of Paul Brainard,* ed. John Knowles (Amsterdam: Gordon and Breach, 1996), 177.

36. "Der Geist der musikalischen Technik," 147–148.

sical logic that Adorno deemed chamber music's "vital element, motivic-thematic work or its residue, that which Schoenberg called 'developing variation.'"[37] Dahlhaus noted that "music appears with Brahms as the development of [motivic] ideas, as sounding discourse."[38] Writing in more concrete terms than the young Schenker, he likewise recognized the historicity of musical logic:

> That the motivic-thematic and harmonic development of a movement could be compared to discourse, in which every detail forms a consequence to what has been presented previously and a premise for what follows, is not altogether self-evident. Yet since the late nineteenth century it has become a firmly rooted aesthetic principle.[39]

While Brahms never expressed as articulate a position as most of these writers, he was deeply committed to the artistic deception that Schenker eloquently describes. Brahms's recorded comments about musical coherence and other aspects of his art, like those of Schenker, also a composer at that point, stress human agency over nature: it is the *artist* who makes an organic composition. But he offers a slightly different perspective in the emphasis he places on musical intellect. Evidence of Brahms's compositional creed comes especially from his students Gustav Jenner and Prince Heinrich Reuß. Jenner began to study with Brahms in the late 1880s and wrote an account of those lessons in 1905. His report of Brahms's reaction to a piano trio he took to the first lesson implies an organic model: "The whole . . . lacked that broad and full undercurrent of feeling that creates unity . . . by expressing itself in an equally lively manner throughout the various parts and giving all the details, even if disparate and at a distance from each other, its particular stamp."[40] In his own daily composition, according to Reuß, Brahms never lost sight of "his 'arch' [seine 'Bogen'], the rounding off of the whole."[41]

In preparation for composing their own works, Brahms had his students analyze the relationship between part and whole (the "organic" structure) in works by classical masters. Jenner's account demonstrates how strongly the older composer felt about the need for proper musical *Bildung*. Composing sets of variations was particularly appropriate for his pedagogical purposes because "no [other] form is so well suited to teach the beginner to distinguish the essential from the unessential, to educate him in artistic, strictly logical thinking" (48). When Jenner first showed Brahms his compositions, the older composer pointed out its "illogical" features. He directed Jenner's attention "from the surface of a dreamy sentiment downward into the depths, where I could but sense that in addition to feeling another factor must be active, which because of lack of ability and knowledge assisted me only very imperfectly: the intellect" (8). He recalls Brahms's subsequent recommenda-

---

37. *Einleitung in die Musiksoziologie: Zwölf theoretische Vorlesungen* (Frankfurt am Main: Suhrkamp Verlag, 1973), 111.

38. "Brahms und die Idee der Kammermusik," in *Brahms-Studien*, vol. 1, ed. Constantin Floros (Hamburg: Brahms-Gesellschaft, 1974), 46.

39. "Musikkritik als Sprachkritik: Musikalische Logik," in *Klassische und romantische Musikästhetik* (Laaber: Laaber-Verlag, 1988), 283.

40. *Johannes Brahms als Mensch, Lehrer und Künstler: Studien und Erlebnisse* (Marburg in Hessen: N. C. Elevert, 1905), 7.

41. Kalbeck, *Brahms*, 4:89.

tion that he study and imitate sonata form movements by Beethoven and Schubert: "He intended that through this composition of pieces after models . . . I would learn to think logically in music" (57).

References to musical logic tend toward redundancy, as Hans-Heinrich Egge-brecht noted in comments on writings by Schoenberg and Hugo Riemann, the theorist most obsessed with the concept: "Logic is a property of musical thinking, which, as a consequence, 'infallibly' proceeds in a logical manner, according to Schoenberg. The concept of musical logic is dissolved into that of musical thinking: musical thinking proceeds logically (consistently), otherwise one does not think musically."[42] Certainly, in the sentences quoted here, Jenner could have written simply "to educate him in artistic thinking" and "He intended that . . . I would learn to think in music." Rather than "thinking logically in music," what Brahms taught could have been described as "artistic discrimination."

Still, the redundant usage linked to Brahms is significant as a cultural artifact, for the view of the artist as intellectual agent that Jenner conveys is fully consonant with Liberal values. Brahms's compositions can be understood to have projected those values through the marked discursive quality Dahlhaus observes, through the strong "impression" of coherent and "self-contained thought" in his works, a product of the artifice or second nature Schenker saw behind the seeming naturalness and inevitability of music.

BRUCKNER'S STRING QUINTET
AND MUSICAL ILLOGIC

The association between chamber music and musical logic made the genre Brahms's acknowledged domain. Inevitably, one of the few significant chamber works by a "progressive" composer, Bruckner's String Quintet, occasioned the first important skirmish between the factions around the two composers. Bruckner undertook the work at Josef Hellmesberger's suggestion and completed it in 1879, but the Hellmesberger Quartet delayed scheduling it. By the time the group decided to play the official premiere, Bruckner's fortunes had already started to improve. Interest in the String Quintet itself had grown after private performances in 1881 and 1884 earned favorable notices in the few Viennese newspapers that reviewed them.[43] When the Hellmesberger Quartet eventually set the premiere for January 1885, it opted for the large rather than the small hall of the Musikverein building, which meant that Bruckner's supporters could appear en masse.[44] The work's success was all the more significant because his Seventh Symphony had triumphed only the week before in Leipzig. With the sudden recognition of Bruckner as a com-

42. "Musikalisches Denken," in *Musikalisches Denken: Aufsätze zur Theorie und Ästhetik der Musik* (Wilhelmshaven: Heinrichshofen, 1977), 143–144.

43. The Winkler Quartet played the first three movements at a meeting of the Academic Wagner Society; full private performances took place in February 1883 and April 1884. See Wagner, *Bruckner,* 132 and 158–159.

44. Robert Maria Prosl, *Die Hellmesberger: Hundert Jahre aus dem Leben einer Wiener Musikerfamilie* (Vienna: Gerlach und Wiedling, 1947), 63.

poser of both symphonies and chamber music, inroads into the Classical genres by progressive composers had to be taken seriously; as the Viennese critic Theodor Helm noted, whether his colleagues liked Bruckner's music or not, they could no longer ignore him.[45]

Both Bruckner's critics and his supporters found the Adagio ineffably beautiful, while they also agreed on the weakness of the musical logic in the String Quintet as a whole. Kalbeck thus called the work *Offenbarungsmusik:* "pure music of revelation . . . composed without any worldly addition of profane logic, art, or reason." Although Kalbeck was in part deriding Bruckner's Catholicism by referring to his compositional approach as a kind of musical automatic writing, he was not simply being malicious, for he named Bruckner "by far the most dangerous of today's musical innovators."[46]

Hanslick wrote a uniformly satirical review, describing as "a psychological mystery, how this most gentle and peaceable of persons . . . becomes in the act of composition an anarchist who pitilessly sacrifices everything that signifies logic and clarity of development, unity of form and tonality."[47] Dömpke and Kalbeck expressed similar outrage about the Quintet but also gave the work more detailed and careful consideration than Kalbeck, at least, would afford one of Bruckner's compositions for many years.[48] Most likely they did not dismiss the Quintet with a brief rebuff because of the audience's positive reaction; the sense of "danger" surely stemmed from the obvious effectiveness of a work that both critics deemed wildly illogical. Their comments indicate further that what disturbed them was Bruckner's approach to harmony and his conception of tonality and, moreover, that his offenses had less to do with the construction of individual chords than the ordering of events. Although Dömpke made passing reference to "harmonic harshness," he emphasized "the unnaturalness of Brucknerian harmonic successions and formal construction."[49] Kalbeck likewise exclaimed: "all the elements of music are found here in the wildest disorder," adding that "the harmony denies any commitment to tonality's basic character and the identity of the key is proved only by the signature and the ending."

Both critics found the first movement particularly transgressive. The most notorious moments are the massive *Steigerungen* (intensifications) in the exposition and recapitulation followed by a quiet semitonal shift (mm. 65–73 and 223–229). But there are precedents—of sorts—for these passages in the music of Schubert.[50] What did they hear that moved them to such strong expressions of outrage? From their perspective, he lacked the discernment that Brahms referred to as "thinking logically in music." In particular, the dramatic rising sequences are rarely coordinated

---

45. *Deutsche Zeitung,* 14 January 1885.

46. *Die Presse,* 28 January 1885.

47. *Neue Freie Presse,* 26 February 1885.

48. Dömpke moved back to Königsberg in 1887. See the entry for him in *Anton Bruckner: Ein Handbuch,* ed. Uwe Harten (Salzburg: Residenz Verlag, 1996), 133. But Kalbeck wrote a favorable review of Bruckner's Eighth Symphony in *Montags-Revue,* 19 December 1892.

49. *Wiener Allgemeine Zeitung,* 17 January 1885.

50. See, for example, the first movements of the G Major String Quartet, D. 887, and the B-flat Piano Sonata, D. 960.

with important harmonic goals here. Consider, for instance, the lengthy passage that precedes the first of the famous *Steigerungen*. The movement has *already* modulated from F to C major by m. 29, the beginning of the secondary thematic group.[51] In mm. 40–44, a rising chromatic sequence set to a crescendo leads to suddenly reduced dynamics in m. 46 and then another brief crescendo, followed by quiet closure (marked "pp" and then "ppp") in C major. Only at this point does Bruckner begin the succession of crescendos that culminate in a prolonged dominant of C and the sudden shift to F-sharp. As Kalbeck remarked, not only Bruckner's harmonic progressions, but also his dynamics sound "capricious and arbitrary," as do, I would add, his declamatory pauses and unison textures: the use of these, as of the *Steigerungen,* has little to do with formal considerations. To ears accustomed to Brahms's compositional choices, many passages in Bruckner's first movement sound, as they did at the time, perplexing, "illogical."

Dömpke prefaced his review with a lengthy disquisition on the current crisis in music, "unprecedented in its kind and scope compared with controversies in other arts." By its nature, chamber music "had remained protected from futurist excesses the longest," because one can discriminate "organic" musical quality more clearly in a concert hall than an opera house:

> Here it is necessary to show one's cards and differentiate between the logical and the merely "gifted" artists; those who create organic works of art from those who gush subjectively. . . . The true basis of the new musical religion is to be sought at least as much in an unmistakable coarsening and arrogant overstimulation of direct musical sensation as in the theory of the unified work of art.[52]

In a straightforward affirmation of what might well be called the Liberal aesthetic creed, Dömpke assumed the obvious superiority of the logical maker of organic works. For those on the other side, however, what he described pejoratively as "arrogant overstimulation of direct musical sensation" suggested positive attributes: expressive immediacy, power, and vividness.

VIENNESE WAGNERISM AND "SHARPER-KEY" POLITICS

What one historian calls the "dreary rationalism" of the Liberals had produced a reaction, an antirational cult of emotion and instinct that became increasingly prominent during the 1880s.[53] While the reaction drew on many sources, among

---

51. Leopold Nowak, "Form und Rhythmus im ersten Satz des Streichquintetts von Anton Bruckner," in *Festschrift Hans Engel zum siebzigsten Geburtstag*, ed. Horst Heussner (Kassel: Bärenreiter, 1964), 262. Janet Schmalfeldt suggested a similar view of the form to me.

52. See also Hugo Riemann's obituary for Brahms. He wrote: "What partisans of the modern miss in Brahms is what they prize in their new idols as the highest virtue, that is that naturalistically crude recklessness, the thoughtless asserting of one's own will, the explosion of feelings, in a word the *unrestrained rule of the sensual.*" In *Präludien und Studien: Gesammelte Aufsätze zur Aesthetik, Theorie und Geschichte der Musik*, 3 vols. in 2 (Wiesbaden: Kraus Reprint, 1976), 3:217.

53. Robert A. Kann, *The Multinational Empire*, 2 vols. (New York: Columbia University Press, 1950), 1:101.

them Schopenhauer and Nietzsche, Wagnerism created the most immediate link between politics and music in late nineteenth-century Vienna. Reception of Wagner's music and, even more, his writings had a direct impact on the volatile brands of mass politics that evolved in the city during the 1880s. Three parties of lasting importance developed out of the chaotic anti-Liberal movement of that decade: the right-wing Pan-Germans and Christian Socials and the left-wing Social Democrats. During that decade, leaders or future leaders of all three parties belonged to the Wiener Akademischer Richard Wagner-Verein (Viennese Academic Richard Wagner Society). Adam Wandruszka writes, moreover, that the parties' origins can be traced back "until one finally finds the 'founding fathers' of all three camps—and thus of Austrian party and domestic history in the 20th century—gathered together in a single circle around the young Georg von Schönerer."[54]

The basic condition that permitted political change was a gradual transition to universal male suffrage that began in 1882, when the vote was extended on the national level to lower middle-class men. But the insurgents succeeded because they refused to accept as a discursive premise the appeals to reason that supported the Liberal worldview. In the late 1870s, Schönerer and his circle came up with a political style they called the "sharper key," calculated to excite emotion rather than engage the intellect. Schönerer's youthful followers came from the same middle-class backgrounds as most establishment politicians; Schorske analyzes their anti-Liberalism as to some extent a rebellion against their fathers' generation.[55] Populism, cultural anti-Semitism, and jingoistic pride in German culture—like that of Liberals, but more extreme—all bolstered and in part inspired by Wagner's legacy, formed the foundation of their program. Because of the ties between Jews and Liberalism, the deliberate arousal of anti-Semitic feelings became the most potent tool in the fight to dislodge the Liberals from power.

An effective anti-Liberal movement began to coalesce in Vienna shortly after lower middle-class men gained the vote at the local level in 1885. The historian John Boyer attributes the changed style of politics to this new class of voters: "Much of the irrational behavior which has been imputed to [Lueger and other Christian Social leaders] on the basis of their wild rhetoric was actually a commonly understood and accepted system of public discourse current among the particular strata to which the Christian Socials appealed."[56] This does not fully explain the new political style's origins. Although Lueger, often portrayed as the ultimate pragmatist, habitually resorted to the "sharper key" to exploit a tense political situation, the earlier group around Schönerer had conceived it. Some of the most prominent members were Jewish and

> had long accepted a form of cultural anti-Semitism as part of their völkisch reaction against the bourgeois liberalism of their parents. . . . Since they saw themselves as members of the German Volk, even the Jewish members . . . felt it essential to reject what

54. "Oesterreichs politische Struktur," in *Geschichte der Republik Oesterreich*, ed. Heinrich Benedikt (Munich: R. Oldenbourg, 1954), 292–293; quoted and translated in McGrath, *Dionysian Art and Populist Politics*, 166.

55. "Generational Tension and Cultural Change," in *Thinking with History*, 141–156.

56. *Political Radicalism in Late Imperial Vienna: Origins of the Christian Social Movement, 1848–1897* (Chicago: University of Chicago Press, 1981), 206.

they regarded as Semitic cultural traits. As [George] Mosse observes, the Jew was seen in stereotype as being intellectual and artificial, rootless and alienated from nature.[57]

Only when the racial cast of Schönerer's anti-Semitism became obvious in the spring of 1883 did these Jewish members break with him. Schönerer's public avowal of racial anti-Semitism virtually coincided with the Maaßen incident, in which the Liberal elite's own German-nationalist prejudice came to the surface. Shortly thereafter, Schönerer founded his own organ, *Unverfälschte Deutsche Worte* (Unadulterated German Words), in contradistinction to the *Deutsche Worte* published by his erstwhile followers.

Schönerer's new scandal sheet offered running commentary on the marked presence of Jews in the city's music life, for example in the Wiener Tonkünstler-Verein (Viennese Musicians' Society). (Brahms was closely associated with this organization, which formed a kind of classicist or "Liberal" counterpart to the Academic Wagner Society.) In 1887, Schönerer's periodical, not a paper given to subtlety, named some members of the Tonkünstler-Verein and remarked on how *verjudet* it had become in the year or so of its existence: "This list of names at the same time shows the complete Jewish domination of art in Vienna, in the conservatory, and in the music shops. Indeed, the Viennese Tonkünstler Society should really be called Cohnkünstler Society."[58]

The following year, 1888, Schönerer and some of his associates went much further. They physically attacked the staff of the *Neues Wiener Tagblatt* because the paper had issued a premature report of the German kaiser's death. Schönerer's subsequent conviction for the assault led to a five-year ban on his participation in politics. Following his trial, the government cracked down on German nationalist groups, which meant that most Pan-Germans put their support for the time being behind Lueger and the emerging Christian Social party to bring about the collapse of Viennese Liberalism.[59]

The role of Wagnerism in the new parties' origins is better known than are later developments that show the continuing connections between Wagnerism and Viennese politics. After Wagner's death in 1883, the number of members in the Viennese Academic Wagner Society increased dramatically, with many members advocating both active involvement in anti-Liberal politics and the exclusion of Jews from membership.[60] When the Wagner Society finally rejected these proposed measures in March 1890, Schönerer and a splinter group of Pan-German sympathizers left to form the Neuer Richard Wagner-Verein (New Richard Wagner Society). According to the music critic Josef Stolzing, the Academic Wagner Society had forced out those like himself "who reminded the directorate whether in a subtle or blunt manner that Wagner was an anti-Semite until the end of his life."[61]

57. McGrath, *Dionysian Art and Populist Politics*, 196–197.

58. "Vom Wiener Tonkünstlerverein" (signed "r."), *Unverfälschte deutsche Worte*, 16 March 1887.

59. Wistrich, *The Jews of Vienna*, 219; and Peter Pulzer, *The Rise of Political Anti-Semitism in Germany and Austria*, rev. ed. (Cambridge, Mass.: Harvard University Press, 1988), 153.

60. This information came from my own study of the *Jahresberichte* of the Wagner Society for the years 1873 through 1910.

61. Review in the *Ostdeutsche Rundschau*, 11 January 1891, of a performance by the Vienna Philharmonic of Bruckner's Third Symphony.

Members of the new organization took an oath to conduct themselves in Wagner's spirit and to associate only with other followers of Wagner and Schönerer. And they accepted extreme German nationalism and anti-Semitism as articles of faith: "Since Richard Wagner as a nationalistic artist was himself an anti-Semite, every Wagner society must also be unadulteratedly German, so as not to become a caricature of an artistic association bearing the name Wagner." Bruckner was named honorary member, and Göllerich, his official biographer and the "spiritual creator" of the group, became its honorary chairman. Along with Göllerich and Stolzing, founding members included Camillo Horn and Hans Puchstein.[62] All four of these men from Vienna's lunatic fringe worked as music critics for two new anti-Semitic newspapers, the *Deutsches Volksblatt* and the *Ostdeutsche Rundschau*. (See fig. 1.1.)

A "Probeblatt" for the *Deutsches Volksblatt* (15 December 1888) included a front-page article that borrowed the title of Wagner's essay "Was ist deutsch?" and quoted at length from it.[63] Proclaiming that the *Deutsches Volksblatt* was the belated realization of Wagner's wish for a newspaper representing "true Germanness," the anonymous author articulated a belief that German music could heal modern society's ills, but stressed the extremity of those ills. That this article projecting an attitude of twisted idealism toward music appeared on the very first page of a newspaper later deemed "the most significant German-national, anti-Semitic organ in Austria" underscores the continuing presence of Wagnerism in Viennese politics.[64]

While the Academic Wagner Society had ostensibly chosen a nonpolitical stance, the group's report for the year 1891 suggested otherwise. Thanking "the progressive champions for our cause in the Viennese press," in particular Helm, the report reiterated the frequently observed connection between Liberal politics and conservative tastes in art. A contradiction was noted, in that the "politically 'most Liberal organs' believe they must behave in a thoroughly reactionary manner in artistic and especially musical questions, even today."[65]

Bruckner had for some time been receiving support in the press from Helm and another critic associated with the Academic Wagner Society, Hans Paumgartner (as well as from a third critic, Ludwig Speidel, who had no use for Wagner). As we shall see, while Helm and Paumgartner, critics for long-established newspapers, couched their reviews of Brahms in language with anti-Liberal overtones, critics for the new papers borrowed the linguistic innovations of sharper-key politics. Indeed, in 1901, Carl Hruby, a student of Bruckner in the years around 1890, explicitly connected the gains that had finally been made on that composer's behalf to the political changes. "During the Liberal era, now defunct, one believed . . . that everything must be handled with kid gloves and that in all things one had to maintain the wonderful so-called 'parliamentary tone.' . . . That has fortunately changed in recent times." According to Hruby, the sober uses of language previously consid-

---

62. Herwig [Eduard Pichl], *Georg Schönerer und die Entwicklung des Alldeutschtumes in der Ostmark: Ein Lebensbild*, 4 vols. (Oldenburg: Gerhard Stalling, 1938), 2:59.

63. The first numbered issue appeared on 1 January 1889.

64. Kurt Paupié, *Handbuch der österreichischen Pressegeschichte 1848–1859*, 2 vols. (Vienna: Wilhelm Braumüller, 1960), 1:107.

65. *Jahresbericht* from 1891, 16.

Anton Bruckner.

(Die beim Bruckner-Commers nicht gehaltene Festrede von August Göllerich.)

Geehrte, liebe Festgenossen!

Zu allen Zeiten haben in hervorragender Zahl deutsche der Ostmark tapfer mitgeholfen an der Gewinnung jenes geistigen Mitteldeutschland, das durch keine politischen Grenzen beengt, das echteste Schaffen unseres Volksthums auf allen Gebieten der Kunst und des Lebens bergend, eine ideale Macht geworden, der sich heute die ganze Culturmenschheit beugt.

In Kampf und Streit, in Lust und Leid waren es oft und oft der Ostmark deutsche Söhne, die den eingeborenen deutschen Geist hoch und rein erhielten im Ansturme fremder Art, die in rechten Überzeugungstreue mit ihm fochten, bis er, in Reine treu bewahrt, siegend und von Fesseln frei, sein befreiendes Licht auf's Neue entfachen konnte. Einem solchen Kämpfer, einem solchen deutschen Helden gilt unsere heutige Feier. Auf den sein selbe deutsche Bethätigung, im Reiche der Musik, hat er gerungen und erreicht, ein Befestiger eigenst deutschen Fühlens, ein Prediger echtest deutschen Glaubens, der immerdar der Welt verkündet, daß das Edle, Schöne mitten in die Welt tritt, daß es beutsch sei, eine Sache, die man treibt um ihrer selbst willen und aus Bortheiles wegen in die Welt tritt. Dieser Glaube hat unseren Meister Freude an ihr zu treiben. Dieser Glaube hat unseren Meister Anton Bruckner zeitlebens durchglüht, gestählt und erhalten! — Unbeachtet, aber auch unüberhör brachte er seine Originalität zur herrlichsten Entwicklung. Abseits vom Geräusche des Lebens, lauschte er einzig den Harmonien seines Innern und sprach, ein zäher Oberösterreicher, zu einer Welt, die ihm Nichts zu sagen hatte, nur aus seiner Tiefe, ganz bei sich, ganz in sich.

Ein Volkskind im echtesten Sinne des Wortes wuchs

Anton Bruckner in der Stille und Schlichtheit des oberösterreichischen Landlebens auf. In kleinen Orten seiner Heimat schleppte sich der junge Bruckner als Schulmeister und Küster, später als Organist in kürzlichen Anstellungen durch's Leben, gleich dem großen Sebastian Bach, der ebenso unbeachtet und mühsam als Cantor sein Brot in thüringischen Flecken zu suchen hatte, die man heute kaum dem Namen nach kennt. Durchforschen wir die Tage seiner Kindheit, so zeigen sich in ihnen schon köstliche Keime späteren Werdens, brollige Beziehungen zur einstigen Entwicklung.

Als Schullehrersohn von Ansfelden trieb es der kleine Tonerl, ein rechter oberösterreichischer Lausbuben, nämlich schon in seiner ersten Schulstunde so bunt, daß er gleich am ersten Tage seiner Laufbahn "hinausstehen" mußte und richtig Prügel bekam. Er hatte auch richtig während seines ganzen Lebens außer den Weistern seiner "braven" Genossen zu stehen und kritische Schläge auszuhalten. Mit 4 Jahren schon zeigte Anton leidenschaftlich seinem lieben Herrn Pfarrer auf einer kleinen, rothen Singstunde vor. In die Schule ging er gerne nur zur Einbergeige, wie es ihm denn auch herannadhend eine besondere Freude war, am Chore der Kirche singen zu dürfen. Im Uebrigen spielte er an den Rieschen Soldaten, und erhob sich damals schon gerne über den Boden, entweder auf Rossen reitend oder auf Zimmerleuten predigend. Immer mehr stellte sich als Ideal des stürmischen Jungen der "Beruf" des "Gutsbesitzers" fest — ein Ideal, das sich ihm freilich nie erfüllen sollte. Bald sollte der Ernst des Lebens an ihn herantreten. Mit 12 Jahren mußte er, als Melzeller von zwölf Geschwistern, nach dem Tode des Baters dessen Stelle übernehmen, und zwar alle darauf lastenden Verpflichtungen, also Schule halten, Meßner- und Organistendienst leisten. Hatte der kleine Anton schon bevor er noch irgend einen Ton gekannt, nach seinen eigenen

Worten "**fürchtbar**" auf einem kleinen Spinett des Baters gespielt und gesungen, so hatte er mit 10 Jahren das erstemal sich öffentlich auf der Orgel in Hörsching mit dem Fahenliebe produciren dürfen, wobei er schon mit Stolz das Pedal behandelte und für seine Leistung einen Groschen bekam.

Im Uebrigen war es der höchste Festtag für Bruckner und seinen Vater, wenn am Fröhnleichnamsfeste Pauken und drei Trompeten aus Linz kamen, — denn in Ansfelden gab es als Höchstes nur ein Horn! — Bruckner war mit den genannten Instrumenten schon damals "gut Freund!" In St. Florian, wohin ihn der Prälat des Stiftes als Sängerknabe berief, oblag unser Meister den ersten ernsten Studien in Generalbaß, Clavier und Violine, und begleitete oft schon die Kirchenmessen auf der Orgel, als er im Jahre 1840 in die Beipräandencur in Linz eintrat. Charakteristischerweise absolvirte Bruckner in Linz diesen, auf zehn Monate berechneten Curs unerhört gut, obwohl es Regel zu sein schien, daß Jeder einmal fiel, um zwei Jahre beim Director zu bleiben. Im Orgelspiel jedoch wurde ihm bloß die Note "gut" zuertheilt! — eine Qualificirung, für welche ihm der Lehrer vier Jahre später feierlige Abbitte leistete, als Bruckner bei einem Orgelconcurse, bei dem er das Lehrerzeugniß gewann, ein Thema von Preindl schon contrapunktisch bearbeitete.

Nun sehen wir unseren Meister nach dem erworbenen klingenden Zeugnisse mit zwölf Gulden jährlicher Besoldung in Schulgehülfe in Windhag, wo er dieselben Dienste wie in Ansfelden zu verrichten, alle Werck-Gänge zu begleiten hatte, auf einem Corridor seine Wohnung bekam und eine nicht sehr beneidenswerthe Behandlung erdulden mußte. Obendrein sollte Bruckner dem Herrn Lehrer immer Noten abschreiben und Feldarbeit leisten. Da er die letztere einst unterließ, wurde er 1843 nach Kronstorf bei

☞ Kauft nur bei Christen! ☜

FIGURE 1.1. *Deutsches Volksblatt*, 13 December 1891, bottom of page 1. Göllerich, as Bruckner's official biographer, had been scheduled to speak to a student gathering on 11 December; the occasion was the University of Vienna awarding the composer an honorary doctorate. The university asked Göllerich to withdraw because his outspoken anti-Semitism made him too controversial a figure. The *Deutsches Volksblatt* subsequently published the speech as the "formal address by August Göllerich not delivered at the Bruckner celebration." Below the beginning, shown here, a note urges readers to "buy only from Christians": an economic boycott of Jewish merchants was underway.

ered appropriate had been inadequate to counter the attacks on Bruckner.[66] As part of the contemporary dialectic of action and reaction, the Liberal critics' reception of Bruckner had given rise to anti-Liberal reception of Brahms, expressed in the idioms of the new political style.

ANTI-LIBERAL RECEPTION OF BRAHMS

Like the political crisis, the polarization in the city's music worlds had clearly deepened in the late 1880s. "Talk of a potential anti-Liberal coalition soon filled Vienna's political clubs and salons in the autumn of 1887," after Lueger gave his first anti-Semitic speeches in June and September of that year.[67] And in April 1889, Helm noted that "in Vienna it seems to be even more difficult to reach reconciliation in music than in politics."[68]

Echoing recurring complaints about Liberal culture in general, Brahms's critics often found his later compositions to have become contrived and cerebral. Paumgartner's critique of the 1890 premiere of the G Major String Quintet is typical: "The themes, although treated so effectively and elaborately, nonetheless increasingly seem thought rather than felt, more constructed than discovered. Brahms so seldom touches our innermost soul and the specific mood in which he puts us is always only one of a reflective pleasure."[69]

Manipulation of the language of feeling made for effective politics in the Vienna of the 1880s. Although somewhat different motives may have underpinned the emphasis on unleashed expressiveness in music, part of the purpose there, too, was to break through the artifice of modern culture and connect with a broader audience. Many musicians believed that the greatest music has a powerful emotional impact without the mediation of the intellect, and that this was its salutary democratizing feature. And they saw Brahms as virtually incapable of such an effect. Paumgartner wrote in 1890 that Brahms's symphonies

> do not inspire and delight the human heart and will therefore never become popular. But anything that would be lasting must be popular. This is the case with all art, perhaps all human action. Art, but especially music, that wins the admiration of experts but not humanity's beating heart will endure only with difficulty.[70]

From its inception in the eighteenth century, the symphony had been the instrumental genre expected to have the widest appeal, which made Brahms's supposed weakness in melodic invention acute precisely there.

Beyond the anti-Liberal stance apparent in his reviews from around 1890, Paumgartner also revealed a German nationalist slant that he likewise turned against Brahms—ironically, given the composer's chauvinism. Paumgartner touched ex-

---

66. *Erinnerungen an Bruckner* (Vienna: Friedrich Schalk's Verlag, 1901), 27.
67. Boyer, *Political Radicalism in Late Imperial Vienna*, 217–218.
68. *Deutsche Zeitung*, 13 April 1889.
69. *Wiener Abendpost*, 19 November 1890.
70. *Wiener Abendpost*, 14 March 1890.

plicitly on this when he wrote about a concert that Joseph Joachim and Brahms performed in February 1889:

> Herr Joachim received a great deal of applause; nevertheless, the enthusiasm of a deeply stimulated and inspired audience was lacking. Brahms as composer, Joachim as performer—that is the new German music. It is clever and learned, interesting and tasteful; still, if the German people had never felt and heard any music but this, they would never in all eternity have been permitted the experience of a Sedan.[71]

Referring to the culminating victory over the French that led to the Second Reich's formation, Paumgartner strongly implied that a non-German emotional superficiality was now defiling German music. (Joachim had grown up in an observant Jewish household.)

No holds were barred in the new anti-Liberal, anti-Semitic newspapers that began to appear at the end of the 1880s. Critics in both the *Deutsches Volksblatt* and the *Ostdeutsche Rundschau* lost no opportunity to revile Brahms in their reviews, even when the concert supposedly under review included no music by him. Göllerich, for example, gratuitously compared Bruckner and Brahms when reviewing a concert of chamber music by Schubert and Beethoven. In his words, "only this master [Bruckner] is capable today of elevating his melody to the eternally effective, purely human type of his predecessors, while contemporary talents—even those of the most imposing natural gifts [i.e., Brahms]—are for the most part understandable only through the mediation of art-historical reflection."[72] Critics in the new papers, furthermore, were shamelessly direct in their expression of *völkisch* sentiments. In January 1891 Hanslick had praised the artistic development manifest in Antonín Dvořák's G Major Symphony (Op. 88) thus: "And this natural, blooming development is what in our time of prevailing reflection wins us quickly and holds us willingly." Horn quoted these words, inserting parenthetically after them: "the racial fellows of Mr. Hanslick may thank him." After thus linking Hanslick to the Jews, Horn added a gratuitous slur against Brahms: "And what does Mr. Brahms, 'embodied reflection,' say to that?"[73]

Along related lines, Göllerich showed contempt for Brahms's apparent attempts at a simpler, more accessible style, especially as heard in the Third Symphony. He asserted in March 1889 that the composer "wants at any cost to be popular":

> One of the cleverest critics in Vienna, L. Speidl [*sic*], in an ingeniously apt way writes that when Brahms wants to be popular, he displays a kind of "desperate naiveté." We were reminded of this choice expression again while listening to the Andante of the [Third] Symphony—what wretched barrenness of ideas reigns in this *Zampa*-like movement, which does not even disdain Jewish-temple triplets simply to appear properly "understandable"![74]

71. *Wiener Abendpost,* 13 February 1889.
72. *Deutsches Volkblatt,* 25 December 1889.
73. *Ostdeutsche Rundschau,* 17 January 1891. Hanslick's review is reprinted in *Aus dem Tagebuche eines Musikers* (Berlin: Allgemeiner Verein für Deutsche Litteratur, 1892), 340–341.
74. *Deutsches Volkblatt,* 28 March 1889.

The historian Steven Beller notes that in the declining days of Liberalism, "anyone could be discredited by being associated with the Jews," and that Liberals were the usual targets.[75] In a veiled way, Paumgartner may have intended and both Horn and Göllerich certainly did intend to link Brahms with the Jews. But Stolzing, the music critic of the *Ostdeutsche Rundschau,* was utterly blunt. In a sarcastic article in October 1890 about the conservative Viennese symphonic programs, he remarked that Goldmark and Brahms were "in any case the right composers for the predominantly Jewish audience of the midday concerts." Moving his survey from the Gesellschaft der Musikfreunde concerts to those of the Philharmonic, in a rhetorical flight of fancy Stolzing transformed Brahms into a Jew:

> We are very curious about the Philharmonic repertoire, which will be assembled, as ever, from some frequently heard symphonies of Beethoven, Schubert, and Schumann, along with the most recent works by Jews. . . . What a pleasing spectacle awaits us when Hanslick, Hirschfeld, Königstein, and Kalbeck again offer the palm to their great (?) fellow-clansmen Goldmark, Goldschmidt, Brahms etc. and lead them into the temple of immortality. Long live the music-loving and music-making Jewry!
> Strange! In the realm of politics Jewry is liberal, in that of music, conservative.[76]

Brahms of course was not a Jew, but he *was* a Liberal. The motivic-thematic elaboration, chamber style, and reflective aesthetic experience associated with his music were linked more generally with Liberal intellectual elitism. Tribalist critics who supported Bruckner espoused an irrationalist aesthetic that valorized melodic invention and the expressive immediacy of symphonic style. To be sure, the black-and-white categories established by the polemicists did not always hold. Thus Speidel, a Jewish journalist who wrote for the *Fremden-Blatt* and the *Neue Freie Presse,* admired the music of Bruckner but was critical of both Wagner and Brahms.[77] Moritz Szeps, the Jewish editor of two leftist-Liberal newspapers, first the *Neues Wiener Tagblatt* and then the *Wiener Tagblatt,* was both a Francophile and an ardent Wagnerite.[78] Even Hanslick, at least in his review of Dvořák's G Major Symphony, privileged immediacy over reflection. Furthermore, musicians and critics on both sides of the musical divide considered a particular melodic ideal to be crucial to the symphony (an aesthetic I shall discuss in chapter 5). The reviews also raise many questions, such as what, exactly, does "melodic invention" *mean?* For Schenker, it approached first nature, but for Brahms, it was something quite different, as will become clearer in chapter 3. And I shall argue in chapter 2 that Brahms did in fact model reflectiveness and more overtly cultivate musical artifice in his later music, as his critics claimed.

Still, the skewed critiques reflect a real conflict that culminated in the collapse of Viennese Liberalism in 1897, the year of Brahms's death. His rehabilitation as an

75. *Vienna and the Jews 1867–1938: A Cultural History* (New York: Cambridge University Press, 1989), 200.

76. *Ostdeutsche Rundschau,* 19 October 1890.

77. For Speidel, see Charlotte Pinter, "Ludwig Speidel als Musikkritiker," 3 vols. (Ph.D. diss., University of Vienna, 1949).

78. For Szeps, see Berta Szeps Zuckerkandl, *My Life and History,* trans. John Sommerfield (New York: Knopf, 1939).

echt deutscher composer began quickly thereafter—it helped that he was not actually Jewish.[79] Although the Liberal party had little political power after 1897, Albert Fuchs notes that important (Jewish) intellectuals in Austria such as Freud, Stefan Zweig, and Arthur Schnitzler continued to view the world from essentially Liberal perspectives.[80] To his list we could add Schoenberg, whose emphasis on "musical logic" and composing "after models" surely derives from the Liberal tradition (invoked now by a "progressive" composer). Moreover, Alban Berg's polemic against Hans Pfitzner in 1920 took up the crucial aesthetic question ("inspired invention" versus "'rational' elaboration"), still imbued with political meaning, that had engaged the factions around Brahms and Bruckner in *fin-de-siècle* Vienna.[81] The rhetoric in the original musical controversy had often been petty. But the central issue was not trivial, and its aesthetic and political aspects had become inseparable.

79. Hruby, *Erinnerungen an Bruckner,* 37.

80. Fuchs, *Geistige Strömungen,* 10.

81. "Die musikalische Impotenz der 'neuen Ästhetik' Hans Pfitzners [1920]," in Willi Reich, *Alban Berg: Mit Bergs eigenen Schriften und Beiträgen von Theodor Wiesengrund-Adorno und Ernst Křenek* (Vienna: Herbert Reichner Verlag, 1937), 181–192.

CHAPTER 2

BRAHMS AND THE PROBLEM
OF LATE STYLE

Does Brahms have a late style? Consider first a passing reference by Adorno to the "Brahmsian 'tone,' the laboriously loosened muteness, the heavy breath-taking of a more or less unremitting aging of music," in an essay written less than four decades after the composer's death.[1] From Adorno's perspective in 1934, music itself appeared to have entered a late phase by Brahms's time. Because the tonal language had grown old, Adorno's comments imply, musical expression sounds difficult in Brahms's compositions, and he did not limit his observation to the later works. In a related vein, Karl Geiringer wrote, in a study published likewise in 1934, that the composer's "'twilight' style, with its particular blending of moods, was already in evidence" in compositions from the mid-1850s.[2] The character of much of Brahms's oeuvre noted by writers as different in their outlooks as Adorno and Geiringer, the autumnal qualities or sense of expressive constriction often mentioned in the literature on Brahms, makes the concept of stylistic change more questionable even than usual. If music itself had aged, and if most of Brahms's works sound twilit, what meaning might a late period have with respect to his lifework, and how might one go about finding its beginning?

Other interpretive traditions and contextual factors add to the difficulties. For example, the perception of the final decade or so of the nineteenth century as not just a *fin de siècle* but in other respects a historical late period also complicates the issue. Beyond the personal sense of lateness articulated by Brahms and his contemporaries, these decades merit designation as a late period in European social history.[3] The general "aging of music" Adorno heard in his works can be understood as one manifestation of a culture's final phase. In a number of broad historical nar-

---

1. "Brahms aktuell," in *Musikalische Schriften V,* 201.
2. *Brahms,* 202.
3. See Werner Kohlschmidt, "Die Problematik der Spätzeitlichkeit," in *Spätzeiten und Spätzeitlichkeit: Vorträge, gehalten auf dem II. Internationalen Germanistenkongreß 1960 in Kopenhagen,* ed. Kohlschmidt (Bern: Francke Verlag, 1962), 16–26; and Brinkmann, *Late Idyll.*

ratives, Brahms represents the disillusioned end of the nineteenth century, Beethoven the more idealistic early years.[4]

While historical lateness suggests decline, the late style of an artist, at least since the mid–nineteenth century, has tended to have positive connotations. Beethoven provides a frequent point of reference for Brahms in this type of interpretation as well. Especially after the middle of the nineteenth century, many writers saw Beethoven's late style as the climax of his lifework, perhaps of music history. "Late style" had gained a new stature, more likely than before to be taken as signifying culmination rather than deterioration. As a consequence, for some critics it became an honorific, even politically charged category that might not apply to the last works of all artists, including Brahms at times.

Critics had begun to divide Brahms's compositions into periods very early in his career, with Adolf Schubring already construing three periods in a series of articles written in 1862, when Brahms was only twenty-nine years old.[5] Although this was an odd and isolated instance, a pattern emerges in documents from the early to mid-1880s in which many more writers discerned signs of a new style, viewed by some as initiating his late—or at least his third—period. From our wider perspective, we can see that the perceived stylistic shift in Brahms's music coincided with the inception of the twilight years of Liberal politics and culture in Vienna, which thus offers one compelling context for stylistic change, if also one that must be interpreted cautiously.

Many, probably most, twentieth-century writers understood Brahms's final period to have begun only after his completion of the G Major String Quintet in 1890 and a short interlude in which he thought his creative life over. But Malcolm Mac-Donald and certain other recent writers place his last period's onset at about the same time his contemporaries place it, at the Third Symphony, composed in 1883, the year in which Brahms turned fifty, often considered a watershed in anyone's life. In a striking reversal, several of these critics take a position diametrically opposed to that of critics in his own time. Whereas Brahms's contemporaries saw his new style from the mid-1880s on as more accessible than his earlier styles, writers such as Schmidt and Siegfried Kross interpret the late style as surpassingly difficult.

As the array of complexities and contradictions I have assembled suggests, the possibility of a late style in Brahms's music raises questions that go well beyond the inevitable artificiality of such constructs. Still, most of the observations do stem from a shared perception of difference in certain later works. Despite the divergent views of the various writers as well as the continuities in expressive qualities implied by Adorno and Geiringer, late style remains a meaningful category with respect to Brahms's lifework.

---

4. Thus Schering writes that in Beethoven's time, "when idealism constituted the German people's spiritual breath of life, it was still possible to feel oneself at once an individual and a member of a collective." "Brahms und seine Stellung," 15.

5. On these articles, see Walter Frisch, "Brahms and Schubring: Musical Criticism and Politics at Mid-Century," *19th-Century Music* 7 (1984): 271–281.

RECENT APPROACHES TO THE PROBLEM

As artists' late works rose in status during the late nineteenth and early twentieth centuries, a type of critical discourse evolved peculiar to *Altersstil* or *Spätstil*—"style of old age" or "late style," respectively, but used as virtual synonyms. While these efforts yielded many insights, no coherent or universally valid theory of late style resulted—such a theory is surely impossible. Thus late style "embraces a changing complex of critical categories, including, prominently, 'anachronism,' 'attenuation,' 'fragmentation,' abstraction,' and 'concision.'"[6] Indeed, although anachronisms are observed in some works, modernism ahead of its times is seen in others. And critics note in certain late works a single-minded focus on technical problems and in others a disregard for the technical perfection evident in the artists' earlier works.[7] Consequently, late-style criticism invites an approach that tries to find meaning despite the contradictions rather than expecting to resolve them.

At present, Adorno is the most celebrated representative of an originally German critical tradition that also includes the writers Georg Simmel and Hermann Broch and the early twentieth-century art historians Albert Brinckmann and Hans Tietze, among others. In attempting to limit the meaning of "late style," some critics reserve it for artists whose final works suggest both an absence of the ambitious striving for worldly success evident in their earlier works and a resulting unconcern about pleasing their audience. Tietze, for example, writes that the "aged artist has grown indifferent towards the . . . public which has perhaps already begun to cast its approval on younger artists," and he remarks on the productive independence that sometimes results from "being outdated."[8]

A sense of isolation, psychological or stylistic, comes up repeatedly in commentary on *Alterswerke* (works of old age). In a recent, wide-ranging study, Klaus Wolfgang Niemöller concludes: "If one views the complex 'late style' as an overriding field of problems . . . the late style of significant composers appears as shaped expression of a creative personality that has largely freed itself from the pressure of historical and social forces."[9] He observes two, potentially overlapping categories of features common to various composers' late styles. On the one hand, an "experimental breakthrough into a new tonal world" sometimes sets artists' late styles apart from their previous mature styles. On the other hand, artists have often broken new

---

6. Anthony Edward Barone, "Richard Wagner's *Parsifal* and the Hermeneutics of Late Style" (Ph.D. diss., Columbia University, 1996), 15. Barone's dissertation includes a valuable bibliography of work concerning late style.

7. The abstractness sometimes noted in late works accounts for both possibilities. On the first tendency, see Hermann Broch, "The Style of the Mythical Age," introduction to *On the Iliad,* by Rachel Bespaloff, trans. Mary McCarthy (Washington, D.C.: Pantheon Books, 1947), 10–13; on the second, see Julius S. Held, "Commentary," *Art Journal* 46 (1987): 127. Held cites a famous remark by Goethe about Titian's late works. See also David Rosand, "Editor's Statement: Style and the Aging Artist," *Art Journal* 46 (1987): 92. Rosand quotes Barbara Herrnstein Smith's phrase "the senile sublime."

8. Tietze, "Earliest and Latest Works of Great Artists," *Gazette des Beaux-Arts* 26 (1944): 280–281; and Brinckmann, *Spätwerke grosser Meister* (Frankfurt am Main: Frankfurter Verlags-Anstalt A.-G., 1925).

9. "Spätstilaspekte," in *Festschrift Arno Forchert zum 60. Geburtstag am 29. Dezember 1985,* ed. Gerhard Allroggen and Detlef Altenburg (Kassel: Bärenreiter, 1986), 183.

ground in their late works by turning increasingly to compositional procedures associated with the remote past. As a result, a late style "reveals itself in many instances through a certain emancipation from the general style of the time."[10] Niemöller sees Brahms's music from the Fourth Symphony, with its concluding chaconne, to the posthumous Eleven Chorale Preludes for organ in this light as manifestations of a late style.[11] Both Hans Mersmann and Peter Gülke—the latter with some reservations— place the inception of a late style, in a strong sense similar to that articulated by Niemöller, later than he does, at the chamber music with clarinet that Brahms composed in 1891 after a brief hiatus.[12] These points of view do allow reconciliation: signs of lateness may have taken a different form or became more strongly marked in the final works.

Certainly, the sense of far-reaching changes occurring in Brahms's Viennese milieu deepened around 1890, suggesting a connection between external circumstances and the resistance to their pressures that Niemöller and Tietze impute to artists cultivating a late style. In other words, as the composer's feelings of isolation increased, the "lateness" of his work became more pronounced. And, indeed, the final chamber music takes late-style traits to a new level. The mode of critical writing that subsumes Brahms's oeuvre into overarching accounts of the lateness of the time itself originated in the European culture that slowly faded around the turn of the twentieth century. This chapter will therefore conclude with a brief discussion of lateness as a historical category and the related topos of the composer's autumnal style.

Most of the literature on artists of course does not problematize "lateness." Instead, the late period of, say, a composer typically fits into a framework of three or four stylistic periods. Dividing a composer's lifework does not usually involve self-evident choices, nor do the compositions tend to be easily separable into discrete chronological groups. Despite the difficulties of making such decisions, difficulties that are more noticeable in the case of Brahms than some other composers, grouping an artist's works into stylistic periods is, if nothing more, a necessary evil for biographers and others who survey an entire oeuvre. Geiringer admits that "Brahms's artistic development proceeded slowly and steadily" but finds it possible to discern four periods based on creative "landmarks" that can be "coordinated with special events in his life."[13] In his scheme, the few works from the 1890s after Brahms's short-lived retirement are the products of the last period.[14] While Michael Musgrave comes up with the same final group of works, he construes four periods exclusively from Brahms's professional actions and ignores his personal life altogether.[15] Consequently, his scheme has the rare virtue of internal consistency.

10. "Spätstilaspekte," 179.

11. "Spätstilaspekte," 181.

12. Mersmann, "Alterswerke der Kunst," in *Lebensraum der Musik: Aufsätze–Ansprachen* (Rodenkirchen: P. J. Tonger Musikverlag, 1964), 118; and Gülke, *Brahms–Bruckner: Zwei Studien* (Kassel: Bärenreiter, 1989), 63.

13. *Brahms,* 201.

14. *Brahms,* 203.

15. Unremarkably, he placed one division after the Four Ballades (Op. 10; completed in 1854), when Brahms temporarily decided to cease offering his works for publication, and another after the composition of the G Major String Quintet in 1890. More unusually, Musgrave saw a second period extend-

In a book devoted solely to Brahms's chamber music, Daniel Mason also postulates a four-period framework. For Mason's purposes, the final stylistic phase begins with the D Minor Violin Sonata.[16] This grouping may seem idiosyncratic, since Brahms drafted at least the first movement of the D Minor Violin Sonata during the summer of 1886, when he also wrote the F Major Cello Sonata, A Major Violin Sonata, and C Minor Trio. Mason's division obviously raises the question of whether a change in style might occur within the composition of a group of works. I shall argue nonetheless that the D Minor Violin Sonata's first movement does stand apart from the other three first movements, that one sign of lateness is more prominent in it than elsewhere in the chamber music.

In his laudable study of the life and works of Brahms, MacDonald acknowledges the inevitable arbitrariness of style periods but devises one that groups the Third Symphony with all the compositions that follow it.[17] Taking a stronger stand, Kross posits that a "retreat" from the genres of symphony and string quartet marks the beginning of the final creative period, which he therefore places after the Fourth Symphony's completion, at the chamber works from 1886.[18] He focuses on the intricacy of the motivic patterns in Brahms's late works, referring to "techniques of developing his thematic material out of pre-thematic shapes" as a predominant feature.[19] Stressing the difficulty of the late works, Kross asserts that even such close friends as Billroth and Clara Schumann were unable to understand and appreciate them. Rather than probing possible contexts for a late style, he makes stylistic change itself an agent in the composer's life. According to Kross, "unquestionably his late style caused" the estrangement that occurred between Brahms and Billroth toward the end of the 1880s.[20]

Like Kross in both respects, Schmidt disregards possible contexts for Brahms's late style and stresses its difficult aspects. For him, the Third Symphony simultaneously marks a turning point in the composer's treatment of the genre and "the transition to the late style." Schmidt describes this style as "characterized by an uncompromising prominence of artifice, by the far-reaching penetration of the musical details, which makes no allowance for effectiveness and easy perceptibility;

---

ing until Brahms had finally completed several longstanding compositional projects (all in C minor): the First String Quartet, the Third Piano Quartet, and the First Symphony. Musgrave divides his book into four parts, one for each period. *The Music of Brahms* (Oxford: Clarendon Press, 1994).

16. *The Chamber Music of Brahms* (New York: Macmillan, 1933). Other authors have offered further variations on the schemes I have described. Arno Mitschka placed the G Major String Quintet into the final of four periods, whereas Viktor Urbantschitsch saw a fourth period beginning with the Fourth Symphony, and August Sturke divided Brahms's works into three periods, the Third Symphony initiating the final one. See Mitschka, "Der Sonatensatz in den Werken von Johannes Brahms" (inaugural-diss., Johannes-Gutenberg-Universität zu Mainz, 1961); Urbantschitsch, "Die Entwicklung der Sonatenform bei Brahms," *Studien zur Musikwissenschaft* 14 (1927): 265–285; and Sturke, *Der Stil in Johannes Brahms' Werken: Eine stilkritische Untersuchung seiner Klavier-, Kammermusik-, Chor- und Orchesterwerke* (Würzburg: Konrad Triltsch, 1932).

17. *Brahms* (New York: Schirmer Books, 1990), 157 and 302.

18. *Johannes Brahms: Versuch einer kritischen Dokumentar-Biographie*, 2 vols. (Bonn: Bouvier Verlag, 1997), 2:927.

19. *Johannes Brahms*, 2:962.

20. *Johannes Brahms*, 2:966–967.

in short, by the undisguised realization of Brahms's chamber-music ideal of composition." While Schmidt's description brings to mind the emphasis on technical problems observed in many late works, the implications of this trend for ideas of genre are his primary concern. According to him, throughout much of the Third Symphony Brahms rejects the "monumentality" and expressive immediacy considered crucial for the symphony at the time. For Schmidt, the transition to the late style is complete in the Fourth Symphony, for in that work the composer no longer resists his inclination to adhere at all times to his "chamber-music ideal." In doing so, Brahms reveals an "utterly unmistakable" contradiction between his personal standards as a composer and his audience's expectations of the symphony.[21] Although Schmidt does not explicitly make this point, chamber style lends itself to technical experimentation and other late-style features such as introversion.

In considering late style in Brahms's music here, I take these as central issues: What were the contexts for change and the perception of it, and how does the music sound different from before? This chapter moves between discussions of the music from the perspective of these three concerns, beginning with chamber works from the mid-1880s. Regarding the inception of a late period, I assume that various factors are likely to have determined both stylistic change and the reception of it. Connections that correspond "to a zigzag-like devious line" or "to a ramifying and especially to a converging system of lines," to invoke Freud's explanation of a word that he introduced in the Vienna of Brahms's final years, "overdetermine" stylistic change.[22] Because of the focus of this book, I privilege political factors, in particular Brahms's German nationalism and the increasing untenability of that bias. In addressing the sound of his late compositions, I discuss the overt density of the motivic work that Schmidt and Kross note. But I focus more on Brahms's mastery of harmonic/tonal subtleties, a feature he took as far as it could go in this late period of tonality, in music at a level of compositional virtuosity so high as to call to mind the mannerism of other late styles. Artifice is nevertheless only one side of his late style. Thus at certain moments, Brahms uses his supreme technical command to convey psychological states unlike any heard in his earlier music or indeed in music by any other composers. In these moments, the music models the reflectiveness that critics frequently complained about, creating a sense of unprecedented expressive complexity that is evocative at times of Freud's Vienna. This suggests an addendum to late-style dialectics: late works are at once an expression of their time and out of step with it, alienated from the contemporary context.[23]

21. *Brahms und seine Zeit,* 89. I discuss symphonic monumentality in chapter 5.

22. Josef Breuer and Sigmund Freud, *Studies in Hysteria,* trans. A. A. Brill (Boston: Beacon Press, 1937), 219. The passage is from "Psychotherapy of Hysteria," a chapter Freud wrote. In 1900, Freud elaborated the idea in *On the Interpretation of Dreams,* which recently appeared in a new translation by Joyce Crick (New York: Oxford University Press, 1999). See also Louis Althusser, "Contradiction and Overdetermination: Notes for an Investigation," in *For Marx,* trans. Ben Brewster (New York: Verso, 1996), 87–128.

23. Along related lines, Edward Said writes: "Lateness is being at the end, fully conscious, full of memory, and also very (even preternaturally) aware of the present." "Thoughts on Late Style," *London Review of Books,* 5 August 2004, 5.

OBSERVATIONS ON THE GENESIS OF THE
CHAMBER MUSIC FROM THE MID-1880S

In a pocket notebook, Brahms indicated that he had completed nine works in August 1886: four lieder and the part song *Im Herbst,* along with the F Major Cello
Sonata, the A Major and D Minor Violin Sonatas, and the C Minor Piano Trio.[24]
These entries obscure various complicating factors in the origins of the chamber
pieces. While he must have been unusually productive that summer, the Adagio
affettuoso of the F Major Cello Sonata may derive from the E Minor Cello Sonata's
adagio, a movement he composed in 1862 and then suppressed, and he may not have
completed the D Minor Violin Sonata until 1888.

Comments in his correspondence, moreover, make it clear Brahms had begun
the A Major Violin Sonata three years before, during the summer of 1883, when he
composed the Third Symphony. Remarkably, each of these works contains an unmistakable reference to music by Wagner, possibly in tribute to the composer, who had
died in February: the symphony to *Tannhäuser* and the sonata to *Die Meistersinger.*[25]
Although Donald Tovey complained that the A Major Violin Sonata is "sometimes
known by the 'mutton-head' title of '*Meistersinger*' sonata because of its first three
notes," critics had immediately linked the sonata to Walter's "Prize Song."[26]

The months after Wagner's death had been unusually eventful in Vienna. While
the anti-Liberal politician Schönerer unveiled the uncompromising racial cast of
the Germanic worldview he embraced, mainstream Liberals expressed their outrage
in the *Neue Freie Presse* about concessions to the empire's Slavs. Kalbeck connected
the Third Symphony's origins to Brahms's heightened feelings of German nationalism and used that observation as the basis for a programmatic reading of the music.
He made a number of subsequent observations about the composer's reactions to
various political currents, but he did not try to fit this commentary and his reading
of Brahms's Third into a single linear narrative. In fact, no overarching interpretation of the composer's later years structures the final portions of Kalbeck's biography.
Consequently, he avoided the potential trap the late twentieth-century art historian
Julius Held implies in remarks about topoi "that shape biographies in general" and
in particular "the role a mid-life conversion or crisis may have played in the emergence of the Altersstil of some artists."[27] The concept of overdetermination offers
an alternative to a scenario of cause and effect.

After celebrating his fiftieth birthday on 7 May 1883 in Vienna, Brahms traveled
to Wiesbaden, where he spent the summer close to the home of Rudolf von Beck-

---

24. Kalbeck, *Brahms,* 4:92. Brahms revised *Im Herbst* before publishing it in 1888.

25. On the reference to *Tannhäuser,* see David Brodbeck, "Brahms, the Third Symphony, and the
New German School," in *Brahms and His World,* ed. Walter Frisch (Princeton, N.J.: Princeton University Press, 1990), 65–80.

26. "Brahms's Chamber Music," in *The Main Stream of Music and Other Essays,* 262. Speidel wrote
that a whisper went through the concert hall at the beginning of the sonata's premiere, "out of which
the words 'Morgenlicht leuchtend' could be clearly heard," *Fremden-Blatt,* 7 December 1886. Helm also
noted the resemblance, but downplayed its importance, *Deutsche Zeitung,* 11 December 1886.

27. "Commentary," 132.

erath, a gentleman winegrower and an accomplished amateur violinist. Kalbeck attributed great importance to the composer's having attended the dedication nearby of a monument to "Germania," at which Wilhelm I and various other high-level German dignitaries were also present, on 28 September, the thirteenth anniversary of Strasbourg's capitulation. His biographer went so far as to refer to the Third Symphony as the *Germaniasymphonie*.[28] Kurt Stephenson, however, calls these remarks "exaggerated," noting that Brahms's hostess, Laura von Beckerath, did not even mention the event in the detailed diary she kept of that memorable summer.[29] More straightforwardly significant, given Brahms's intense cultivation of chamber music in the final decade and a half of his life and the Third Symphony's late-style/chamber-style features, was the frequent music making in the von Beckeraths' house.

Throughout the summer, Brahms and Rudolf collaborated on sonatas by Bach, Haydn (arrangements of piano trios, string quartets, and piano sonatas), Mozart, and Beethoven, and by later composers such as Edvard Grieg and Friedrich Kiel. Letters between Brahms and his hosts after his departure show that he drafted the middle movement of the A Major Violin Sonata and almost certainly the first, as well, that summer.[30] Moreover, in composing that middle movement, Brahms took a thematic idea from one of the Grieg sonatas he and Rudolf had played.[31] The chamber music Brahms attributed to 1886 thus had one source in a summer of *Hausmusik* three years earlier. Beyond the specific connection to the Grieg sonata, the chosen repertory surely influenced the modest dimensions and ostensible simplicity of the A Major Violin Sonata.

Brahms clearly had decided to write a group of chamber works with piano long before his arrival in Thun on 27 May 1886. With the A Major Violin Sonata, the F Major Cello Sonata must date back the furthest of the four works, since Brahms seems to have completed these two first. Other circumstantial evidence, most of it concerning his earlier E Minor Cello Sonata, suggests that he had begun the second cello sonata before the piano trio and D Minor Violin Sonata. Kalbeck reports that the cellist Robert Hausmann asked Brahms to compose a second sonata in 1884 and that Hausmann's March 1885 performance of the first one in Vienna convinced Brahms to acquiesce. But Brahms had already played the first sonata with Haus-

---

28. *Brahms*, 3:384–386.

29. *Johannes Brahms und die Familie von Beckerath mit unveröffentlichten Brahmsbriefen und den Bildern und Skizzen von Willy von Beckerath,* ed. Kurt Stephenson (Hamburg: Christians Verlag, 1979), 25. In a letter to Brahms of 1 October 1883, Heinrich von Herzogenberg playfully referred to the monument. He alluded to a rumor that Brahms wanted to move from Vienna to Germany because of the perceived anti-German bias of Austria's prime minister, Count Taafe. *Brahms Briefwechsel,* 2:8.

30. For the musicales, see *Brahms und die Familie von Beckerath,* 29–39. For the letters referring to the gestating violin sonata, see 26 and 47.

31. Herzogenberg referred to the source of the scherzando sections of the A Major Violin Sonata: "At first, I didn't really like it that this lovely F major countenance [*Gesicht*] brought along a groom, a cheerfully melancholy Norwegian," *Brahms Briefwechsel,* 2:147. I discuss the connection between Brahms's movement and Grieg's G Major Violin Sonata in "Discourse and Allusion: The Chamber Music of Brahms," in *Nineteenth-Century Chamber Music,* ed. Stephen E. Hefling (New York: Schirmer Books, 1998), 262–264.

mann in September 1883, when Hausmann visited the Wiesbaden area and joined Rudolf von Beckerath and him in a succession of domestic performances.[32]

Among all of Brahms's works for the various chamber media, the E Minor Cello Sonata stands out for its odd proportions: two brief movements, a Quasi Menuetto and a fugal finale, follow a very extended and lyrical first movement. The sonata originally included an adagio that Brahms removed before publication, which led Kalbeck to speculate that the composer revived it as the impressive Adagio affettuoso of his much later F Major Cello Sonata.[33]

It is likely that the F Major Cello Sonata's genesis was further overdetermined. For another possible factor, in addition to the cast-off slow movement and Hausmann's request, has gone unnoticed: the documented impact, two months earlier, of the premiere of Bruckner's String Quintet both on Vienna's music worlds and on Brahms personally. Kalbeck did not associate Brahms's F Major Cello Sonata with Bruckner's Quintet. But in the chapter after his interpretation of the Third Symphony, he picked up the thread of Brahms and the political situation in Vienna when he discussed the battles between the factions around the two composers. According to Kalbeck, the first incident occurred in December 1883 at the Third Symphony's premiere in Vienna, when Bruckner's supporters booed the performance, only to be drowned out by the applause of Brahms's supporters.[34] Reviews did not mention these behaviors; rather, the conflict came out into the open in the press when Bruckner's Quintet premiered slightly more than a year later in January 1885, two months before Hausmann's public performance of Brahms's E Minor Cello Sonata in Vienna. Even critics who expressed reservations about Bruckner's String Quintet as a whole lavished praise on the Adagio, and Bruckner's success manifestly rankled Brahms. What is striking is that an unusual shared technical feature connects Brahms's F Major Cello Sonata, and especially its Adagio affettuoso, to Bruckner's String Quintet, also in F major, and its Adagio.[35] Responding to several influences, Brahms may well have begun to conceive a second sonata in the spring of 1885 around what would have to have been an extensively revised version of the first sonata's unused adagio.

Various factors no doubt also played a role in Brahms's increasing commitment to his "chamber-music ideal," among them Bruckner's emergence as a rival and the escalating political crisis. Brahms had also reached the critical age of fifty: chamber style is a natural vehicle for the introversion often ascribed to older artists. In any case, he made rapid progress on his compositional project and on 8 August 1886,

32. Kalbeck, *Brahms*, 4:33; and *Brahms und die Familie von Beckerath*, 37–38. At the Viennese home of Brahms's friends Richard and Maria Fellinger, Hausmann and the composer played the first cello sonata at least two more times before the summer of 1886: in the fall of 1884 and then in April 1886. See Richard Fellinger, *Klänge um Brahms: Erinnerungen* (Berlin: Deutsche Brahms-Gesellschaft, 1933), 25 and 48.

33. I explore Kalbeck's hypothesis in "Brahms's Cello Sonata in F Major and Its Genesis: A Study in Half-Step Relations," in *Brahms Studies*, ed. David Brodbeck (Lincoln: University of Nebraska Press, 1994), 1:139–160. Kalbeck presented his idea in *Brahms*, 4:33.

34. *Brahms*, 3:412.

35. I discuss the connections between the two cello sonatas and those between the F Major Cello Sonata and Bruckner's String Quintet in chapter 6.

less than two and a half months after his arrival, sent the first movements of all four chamber pieces to Billroth. Five days later, before Billroth could relay his reaction to the works, Brahms requested that his friend have the movements copied, but only in score and with preference given to the cello sonata and the A Major Violin Sonata.[36] Before he left on 4 October, he wrote a letter directly to the copyist, William Kupfer, instructing him to prepare the rest of the cello sonata in score and write out the complete cello part.[37]

Brahms was already moving toward performances of the new chamber music. As soon as he returned to Vienna on 8 October, he began making further arrangements for the premieres of both sonatas, to be played there from the manuscripts. The performances happened within a short interval: Hausmann and Brahms played the cello sonata on 24 November; Josef Hellmesberger and Brahms played the A Major Violin Sonata on 2 December. The premiere of the C Minor Piano Trio took place in Budapest on 22 December, and the first Viennese performance on 26 February 1887. By offering three compositions of closely related types to the public in one season, Brahms allowed critics to make a more convincing case for stylistic change than otherwise would have been possible.

Despite the relatively low status of duo sonatas and piano trios, early performances of these works led to a brief period of almost unanimous acclaim for the composer and his "new style." Contrary to his previous practice, Brahms postponed publication of the compositions until April 1887, at the end of the regular concert season, explaining to his publisher, Fritz Simrock, that he wanted to ensure that adequate practice and rehearsals preceded performances of them.[38] But the composer did give Hausmann permission to perform the cello sonata at least one more time before publication, and he also allowed Amalie Joachim to present the violin sonata and piano trio in Leipzig and Berlin before these pieces were generally available.[39] Brahms in this way carefully controlled performances of the new works, while at the same time making certain that they were heard in several important central European cities.

PERCEPTIONS OF BRAHMS'S "THIRD PERIOD" IN HIS LIFETIME

Even before critics had discerned signs of a third or late style in Brahms's music, at least one writer, Louis Köhler, was using the example of Beethoven to prepare the reception of such a style should it develop. In a polemical pamphlet about Brahms's "place in music history" published in 1880, Köhler wrote that Brahms "reminds us

36. For the two letters by Brahms, see *Brahms-Billroth Briefwechsel,* 396 and 398.

37. The letter is held in the Gesellschaft der Musikfreunde. I thank Prof. Dr. Otto Biba and Dr. Dexter Edge for helping me decipher Brahms's handwriting. An excerpt from the letter appeared in Biba, *Johannes Brahms in Wien* (Vienna: Gesellschaft der Musikfreunde, 1983), 79–80.

38. *Brahms Briefwechsel,* 11:140, letter of 23 January 1887.

39. Hausmann performed Op. 99 on 23 March 1887 in Berlin with Richard Barth. On the performances organized by Amalie Joachim, see Willi Rehberg, "Brahms-Erinnerungen," *Der Weihergarten: Beilage zu Melos* (July/October 1933): 26.

with good reason of Beethoven. But at the same time he has such an enigmatic nature we can not be certain: are we unable to penetrate the depths, or are the depths empty, or are there no depths whatsoever?"[40] Mining a familiar vein of quasi-Hegelian determinism, Köhler told a tale that merged biographical factors and historical forces in an attempt to preclude any possibility that a late style in the Beethovenian sense could emerge in Brahms's music. He noted not only Beethoven's "unparalleled individuality" but also the gradual development, "on the basis of a particular historical period and a tragic personal fate," of a unique style, "above all in the so-called 'late Beethoven.' "[41] Brahms's personal fate did not appear tragic, and rather than living with similar intensity in his own time, according to Köhler, Brahms lived in the music of past composers, above all Beethoven. Like other critics then and more recently, he saw Brahms as an artist unaffected by contemporary history, someone who composed "music about music."[42] From Köhler's perspective, the composer could never develop a true late style. And he implied congruence between biographical events and broader historical currents, rather than the artist's alienation from the outside world that twentieth-century writers on late style observe.

In other respects, late nineteenth-century writers viewed late style differently from the critics who would refine the concept slightly later. Thus twentieth-century discussions of composers' late styles, above all those of Bach and Beethoven, frequently dwell on a tendency toward abstraction, toward a sense of spirituality achieved perhaps paradoxically through concentration on technique.[43] But earlier critics often focused instead on lyricism, which they considered to be the source of an unparalleled expression of transcendence in late Beethoven. Kalbeck drew on this topos in remarks about Brahms's piano works from the 1890s: "Like the 'final Beethoven,' the 'final Brahms' is completely saturated by melody and with him [the music] also becomes, as he used to say about the Beethoven quartets, 'increasingly transfigured.' "[44]

Brahms's contemporaries had heard a new melodiousness in the Third Symphony in 1883 and the F Major String Quintet the previous year;[45] and critics on both sides of the musical divide discerned that agreeable change continuing in two of the new chamber pieces performed during the 1886–87 season. Indeed, the prominent Wagnerite Wilhelm Tappert wrote a rave review of the Berlin premiere of the A Major Violin Sonata and C Minor Piano Trio. Calling the former "a tranquil, euphonious, one could almost say an unpretentious work," he explicitly noted

40. *Johannes Brahms und seine Stellung in der Musikgeschichte* (Hannover: Verlag von Arnold Simon, 1880), 22.

41. *Johannes Brahms und seine Stellung,* 20.

42. *Johannes Brahms und seine Stellung,* 21. See also J. Peter Burkholder, "Museum Pieces: The Historicist Mainstream in Music of the Last Hundred Years," *Journal of Musicology* 2 (1983): 115–134.

43. In addition to the previously cited discussion by Broch, see the chapter "Late Works" in Carl Dahlhaus, *Ludwig van Beethoven: Approaches to His Music,* trans. Mary Whittall (Oxford: Clarendon Press, 1991), 219–237.

44. *Brahms,* 4:285.

45. Two correspondents for the *Musikalisches Wochenblatt,* for example, perceived the F Major String Quintet as having broader appeal than earlier music by Brahms. *Musikalisches Wochenblatt* 14 (1883): 57 and 67–68. Even Hugo Wolf praised this work. See *The Music Criticism of Hugo Wolf,* ed. and trans. Henry Pleasants (New York: Holmes and Meier, 1979), 27–28.

the absence of the brooding and austerity that critics had often singled out in their complaints about Brahms's music. As was frequently the case then, Tappert framed his remarks directly in terms of the composer's assumed personal outlook: "from beginning to end pleasant contentment—no gloomy pessimism, but rather cheerful zest for life." According to Tappert, "contact with the Brahmsian muse had become painful" to him until the Third Symphony. He speculated that listeners making their first acquaintance with the composer through the violin sonata might ask "How could the music world have been resistant to Brahms for so long?"[46]

The more "popular" manner also inspired praise elsewhere, as in an anonymous review of the piano trio's Viennese premiere: "This time the composer has drawn from the depths of his undeniably great lyric talent and given us a work that offers pleasure not only to the expert through its artistic working out, but also to the soul and ears of the naïve listener."[47] Although the "artistic working out" in Brahms's compositions had usually pleased the musically educated, supposed deficiencies in his melodic style had previously made his works inaccessible to the public at large. Critics thus welcomed the new melodiousness.

Even the veteran New German (thus at this point anti-Liberal) apologist Richard Pohl begrudgingly acknowledged the effectiveness of the C Minor Trio when he reviewed a performance at the Tonkünstlerfest des allgemeinen deutschen Musikvereins in June 1887:

> Salient features of this work are the conciseness of its forms, at least in the last three movements, and a certain striving for easy intelligibility—for popularity, if one may speak in this way about Brahms. . . . The trio, to be sure, does not belong to the most distinguished chamber music works by Brahms, but it is balanced in mood throughout and readily understood even on first hearing.[48]

Pohl's qualifying remark, that while the changed style was more accessible it was also less distinguished than that of his earlier chamber works, would become a recurring theme in assessments of this music. For many critics, the composer simply could not win.

Some critics did continue to consider the transparency and optimism they heard in this third style a positive development. After an 1895 performance of the Third Symphony, Kalbeck asserted: "the period of the composer's uncontested mastery in Vienna in fact dates only from the symphony's first performance. With it he won the Viennese public, which earlier more admired than loved the 'North German great man of music.' "[49] This bland assessment, however, glosses over many negative reactions to Brahms's works from the 1880s and 1890s. To be sure, Hanslick, who vocally disliked Beethoven's late works for what he heard as their pessimism, wrote that in his own later music Brahms increasingly resembled second-period Beethoven, going "in the reverse direction: from storminess to peace, from night

46. *Musikalisches Wochenblatt* 18 (1887): 17.

47. *Illustrirtes Wiener Extrablatt,* 27 February 1887.

48. *Musikalisches Wochenblatt* 18 (1887): 365. At midcentury, New German composers had been associated with a revolutionary kind of Liberalism.

49. *Montags-Revue,* 28 January 1895.

to light."[50] But other writers, including some who initially hailed Brahms's new style, began to interpret it as a symptom of decline.

The Leipzig-based critic Bernhard Vogel performed the most startling about-face. In an April 1887 review, he praised Brahms for no longer "addressing the listener with tonal puzzles, but rather with intimate, heart-winning melodic openness" and linked this to a new and "salutary optimism" in the composer's outlook.[51] Yet when Vogel finished a monograph on Brahms in August that same year, he took a negative position on the composer's apparent attempts at a more popular style. He still saw the three recently published chamber works as inaugurating a new style, that of Brahms's third period. But only four months after first hearing two of these pieces, he suggested that Brahms had compromised his integrity with the style change.

For Vogel, Brahms's most individual works were "stamped with deep seriousness to the point of unearthly darkness and obscurity." While knowledgeable listeners sensed something significant in those compositions, the public, "half-terrified," avoided them. Drawing Beethoven—of course—into the discussion, Vogel argued that while "the most characteristic Beethoven is always the truest and most imposing, the most characteristic Brahms is understood by only a few: that is the problem with his individuality." Using as his examples of Brahms's three periods the piano sonatas, the F Minor Piano Quintet, and the recent chamber music, respectively, Vogel acclaimed the "bold impetuosity" of the first and the "taciturn defiance" of the second period. And he concluded that Brahms at present "allows more peaceful powers dominion over himself; pleasantness wields the scepter and chases away the dark creatures of night" but that in allowing this, the composer is not true to himself.[52] Once he had developed this interpretation of Brahms's lifework, Vogel stuck with it. Still regarding these chamber pieces as the beginning of the composer's "third style," he reused much of the passage, virtually unchanged, in an obituary.[53]

How are we to account for the abrupt change in Vogel's position? Perhaps he had discussed the new works with colleagues such as Pohl during the summer. Given the increasingly politicized polarization within Austro-German music worlds, it was inevitable that some critics would come to interpret any imagined change of style as signifying deterioration rather than apotheosis. Within Vienna itself, furthermore, the question of a late style had become one more tool in polemical attacks on the composer, which increased toward the end of the 1880s. In his role as music critic for the *Deutsches Volksblatt*, Bruckner's biographer Göllerich wrote—albeit in a skewed, overtly biased fashion—about central questions in Brahms reception during the years around 1890, mixed at times with expressions of anti-Semitic or xenophobic sentiments. One issue was the new "popularity," in both meanings of the word, of his works: some of the music seemed more accessible to a broader public, but it was also "popular" in the secondary sense of "frequently encountered." In

50. From a review of Brahms, G Major String Quintet (1890), reprinted in *Aus dem Tagebuche eines Musikers*, 317.

51. Concert report from Leipzig, *Neue Zeitschrift für Musik* 54 (1887): 196.

52. *Johannes Brahms: Sein Lebensgang und eine Würdigung seiner Werke* Leipzig: Max Hesse's Verlag, 1888), 76. The preface indicates that Vogel completed the book in August 1887.

53. *Neue Zeitschrift für Musik* 64 (1897): 169–171.

one review, Göllerich claimed: "Today, besides foreign trinkets, we hear nothing but larger indigenous works by Brahms." According to him, if the public had the opportunity to hear "the real thing," music by Bruckner, "the whole, laboriously constructed popularity of Johannes the new evangelist in music would irretrievably be lost."[54]

Along with ongoing insistence that, despite his technical mastery, Brahms's works were weak in melodic invention, other topoi include the notion that the composer had entered a final period of creative decline. Thus Göllerich attacked Brahms as "never at any time a creator in the sense of our great masters, but undoubtedly a gifted, only all too brooding talent who has left behind him the period of his best inspirations."[55] From the perspective of Göllerich, like Köhler, Pohl, and Vogel, a late style in Brahms's oeuvre could never mean culmination, but rather only a falling-off; the very concept of late style had become politicized.

Certainly, a perception that Brahms's creativity was waning must have become widespread, since Schenker felt moved to counter it in an 1891 review. He attributed this to premature, misguided efforts to divide the composer's artistic output into periods:

> For some time now, critics and readers have whispered to themselves that Brahms has entered his third and weakest creative period. Now if feuilletonistic criticism, instinctively recognizing the greatness of the composer (it seldom offers evidence), wants to prepare the ground for music history and concern itself with periodization, then references even to the most splendid manifestations of the Brahmsian genius in this period will scarcely be proof enough for it. How can a Violin Sonata in A major, a String Quintet Op. 111, a Fourth Symphony in E minor be aligned to such a standard?[56]

Schenker's remarks also indicate that observations of a third style having evolved in the mid-1880s were commonplace.[57] As wrongheaded or even malicious as the comments about Brahms's new style were, the critics were correct in hearing a difference in the later music.

DEGREES OF TONAL/HARMONIC DEFINITION
AND MOMENTS OF EXPRESSIVE COMPLEXITY

Because of the emphasis on expressive qualities and their connection to the composer's conjectured personal outlook, the critical approach of Brahms's contemporaries may appear naïve to us today. In the essay quoted at the outset of this chapter, Adorno wanted, already in 1934, to deflect attention away from the "tone" of the music toward questions of compositional technique.[58] Whether acknowledged

---

54. *Deutsches Volksblatt,* 7 February 1889.

55. *Deutsches Volksblatt,* 9 February 1889.

56. "Johannes Brahms: Fünf Lieder für eine Singstimme mit Pianoforte, Op. 107," *Musikalisches Wochenblatt* 22 (1891): 514.

57. Heuberger referred to this in a review of the Clarinet Quintet: "Those who again and again parrot the nonsense that Brahms now writes in a colder, more reflective manner than in younger years will have to put a stop to their remarks before this Quintet." *Wiener Tagblatt,* 11 January 1892.

58. Yet tone is a central category in Adorno's monographs on Berg and Mahler.

or not, however, similar factors underlie most assessments of an artist's style; even in high-level discussions of style, personality and expression seem to be unavoidable topics. In one well-known recent study, the art historian Meyer Schapiro calls the style of an individual artist "a system of forms with a quality and a meaningful expression through which the personality of the artist" is discernible.[59] Brahms's melodies and his complex motivic work, for example, are two aspects of one "system of forms"—motives can develop into melodies—the style that projects his artistic personality, related to but not identical with his personality as a private individual.

The heightened lyricism noted by Brahms's contemporaries and the increasingly overt motivic density stressed by recent writers are both conspicuous in his later music, as are the apparent simplicity and greater conciseness that sometimes come up in discussions of artists' late styles. For each of the four first movements he sent to Billroth, furthermore, Brahms found an original approach to the connection between development and recapitulation, perhaps a tentative manifestation of the "experimental breakthrough into a new tonal world" that Niemöller notes in certain *Alterswerke*. Thus in the C Minor Piano Trio, while the opening group's first phrase (mm. 1–4) returns, transformed but in the tonic, to begin the development section, the powerful prolonged dominant from the center of the group (mm. 5–11) eventually becomes part of a markedly long retransition dominant.[60] This does not lead to another statement of the opening phrase but rather to the recapitulation of the second thematic group, set dramatically in relief.[61]

Reception of this second theme reflects the changing priorities among critics. In contrast to a contemporary of Brahms who referred to the "noble, long-breathed song" of that theme, recent writers often cite its head-motive as an example of his ingenuity at manipulating motives.[62] For the opening of the second theme, Brahms augments a motive from m. 1, called motive *a* here, chromatically inflecting the pitches (B-natural–C–D–E-flat) to fit into E-flat major (B-flat–C–D–E-flat), where they represent different scale degrees. Although the half-step cell *x*, formed from a chordal pitch and an adjacent pitch, mutates, the four-note motive that opens the second theme is audibly connected to the original configuration. (See ex. 2.1a and b.) Brahms in this way maintains most of the basic shape of motive *a* while fundamentally reinterpreting its harmonic and tonal meaning. Without having to force the point, moreover, the entire second group can be heard as arising through developing variation of both motives from m. 1, always permuting or shadowing at least the contour of one of the motives or a derivative of one.[63] Yet the theme as a whole is as songlike as the earlier critic observed.

While the later compositions, as Kalbeck asserted and this theme illustrates, often sound more melodious than the earlier music, they do not, contrary to Kalbeck's

59. "Style," in *Theory and Philosophy of Art: Style, Artist, and Society* (New York: Braziller, 1994), 51.

60. The third part of the opening thematic group (mm. 12–20) reappears to bring full closure at the end of the recapitulation (mm. 200–208) before the coda.

61. Another work in C minor, the first movement of the Piano Quartet, Op. 60, prefigures Brahms's treatment of form here.

62. Review of the Budapest premiere, *Pester Lloyd,* 23 December 1886.

63. On developing variation and its application to Brahms's music, see Walter Frisch, *Brahms and the Principle of Developing Variation* (Berkeley: University of California Press, 1984).

EXAMPLE 2.1a. Brahms, C Minor Piano Trio, Op. 101 / I, mm. 1–4

further claims, recall Beethoven's late works. Brahms tended to shy away from ex-pressions of transcendence.[64] On the other hand, certain moments in late Brahms convey affective states or mental processes that have no real parallels in Beethoven. As Geiringer notes, Brahms developed early on the "blending of moods" we asso-ciate with his music. But in some later works—indeed, already at the end of the F Major Quintet's middle movement—he concentrates expressive complexity in brief passages. These moments make it clear that Brahms was the contemporary of Adolph Menzel and Theodor Fontane in Germany and Robert Browning and Henry James in England, and they remind us that in the 1880s and 1890s he was living in the Vienna of Freud and Breuer.[65]

Various elements contribute to the power of these moments: Brahms's use of dy-namics, the nature of his motivic work, and above all his unprecedented mastery of degrees and types of tonal or harmonic definition. The latter facet of his style has received little attention. To be sure, late twentieth-century commentaries some-times single out "ambiguity" as a basic premise of his compositional approach. Kofi Agawu, however, argues that the concept of ambiguity in tonal music does not stand up under scrutiny, since harmonic meaning is always determinable in that music.[66] What has typically been seen as Brahms's cultivation of harmonic or tonal ambiguity, especially in his later works, can often be framed more precisely in dif-ferent terms. One characteristic strategy is to underscore that a key and its relative

64. Gülke, *Brahms–Bruckner*, 19: "apotheoses were never Brahms's thing."

65. Brinkmann discusses Fontane and Menzel in *Late Idyll,* and Roland Jordan and Emma Kafalenos compare Brahms to James in "The Double Trajectory: Ambiguity in Brahms and Henry James," *19th-Century Music* 13 (1989): 129–144.

66. "Ambiguity in Tonal Music: A Preliminary Study," in *Theory, Analysis and Meaning in Music,* ed. Anthony Pople (New York: Cambridge University Press, 1994), 86–107.

EXAMPLE 2.1b.   Brahms, C Minor Piano Trio, Op. 101 / I, mm. 38–41

major or minor are aspects of each other, as in the first movement of the D Minor Violin Sonata and the Clarinet Quintet's third movement, both of which I shall discuss in this chapter.[67]

In a number of his later works, Brahms also creates evocative moments that seem on paper to prolong a tonic yet sound unmistakably like a dominant. A beautiful example of this second strategy appears at the end of the development section in the F Major Cello Sonata's first movement. According to Schoenberg, early audiences had difficulty understanding this work because the opening motivic interval, a rising fourth, evolves so quickly and immediately.[68] But throughout most of the development section, Brahms avoids conventional motivic work until the head-motive comes to the surface, pianissimo, like something faintly remembered (m. 94); the impression of a sentient subject is strong.[69] Eventually all the pitches from the opening four measures return (mm. 112–118), with the rhythms equalized and expanded to fill seven measures. This passage looks as if it starts on the tonic yet audibly prolongs the retransition dominant. Like the theme's notes, the tonic sounds like a distant recollection that becomes vivid again when the recapitulation begins. Similar effects of "recovered memory" occur in other late Brahms works.

A third, more general strategy, which can encompass the other two, is to stress a key's instability. This strategy underlies a passage from the development section of the C Minor Piano Trio's first movement, in particular mm. 98–101. As noted earlier, the development begins with a variant of the movement's opening phrase: mo-

67. Grieg does this as well in the middle movement of the G Major Violin Sonata, which caught Brahms's interest in the summer of 1883.

68. "The Orchestral Variations, Op. 31: A Radio Talk," *Score* 26 (July 1960): 28. See also Frisch's discussion of Schoenberg's analysis in *Brahms and Developing Variation,* 4–5 and 146–147.

69. See James Webster, "The General and the Particular in Brahms's Later Sonata Forms," in *Brahms Studies: Analytical and Historical Perspectives,* ed. George S. Bozarth (Oxford: Clarendon Press, 1990), 74–75; and Peter H. Smith, "Liquidation, Augmentation, and Brahms's Recapitulatory Overlaps," *19th-Century Music* 17 (1994): 247–253.

EXAMPLE 2.1C.   Brahms, C Minor Piano Trio, Op. 101 / I, mm. 81–85

tives *a* and *b*, presented simultaneously in mm. 1–4, now appear successively and otherwise transformed (mm. 81–85; see ex. 2.1c). The reworked opening in C minor emphasizes the distance and the fragility of the keys that follow. Jenner, Brahms's student, quoted remarks by the composer on the first quality:

> An integrated modulation does not in any way rule out the use of the most remote keys. Quite the contrary, these remote keys become so only because another is the governing one. They receive true power of expression in that way, they say something else. They are like colors in a picture that separate from the background color, which both contains and enhances them.[70]

Here Brahms begins the process of "separation from the background color" after the extended half cadence of mm. 85–87 by freezing A-flat as a temporary new tonic, a half-step move upward derived from the semitonal cell *x*. From this point through m. 113, the various implied keys sound remarkably unstable in ways that have little to do with traditional developmental procedures. The effect derives in part from the reduced dynamics and even more from the deceleration of both rhythmic values and harmonic rhythm that begins with the augmented A-flat in m. 87: the notes and harmonies move more slowly, but the key is never made secure. As in the cello sonata, rhythmic augmentation intensifies the impact of the harmonic strategy.

Brahms bases the first part of the development (through m. 113) on transformations of motives *a* and *b*. In the central transformation of mm. 98–101, a different counterpoint between the two motives comes about through their changed position in the measure (see ex. 2.2). But why does the key, C-sharp minor, seem especially unstable here? Although an A-flat/G-sharp triad is prolonged throughout mm. 87–113, most obviously in mm. 87–101, briefly as tonic (mm. 87–92) and then as dominant, it never sounds secure in either role, and certainly not in mm. 98–101.

70. *Brahms als Mensch,* 39.

EXAMPLE 2.2.   Brahms, C Minor Piano Trio, Op. 101 / I, mm. 86–102

A partial explanation for the effect of these measures is possible. To begin with, the surface harmonic rhythm is more rapid than before. Because of the quicker harmonic rhythm, the original harmonic meaning of motive *a*—the second and fourth pitches taken as chordal tones—appears to hold on the downbeats of mm. 98 and 99, but then changes. For example, although the C-sharp-minor six-three on the downbeat in m. 98 momentarily seems to resolve the diminished-seventh chord from the preceding measure (m. 97), it is immediately absorbed into the cadential six-four that follows on the second beat of m. 98. There is thus a passing conflict between levels of harmonic significance: while the chord on the downbeat of m. 98 seems to be a tonic, it merely prepares the cadential six-four and therefore has only the most fleeting status as a tonic. The entire passage prolongs the dominant of C-sharp minor.

Measures 98–101 represent the moment of greatest expressive and harmonic/tonal complexity in a long passage marked throughout by the tenuous sound of chords and keys. Motive *a* subsequently appears in a D major that is even less stable than the C-sharp minor (mm. 103–104), arrived at through a deceptive cadence (therefore related to both cell *x* and the semitonal shift in m. 87). A briefly implied G major (mm. 105–108) leads via chromatic and enharmonic mutation (D becomes D-sharp, C, B-sharp) and another change in meaning—B-sharp and G-sharp, embellishments in mm. 109–110, become harmonic tones at the upbeat to m. 111—to a restatement of the G-sharp (A-flat) major triad. From m. 114, Brahms uses harmonic instability for a more traditional purpose: with fragmentation and sequences to produce a sense of the music driving toward the lengthy retransition dominant that begins in m. 126.

But the effect in mm. 87–113 is far removed from that made by development sections in Haydn and early and middle-period Beethoven, described by Adorno as based on a principle of "'doing,' accomplishing, something."[71] For the "bustling eagerness to get something done" in that music Brahms substitutes an evocation of memory. Slowing down the sense of time through prolonged and at the same time audibly untenable harmonies, to the same end he also uses devices such as augmentation and the flattening of previously differentiated rhythmic figures (e.g., in mm. 87–91) as part of ongoing reconfiguration of motives.[72] Throughout the passage from m. 87 to m. 113, the motivic work creates an image in sound that resembles psychological association far more than it does logical thinking or any other purposeful activity. Because of the slight changes in motive forms from one measure to the next (e.g., in mm. 91–97) against the background of sustained but obviously provisional keys, the effect is of one motive form bringing to mind another.[73] As in the passage from the F Major Cello Sonata, the music models a kind

71. *Beethoven*, 37–38.

72. Similar moments occur in the development section of the G Major String Quintet's first movement. See my discussion in "Discourse and Allusion," 278, and Elisabeth Reiter, *Sonatensatz in der späten Kammermusik von Brahms: Einheit und Zusammenhang in variativen Verfahren* (Tutzing: Hans Schneider, 2000), 171–172.

73. Mitschka writes of the "irrational" treatment of this part of the form in certain works of Brahms, as of Schubert and Schumann, in "Sonatensatz in Brahms," 156.

EXAMPLE 2.3a.   Beethoven, First Symphony / I, mm. 13–25

of unwilled thought process. The expressive qualities in these moments are as characteristic of the later Brahms as the virtuoso technique that makes them possible.

OSTENSIBLE SIMPLICITY VERSUS MANNERISTIC ARTIFICE IN THE LATER CHAMBER MUSIC

Composers have often focused on chamber music late in life, in part because the genre encourages probing the limits, the arcane aspects of their craft. In a discussion of Brahms, Dahlhaus amplifies the latter point: "musical artifice is an element basic to chamber music, defining its character as a music for private rather than public performance; but it was supposed to remain half concealed, in accordance with the motto *nascondere l'arte*."[74] An aesthetic partially based on concealing fine points of musical craft would certainly help account for contemporary reception of the A Major Violin Sonata and C Minor Piano Trio, which stressed the music's direct appeal rather than its—to some extent—hidden technical complexities.

Consider the sonata's beginning. Without drawing attention to the artifice involved, Brahms transforms a conventional opening move in which the second phrase rises a step to present a tonal sequence of the first phrase. The Allegro con brio of Beethoven's First Symphony begins with a more typical example: the tonic chord progresses to an applied dominant seventh, which is strongly connected through a crescendo and upbeat figuration to the supertonic triad that opens the second phrase (see ex. 2.3a, mm. 17–19). Giving the construction a different emphasis, Brahms stresses the relationship between the applied dominant seventh and the chord that *precedes* it, which he strengthens in the second phrase by artfully bringing back the same pair of chords transposed down a whole step (see ex. 2.3b, mm. 3–4 and 8–9).

---

74. *Nineteenth-Century Music,* 260.

EXAMPLE 2.3b.   Brahms, A Major Violin Sonata, Op. 100 / I, mm. 1–12

In Brahms's reworking of this standard construction, the chord that precedes the dominant seventh sounds like a subdominant of the subdominant, especially in mm. 8–9. (In m. 8 he reaches that chord via a Neapolitan sixth in m. 7.) Measures 10–11 briefly allude to the plagal implications, which are eventually expanded to great effect in the coda (mm. 219–242). While the consequences are thus dramatic, Brahms deemphasizes the ingenuity involved in transforming a much plainer construction into the one that opens this movement.

He likewise downplays the artifice in the sonata's middle movement. As in the F Major String Quintet, this movement consists of alternating slow and fast sections: here three F major Andantes, two D minor scherzandi, and a scherzando coda in F major. No process of modulation leads from the F major of the Andantes to the D minor of the scherzandi; a bare 5–6 voice leading motion prepares the D minor of each Vivace (see ex. 2.4). Demonstrating again Brahms's mastery of ways (and degrees) of asserting a key, the movement goes between the tonic major and its relative minor in an understated fashion that shows each key to be an aspect of the other while simultaneously supporting the aura of pastoral naturalness.[75]

The aesthetic Dahlhaus describes would help account not only for the positive reception of the A Major Violin Sonata and C Minor Piano Trio but also for the

75. Tovey called this movement "a counterpart in pastoral comedy" to the "sublime mystery" of the F Major String Quintet's middle movement. "Brahms's Chamber Music," in *The Main Stream of Music and Other Essays*, 262.

EXAMPLE 2.4.   Brahms, A Major Violin
Sonata, Op. 100 / II, mm. 14–15

less positive reaction to the F Major Cello Sonata and D Minor Violin Sonata. In their response to these, critics emphasized the obscurity of the cello sonata's first movement and the overt reliance on artifice in that of the D Minor Violin Sonata.[76] One critic wrote that the D Minor Violin Sonata's opening Allegro "repeatedly starts in a song-like manner but ends over and over again in the sands of rhythmic-harmonic artifice."[77] Another deemed the first movement "genuine Brahms," adding: "the idea works with audible difficulty, and none of the motives, once touched upon, succeeds in artistic, vivid elaboration; it is a perpetual playing with techniques."[78]

Brahms's contemporaries were hardly infallible critics of his music, and they were most likely referring to features other than the one I shall discuss. Still, in this movement, unlike much of the other chamber music, he dwells on the artifice to a degree that justifies calling the movement mannerist. Historians of various arts typically invoke the concept, which implies exaggeration, preciosity, esoteric procedures, elitist art, in reference to the final phase of the Renaissance—and an earlier chamber-music ideal than that described by Dahlhaus—but sometimes also to other late styles.[79] In one of the most pertinent discussions of musical mannerism, James Haar advocates reserving the term for instances in which composers are narrowly concerned with various techniques or "manners" for their own sake, understood against the norms of an unchallenged classical style.[80]

76. About the cello sonata, Helm wrote: "many of the intermediate links remain unclear to the unprepared listener," *Deutsche Zeitung*, 27 November 1886. Schoenberg asserted that "at the time of Brahms's death this sonata was still very unpopular and was considered indigestible" because of its unusual opening theme. See the references in note 68.

77. "k. st.," *Illustrirtes Wiener Extrablatt*, 14 February 1889.

78. "W. Fr.," *Neues Wiener Tagblatt*, 15 February 1889.

79. Dahlhaus himself connected later chamber music to Renaissance madrigals in "Brahms und die Idee der Kammermusik."

80. "Classicism and Mannerism in 16th-Century Music," *International Review of the Aesthetics and Sociology of Music* 25 (1994): 5–18. This article appeared twenty-five years earlier in the journal's first issue. The literature on musical mannerism is vast. For a discussion of various approaches to defining it and

Charges of artificiality in Brahms's music are often unmistakably polemical and tendentious. In his later years, however, he did compose several works concerned with compositional speculation and virtuosity, the "prominence of artifice" Schmidt notes, to an extent that supports calling them mannerist. Brahms is not alone in this respect among older composers; other composers have likewise become obsessed with technical aspects of art—that is, with artifice—most commonly with counterpoint, late in life.[81] Bach provides an obvious example of an almost single-minded focus on "playing with techniques" of counterpoint toward the end of a life. But the gnarled textures and other anticlassical distortions in the *Grosse Fuge* and the *Hammerclavier* Sonata's finale make Beethoven especially open to the specific charge of mannerism. Brahms himself took musical artifice to an extreme in works such as the E Minor and F Minor Intermezzos for piano solo (Op. 116, No. 5, and Op. 118, No. 4). In each of these pieces composed after his fleeting retirement, he clearly valued the possibilities offered and problems posed by particular techniques—syncopation and hemiola in the former and close, pervasive canonic writing in the latter—above other considerations.

Among the late chamber compositions, the first movement of the D Minor Violin Sonata, the work that Mason viewed as inaugurating Brahms's final period, fits into the same category. Unlike the A Major Violin Sonata's middle movement with its façade of naturalness, this Allegro openly suggests studied experimentation in ways of moving between a key and its relative major or minor. Furthermore, it is a minor-mode sonata-form movement, a type predicated on establishing contrast between the minor key and its relative major. In this first movement, Brahms pursues effects of referring briefly but conspicuously to each of the keys in a formal section governed by the other.

D minor sounds unstable at the beginning because of the initial emphasis on F major (see mm. 4 and 8 in ex. 2.5). Throughout most of the movement, moreover, the status of D minor as tonic is projected by its dominant, notably by a pedal point throughout the entire development section. The first group even cadences on a tonicized A minor triad (with a Picardy third, m. 24). And, just as F major makes an appearance in the first group as a facet of D minor, the dominant of D minor (mm. 56–61) returns in the middle of the F major second group.

Such interpenetration of the form-defining keys in a minor-mode work must have fascinated Brahms, since he (and other composers) used this as a formal premise many times, with striking consequences above all in his later music. Why, then, might this movement deserve the label "mannerist" more than others? Within the field of similar works by him, here he took the experiment to a kind of logical extreme while deliberately drawing attention to his procedures.

Two pitches play central roles in this study in tonal ambivalence. The first is A, especially as a treble note, common to D minor, F major, and A major/minor triads, but when placed at the top of the texture not indicating full closure in either

---

their different drawbacks, see Hellmut Federhofer, "Der Manierismus-Begriff in der Musikgeschichte," *Archiv für Begriffsgeschichte* 17 (1973): 206–220.

81. Stravinsky offers another example of a composer obsessed with counterpoint late in life.

EXAMPLE 2.5.   Brahms, D Minor Violin Sonata, Op. 108 / I, mm. 1–10

D minor or F major. A pattern of A reappearing in the treble at important formal junctures until well into the recapitulation (mm. 1, 24, 25, 45, 83, 84, 130, and 153) undermines a sense of conclusive harmonic-contrapuntal progression. The second important pitch is D-flat, the flattened sixth degree in F major and enharmonically equivalent to C-sharp, the leading tone in D minor. This pitch relationship, increasingly prominent in Brahms's music and late nineteenth-century music in general, epitomizes the likewise increasing emphasis on plagal harmony in his oeuvre and in music by his contemporaries.[82] Especially in many late works, Brahms uses the equivalence to move between a key and its relative major or minor. Here he introduces the enharmonically equivalent pitches with their different resolutions, which connect the keys of D minor and F major, already in mm. 3 and 4, as shown in example 2.5.

Two formal anomalies in this movement are well known: (1) as already noted, the singular, hypnotic development section occurs from beginning to end over a dominant pedal; and (2) the first group reappears (is recapitulated) twice thereafter. In part because the dominant chord has almost invariably projected D minor up

82. According to some theories, the sixth scale degree in the minor mode, associated with subdominant harmony and resolving downward by semitone to scale degree five, is as characteristic of that mode as the leading tone is of major keys. See Daniel Harrison, *Harmonic Function in Chromatic Music: A Renewed Dualist Theory and an Account of Its Precedents* (Chicago: University of Chicago Press, 1994).

EXAMPLE 2.6.   Brahms, D Minor Violin Sonata, Op. 108 / I, mm. 202–205

until that point, the development pedal carries little weight, certainly not enough to make it qualify as the "structural dominant" that typically appears by the close of the development, if not earlier.[83] But with the recapitulation of the second group (mm. 186–203), a tonic triad is finally representing D (now major).[84] Toward the end of this group, definitive motion away from D major (to F major, in m. 204) and back to a chord with the full dramatic force of a structural dominant (m. 214) at last takes place. Logically enough, this dominant leads to the second, "true" recapitulation of the opening theme (mm. 218–236), which for the first time closes in D rather than A minor; the first theme, too, requires resolution.

While these unusual formal features, based on the premise that the two keys are aspects of each other, in themselves might justify the designation "mannerist," at several points Brahms underscores the artifice involved in carrying out his idea. Most obviously, at the climax of the second group's recapitulation, the dominant of D major moves dramatically to F major through enharmonic resolution, again, of C-sharp as D-flat. (See m. 204 in ex. 2.6.) This motion away from the dominant of D and subsequent return to it as a structural dominant was necessary for Brahms's overall plan. Yet the moment is also exaggerated, mannered, self-reflexive.

Earlier, when the dominant of D minor reappears in the second group (mm. 56–61), Brahms transposes material presented shortly before, at the end of the transition, to prolong the dominant of F (mm. 40–44). The sound of this suddenly softer passage—music already heard but now stated conspicuously in the wrong key—seems to place quotation marks around what is after all quoted material. But the

83. Heinrich Schenker calls this the "divider dominant." *Free Composition (Der freie Satz): Volume 3 of New Musical Theories and Fantasies,* trans. Ernst Oster, 2 vols. (New York: Longman, 1979), 1:37.

84. Musgrave notes that the nature of the development section "has profound consequences for the movement, since the normal tonal exploration of the section has to take place in the recapitulation," by which he means the recapitulation of the transition (*Brahms,* 191). Since most of the recapitulated transition is audibly an almost exact transposition of the transition in the exposition (mm. 168–185 are the same as mm. 30–47 down a minor third), however, the dominant at the end does not carry sufficient weight to function as a structural dominant.

EXAMPLE 2.7a.   Brahms, D Minor Violin Sonata, Op. 108 / I, mm. 40–44

C-sharp implicitly resolves as if it were D-flat (mm. 60–61), and the group continues in F major as if nothing out of the ordinary has happened. (See ex. 2.7a and b.)
And after full closure in F major at the end of the second group in the exposition—
thus, with F (scale degree one) in the treble at the cadence (m. 74)—a treble D-flat
repeatedly appears in the closing group, resolving normatively each time to C, scale
degree five. Nothing in the immediate context motivates the subsequent reinstate-
ment of A, scale degree three in F major, at the end of the section. Thus this
moment, too, despite its quiet dynamic level, stands out from the music that surrounds it. Brahms does not model reflectiveness in any of these moments. Rather,
he exaggerates the elements—the artifice—that support his conception of this
movement. In cultivating technical devices that disturb the smooth surface of a classical style without undermining it, he displays an attitude consistent with late-style
mannerism.

LATE STYLE IN A STRONGER SENSE:
THE CHAMBER MUSIC WITH CLARINET

Mersmann writes: "we speak of the old-age works [*Alterswerke*] of an artist and in
this concept confront a complex of traits that is intricate and difficult to grasp." List-
ing attributes such as "venerable patina, distant removal from life, a changed atti-

EXAMPLE 2.7b.   Brahms, D Minor Violin Sonata, Op. 108 / I, mm. 56–61

tude toward the elements of artistic expression," he concludes that these have in common a tendency to isolate an artist's old-age works from those of the previous period of ripe maturity. To illustrate his point, he cites Brahms's belief that with his G Major String Quintet he had reached the end. According to Mersmann, the chamber music with clarinet that followed was "only outwardly conditioned by his acquaintance with Mühlfeld," adding that these four compositions "breathe in a pure sphere removed from their own past."[85] Certainly, in these final chamber works, late-style traits such as introversion and conciseness are more pronounced than in the chamber music from the previous decade.

Accounts of the works' genesis typically do credit the playing of the clarinetist Richard Mühlfeld with having inspired Brahms to compose again after his short-lived decision to retire. Gülke, however, takes a position similar to that of Mersmann and words it more provocatively: "as if he does not want to bear the responsibility alone, [the composer] blames . . . Mühlfeld's art for the late chamber music's having come into existence."[86] Brahms himself told a friend, the musicologist Eusebius Mandyczewski, that after completing the G Major String Quintet he had begun other compositions, "but nothing would turn out right." Recognizing that he had been industrious throughout his life and faced no financial worries in old age, Brahms absolved himself of the need to compose anything more: "And that made me so happy, so satisfied, so pleased, that all at once it worked again."[87] Brahms's anecdote suggests that by briefly relinquishing all further ambition he gained a sense of freedom. This resonates with observations regarding contexts for late works.[88]

The sources of creativity are too mysterious for any simple explanation to be able to account fully for the transitory feeling of artistic barrenness that preceded Brahms's composition of the chamber music with clarinet. But in his discussion of works from the mid-1880s, Kalbeck imputed fundamental importance in the composer's creativity to his sense of German cultural superiority. Indeed, his biographer first presented Brahms as having mapped his own evolution as an artist onto the progress of the German nation and then proceeded to forgive him for having done something that Kalbeck personally viewed as foolish. He concluded: "And who wanted to laugh at his innocent artist's delusion, which measured the course of things against his own development until both coalesced for him into one inseparable historical process?" Although he did not raise them himself, Kalbeck's commentary should provoke questions concerning the emergence of a late style in Brahms's music. For example, to what extent did he feel alienated from the extreme forms of German nationalism that became a clear threat around 1890? How might such estrangement—an estrangement, as will be discussed in the epilogue, that seems indisputable—have affected him and his work? For if we accept Kalbeck's claim that Brahms had required the "fine superstition" of German superiority to compose, we

85. "Alterswerke der Kunst," 118.
86. *Brahms–Bruckner,* 63.
87. Kalbeck, *Brahms,* 4:247, n. 2.
88. See, for example, the remarks by Tietze cited earlier.

must assume that the increasing indefensibility of that position would have had an impact on his creativity.[89]

Beyond that crisis, beyond even the undeniable effects of aging, other factors no doubt contributed to the psychological isolation often associated with the development of a late style and implied in a number of stories about Brahms. One factor would have to have been the irrelevance of his own work, and of aspects of craft that mattered a great deal to him, to some of the most talented younger composers, including Mahler and Richard Strauss. The rise of modernism in the arts around 1890, like the sociopolitical crisis that peaked more or less simultaneously, would have tended to give Brahms the appearance of someone who had outlived his time, a view supported by contemporary reception of his music I have cited. In comments quoted earlier, the art critic Tietze notes that such a sense of "being out-dated" sometimes leads older artists to a productive attitude of indifference toward their public.

Feelings of isolation must account for some unusual late-style features. In essays on Beethoven and Goethe, Adorno writes about each artist's use of archaisms in the final phases of his career, claiming that expressiveness adheres more to that device, which conveys alienation, than to others.[90] (He makes similar comments about the modally tinged harmonies in Wagner's *Parsifal* that for Adorno, as for other listen-ers, bear an audible resemblance to passages in Brahms.)[91] I shall argue in chapter 3 that such features in the Clarinet Trio's first movement likewise create an atmo-sphere of estrangement. Because of the context in which Brahms introduces the ar-chaisms, the effect is more pronounced than in either the Fourth Symphony or the Chorale Preludes, the works Niemöller mentions in related remarks.

Other writers note stylistic features that look to the future. About Beethoven's final quartets and Liszt's late piano music Dahlhaus writes: "The correlative of the chronological 'homelessness' of late works is an anticipatory modernity."[92] Al-though a famous critical tradition deriving from Schoenberg himself stresses that "progressive" traits in Brahms's music, above all its total thematicism, anticipate his own brand of modernism, this literature does not single out the late works.[93] Thus both Adorno and Ernst Křenek connect the complex motivic development in Bee-thoven's late quartets to Brahms (in general) and ultimately to Schoenberg.[94] At one point Adorno does remark on "the infinite motivic economy that character-izes the technique of the later Brahms," without clarifying where he places "the later Brahms."[95] Elsewhere he asserts that "the principle of universal thematic work

89. *Brahms*, 3:385.

90. "On the Final Scene of *Faust*"; and "Alienated Masterpiece," in *Essays on Music*.

91. "On the Score of *Parsifal*."

92. *Beethoven*, 219.

93. See Frisch, *Brahms and Developing Variation*, 1–18, for a summary of relevant writings by Schoen-berg.

94. "Schoenberg logically follows the last quartets of Beethoven and ties up to them, with Brahms serving as the connecting link." Křenek, *Music Here and Now*, trans. Barthold Fles (New York: Norton, 1939), 83.

95. "On the Problem of Musical Analysis," trans. Max Paddison, in *Essays on Music*, 163.

was already achieved in Brahms as early as in the Piano Quintet."[96] Could the Piano Quintet, completed in 1864, be what Adorno means by "the later Brahms"?

Had Adorno attempted to define style periods in Brahms's oeuvre, it is likely he would have encountered even greater problems than other writers because of his inclination to focus narrowly on motivic/thematic techniques, which Brahms did in fact master at an early age. (Adorno did not bring such a narrow technical focus to his work on Beethoven.) If Brahms had achieved "the principle of universal thematic work" in the Piano Quintet, however, the chamber music with clarinet from more than a quarter-century later takes such virtuosity to another level altogether. And while the motivic work may be considered to anticipate Schoenberg's reliance on thematic development in his posttonal music, the motives in certain of Brahms's last chamber movements are more intimately connected than ever before to particular tonal/harmonic meanings.

In any case, style, as Schapiro suggests, goes beyond a single type of technique; it encompasses a complex of technical features and an individual mode of expression, both of which change as artists mature and then grow old. The visual artists Brinckmann studied tended in old age toward "a bending back into the self." The objective correlative of this psychological tendency is a stylistic tendency to which he applied the word *Verschmolzenheit,* "a blending of all the formal and expressive elements." Conveying as it does introversion, this "blended" style lacks the dynamism and contrasts of the artists' previous styles.[97] Many writers note changes of these kinds in Brahms's chamber music with clarinet.

The most popular of the works has always been the Clarinet Quintet. Blended affects had long been characteristic of Brahms's music, but here he achieved a new sound that critics immediately recognized. Several reviews mentioned the mixed sentiments approvingly; the Clarinet Quintet's first performance seems in fact to have been the most successful premiere of a Brahms composition in Vienna. Some critics linked the expressive effect in the first and third movements to the frequent motion between the tonic triad (B minor and D major, respectively) and its relative major or minor. Thus after interpreting expression of "sorrow for the transience of all earthly things" in the quintet, Kalbeck wrote: "Characteristic of the conciliatory, in the best sense humorous, basic mood of the work is the free play the composer makes with the relative major of B minor." Robert Hirschfeld likewise referred to the "changing mood, which never wearies and keeps the listener constantly in suspense" and to the "chiaroscuro of the tonality."[98]

The "chiaroscuro of the tonality" helps create the sound that marks the Clarinet Quintet as an *Alterswerk.* Twenty-five years before, Brahms similarly mixed an E-flat triad into the tonic triad at the beginning of the G Major String Sextet, an early work exhibiting "autumnal" qualities. The autumnal sound, closely linked to his harmonic style, remained consistent despite other sorts of stylistic changes evident

---

96. *Einleitung in die Musiksoziologie,* 119. He links this aspect of the Piano Quintet to Beethoven's final quartets, as he does Brahms's music more generally elsewhere.

97. *Spätwerke grosser Meister,* 41. I use the (free) translation of *Verschmolzenheit* in Held, "Commentary," 127.

98. Kalbeck, *Montags-Revue,* 18 January 1892; and Hirschfeld, *Die Presse,* 12 January 1892.

EXAMPLE 2.8a.   Brahms, Clarinet Quintet, Op. 115 / I, mm. 3–4

in the final chamber works: pronounced reduction in length, diminished contrast between thematic groups, and so on. In the first and third movements of the Clarinet Quintet, he tied longstanding features of his harmonic style to constant, overt reinterpretation of motives, and in a manner transparent enough that critics immediately discerned much of his modus operandi.

The acuity of the critics' comments supports the idea that Brahms's late music was not in general considered difficult to understand. On first hearing, Hirschfeld,

EXAMPLE 2.8b.   Brahms, Clarinet Quintet, Op. 115 / III, mm. 140–146

EXAMPLE 2.9a.   Brahms, Clarinet Quintet, Op. 115 / III, mm. 1–2

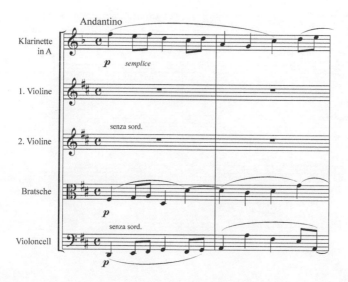

in particular, noted a number of fine points; he wrote, for example, that the opening four measures of the first movement provide "in a highly original manner a microcosm of the work." Regarding the third movement, an intermezzo, he heard that the theme of the scherzando middle section derives from the movement's opening theme through diminution, as did Kalbeck. More impressive, Hirschfeld detected a subtle motivic connection between the third and first movements. (See ex. 2.8a and b.)

EXAMPLE 2.9b.   Brahms, Clarinet Quintet, Op. 115 / III, m. 34

EXAMPLE 2.9c.   Brahms, Clarinet Quintet, Op. 115 / III, mm. 14–16

Furthermore, he perceived the plagal inclinations of the third movement's basic motive, D–C-sharp–D–B, the last note of which Brahms harmonizes with a subdominant triad in both the opening D major Andantino and central B minor Presto non troppo, respectively G major and E minor triads. (See ex. 2.9a and b.) Within the D major of the Andantino, the motive also permits several cadences in B minor, as shown in example 2.9c, thus supporting the frequent motion between the two keys. And the motive has further harmonic implications. After the Andantino, the Presto non troppo serves as a kind of sonata-form trio. In the exposition, the basic motive (m. 34) is not harmonized until its second pitch, C-sharp, at which point the dominant of B minor appears (ex. 2.9b). As a consequence of this harmoniza-

EXAMPLE 2.9d.   Brahms, Clarinet Quintet, Op. 115 / III, mm. 116–122

tion, Brahms prepares (in mm. 114–121) the recapitulation with the *secondary* dominant ninth—C-sharp–E-sharp–G-sharp–B–D—three notes of which belong to the
basic motive, eventually presented in the first violin (mm. 118–121); see example
2.9d. Motivic and harmonic features again have everything to do with each other:
Brahms no doubt chose the dominant as the exposition's initial chord because of
the motivic/harmonic possibilities in the retransition.

Other motives are likewise prominent in both the Andantino and Presto non
troppo. In the Andantino, a treble-line figure from the B minor cadences (mm. 6–7,
14–15) is reconfigured in mm. 20–21 and 21–22. This derived form opens the transition theme in the Presto non troppo (mm. 44–47, 132–136), and a version, in turn,
of its head-motive begins the second theme (mm. 54–55, 140–141). Brahms has
composed a movement of utter, overt motivic integration. And rather than closing
in B minor, the sonata-form trio leads into a coda (mm. 162–193) that restores the
key of D major and thematic material from the opening Andantino (mm. 19–33).
Brahms in this way alludes to but does not observe the principles of contrast and
closure that help define the umbrella type of scherzo and trio to which the movement belongs.

In phrases that close the Andantino (mm. 19–33) and return in the coda (mm.
166–192), he uses a different kind of refinement. Here, as in the C Minor Piano
Trio and F Major Cello Sonata, two harmonic meanings are implied. Although the
dominant in mm. 19–23 looks as if it resolves to the tonic pedal that begins in m.
24, aurally it has a different effect. The circle-of-fifths progression (mm. 24–26), the
plagal harmony in m. 32, and, most remarkably, the "apparent four-two" in mm.
27–28 seem to prolong the tonic. But the dominant pedal that enters in m. 19 does
not sound as if it resolves until the final chord.[99] In a passage of extreme harmonic
beauty, these devices, ostensibly introduced to sustain the tonic, prolong the dominant instead.

By suggesting tonic and dominant at once, by moving frequently between the
tonic and its relative minor, by connecting one pervasive motive to several harmonic
meanings, and by referring to formal boundaries and sectional contrasts and then
blurring them, this intermezzo suggests the "Verschmolzenheit" of a late work. Instead of striving for tension and contrast, Brahms blends the various technical elements, projecting an affect of serene, at times perhaps nostalgic introspection. Taken
together, these features offer a concrete example of the "complex of traits . . . intricate and difficult to grasp" that Mersmann struggled to describe in general terms.
As we shall see in succeeding chapters, other aspects of the chamber compositions
with clarinet support the idea that they are late works in a stronger sense than the
earlier chamber pieces.[100]

---

99. On the concept of an "apparent four-two" and its association with prolonging a tonic chord,
see Edward Aldwell and Carl Schachter, *Harmony and Voice Leading,* 2nd ed. (Fort Worth: Harcourt
Brace Jovanovich, 1989), 391.

100. Phillip Spitta, who had not liked several of Brahms's works from the early 1880s, wrote approvingly of the new style he heard in the Clarinet Trio and Quintet, "The man appears only now to
enter his autumn, and he is still at a far distance from winter." Quoted from a letter of 21 December
1891 to Heinrich von Herzogenberg in Ulrike Schilling, *Philipp Spitta: Leben und Wirken im Spiegel seiner
Briefwechsel: Mit einem Inventar des Nachlasses und einer Bibliographie der gedruckten Werke* (Kassel: Bärenreiter, 1994), 178.

In this chapter I have drawn attention not only to a "blending of all the formal and expressive elements" and an "anticipatory modernity" in the Clarinet Quintet's intermezzo but also to other, contradictory features noted in late-style criticism, such as seeming simplicity and artifice pursued for its own sake. Another aspect of Brahms's late works, the moments that model psychological process, has not to my knowledge appeared in the literature on him or other artists cultivating a late style. Underlying most of these effects of lateness is his complete mastery of ways and degrees of defining keys and harmonies, a topic I shall return to in subsequent chapters.

BRAHMS IN A WANING CULTURE AND THE TOPOS OF AN AUTUMNAL STYLE

In his work on visual artists' late styles, Brinckmann cautioned against melding individual and art-historical development; he considered the changes he observed to be psychologically rather than historically determined.[101] The lives of certain artists, Beethoven prominently among them, do seem to invite combining one teleological narrative, that of an artist's own development, with another, that of a chain of historical events. Perhaps too easily, the dissolution of the heroic style and the inception of Beethoven's late period map onto the end of the Napoleonic Wars and changes in the system of musical patronage.[102] In a similar fashion, Brahms's maturity and cultivation of the larger choral and orchestral genres correspond to the *Gründerzeit* in Germany and Austria. During that brief period of middle-class optimism, beginning in the 1860s with the Liberals' political dominance finally achieved, Vienna underwent the grandiose modernization that resulted most strikingly in the Ringstrasse and its buildings. (With reference to Austria, the period is sometimes also called the *Ringstrassezeit*.) And any late period in Brahms's lifework would have to be placed in the decades of decline that followed.

For many listeners, Brahms's music does seem to have become inseparable from their knowledge of his historical position, of his compositions' general lateness. Thus, at some point in the early twentieth century, the familiar notion of his so-called autumnal style joined, and eventually almost supplanted, that of him as a cold and calculating composer. For unlike the latter topos, the former does not seem to have become an important theme until after his death. In 1909 Louis made one of the first published references to the "feeling of autumn" in Brahms. Louis connected this to the composer's consciousness of having been born in "a fundamentally uncreative and inartistic time": "it is the sense of artistic decline, the feeling of autumn . . . that comes through in the melancholy of Brahms's musical language."[103] In Louis's view, the autumnal quality derived from the composer's own awareness of living in a late period.

By the time of the Brahms centennial in 1933, attributing autumnal qualities to his music had become commonplace enough for Adorno to think that he had to

---

101. *Spätwerke grosser Meister*, 41.

102. Maynard Solomon, *Beethoven*, 2nd ed. (New York: Schirmer Books, 1998), 293–294.

103. *Die deutsche Musik der Gegenwart* (Munich: Georg Müller, 1909), 149.

downplay the significance of that sound while tacitly acknowledging its expressive power. Even performers, he implied in the 1934 essay, should focus on constructive principles in the music, rather than the "academic heritage or the autumnal colors." Adorno saw the "Brahmsian tone" as "profoundly associated with the Brahmsian source, and that means at the same time his procedure." But he separated the two in the interest of demonstrating the music's continuing value, which he considered to lie above all in the motivic/thematic work.[104] Moreover, while the autumnal sound of Brahms's music might call to mind a late culture, a longstanding critical tradition based on the relationship between themes and sonata form suggested stronger connections between music and social history. Examining and applying that tradition is the undertaking of chapter 3.

104. "Brahms aktuell," in *Musikalische Schriften V,* 203 and 201.

THEMES AND FIRST MOVEMENTS: QUESTIONS OF LATENESS AND INDIVIDUALISM

Adorno: "That Brahms . . . bears the mark of middle-class society's individualistic phase is indisputable to the point of triteness. The category of totality, which in Beethoven still maintains an image of a proper society, in Brahms fades increasingly into a self-sufficient aesthetic principle of organization for private feelings: that is the academic side of him."[1]

As the reference to triteness indicates, this bleak view of Brahms and his time follows a well-defined tradition that construes nineteenth-century Austro-German history as decline. For Adorno, the changing nature of "totality" reflects that downward trajectory, Beethoven and Brahms representing the changes in music from one end of the century to the other. Let me briefly unpack his remarks. A work such as the first movement of the *Eroica* Symphony expresses a utopian moment in music and social history. Reflecting the optimism Beethoven and others felt after the collapse of feudalism in France, theme and form stand in perfect equilibrium: the needs of individuals and society as a whole might be reconciled, or so it seemed. The Napoleonic Wars and subsequent repression quashed that illusion.[2] In German-speaking lands, the disappointments of the middle class lasted until well after the failed midcentury revolutions. When the society envisioned at the start of the century finally became a possibility in the 1860s, a system emerged that placed too much emphasis on the individual—and by no means all individuals. From Adorno's perspective, the loss of ideals and illusions manifested itself in music as on the one hand an academic approach to form and on the other themes complete in themselves and thus insufficiently involved in the course of the movement in which they appear.

The connections Adorno makes in the opening excerpt and in related passages from *Philosophie der neuen Musik* are at once cogent and flawed. Historians do routinely discern increased emphasis on the individual in later nineteenth-century cul-

---

1. *Einleitung in die Musiksoziologie,* 81–82.
2. See Gülke's remarks on the emergence of Beethoven's late style in "Introduktion als Widerspruch im System: Zur Dialektik von Thema und Prozessualität bei Beethoven," *Beiträge zur Musikwissenschaft* 14 (1969): 37.

ture. And it does not require an extravagant hermeneutic leap to correlate this trend to tendencies in music: striking harmonic effects and lyrical, self-contained melodies at the expense of a complex formal whole. The difficulty lies in Adorno's excessive privileging of historical forces over personal creativity and choice.

In passages from two posthumously published writings, the 1934 essay and the Beethoven book, Adorno gives Brahms the agency he denies him elsewhere. Thus in one fragment from the Beethoven book he notes: "once the theme has taken on substance, the totality becomes a *problem* (not simply impossible). The whole of Brahms's music later crystallized around this problem."[3] Here Adorno implies that the composer grappled with a dilemma caused by music-historic lateness. He also offers, without developing it, a more positive way of interpreting the composer within his middle-class culture. To wit, Brahms acknowledged the musical problem, if not the broader societal emphasis on the individual from which it derived, and made it central to his work.

As was usually the case when he wrote about Brahms, Adorno did not ground these remarks in observations about particular pieces. The vagueness of "the category of totality . . . in Brahms fades increasingly" and "the whole of Brahms's music" is especially frustrating. In such comments it becomes obvious that Adorno's preoccupation with Brahms's place in music history made him overlook stylistic development within the composer's oeuvre.

Yet Brahms's treatment of theme-form relations itself changes, and late style becomes a compelling factor in his last sonata-form movements. Summoning the will to keep composing required more of an effort after about 1890. He faced not only old age, but also the realization that his was an outmoded style, that what mattered to him was of diminishing importance to other musicians. Recognizing his own irrelevance must have played a role in his newfound sense of freedom and creativity and in the innovative approaches to the theme-form problem apparent in his final chamber music. Late style and music-historic lateness converge in these works.

VIEWS OF BRAHMS AND THE
MIDDLE-CLASS MILIEU

Topoi I have mentioned—the sense of lateness and decline, excessive individualism as a tenet of middle-class culture, and the academic art favored within that culture—recur throughout literature on Brahms that considers his place in social history. For contemporary critics antagonistic toward Brahms, his use of Classical forms and genres and his apparent conservatism in artistic matters—the "academic-epigonous classicism" mocked by Louis—corresponded to what they saw as the superficial and safe artistic tastes of the dominant class. Already in 1874, Cosima Wagner wrote that she and her husband had had evening conversations with friends "about Herr Brahms and his damaging and bigoted influence on the educated middle classes."[4]

---

3. *Beethoven,* 24.
4. *Cosima Wagner's Diaries,* ed. Martin Gregor-Dellin and Dietrich Mack, trans. Geoffrey Skelton (New York: Harcourt Brace Jovanovich, 1978), 1:778.

While we do not expect unbiased remarks about Brahms from either Louis or the Wagners, the tenor of Brahms's milieu, and in particular the Viennese milieu, continues to present difficulties for critics attempting favorable interpretation of his music within it. Not only did he reside in Vienna during a period of extreme disparities in its inhabitants' living conditions, but he became wealthy and developed close ties to the city's upper middle-class elite, a group, moreover, that had aesthetically questionable tastes in art. Louis's "academic-epigonous classicism" applies also to literature deriving from a cult of Goethe and other German Classical authors and to visual art that imitates various historical styles.[5] The imposing—to some of us, monstrous—buildings completed during the 1870s and 1880s on the Ringstrasse memorialize the artistic preferences of Vienna's newly rich for posterity.

Sympathetic critics naturally emphasize the more defensible aspects of Brahms's milieu. Schering notes Brahms's importance for that segment of the *Bürgertum* "whose members belonged to the higher, intellectual professions."[6] He is referring to the "Bildungsbürgertum," a word scholars often oppose to "Besitzbürgertum" to indicate the relative importance of education and property to different segments of the middle classes. And ignoring the academicism imputed to late nineteenth-century classicism, Gülke instead links Brahms to the original Classical style. According to him, Brahms's advocacy of the "enlightened, Classical traditions of 'thinking in tones'" found little resonance in music, but rather placed him with the "great realists in other fields, Keller, Fontane, and Menzel." For Gülke, "sober professionalism" most basically connects the four artists.[7] Along related lines, Kneif and Schmidt stress the middle-class ethos of individual accomplishment through hard work that Brahms's lifestyle and compositional approach epitomize. Schmidt writes: "not only do hard work and willed achievement characterize Brahms's personal behavior, but also the concept of work . . . shaped his understanding of the compositional process."[8] Kneif ties this attitude to the music's very substance, drawing attention to the specific techniques of open*work* and thematic-motivic *work* so prominent in Brahms's compositional style.[9]

Kneif refers to the thesis that the composer personifies middle-class qualities to an unparalleled degree as not "specifically Marxist." In any case, a twentieth-century socialist perspective did not necessarily entail devaluing all aspects of nineteenth-century culture. As he notes, twentieth-century Marxists tend to differentiate "between an early and progressive and a later and declining *Bürgertum,*" thus distinguishing, as Schering does, between better and worse sides of middle-class culture. Kneif observes that even in the twentieth century, many Marxists professed

5. On literary trends, see Lukács, *Die Grablegung des alten Deutschland: Essays zur deutschen Literatur des 19. Jahrhunderts* (Neuwied: Rowohlt, 1967). On the visual arts, see Richard Hamann, *Gründerzeit,* ed. Jost Hermand (Munich: Nymphenburger, 1971). Hermann Broch wrote of "Vienna's Gay Apocalypse of 1880" and the "value vacuum" between 1870 and 1890. *Hugo von Hofmannsthal and His Time: The European Imagination, 1860–1920,* ed. and trans. Michael P. Steinberg (Chicago: University of Chicago Press, 1984), 59.

6. "Brahms und seine Stellung," 10.

7. *Brahms–Bruckner,* 60 and 61.

8. *Brahms und seine Zeit,* 59.

9. "Brahms—Ein bürgerlicher Künstler," 12.

their loyalty to that culture's positive aspects, "to *bürgerlich* ideas of revolution, to maintaining the valuable 'bürgerlich' heritage."[10]

The Marxist musicologist Georg Knepler, for instance, interprets Brahms as having clung to the *bürgerlich* humanism of the Josephinist era that had also inspired Beethoven even after Joseph II's death in 1790. Knepler in this way allies the composer with Beethoven and the early, better form of middle-class culture, overriding the narrative of decline that aligns Beethoven and Brahms with socially idealistic and overly self-focused versions of Liberalism, respectively. He also accurately notes that Brahms rejected the ostentatious aspects of contemporary middle-class culture embraced by Wagner and Liszt. But his Marxist-universalistic perspective leads him to unwarranted conclusions regarding Brahms's unattractive penchant for jingoistic pronouncements. Knepler—and he is not alone in this—goes so far as to attribute the composer's not having set foot in either England or France to German chauvinism. (One likelier explanation is his inaptitude for foreign languages.)[11] He then makes a distinction between Brahms's expressed opinions and what his compositions mean. While as a private individual the composer might have shared the limited, nationalistic outlook of his class, his music intimates another point of view. Knepler observes that a resigned tone became more and more pronounced in the decades after the German Reich's founding.[12]

Adorno may have attempted to set aside questions of tone in his 1934 essay, but they seem to be almost inescapable in the Brahms literature. By interpreting expressive qualities in the later music, Knepler suggests the composer's estrangement from a dubious cultural trend, the tribalism that attracted many people after the Franco-Prussian War and even more in the 1890s as Liberal individualism appeared progressively more bankrupt. From a different perspective, I have mentioned the natural affinity between late-style inwardness and chamber music. Brinkmann, in contrast, connects the introverted tone of chamber style to music-historic lateness, and he writes about the melancholy of middle-class life conveyed by Brahms's music, as by works of Fontane and Menzel. He emphasizes all three artists' sense of their historical lateness and the resulting emphasis on craft and industry noted by Gülke and others: "The historical latecomer's excess skill and knowledge beget reflection."[13] For Brinkmann, the basic fact of lateness ties the tone of melancholy reflection to the hard work that Kneif locates in the music itself.

Because he is focusing on music-historic lateness, Brinkmann dwells on the temporal gap between Beethoven and Brahms and its consequences;[14] whereas Gülke and Knepler stress the philosophical continuities between the two composers. Positioning Brahms with respect to Beethoven is, predictably, a fundamental concern

---

10. "Brahms—Ein bürgerlicher Künstler," 10.

11. See, for example, the anecdote about Brahms's election to the French Academy in 1896, recounted here in the epilogue.

12. "Brahms historische und ästhetische Bedeutung," (1961), reprinted in *Johannes Brahms, oder, die Relativierung der 'absoluten' Musik,"* ed. Hanns-Werner Heister (Hamburg: Bockel, 1997), 50 and 53–55.

13. *Late Idyll,* 139.

14. Thus the rhetorical question "Is the subject of Brahms's symphony [the First] still the same as the subject of Beethoven's Ninth?" *Late Idyll,* 35.

in the critical tradition concerned with the theme-form relationship, as are several interconnected concepts: along with individualism, Hegelian dialectics and work in its various meanings and ramifications.

THE F MAJOR CELLO SONATA'S ALLEGRO VIVACE AND CONCEPTIONS OF SONATA FORM

Ideas about the theme–form relationship in Brahms's music follow from the enormous significance that critics assign to Classical sonata form. Like many other writers, Zofia Lissa connects Beethoven to Hegel and notes: "In Beethoven the *dialectic as principle of integration* achieves its high point: the principle of oppositeness (contrasts) operates here even within the smallest cells of the process."[15] Writers such as Adorno and Gülke regard sonata principles, especially as instantiated in Beethoven's music, as capable of conveying in dramatic form an image of an inclusive, whole society and, simultaneously, the striving for self-actualization characteristic of the period following the French Revolution.[16] This interpretation goes well beyond formalist analysis, and it depends above all on the relationship between particular themes and sonata-form process, which in this tradition correspond roughly to the philosophical concepts of subject and object or, alternatively, being and becoming. Regarding the last concept, Lissa writes: "the experience of past phases of the work endows the currently experienced phase, thus the form in its becoming, with the sense appropriate to it. The form as a whole is only given to us when all its phases are past."[17] To this Gülke adds: "The Marxist concept of the working subject realizing itself only in renunciation is altogether pertinent; not without reason did Beethoven secure new significance in music, as Hegel did in philosophy, for the concept of work as a principle of realization."[18]

Long before Brahms's time, an idea had taken hold that a theme or melody is the most direct expression of a composer's individuality and can, in that respect, also be considered a composition's "subject." But when Gülke refers to the "quasi-anthropomorphization of the theme," he has in mind its role-like nature. And he notes that conceptualizing the theme "as an acting subject would be inadmissible if the analogy did not lead further": that is, to a consideration of the theme's relationship to the overall form, of "whether the subject realizes itself in work and renunciation of the self or becomes alienated."[19] In the latter instance, presumably, the subject would sound isolated, not sufficiently involved in the movement's course, while the

---

15. "Die Prozessualität in der Musik," in *Aufsätze zur Musikästhetik: Eine Auswahl* (Berlin: Henschelverlag, 1969), 44–45.

16. *Einleitung in die Musiksoziologie*, 80. See also Christopher Ballantine, "Beethoven, Hegel and Marx," in *Music and Its Social Meanings* (New York: Gordon and Breach, 1984), 30–48; and the discussion of August Halm's *Von zwei Kulturen der Musik* as an influence on Adorno in Max Paddison, *Adorno's Aesthetics of Music* (New York: Cambridge University Press, 1993), 73–74.

17. "Die Prozessualität," 45.

18. "Kantabilität und thematische Abhandlung: Ein Beethovensches Problem und seine Lösungen in den Jahren 1806–1808," *Beiträge zur Musikwissenschaft* 15 (1970): 252–253.

19. "Kantabilität und thematische Abhandlung," 253.

first scenario applies above all to middle-period Beethoven, where the subject's identity emerges only as it fulfills its function in formal process.[20]

Many formalist critics likewise assume that sonata form reached its high point in Beethoven's music and then went into an irreversible decline, an observation usually supplemented with a statement to the effect that this holds true "even" for Brahms. This vein of criticism focuses on the problems that Adorno singles out, academic form and insufficiently functional content, as evidence that post-Classical composers misunderstood sonata form. Charles Rosen takes a straightforward position based on the theoretical codification of Classical forms by about 1840, after which sonata form was "no longer a free development of stylistic principles, but an attempt to reach greatness by imitation of classical models." He notes the "academic beauty" of some early post-Classical works and the intensified and more successful academicism of the following generation, that of Brahms. Rosen nonetheless judges Brahms's formal patterns to "lack the variety of those of Haydn, Mozart, and Beethoven," seeing him as having limited his choices to just a few (frequently noted) procedures having to do with "the possibilities of overlapping sections, the ambiguities of the boundaries of sonata form."[21]

Friedrich Blume does not charge Brahms with academicism. Rather, he observes changes from sonata form's original conception, which—resembling Lissa in this regard—he takes to be "the struggle of opposites and their conflict in the developing elaboration of the initial thematic material."[22] Interpreting the "emphatically lyric character" of nineteenth-century instrumental music, again including that of Brahms, as a "consequence of the decay of formal construction," Blume implies that Romantic composers were at their best in genres such as the lied and the lyric piano piece. From this vantage point, these kinds of small-scale works allowed composers to display their melodic gifts without requiring them to tailor their ideas to the formal demands of larger Classical genres such as the symphony and piano sonata.[23] Blume's criticism thus has to do with the other basic problem ascribed to post-Classical sonata form, self-sufficient content.

In the 1934 essay, Adorno acknowledges that sonata form had changed but argues that Brahms understood how to work with the changes, that Schumann's innovations in particular caused him to rethink the form. Adorno stays focused here on technical problems, praising Brahms for confronting those posed by the musical material that served as his point of departure, "that melodious homophony, which for the sake of song and harmonic discovery had softened the grand Beethovenian sonata construction." Brahms redefined sonata form in part by removing "Schumann's harmonic findings from their expressive isolation" to create "autonomous scale

20. On Beethoven's D Minor Piano Sonata and one aspect of this critical tradition, see Janet Schmalfeldt, "Form as the Process of Becoming: The Beethoven-Hegelian Tradition and the 'Tempest' Sonata," *Beethoven Forum* 4 (1995): 37–71.

21. *Sonata Forms*, rev. ed. (New York: Norton, 1988), 394 and 395.

22. *Classic and Romantic Music: A Comprehensive Survey*, trans. M. D. Herter Norton (New York: Norton, 1970), 143.

23. Blume considered the procedures of "New German" composers such as Bruckner and Wagner far more successful; *Classic and Romantic Music*, 143–144.

steps" capable of lengthy expansion.[24] In this way he objectified means that Schumann used for subjective expression.

The altered harmonic style entailed other changes: Beethoven's "sequencing of exactly maintained motives . . . is as incompatible as the Wagnerian chromatic sequence with this kind of harmonic consciousness." Brahms's solution was to transform Beethoven's developmental techniques into "an art of variation" for exposition and recapitulation. Describing his mastery of "economical partition of themes into the smallest motives" as a feat achieved "without sacrificing the formative theme as material medium between motive and large-scale form," Adorno finally praises the "melting down and rebuilding of the sonata [form] itself."[25] In this early essay, he considers Brahms—and only Brahms—to have succeeded in revivifying form in tonal music's late period by adapting it to a changed harmonic language and its thematic-motivic requirements.

Adorno began the Beethoven manuscript in 1938. One early entry concerns "the specific formal concept" in Beethoven, which "arises from the collision between the act of composing and the pre-existing schema."[26] Adorno makes it clear he conceives sonata form thematically. But here he presents formal process as a dialectical relationship between composer as subject and sonata-form schema, a set of widely accepted and therefore manifestly social norms, as object.

Within Brahms's oeuvre, the F Major Cello Sonata's Allegro vivace can serve to illustrate both this conception of formal process and the "art of variation" Adorno discusses in the 1934 essay. Regarding this movement, Mersmann writes, the "musical language becomes here completely subjective (not as to content, but as to style)," which he associates with a "design that avoids every firmly imprinted shape."[27] This description suggests the "collision between the act of composing and the pre-existing schema" Adorno attributes to Beethoven. Indeed, the flexibility with which Brahms uses sonata procedures refutes characterizations of his formal approach as "academic." Thus he places the modulation expected of a sonata-form exposition in an unorthodox passage that sounds improvised (mm. 22–33), fulfilling a transition's function in a manner that never suggests "imitation of classical models," while continuing the motivic variation from the preceding thematic statements. Brahms composes this transition against the grain, for it is the exposition's most relaxed passage.

When a secondary theme opens shortly thereafter in the key of the dominant, C major, it does not cadence. Undergoing continuous variation, it moves to a re-

---

24. "Brahms aktuell," in *Musikalische Schriften V,* 201 and 202.

25. "Brahms aktuell," 202. Adorno later emphasizes that no one else had effected the "necessary reorganization of the large-scale form [seen] in Brahms's best works," 203. In this essay, Adorno might appear to anticipate Schoenberg's essay "Brahms the Progressive." Although this essay was not published until 1950, in February 1933 he gave an early version as a radio talk in Frankfurt, where Adorno lived. He surely would have listened to Schoenberg speak. For the original radio address, see "Vortrag, zu halten in Frankfurt am Main am 12. II. 1933," trans. Thomas McGeary, *Journal of the Arnold Schoenberg Institute* 15/2 (November 1992): 22–90. "Brahms the Progressive (1947)" is reprinted in Schoenberg, *Style and Idea,* 398–441.

26. *Beethoven,* 60. An appendix gives the chronology of the entries, which the editor has rearranged thematically.

27. *Deutsche Romantik,* vol. 3 of *Die Kammermusik* (Leipzig: Breitkopf und Härtel, 1930), 111.

lated theme in E minor and then A minor and on to a "closing" section, likewise in A minor, which also does not conclude.[28] Except for the transition, the exposition is always striving, "working," constantly being turned in a new direction and thus avoiding "every firmly imprinted shape." By itself, the absence of closure might be shrugged off as an exploration of "the possibilities of overlapping sections" Rosen cites. But as a whole, the exposition—in fact, the entire movement— shows an individualized, even idiosyncratic, control of flow and articulation that belies his claim of a lack of variety in Brahms's approach to form.

In 1939, Adorno entered into the Beethoven manuscript the first reference to Brahms and the specific problem of the theme–form relationship: "Beethoven recognizes the incompatibility of the 'theme,' as a melody sufficient in itself, with the grand design. The mature Brahms had a very sensitive ear for this critical moment in Beethoven."[29] A half-century later, Gülke explicitly invokes the Hegelian concept "Für-sich-Sein": the subject or being for its own sake, considered without reference to an object or the process of becoming. According to Gülke, he "did not willingly grant [his themes] the Für-sich-Sein of a shape, the autonomy of an already self-evident structure."[30]

The Allegro vivace of the F Major Cello Sonata again illustrates Brahms's awareness of thematic qualities that suit, as Adorno notes about Beethoven, a "specific formal concept." Despite the ongoing transformation of motives that drew Schoenberg's attention in this movement, Brahms does retain themes as the "material medium" between motives and sonata-form schema. These themes are emphatically not self-sufficient or lyrical melodies: each of the posttransition themes is interrupted, and the two four-bar phrases that make up the first theme have neither a conventional contour nor a balanced shape.[31] The opening phrase's very angularity makes it immediately recognizable, even without its characteristic dotted rhythms, when it returns at the close of the development section. Mersmann observes that the *style*—improvisatory and contemplative in the transition and most of the development, purposeful-sounding elsewhere—rather than the (thematic) content is subjective. The "subject" strains against sonata-form expectations but submits to them. In Mersmann's words, the Allegro vivace is "dominated by thrusting short motives that resist every firm bond," suggesting both the unstable, idiosyncratic nature of the themes and the dynamic reciprocity between motives, themes, and formal schema audible in the movement.[32]

The evidence we have for Brahms's conscious position toward theme–form questions resonates with later commentaries by Gülke and Adorno. In the monograph devoted to his lessons with the composer, which began in the late 1880s, Jenner wrote: "the nature of form began to reveal itself." Brahms's ruminations on the

28. See Roger C. Graybill, "Harmonic Circularity in Brahms's F Major Cello Sonata: An Alternative to Schenker's Reading in *Free Composition*," *Music Theory Spectrum* 10 (1988): 43–55.

29. *Beethoven*, 40.

30. *Brahms–Bruckner*, 26.

31. This movement's thematic content and intimately connected formal anomalies may well be the result of Brahms's tailoring it to precede a revised version of the first cello sonata's discarded adagio. A comparison of the opening theme of the E Minor Cello Sonata's first movement with that of the F Major Cello Sonata is certainly instructive.

32. *Deutsche Romantik*, 110–111.

meaning of sonata form and the reciprocal relationship between form and theme became an important thread in recounting those lessons. According to Jenner, he learned that a sonata-form movement "must of necessity result from the themes," that "form and theme exert an intrinsically decisive influence on each other," and that "only one who creates in the spirit of a form, creates freely."[33] These remarks express an attitude that goes beyond the work ethic that Kneif, Brinkmann, and others observe. Indeed, the choice of words suggests an ethics of composition based on the theme–form relationship, and this of course supports the larger meaning Adorno and Gülke ascribe to Brahms's compositional choices.

THEMES, FORM, AND LATENESS IN THE CLARINET QUINTET

After his momentary attempt to retire, Brahms composed the four chamber works with clarinet. Not surprisingly, the sound of that instrument, the possibilities afforded by ensembles that include it, and the sense of freedom he gained from his short-lived retirement all left their mark on the music. In the substantial literature on this movement, two commentaries in particular, by Gülke and another distinguished musicologist, Rose Rosengard Subotnik, reveal the influence of the models of late style and music-historic lateness. Subotnik, like Gülke, conceives sonata form in Hegelian terms, that is, as a dynamic process that involves ongoing contradictions and contrasts until the shape of the whole emerges at the end, and both authors recognize the changes that occurred in the nineteenth century. Subotnik writes: "For Brahms, as for most nineteenth-century composers, the sonata structure functions as a preexistent, static structure."[34] But Gülke, as we have seen, differentiates Brahms from his contemporaries, asserting that from the beginning he composed into his themes their connection to the whole.

Brahms's observations about the theme–form relationship, as passed along by Jenner, have a bearing on the Clarinet Quintet's first movement and Subotnik's and Gülke's commentaries on it. Subotnik describes Brahms's Allegro as "a 'textbook' sonata heavily reliant on motivic transformation—in which all the expressivity of line, color, chromatic inflection, and tonal ambiguity cannot overcome a profound impression of nonimplicative, atemporal immobility."[35] In certain respects, Gülke suggests a contrary view, remarking that Brahms alludes to sonata-form principles rather than adhering to them.[36]

Like Subotnik, Gülke considers the work to be nonimplicative: "the events are ordered sonata-like but almost devoid of that surplus of significance and meaning extending beyond them that sonata form requires because it must argue. The music . . . knows nothing of oppositions and the agony of choice and elimination." But instead of finding Brahms's movement to be a textbook sonata, he calls it both

---

33. *Brahms als Mensch*, 6 and 61.

34. "Tonality, Autonomy, and Competence in Postclassical Music," in *Developing Variations: Style and Ideology in Western Music* (Minneapolis: University of Minnesota Press, 1991), 202.

35. "Tonality, Autonomy, and Competence in Postclassical Music," 202.

36. *Brahms–Bruckner*, 64.

EXAMPLE 3.1.   Brahms, Clarinet Quintet, Op. 115 / I, mm. 69–6 (the
exposition's first ending and the beginning of the repeat)

"a free-floating 'fantasy on . . .' resulting from the principle of respecting rules
without being submissive to them" and "a final music."[37] He does not deny that
Brahms created the movement "in the spirit of" sonata form, to invoke the composer's own position; rather, he emphasizes that Brahms created it "freely" in that
spirit. For Gülke, the effacing of sonata-form oppositions points to the movement's
lateness within Brahms's oeuvre—recalling Brinckmann's *Verschmolzenheit*—rather
than the historical lateness Subotnik's comments imply.

I would like to develop Gülke's observations. As he writes, Brahms minimizes
oppositions, notably between the exposition's two keys. In the opening measures,
B minor and D major sound equally possible as the tonic. And, as has been widely
noted, Brahms stresses the mediant (in m. 5)—it remains a chord, but could have
become a key—well before the entrance of the tonic triad (in m. 18) or even the
dominant (in m. 9). Consequently, the exposition, which does not close, can lead
directly into its repetition, D major as secondary key becoming D major as triad
again (see ex. 3.1). The smoothness with which the exposition's end joins with the
repetition's beginning demonstrates the ingenuity in eliding normative formal divisions that Rosen and others have emphasized, and at the same time underscores
the weakening of one aspect of sonata-form dialectics, the contrast between keys.

But themes and form still have a "decisive influence" on each other: Brahms can
deviate from sonata-form expectations of implication and argumentation because of
the nature of the themes. While Adorno's word "collision," which suited the
theme–form (or composer–schema) relationship in the F Major Cello Sonata, is too
aggressive to describe the effect here, the themes again do not become self-sufficient. For the second theme flows into the middle of the first when the exposition

37. *Brahms–Bruckner*, 64.

EXAMPLE 3.2a.   Prototype of progression in Brahms, Clarinet Quintet, Op. 115 / I, mm. 5–10

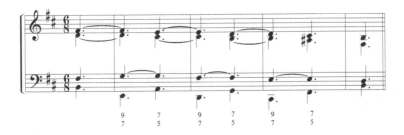

repeats, and the very opening has an improvisatory quality because Brahms problematizes the formation of a discrete theme. Kalbeck writes perceptively, with only slight exaggeration, that "the secret of the movement is that it has many ideas but no closed theme": becoming occurs within the themes themselves.[38] The opening "thematic complex" fills twenty-five measures but does not acquire a conventional thematic shape until m. 18, a process the initial tonal uncertainty supports.

The opening is as overtly motivic as that in the F Major Cello Sonata, but motivic development is languorous and extended compared with the earlier work's volatile, intensive elaboration. Four introductory measures present the essential motives, two versions of one (x and x^1 here) in mm. 1–2 and two versions of the other (y and y^1 here) in mm. 3–4. Thereafter Brahms coordinates ongoing expansion and development of the motives, as he originally orders them, with other formal processes such as the incomplete harmonic progression that underlies the opening. (An incomplete harmonic progression does not begin with tonic harmony.) Lengthening the previously unharmonized motive forms from mm. 1–2 by augmenting the F-sharp that opens each (mm. 6–7 and 8–9), he now harmonizes them with alternating ninth and seventh chords in a circle-of-fifths progression. Example 3.2a gives the four-measure prototype. The prototype is changed already in the Clarinet Quintet, in that it is extended to fill five and a half measures, and both begins on the mediant in m. 5 (moving through an applied diminished-seventh chord in m. 6) and ends deceptively in m. 10. (See ex. 3.2b.)

By definition, the underlying sequence is a regular pattern, but by introducing irregularities into mm. 5–10, Brahms avoids the sense of proceeding measure by measure that the sequence otherwise would produce. As he renders it, the progression is thus both tonally open and asymmetrical. One compelling factor in the irregular shape is the hypermetrically ambiguous status of m. 5, in which the clarinetist—the ensemble's natural protagonist—enters. Arpeggiating a D major triad, the clarinetist's line moves from the chalumeau-range F-sharp to the F-sharp two octaves above, the note with which the violins had opened the movement. After the introduction's two-plus-two organization, one expects m. 5 to be hypermetrically

---

38. *Brahms,* 4:249. See also Mason, *Chamber Music of Brahms,* 233; and Brinkmann, *Late Idyll,* 85–87.

EXAMPLE 3.2b.   Brahms, Clarinet Quintet, Op. 115 / I, mm. 1–17

continued

strong. But the clarinet's high F-sharp in m. 6 is the expanded first note of motive *x,* which suggests that m. 6 should have a hypermetric accent. Since the other voices continue to play held notes, they offer no clarification.

After the momentary hypermetric ambiguity in mm. 5–6, Brahms makes the clarinet's elaboration of the opening motives sound as if that motivic process, rather

EXAMPLE 3.2b.   *continued*

than the meter, is determining the rhythmic shape. For between m. 4 and m. 10, the treble (clarinet) and bass (cello) do not come together on a downbeat. These strategies, and the introduction of extra suspensions beyond those the sequential progression creates, keep the thematic material in a state of becoming rather than allowing it to achieve a melody's self-enclosed being, something many critics consider detrimental to sonata form.[39]

Late in the compositional process, Brahms made important revisions here in the movement, for the autograph reads as shown in figure 3.1. He originally intended to prolong the dominant by having the cello play F-sharp from the middle of m. 9 through m. 11 (as these measures would be numbered in the autograph). But in his revision, he chose to prolong the dominant only by implication: in the final version, many listeners will hear the dominant throughout mm. 10–13 despite its literal absence. Paradoxically, sustaining the dominant solely by suggestion—along with other significant revisions, including two added measures in which the clarinet rises dramatically and then plunges into the chalumeau register—makes the impact of the passage immeasurably greater.

Still prolonging the dominant, Brahms expands motives y and y^1 in mm. 14–17. As the structural tonic finally enters in m. 18, these motives become the basis of an eight-bar theme. To summarize, both metric clarity and strong harmonic direction are absent as motives x and x^1 are elaborated in mm. 5–9. Preliminary clarification

---

39. The opening movement of Beethoven's Ninth Symphony offers an immensely influential precedent for dramatizing the genesis of a theme. The contrast between the effect of monumentality in that beginning and the inwardness and motivic detail in Brahms's opening accentuates the differences not just between the two composers but more basically between stylistic premises of the symphonic and chamber genres.

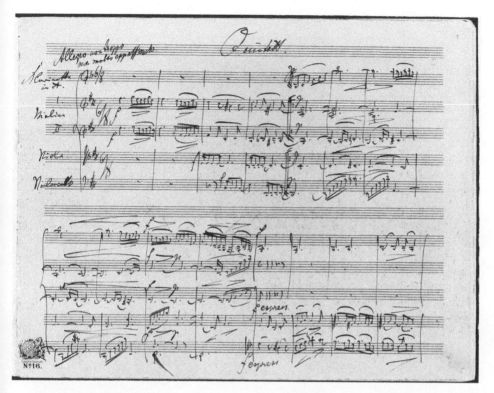

FIGURE 3.1.   Brahms, Clarinet Quintet, Op. 115, first page of the autograph score.
Reproduced by kind permission of the Archive of the Gesellschaft der Musikfreunde,
Vienna.

comes when the dominant enters (in the second half of m. 9) and is prolonged by
implication, motives y and y^i eventually appearing in varied and extended form
over it. Delayed resolution of the harmonic progression concludes in the thematic,
tonal, and rhythmic certainty of mm. 18–25. The recapitulation does not repeat the
extraordinary events of mm. 5–13. Rather, over an understood continuation of the
retransition dominant, a simpler and shorter elaboration of all the opening motives
(mm. 136–41) leads into the discrete "first theme" in which those events concluded.

Brahms uses other kinds of harmonic and rhythmic subtleties in the second
group to support an illusion again of constant becoming. This group begins as continuous variation of a two-bar idea that brings to mind a succession of abbreviated
periods; at the same time, he undercuts the potentially periodic phrase-structure.
Here his strategies include avoided or undermined full authentic cadences—the latter accomplished, for example, by adding a seventh to a cadential tonic (m. 41)—
cadences placed in the weak part of the measure (e.g., mm. 39 and 41), and a succession of appoggiaturas in an irregular pattern. (See ex. 3.3.)

Even as Brahms weakens the opposition between two keys, he also minimizes
affective differences. Allowing only the transition as contrast in the exposition, he

EXAMPLE 3.3. Brahms, Clarinet Quintet, Op. 115 / I, mm. 36–41

subsequently brings that theme closer to the others through an elaborate development-section transformation. Previously harmonized as a quick, almost perfunctory
circle-of-fifths progression in block chords, the theme becomes the basis of an expressively complex passage. Extending the theme sequentially, he embellishes the
voice-leading with suspensions, passing tones, and bass-line anticipations. (See ex.
3.4a and 3.4b: the sequence and the embellishments are marked in ex. 3.4b.) Moreover, he decelerates the tempo to a "Quasi sostenuto" for this most daring—
because of its central placement and the radical changes the theme undergoes—of
his development-section transformations, a meditative, "late" interlude within an
already fantasy-like movement.

Gülke considers this passage in particular to be contrary to sonata form.[40] He
makes relevant remarks in a pair of articles about Beethoven. A slow tempo "con-
fers weight and stress on all the details";[41] for this reason, it causes "the course of
events itself, the lyrical singing and telling" of the immediate present to become
more important than the overall shape to be apprehended only at the end.[42] (He is
again using the Hegelian conception of musical form as his frame of reference.) At
this point in the Clarinet Quintet, Subotnik's observation of "atemporal immobility" seems accurate: the episode creates an impression of disjunction and temporary
stasis as well as audible reflection. If the "subject" appears isolated from the rest of
the movement here, Brahms undoubtedly intended the effect of alienation; in the
exposition and recapitulation, themes and form, despite their idiosyncrasies, do not
seem at odds, for he has rethought both.

40. *Brahms–Bruckner,* 64.
41. "Introduktion als Widerspruch," 13.
42. "Kantabilität und thematische Abhandlung," 254.

EXAMPLE 3.4a.   Brahms, Clarinet Quintet,
Op. 115 / I, mm. 25–27

In the critical tradition represented by Adorno, Gülke, and Lissa, Beethoven's works from the nineteenth century's first decade most perfectly realize becoming, conceived as an attribute more of form than themes. Brahms responded variously to the problems that late nineteenth-century musical materials posed. In this "free-floating fantasy" on sonata form, he correlates late-style underplaying of the form's contrasts and contradictions with keeping the themes themselves in a state of becoming.

ADORNO'S FURTHER FORMULATIONS
OF THE QUESTIONS

One of Adorno's clearest, most extended statements about the theme–form relationship is a long footnote to a disquisition on Schoenberg's twelve-tone compositions. This appears in *Philosophie der neuen Musik,* the Schoenberg portion of which Adorno wrote in 1940–41. Here he directly asserts "the incompatibility of the sculptural song melody Romanticism sought as the symbol of subjectivism with the 'Classical,' Beethovenian idea of unified form." He then compares "the break between the theme and the immediate consequences drawn from it" at the beginning of Brahms's F Major String Quintet with the problem of continuation in many twelve-tone works following the row's initial presentation. Ultimately he claims that the "inconsistency between the theme and what happens to it" represents "the middle-class concept of the individual stand[ing] in perennial opposition to the totality of the social process."[43] More blatantly than elsewhere, Adorno ties Brahmsian themes to middle-class individualism and finds the composer's approach in the quintet problematic and, implicitly, typical.

43. *Philosophie der neuen Musik,* 73–74, n. 23.

EXAMPLE 3.4b.   Brahms, Clarinet Quintet, Op. 115 / I, mm. 98–106

With respect to the F Major String Quintet, Adorno's observation of a "break" is accurate. For the opening, Brahms revived the closed, tripartite thematic type he had used much earlier in the G Major String Sextet's first movement, among others. Although he does attempt a link in the quintet movement by repeating the first theme's final motive (m. 31) as the transition theme's initial motive (m. 32), the effect is awkward because of the first theme's self-sufficiency. Yet the theme is also anomalous in Brahms's music at that point: Adorno's characteristic disregard for stylistic development within the composer's oeuvre is particularly apparent here. The opening themes (or thematic groups) in the slightly earlier C Major Piano Trio and slightly later Third Symphony differ markedly from that in the quintet. Adorno weakens his argument by choosing a first movement that is atypical of the later Brahms and taking it out of stylistic context.

Like the F Major String Quintet's first theme, the Clarinet Quintet's opening thematic complex concludes in a full cadence. But unlike the F Major String Quintet's first theme, it is striving toward a stable thematic shape before closing, and the sharply contrasting transition theme sounds new rather than like a forced continuation. To help keep the long opening section evolving, Brahms uses a basic device that appears elsewhere in the late music: a quasi-introduction, four measures in the Clarinet Quintet, presents essential motives before a theme even begins to take shape. The Third Symphony and the Double Concerto, among other works, also open with prethematic shapes; unlike the approach Adorno found problematic in the F Major String Quintet, this strategy is typical of the composer's later thematic style.[44]

Adorno's attitude toward Brahms clearly vacillated, even within the one book *Philosophie der neuen Musik*. In a better known passage, from the section "Total Development," Adorno approvingly notes the absence of unthematic notes in Brahms's compositions yet later in the same section asserts that conventions of form "lose their meaning" when all notes are thematic.[45] Although the latter remark refers to Schoenberg, the Beethoven manuscript connects it to Adorno's further thoughts about Brahms. In 1948 he entered comments about Brahms's having problematized "increasing subjectivity" and its effect on form. The next fragment (chronologically) indicates that Adorno's previous ideas about form, even those from earlier in that decade, no longer satisfied him. For he writes: "the view I adhered to more or less up to the *Philosophy of Modern Music,* that a subject-object dialectic exists between the composer and the traditional form, is still too one-sided and undiscriminating."[46] As the editor, Rolf Tiedemann, notes, "this view is perhaps most clearly expressed in *Philosophy of Modern Music,* pp. 54 f," that is, at the beginning of "Total Development," which leads into the discussion of Brahms.[47]

According to the revised perspective in the Beethoven manuscript, the "great traditional musical forms already shape" the dialectic. Adorno explains: the "schema of the sonata contains parts—the thematic and developmental parts—which are already *aimed at* the subject and which can accommodate the particular, and others in which, by virtue of the schema itself, conventional generalities emerge."[48] These observations are manifestly pertinent to Brahms because everything is thematic or developmental in his music, and Adorno had stated in *Philosophie der neuen Musik* that in these circumstances, formal conventions "lose their meaning."

A piece such as the *Eroica* Symphony's opening movement shows Beethoven maximizing the dichotomy between thematic and nonthematic to create a work of unprecedented length and vitality: that Allegro con brio contains an abundance of nonthematic figuration, while thematically stable passages are few and brief. Be-

---

44. See Schmidt, *Brahms und seine Zeit,* 117. The first movement of the F Minor Piano Quintet, which Brahms completed in 1864, offers an early example of this kind of opening thematic complex.

45. *Philosophie der neuen Musik,* 59 and 61.

46. Adorno, *Beethoven,* 61 (fr. 146). In the original manuscript sources, fr. 186 on p. 74, which discusses Brahms, precedes the fragment from which I quote. See Tiedemann's "Comparative Table of Fragments" in Adorno, *Beethoven,* 256–257, for these fragments from 1948.

47. Tiedemann, in Adorno, 220, n. 145. In the original German text, the section is at pp. 57–62.

48. Adorno, *Beethoven,* 61.

cause Brahms, unlike Beethoven and his predecessors, assumed every note had to be thematic, he did not consider that distinction an option. To compensate for the lost distinction, he devised new oppositions for the Clarinet Trio and F Minor Clarinet Sonata that produce analogous effects and established these within the opening thematic groups, each time beginning with a quasi-introduction similar to that in the Clarinet Quintet. Brahms's solutions confirm the pervasive emphasis on individual content in late nineteenth-century music, which excluded "conventional generalities" such as stock transitional figuration and closing gestures. He could not change contemporary expectations of a composer, but by devising new kinds of relationships *within* the themes, he could work with the problems the expectations caused.

SONATA-FORM TONALITY AND ITS OTHER: LATE-STYLE ALIENATION IN THE CLARINET TRIO

In his 1908 essay on Brahms, Bahr recalled that in the years around 1890, he and his youthful contemporaries had habitually referred to the composer as "the cold one" (*der Kalte*) because of the emotional reserve they heard in his music. To many listeners, then and more recently, the A Minor Clarinet Trio has seemed one of the very "coldest" of his works. After the first performance, one unsympathetic critic, Paumgartner, remarked that "the melodic invention is sparse, frequently stagnating or running dry altogether." Even Geiringer wrote that "the themes are not quite so inspired, nor is their elaboration quite so captivating as usual," while Mason asserted that the themes "betray an unmistakable apathy of the imagination."[49]

Why would Brahms have composed such unprepossessing themes? One possibility is that, as a composer of late works, he cared less than ever about pleasing the public. Another is that his powers of invention had in fact weakened, since the "sparseness" Paumgartner noted is sometimes seen as characteristic of late works.[50] Yet he composed these themes more or less simultaneously with the Clarinet Quintet's lush themes. Offering a different explanation, Peter Foster observes that Brahms applies contrapuntal devices such as canon, augmentation, and inversion more prominently than usual here. He counters specific charges of "a lack of melodic flexibility," calling these "not a fair criticism of a work whose compositional roots lie in the *alla breve* style of imitative writing."[51] A fourth perspective, which does not rule out the others, is also possible. Adorno suggests that Beethoven (and Haydn) achieve a sense of wholeness "without doing violence to the individual part" by cultivating "bareness" in both part and whole.[52] Let us accept a reasonable premise: Brahms recognized the problems posed by the melodies the nineteenth century favored and deliberately composed plain, unremarkable themes.

---

49. "Brahms," 41; Paumgartner, *Wiener Abendpost*, 23 December 1891; Geiringer, *Brahms*, 243; and Mason, *Chamber Music of Brahms*, 223.

50. Paul Knauth, for example, writes about this in the reception of the older Goethe in *Goethes Sprache und Stil im Alter* (Leipzig: Eduard Avenarius, 1898), 4.

51. Peter Foster, "Brahms, Schenker and the Rules of Composition: Compositional and Theoretical Problems in the Clarinet Works" (Ph.D. diss., University of Reading, 1994), 283.

52. *Beethoven*, 34–35.

The most remarkable moments in the Clarinet Trio's first movement do not appear in the themes as melodic lines, nor do they have to do with essential sonata-form functions such as establishing a secondary key. To the contrary, the movement's most unusual moments are harmonic passages, for the most part brief, that serve no vital formal function because they cannot: they are purely plagal, devoid of the dominant with leading tone that drives common-practice tonality. In placing those passages, so to speak, outside and against the sonata-form framework, Brahms opposes sonata-form tonality and its other, "modal" harmony.

From the beginning, he introduces both a harmonic style that is at odds with sonata-form procedures and an austere melodic style: Mason observes "a sort of poverty, or perhaps intentional bareness, of line" in the opening phrase.[53] Discussing the various contrapuntal techniques apparent in this movement, Foster notes that the first two phrases (mm. 1–4 and 5–13) resemble a fugue subject (dux) and its expanded answer (comes).[54] The pair of phrases also stand in a Classical antecedent and consequent relationship: in the first phrase, the single voice of the cello suggests a motion from tonic to dominant; the second phrase opens with the comes version of the same basic thematic material and closes on the tonic. By making the ascending gestures in both phrases triadic, Brahms manages to avoid the leading tone altogether; in effect, he composes an Aeolian/plagal period, at the end of which the dynamics become softer and the clarinet descends into the chalumeau register. Both uses of the so-called secondary elements of dynamics and timbre also mark subsequent appearances of what I shall call "semiautonomous plagal harmony," semiautonomous because in the absence of the dominant with leading tone, the subdominant takes over its cadential role, but only temporarily.[55]

Chord successions derived from the natural minor sound archaic and passive, especially in a sonata-form movement. Even in a minor key, sonata form dramatizes the tension of dominant function, notably in the retransition but also in the cadences and other fundamental tonal idioms. Here Brahms isolates certain passages, as in the opening, based on the natural minor and its plagal, "modal" harmony, and he makes the alien harmonic style the movement's telos.[56]

The period initiates a three-part thematic complex (a: mm. 1–13; b: mm. 14–17; a': mm. 18–21) that bears little resemblance to the closed tripartite thematic type represented in the F Major String Quintet and earlier works.[57] Melodic style remains severe in the b section; Mason refers to "a rather schematic use of inversion" in this theme.[58] With the b section, however, come other contrasts, for the leading tone appears; moreover, Brahms introduces a constructive opposition between met-

---

53. *Chamber Music of Brahms,* 221.

54. Foster, "Brahms, Schenker and the Rules of Composition," 264.

55. I discuss this at greater length in "Plagal Harmony as Other: Asymmetrical Dualism in Instrumental Music by Brahms," *Journal of Musicology* 22 (2005): 90–130.

56. Although this kind of harmony is often referred to as modal, the scales of only two of the church modes give rise to it. Notley, "Plagal Harmony as Other," 94.

57. The first theme of the F Major String Quintet can easily be related to the Classical small ternary theme, whereas the opening thematic complex in the Clarinet Trio cannot. On the Classical theme type, see William E. Caplin, *Classical Form: A Theory of Formal Functions for the Instrumental Music of Haydn, Mozart, and Beethoven* (New York: Oxford University Press, 1998), chap. 6.

58. *Chamber Music of Brahms,* 221.

ric "dissonance" and its resolution, to use Peter H. Smith's terminology. Smith writes about this aspect of the Clarinet Trio: beginning with mm. 14–17, the bar line sounds in a different place from where it appears on the page in passages based on the *b* motives.[59] To this I add: establishing and resolving such dissonance produces an alternative formal rhythm analogous to that offered by moving between thematic and nonthematic passages, a point I shall return to later.

With the resolution of the metric dissonance in m. 18—the meter as it is notated and as it is heard become the same again—the abbreviated *a'* section opens. While it combines motives from both *a* and *b*, this section recalls the opening harmonic style. The bottom suddenly seems to drop out of the sonata-form sound, based on the opposition between tonic and dominant, introduced only shortly before. Subdominant-function chords precede statements of the tonic, an A minor and A major triad, respectively, in mm. 18 and 20; furthermore, a descending "plagal" line leads to the subdominant-function chord each time.[60] In short, the strangeness of the effect results from the momentary disappearance of dominant function, reinforced again by a softer dynamic level and the clarinet's descent into the chalumeau register.

Each section of the thematic group has distinct qualities. The *b* section most resembles a traditional theme as defined by Schoenberg (in contrast to a melody): "not at all independent and self-determined . . . strictly bound to consequences which have to be drawn"—while *a'* has the character of an aside.[61] As a closed construction, the period (*a*) would seem to pose the greatest danger, in Adorno's words, of "incompatibility . . . as a melody sufficient in itself, with the grand design." But the period never returns as such—how could it? It does not function as a separate theme but rather as an introduction similar to that in the Clarinet Quintet and, as we shall see, F Minor Clarinet Sonata. Harmonically altered versions of the antecedent phrase do reappear at certain important points; one, for instance, provides the basis of the secondary theme in C major that begins in m. 44. In the course of the movement, Brahms brings back all the opening thematic materials except the consequent phrase, whose primary purposes are, with the antecedent, to introduce significant motives and the alternative harmonic style and to place the identity of the subject in question.

Although purely plagal harmony is not well suited to sonata procedures, Brahms manages to use it at certain points in the movement. Remarkably, the exposition ends on a true rarity in tonal music, a plagal half-cadence (mm. 81–82; see ex. 3.5), with softer dynamics and the clarinet once again in the chalumeau register.[62] And

59. "Brahms and the Shifting Barline: Metric Displacement and Formal Process in the Trios with Wind Instruments," in *Brahms Studies,* ed. David Brodbeck (Lincoln: University of Nebraska Press, 2001), 3:191–229. Smith notes that some listeners may not hear the first written metric displacement as such, 213.

60. I discuss such descending lines in "Plagal Harmony as Other," 95–105 and 121.

61. *Fundamentals of Musical Composition,* ed. Gerald Strang and Leonard Stein (London: Faber and Faber, 1970), 103.

62. On plagal half-cadences, see Harrison, *Harmonic Function in Chromatic Music,* 27. I discuss this cadence at greater length in "Plagal Harmony as Other," 114–116.

EXAMPLE 3.5.   Brahms, Clarinet Trio, Op. 114 / I, mm. 79–83

the destiny of the *b* motives is to be set to the "other" harmonic style (just as the antecedent phrase becomes harmonically "normal"). This happens first in the development section. Forte scales in m. 96 lead to the central episode (mm. 97–105), where the appearance of the *b* motives coincides, as always, with metric displacement.[63] The motives have undergone the kind of transformation Brahms favored, especially in his later works. When the movement opens, only the pianist plays these motives, which contrast with the harmonic and rhythmic passiveness of the thematic complex's outer sections. Here Brahms divides the motives in antiphonal scoring between the clarinet and cello, grouped together, and the piano. More important, he turns the incisive rhythmic figures of the opening into even note values and harmonizes the altered motives as parallel six-three chords in a manner reminiscent of fifteenth-century fauxbourdon. Not all successions of six-threes call to mind that historical connection; semiautonomous plagal harmony, based here on the C-sharp Phrygian scale, again creates the sound of otherness.[64] (Ex. 3.6a and b gives the original and transformed versions of the *b* motives.)

Toward the end of the development section, a retransition of the traditional, dominant-driven type takes shape. Atypical of Brahms's later music in its force and harmonic directness, it leads directly into an extended version of the *b* motives (m. 126); no part of the opening period comes back.[65] (See ex. 3.7.) After this forte and fortissimo expression of dominant harmony, the return of *a'* (mm. 132–137), also lengthened, contrasts all the more sharply. Brahms heightens the otherness of *a'* further by having it begin *subito piano* and with the clarinet part suddenly and completely in the chalumeau register. This time, moreover, Brahms does not present the descending lines (mm. 133 and 135) in a unison texture as in the exposition, but

63. Smith, "Brahms and the Shifting Barline," 226.
64. I discuss this aspect of the passage in "Plagal Harmony as Other," 125–126.
65. Brahms problematizes the point of recapitulation in the first movements of, among others, the Fourth Symphony, A Major Violin Sonata, B Major Piano Trio (second version), G Major String Quintet, and F Minor Clarinet Sonata. (He wrote these works between 1885 and 1894.)

EXAMPLE 3.6a.   Brahms, Clarinet Trio, Op. 114 / I, mm. 13–21

rather as parallel six-three chords that intensify the archaic sound of *a'* and recall the development-section transformation.

A similar version of the *b* motives appears in the coda. At the recapitulation's close, Brahms introduces one last section in displaced meter (mm. 201–217) and gradually reverts to harmonic idioms similar to those from the movement's beginning, the last leading tone appearing in m. 205. In another type of archaism, the coda begins with an open-fifth chord (m. 212), which proceeds to the fauxbourdon transformation of the *b* motives, altered to fit the plagal inclinations of, in this case, A Aeolian. With the plagal cadence in mm. 216–217, the meter as heard becomes reconciled one last time with the notated meter.

Brahms thus places the most extended passages based on purely plagal harmony at the movement's beginning and end, with briefer moments in the development section, the plagal half-cadence that closes the exposition, and the *a'* sections of both the exposition and recapitulation. None of these passages impinges on the definitive formal processes in a sonata-type movement. Brahms presumably intro-

EXAMPLE 3.6b.   Brahms, Clarinet Trio, Op. 114 / I, mm. 96–105

duced alien elements into a sonata-form piece because of the challenge and originality involved in doing so. But his approach raises questions beyond those concerning conscious motivation.

Several other well-known late works include similar archaistic elements, which
Adorno connects to the alienation, the sense of estrangement from one's time sometimes associated with late styles. Writing of obsolete word forms that appear in a
very late work by Goethe, the second part of *Faust*, Adorno asserts: "the anachronism increases the power of the passage." And in a fragment from the Beethoven
manuscript, he observes of another late work, the *Missa solemnis:* "A damming up
of expressive means. Expression through archaism; modal elements."[66] In the Clar-

66. "On the Final Scene of *Faust*," 114; and *Beethoven,* 140.

EXAMPLE 3.7.   Brahms, Clarinet Trio, Op. 114 / I, mm. 125–133

inet Trio's opening Allegro, Brahms frustrates many listeners' expectations by likewise suppressing usual nineteenth-century expressive means, such as ingratiating themes and dramatic treatment of them.

The recapitulation here—as opposed to elsewhere in his late music—does sound affirmative, since it begins with the most dynamic part of the opening after a traditional retransition. Adorno considers Beethoven's early and middle-period recapitulations "aesthetically dubious" because of the same quality of self-affirmation.[67] But here the *a′* section that follows brings a sudden intrusion of the alternative harmonic style: the point is the extreme contrast between the two. If this Allegro conveys late-style alienation, and I believe it does, anachronistic moments such as this

67. *Beethoven,* 16–17.

one are responsible for the effect. The themes themselves are not isolated, as Adorno suggests about the F Major String Quintet's opening theme; Brahms does not express subjectivity that way in this movement. In referring to a world decisively not that of sonata form, this Allegro supports a hermeneutic reading of alienation. For listeners attuned to the two harmonic styles, Brahms's ascetic attitude toward melodic invention makes the archaic passages all the more evocative.

COMPOSITIONAL PROCESS/FORMAL PROCESS

The reciprocal relationship between theme and form was a central topic in Jenner's published account of Brahms's teaching; personal communications to Kalbeck after Brahms's death demonstrate the related inseparability of inspiration and work for him. In one such communication, Jenner quoted the composer as follows:

> "Mistrust your ideas [*Einfälle*] and don't write them down right away! One goes for a walk and reflects upon the matter. As a rule, you will then discover that your idea was scarcely the beginning of one. Only through much back and forth, testing and considering, rejecting and reshaping do you arrive at the correct idea, and the theme comes."[68]

This passage indicates that for Brahms, even a theme was the result of work: an inspired idea was only the germ of a theme; hence he took an active role in turning it into one.

Jenner offered additional information to Kalbeck, who again ascribes some sentences directly to the composer:

> "Never write down a piece before it is clear to you from the first to the last measure. Only then does the real work begin." A poor idea can in general be pardoned, since one cannot go beyond one's own limits, but poor elaboration [*Ausarbeitung*] is unforgivable. He valued form, more narrowly sonata form, as the highest, unalterable rule. "Show me any work by Beethoven in which the form is not observed to the strictest degree, even in the final quartets."[69]

Jenner's recollections underscore Brahms's respect for both compositional hard work and schemata such as sonata form. The composer's comments also indicate that the idea had already turned into a mental sketch of an entire piece before he committed anything to paper. This means he must have worked out theme-form connections in his head, developing the relationship as he progressed in the same back-and-forth way through which he arrived at the themes themselves.[70] Although the language is ambiguous, in this account, "Ausarbeitung" seems to mean technical polishing that can be taught rather than the essential mental process suggested

---

68. *Brahms*, 2:183.

69. *Brahms*, 2:183–184.

70. This recalls Schoenberg's abstract concept of the musical idea. See *The Musical Idea and the Logic, Technique, and Art of Its Presentation*, ed. and trans. Patricia Carpenter and Severine Neff (New York: Columbia University Press, 1995), 18. "Beginning with the traditional meaning of musical idea as theme, Schoenberg moved steadily toward an understanding of the idea as somehow standing for the wholeness of a work."

by both sets of remarks: the idea becoming the theme and then the piece in Brahms's head, inspiration begetting work and work further inspiration.

For Brahms, inventing and developing an idea relate to each other in the compositional process much as particular themes and the sonata-form schema do in formal process. In both instances, the relationship is mutual and dynamic. Not only does "the concept of work," as Schmidt expresses it, "shape his understanding of the compositional process" but also his working-out of an idea enters into the music's substance in ways more fundamental than the specific techniques—openwork, thematic-motivic work—Kneif cites. Adorno's 1938 description in the Beethoven manuscript of "the act of composition colliding with the pre-existing schema" conveys how the two processes might come together. The schema as the objective, more or less stable element connects the two: the composer works with evolving ideas against existing formal templates. As we shall see, the relationship between formal and compositional processes has a special bearing on the F Minor Clarinet Sonata's first movement.

In the long footnote to *Philosophie der neuen Musik,* Adorno more fully explains the relationship between an inspired idea [*Einfall*], which he ends up equating with a theme, and the elaboration of it in "the dialectical process that results in the musical form." *Einfall,* in his words, "designates the irreducibly subjective element in this process" and, because it is irreducible, exemplifies being, while "'work' [*Arbeit*] represents becoming and objectivity." At the same time, the latter "contains the subjective element, which propels it," and *Einfall* "as being possesses objectivity."[71] For Adorno, as for Brahms, an inspired idea and the working-out of it, both formally and compositionally, stand in a true dialectical relationship as opposed elements that each take on properties associated with the other, and formal and compositional processes become one.

ALTERNATIVE DICHOTOMIES AND OVERDETERMINED FORM IN THE F MINOR CLARINET SONATA

Composing as he did in the late nineteenth century, Brahms felt compelled to deny himself the contrast between thematic and nonthematic that Beethoven had used to great effect in, for instance, the *Eroica* Symphony's Allegro con brio. Especially in his last works, Brahms applied alternative dichotomies such as the metric dissonance and resolution described by Smith. In the first movement of the F Minor Clarinet Sonata, as in the Clarinet Trio, Brahms drew on that dichotomy and coordinated it with another, between chordal and linear textures, to compensate for what was not available to him as it had been to Beethoven.

Certain critics have considered it problematic that Brahms created a dense network of motivic connections while retaining the form-building harmonic style and formal patterns of the past. According to Schmidt, he in that way "overdetermined" coherence in late works such as the Clarinet Quintet.[72] At one point

---

71. *Philosophie der modernen Musik,* 74, n. 23.
72. *Brahms und seine Zeit,* 119–120.

Dahlhaus says, in similar terms, "Brahms occasionally tended to overdetermine his structures, as though neither architecture nor logic were by themselves sufficient to meet his need for musical solidity." Dahlhaus gives as an example the opening ten measures of the G Minor Piano Quartet—frequently cited in discussions of developing variation—which, according to him, "still reveal the unmistakable outline of a musical period."[73] Both Schmidt and Dahlhaus imply the motivic development by itself would have been able to sustain the form. Neither critic looks closely at how the motivic work shapes themes or more sizable sections, even though Brahms's comments about turning *Einfälle,* subthematic units, into themes indicate the vitality of the link between motive and theme and suggest the same about themes and larger formal units. Nor does either critic note the alternative dichotomies Brahms conceived to cope with the underlying problem.

The Allegro appassionato of the F Minor Clarinet Sonata provides a case in point. Commentaries on the movement usually focus on motivic relationships traceable to mm. 1–4—more basically, to m. 1—but the opening thematic group (mm. 1–24) can be seen, conversely, as elaborating an *Einfall* into a theme. A rare extant sketch further suggests, and the finished work itself demonstrates, Brahms's concern with coordinating the small-scale rhythms arising from motivic development (as in mm. 1–4) with both the more slowly moving rhythms created by the succession of phrases and the placement of important cadences. If the word is applied more in line with the original meaning Freud gave it, Brahms may be said to have formally "overdetermined" this first movement because the various elements converge to determine its form.[74] More specifically, by setting up constructive oppositions that go beyond the standard dualities in the keys and themes, he counteracted the lost distinction between thematic and nonthematic. The two alternative dichotomies, which emerge during the opening thematic complex, were part of his early conception of this movement.

Unlike Beethoven, Brahms frustrated investigation of his compositional process by burning most of his sketches and drafts. Some evidence of how he proceeded nonetheless does survive. Along with similar manuscript materials by Brahms, the Gesellschaft der Musikfreunde in Vienna holds a single page of sketches for the first sixty-eight measures of the F Minor Clarinet Sonata's opening Allegro appassionato and the gist of mm. 1–28 from the third movement. The sketch for the first movement's beginning apparently represents the stage Jenner describes, when the shape of the whole—certainly, of the exposition—had become clear to the composer. (See fig. 3.2; Brahms's sketch of the first movement stops in the fourth measure of the fourth system, where he has drawn a vertical line.)

In this exposition, Brahms puts the greatest formal weight toward the end, demonstrating again a flexible approach to sonata procedures, a matter above all of subtleties in placing or withholding emphasis, in part through careful treatment of cadences. At the exposition's conclusion in several late first movements, such as those of the B Major Piano Trio (second version) as well as the Clarinet Trio and

73. *Nineteenth-Century Music,* 256.
74. "Psychotherapy of Hysteria," 219, in Breuer and Freud, *Studies in Hysteria.*

FIGURE 3.2.   Brahms, sketches for the Sonata for Clarinet and Piano, Op. 120 No. 1.
Reproduced by kind permission of the Archive of the Gesellschaft der Musikfreunde,
Vienna.

F Major Cello Sonata, he avoids complete closure, each time using a different strategy. The exposition of the F Minor Clarinet Sonata lies on the other side of the
spectrum in this regard, concluding very strongly in C minor after having passed
through a theme in a weakly defined D-flat major.[75]

By the time Brahms wrote out the sketch, he had planned the end accentuation
in the exposition (and recapitulation). For the sketch breaks off after a powerful arrival at a half-cadence in C minor (m. 68) already marked forte, the preliminary
goal within the third thematic/tonal section (mm. 53–89). He entered the treble
and bass lines in most of the sketch, but for the D-flat theme (mm. 38–52), he indicated its entire characteristic texture of three distinct lines, likewise already
marked piano. Many motivic details are also in place. For example, in the C minor
section, a four-bar theme is stated twice (mm. 53–56, 57–60) and then is augmented
and metrically displaced (mm. 61–68). In other words, the piano's motives in mm.
61–66 are virtually the same as those in mm. 53–55 and mm. 57–59 but take up
twice as much space/time and begin on the second beat rather than the downbeat.

75. On Brahms's "three-key expositions" see James Webster, "Schubert's Sonata Form and Brahms's
First Maturity (II)," *19th–Century Music* 3/1 (July 1979): 52–71.

In m. 67 a related motive (comparable to the motive in m. 56 and m. 60), not aug-mented but rather presented in an extended version, is realigned with the down-beat, the abruptness of these changes creating the drive to the half-cadence in m. 68. Because the sketch implies that Brahms had thought out various aspects of form—textural distinctions, motivic development, long-range cadential goals, and so on—together, it supports the likelihood that he approached composition as he described to Jenner. In other words, he must have worked out the relationship be-tween motives, themes, and schema before writing out the sketch. He had gone well beyond the initial stage he disdained of inspired idea.

Brahms repeatedly expressed his low regard for invention. Klara Simrock, his publisher's wife, reported a conversation in which Brahms asked her husband the rhetorical question "What does my 'invention' [*Erfindung*] have to do with me?"[76] In any case, no musical idea can be utterly original. Throughout the nineteenth century, "invention" would obviously have presupposed both an internalized framework of common-practice tonality and a composer's knowledge of many ex-isting themes and melodies. Furthermore, certain themes by Brahms, such as the one that opens the F Minor Clarinet Sonata, appear to transmute specific Classical types, precluding the possibility he sought such originality even if we did not know his attitude toward these matters. Themes themselves, like particular adaptations of sonata-form procedures, engage in a dialogue with conventions.

In the Allegro appassionato, Brahms seems to dwell on the relationship between a theme and its predecessors, a dialectical process placed in motion by the opening four-bar phrase, a phrase that ends on the chromatic and therefore significant pitch G-flat. As Schmidt notes, the first four measures, set as bare octaves in the piano, have an introductory function.[77] For the clarinet's entrance, the new texture of melody plus chordal accompaniment, and the tighter organization of what follows all mark m. 5 as the first theme's beginning. Measures 5–12 are readily heard as rep-resenting the Classical thematic type of the sentence, a dynamic phrase-construc-tion often chosen to open a quick sonata-form movement.[78] The *locus classicus* of a sentence appears at the beginning of Beethoven's F Minor Piano Sonata, Op. 2, No. 1. (See ex. 3.8a.) In a sentence such as this one, the so-called presentation states a two-bar basic idea followed by a variation of that idea: here Beethoven shapes the third and fourth measures as a dominant version of mm. 1–2. The "continuation" phrase (mm. 5–8 in ex. 3.8a) seems to move more quickly, its one-measure incre-ments driving to the half-cadence typical of the sentence.

While the organization of mm. 5–12 in the clarinet sonata closely resembles that of Beethoven's sentence, thereafter Brahms extends the basic construction through two varied restatements of the continuation phrase (mm. 13–16 and 17–24), the second doubled in length (see ex. 3.8b). Although m. 13 only slightly alters m. 9, the changes allow the subsequent treble entrance of two measures from the intro-duction to sound logical and lead convincingly to another half-cadence. The con-

76. *Brahms,* 2:182, n. 1.
77. *Brahms und seine Zeit,* 117.
78. On Schoenberg's concept of the sentence, see Caplin, *Classical Form,* 35–48.

EXAMPLE 3.8a.   Beethoven, F Minor Piano Sonata, Op. 2 No. 1 / I, mm. 1–8

tinuation's second restatement (mm. 17–24), twice as long as the first, alters the original treble (clarinet) line much more drastically. Measures 17–18 vary mm. 13–14 through eighth-note figuration and changes in register, after which m. 19 reverts to the rhythm of m. 15, leading to an exact treble restatement of m. 2 in m. 20. Measures 21–24 then present augmented versions of mm. 3–4 in a syncopated hemiola that causes the beat to be perceived as moving half as fast as before and drives the first thematic group to an unorthodox half-cadence.

At least as significant as the motivic and rhythmic sleight of hand is the textural transformation that occurs in this second restatement, for Brahms eventually replaces the chordal style of the original continuation phrase with a markedly linear texture. And he concludes the phrase not, as in the continuation's previous variation, with a conventional half-cadence on a dominant chord with scale degree two in the treble (m. 16), but rather with a Neapolitan sixth with the flattened second degree (m. 24), the G-flat from m. 4.[79]

Through an overt series of motivic transformations, Brahms thus derives a linear variant that is stylistically opposed to his initial continuation phrase. Whether he did so consciously matters little: he would have internalized the small-scale schema on which Beethoven based his theme long before he composed the clarinet sonata. Moreover, the significance lies not only in the final result, the linear variant, but also in the process of developing variation through which it comes into existence. This process guarantees that the first thematic section—resembling the Clarinet Quintet in this respect—remains in a state of becoming, which Brahms sets in motion each time through a quasi-introduction and its motivic content. And the first twenty-four measures as a whole reenact in stages the transformation of an idea into an extended theme.

79. For a pertinent discussion, see Peter H. Smith, "Brahms and the Neapolitan Complex: Flat-II, Flat-VI, and Their Multiple Functions in the First Movement of the F-Minor Clarinet Sonata," in *Brahms Studies,* ed. David Brodbeck (Lincoln: University of Nebraska Press, 1998), 2:169–208.

EXAMPLE 3.8b.   Brahms, F Minor Clarinet Sonata, Op. 120, No. 1/ I, mm. 1–24

Brahms draws on and develops the contrast between the two styles in the course of the movement, most immediately to shape the rest of the exposition. Although critics usually note that he bases the D-flat theme (mm. 38–52) on augmented motives from the introductory four bars, to my knowledge no critic has observed that the D-flat theme's linear style derives from manipulations of the basic sentence (or indeed noted that thematic structure). The second variant of the continuation phrase (mm. 17–24) has also introduced the augmentation and syncopated hemiola that subsequently reappear in the D-flat theme, again slowing down and displacing the perceived beat. With the move to C minor (m. 53) come faster note values and the reintroduction of chordal style along with, as previously discussed, further augmentation and rhythmic displacement, which ultimately lead to the half-cadence that concludes Brahms's sketch.

The opposition between chordal and linear styles offers one substitute for that between thematic and nonthematic. Since chordal style tends to sound weightier than linear style, moving between one and the other creates a kind of formal rhythm analogous to that offered by moving between thematic and nonthematic passages. To similar ends, Brahms introduces rhythmic augmentation associated with metric displacement in all three thematic/tonal sections (in mm. 21–24, 38–43, 46–52, and 61–66), other instances of the metric dissonance and resolution Smith observed in the Clarinet Trio.

At the approach to the recapitulation, Brahms again uses the difference between linear and chordal styles. Traditional harmonic syntax prepares a false return of the introduction, varied and in F-sharp minor (mm. 130–134), related of course again to the G-flat in m. 4 (see ex. 3.9a). But chromatic, linear voice leading precedes the "true" F minor recapitulation of the first theme (mm. 138 and thereafter), which is thereby deemphasized. (At this point, Brahms saw fit to bring back only the basic sentence—mm. 138–145 are the same as mm. 5–12.) The linear approach to the first theme's reentry results in even greater weight than before being placed on what in the exposition had been the C minor theme (mm. 168 and thereafter).

Brahms's autograph reveals that late in the compositional process—long after the "real work" had begun—he made a noteworthy revision of the false recapitulation in F-sharp minor. As Smith observes, the F-sharp minor variant of the introduction takes the form, in fugal terminology, of a "tonal answer" to the conceptually prior "subject."[80] On the third beat of m. 130, the subject version enters in a middle voice imitating the treble's answer. Brahms, however, apparently recognized that the imitative entry was possible only after he had completed his autograph, a so-called clean copy, hence the revision (see ex. 3.9b).[81] The imitation was a refinement, not essential to his conception of the movement. What was essential appears in the sketch: motives shaped into themes, hemiolas and other disruptions of the meter established and resolved, and the opposition between linear and chordal styles, supported already by specific dynamic markings.

All notes are thematic here, but this Allegro manages to replicate the formal rhythms of earlier sonata-form movements using other means. Furthermore, the

---

80. "Brahms and Subject/Answer Rhetoric," *Music Analysis* 20 (2001): 223–226.

81. The autograph of the Clarinet Sonatas is in the Robert Owen Lehman Collection, on deposit at the Pierpont Morgan Library, New York.

EXAMPLE 3.9a.   Brahms, F Minor Clarinet Sonata, Op. 120 No. 1/ I, mm. 130–135

extant sketch for the Clarinet Sonata and the first movement itself suggest that Brahms kept the theme-form relationship in mind at all times. The constant back-and-forth he described to Jenner guaranteed that the themes would suit the form, that the individuality of the initial inspired idea would be subordinated to the demands of the whole as this developed. No passage sounds alienated from the rest of the movement, as occurs in both the Clarinet Trio and Clarinet Quintet. Rather the movement conveys lateness through its conciseness, Brahms's experimentation with the two alternative dichotomies, and the extreme mastery with which he introduced and worked out the new constructive oppositions.

When Adorno writes about "the category of totality, which in Beethoven still maintains the image of a proper society," he is not asserting that such a society ever existed, merely that it briefly seemed possible and Beethoven's music expresses that exalted illusion. For him "the moment of untruth, of ideology" in early and middle-period Beethoven is the recapitulation. Although he considers Beethoven eventually to have moved beyond the middle-class ideology of the heroic works, he

EXAMPLE 3.9b.   Brahms, F Minor Clarinet Sonata, Op. 120 No. 1/ I, mm. 130–131 (original pitches in piano part). From Brahms's autograph manuscript.

observes that the late music "actually *emphasized* the moment" when the recapitulation begins, presumably to show its arbitrariness.[82] Brahms does something similar in the Clarinet Trio when he stresses arrival at the recapitulation and then deflates it, but a more usual strategy in the late works is to deemphasize that moment in the form. In all three of the very late movements discussed here, furthermore, he problematizes the identity of the subject, presenting an opening complex that does not immediately disclose a theme. As Adorno and Gülke suggest, individualism, a social issue associated with nineteenth-century political and economic ideology, became a musical issue. Whereas Brahms as a private person may not have questioned Liberal emphasis on the individual, he did recognize the musical problem.

Beethoven was indisputably Brahms's primary model for the theme-form relationship in his later music.[83] Remarks such as that about always keeping sight of the connecting "arch" when composing a piece of music correspond closely, probably consciously so, to comments by Beethoven that were widely disseminated by the late nineteenth century.[84] But he was no academic epigone of Beethoven, for he worked with the musical material he inherited from immediate predecessors such as Schumann while at the same time holding on to Beethovenian principles such as "thinking in tones." Even more than specific procedures, Beethoven's attitude toward composition served as a model. Brahms's music, it is true, does not have the exhilarating tone, convey the sense of a new world dawning that, say, Beethoven's F Major String Quartet (Op. 59, No. 1) does: it expresses the spirit of a very different age, as many writers have intimated. But Brahms's stance toward composition, modeled on that of Beethoven, ensured that his music expresses more defensible possibilities within that culture—every culture has these.

Beyond his deep understanding of Beethoven's music, Brahms had a broad knowledge of pre-Classical music and its techniques. His particular application of that knowledge in the Clarinet Trio is unique within his oeuvre.[85] Still, in other late instrumental compositions, he did draw on musics from outside the Classical-Romantic mainstream to revitalize various conventions that had become second nature. Thus the emergent field of musicology and his own longstanding study of a particular voice-leading convention left their mark on his late music. That source of renewal is the topic of the next chapter.

---

82. *Beethoven,* 17. See also Subotnik, "Adorno's Diagnosis of Beethoven's Late Style: Early Symptom of a Fatal Condition," *Developing Variations,* 15–41.

83. Webster argues convincingly that Schubert was Brahms's primary model in earlier sonata form movements. "Schubert's Sonata Form and Brahms's First Maturity (II)."

84. Maynard Solomon, "Beethoven's Creative Process: A Two-Part Invention," in *Beethoven Essays* (Cambridge, Mass.: Harvard University Press, 1988), 126–138.

85. Passages in the first movement of the A Major Piano Quartet sound modal, but Brahms did not create a similar constructive dichotomy between harmonic styles.

CHAPTER 4

MUSIC PEDAGOGY, MUSICOLOGY, AND BRAHMS'S COLLECTION OF OCTAVES AND FIFTHS: HISTORICAL DECLINE, PERSONAL RENEWAL

In the last decade or so of his life, Brahms repeatedly vented his dissatisfaction with nineteenth-century music education. Thus in February 1896 he complained about the poor compositional training Schumann, Wagner, and he had received. When Heuberger tried to counter his assertions, Brahms replied, "Look at my first things!—One sees very clearly how I gradually added to my knowledge. No, no, that is nothing! And look at France where certainly still into our day a *school* existed." He voiced his concern that that tradition, too, was in danger, indeed that music itself might come to an end.[1] In his compositions, Brahms expressed lateness and confronted problems caused by music-historical lateness in a number of different ways, but his conscious, verbally articulated sense of lateness centered on lapsed pedagogical traditions.

The older Brahms's fretting had its roots in attitudes and events of several decades before, beginning with the personal sense of inadequacy in the mid-1850s that moved him to initiate a lifelong study of counterpoint. Toward the end of that decade, another crisis developed when "New German" musicians challenged venerable traditions of compositional practice and theory, including the longstanding contrapuntal injunction against parallel fifths. Brahms's public response to outrages perpetrated by futurist theorists and composers was the famous failed manifesto of 1860; a private response, as Robert T. Laudon demonstrates, was to undertake his own study of the disputed contrapuntal rule in his so-called collection of octaves and fifths.[2]

Brahms devoted most of this manuscript to excerpts from other composers' music that seem to violate the convention forbidding consecutive fifths. Various kinds of evidence—letters, markings in his personal library, and patterns in the manuscript—suggest that his final engagement with the collection began in 1893 or 1894 and that the second half of it, roughly speaking, represents a coherent, focused phase of work. The evidence also allows us to trace particular questions that interested him.

---

1. *Erinnerungen an Brahms,* 94, entry for 23 February 1896.
2. "The Debate about Consecutive Fifths: A Context for Brahms's Manuscript 'Oktaven und Quinten,'" *Music and Letters* 73 (1992): 48–61.

This knowledge is significant because, like his other studies, such as writing canons and collecting folksongs, the manuscript was a source of renewal for his own music. Thus his resumed work on it influenced voice-leading decisions in his last chamber pieces, the F Minor Clarinet Sonata and the E-flat Clarinet Sonata, both of which he finished in the summer of 1894.

MUSIC AS FIRST AND SECOND NATURE

A letter to his friend Mandyczewski helps us date when he began the later phase of work. And it provides a point of departure for understanding the older Brahms's attitude toward another, related challenge to musical tradition: musicological work inspired by Hermann Helmholtz's *Lehre von den Tonempfindungen,* first published in 1863. With the emergence of musicology as a clearly defined field in the mid-1880s, scholarly writing in the *Vierteljahrsschrift für Musikwissenschaft* and elsewhere followed Helmholtz's ideas and invoked the overtone series to explain musical conventions or, along related lines, advocate just intonation. (The latter uses the pure perfect fifths and major thirds of the same acoustical phenomenon.) But many sophisticated musicians, including Brahms and Mandyczewski, expressed extreme skepticism about these trends.

In the letter, dated 19 May 1894, at the very beginning of his summer residence in Ischl that year, Brahms wryly suggested that Mandyczewski look at a recent article by Friedrich Chrysander in the *Vierteljahrsschrift* (see table 4.1).[3] In three installments spread over four years (1891, 1893, and 1894), Chrysander translated a late sixteenth-century treatise by Lodovico Zacconi, interspersed with his own lengthy commentary. At the end of the 1893 portion, Chrysander translated Zacconi's discussion of what the latter referred to as "villanelle and other drolleries" (304): works in which composers deliberately violated the rule that forbids parallel fifths. As becomes clear, the article either inspired or resonated with Brahms's own interest in the villanella and, in particular, the villanelle of Luca Marenzio, regarded even then as a composer of uncommon skill and refinement, but Chrysander's explanation of the genre only amused him:

> Don't neglect to read the conclusion of Chrysander-Zacconi on villanelle in the *Vierteljahrsschrift* 1893, p. 304. I have copied many of them (I mean also by Marenzio himself) for myself—only as the strangest, completely incomprehensible examples of fifth progressions. But look at the marvelous elucidation! And the most wonderful part is that an intelligent person used to thinking clearly and seeing far could have come upon it by himself! (That is, Chrysander!) The rest by Z[acconi] I had already read before. It is unbelievably interesting. Since I, however, unlike Chr., cannot make anything definite of them, I simply look and imagine foreign worlds.[4]

Zacconi's description of the villanella offered little that now seems out of the ordinary. Like recent scholars, he attributed the villanella's origins to composers sati-

---

3. Table 4.1 gives bibliographical information for the articles from the *Vierteljahrsschrift* discussed in this chapter. Page references are given in parentheses within the text.

4. Karl Geiringer, "Johannes Brahms in Briefwechsel mit Eusebius Mandyczewski," *Zeitschrift für Musikwissenschaft* 15 (1933): 360. Brahms referred to the journal in shorthand: "4tl J. Schrift 93."

TABLE 4.1.   Brahms and the *Vierteljahrsschrift für Musikwissenschaft*

Volume number	Issues in Brahms's extant personal library	Articles in the *Vierteljahrsschrift* cited in this chapter
1 (1885)	Issue 1 (two copies)	
2 (1886)		Rudolf Schwartz, "Die Frottole im 15. Jahrhundert": 427–466 (includes passages from two villanelle by Giovanni Domenico da Nola that Friedrich Chrysander quoted in modified form in vol. 9)
3 (1887)		Gustav Engel, "Eine mathematisch-harmonische Analyse des Don Giovanni von Mozart": 491–560 (according to Guido Adler, Brahms scoffed at this article, in which Engel analyzes Mozart's opera assuming just intonation)
4 (1888)		Phillip Spitta, "Die Arie 'Ach, mein Sinn' aus J. S. Bach's Johannes-Passion": 471–478 (Spitta suggested that Brahms should read this article in a letter, to which the composer replied that he did not always bother to read the journal)
6 (1890)	All four issues	Shohé Tanaka, "Studien im Gebiete der reinen Stimmung": 1–90 (Eusebius Mandyczewski and Hans von Bülow both reacted vehemently to Tanaka's advocacy of just intonation)
		Reinhard Kade, "Christoph Demant": 469–552 (includes a villanella-like piece by Jacob Regnart that Brahms copied on the same page as a piece by Haßler; he added excerpts from both to his collection)
8 (1892)	Issues 2, 3, and 4	
9 (1893)	Issues 1, 2, and 3	Rudolf Schwartz, "Hans Leo Haßler unter dem Einfluß der italienischen Madrigalisten": 1–61 (Brahms read this article, which includes a discussion of the treatment of parallel or potentially parallel fifths by Luca Marenzio and Andrea Gabrieli; reading the article appears to have inspired Brahms to look for similar passages in works by Haßler for his manuscript collection)
		Friedrich Chrysander, "Lodovico Zacconi als Lehrer des Kunstgesanges (II)": 249–310 (In a letter to Mandyczewski of 19 May 1894, Brahms showed his interest in this article but also made fun of Chrysander's interpretation of the villanelle)
10 (1894)	Issue 1	Heinrich von Herzogenberg, "Ein Wort zur Frage der reinen Stimmug": 133–145 (written in response to the heightened interest in just intonation evident in the pages of this journal and elsewhere)

EXAMPLE 4.1a.   Giovanni da Nola, villanella excerpt (*VfMw* 2 [1886]: 462)

EXAMPLE 4.1b.   Giovanni da Nola, villanella excerpt (*VfMw* 2 [1886]: 462)

rizing airs as sung by the musically uneducated, "in which without any knowledge of music several voices join and sing together in natural consonances" (305). Brahms marked this passage in his copy; the reported folk practice interested him. But Chrysander's subsequent elaboration of Zacconi and the villanella became the display of faulty reasoning Brahms alluded to in his letter. To illustrate his ideas, Chrysander used two passages from villanelle by Giovanni Domenico da Nola that another musicologist, Rudolf Schwartz, had presented in the 1886 *Vierteljahrsschrift* (462; see ex. 4.1a and b). As Chrysander noted, the treble carries the tune, and he thought of the lower voices as "imitating" it, adding: "As long as the melodic motions are imitated in all voices, series of triads result and, to be sure, major" (309).

The implications of Chrysander's statement gradually become clear. He observed that Nola, a well-trained composer, abandoned the pattern of parallel triads when the tune suggests a cadence. But the situation would have been different for the "unschooled common folk," who would have had no choice other than to present simultaneously in all voices the same exact melody, "since they would have lost their only support by straying from it." Chrysander further assumed that in imitating the tune, the imagined peasants gave priority to the "harmony of nature." As he explained, "if one considers every major chord by itself as an immovable column of tones, as it were, the third and fifth of the same result almost by themselves, because both of them already sound at the same time in nature's harmony without being di-

EXAMPLE 4.1c.   Chrysander's version of Nola's first villanella (*VfMw* 6 [1890]: 308)

EXAMPLE 4.1d.   Chrysander's version of Nola's second villanella (*VfMw* 6 [1890]: 308)

rectly intoned" (309). Consequently, Chrysander proposed that rural people singing and inadvertently harmonizing a tune—and therefore, up to a point, composers parodying this practice in villanelle—could have used only major triads because of the overtone series.

As a result, Chrysander strikingly altered the second excerpt by Nola, though he was an educated musician, to conform to the supposed folk practice, turning the initial minor triad into an inappropriate major triad (ex. 4.1d).[5] Brahms voiced his surprise that someone as intelligent as Chrysander could have devised this explanation. Faced with similar, "completely incomprehensible" parallel triads (many of them minor) in villanelle by Marenzio, which he entered in his collection, Brahms

5. The first passage appears in Lionello Cammarota, *Gian Domenico del Giovane da Nola: I documenti biografici e l'attività presso la SS. Annunziata con l'opera completa,* 2 vols. (Rome: Edizioni de Santis, 1973), 2:324. The other passage does not appear in these volumes, which include da Nola's complete extant works. Here and in the other examples taken from the *Vierteljahrsschrift* I have changed the clefs to conform to modern practice. Cammarota gives the first passage as Chrysander does (ex. 4.1c).

could only, as he put it, "look and imagine foreign worlds"; he did not seek an answer in nature.

Chrysander's conception of nature may well seem problematic to musicologists today, who tend to distrust natural explanations and to emphasize instead the cultural determinants of music of a "foreign world." In a similar vein, Lukács asserted that "the growth of *knowledge* about nature is a social phenomenon" and, more strongly: "Nature is a societal category."[6] When Lukács's book was published (1922), the "long nineteenth century" had finally come to a close. He made his remarks in two essays that dwelt on the merely putative naturalness of its capitalist culture, the milieu of Brahms and his contemporaries. From this perspective, it is undoubtedly significant that more than a decade before Lukács's critique appeared, Schoenberg had rejected the ostensibly natural tonal system, a vestige of the same culture.[7] And in *Theory of the Novel,* which he wrote in 1916, Lukács had applied "second nature" to the central literary genre of the middle-class era. His interpretation of this idea gives it a markedly negative cast: "The second nature, the nature of man-made structures, has no lyrical substantiality; its forms are too rigid to adapt themselves to the symbol-creating moment."[8] Adorno took up the concept and repeatedly used it in various contexts, usually without the pejorative connotations apparent in Lukács.

In his music writings, Adorno almost invariably invoked second nature to refer to tonality's seeming naturalness. Thus he wrote about "those features that have become second nature—the triads, the major and minor scales, the distinction between consonance and dissonance, and ultimately all the categories that spring from these."[9] As the young Schenker noted in 1895, the resulting tonal logic is so ingrained in habits of hearing as to seem grounded in nature, an effect to which the link between the major triad and the overtone series lends some support. Chrysander's use of that link, however, calls to mind Lukács's designation of nature as a societal category. For the high estimation of the overtone series that led him astray had less to do with nature than a historical moment, with attitudes particular to his milieu.

In his treatise Helmholtz had called on nature to explain tonal conventions that included the rule prohibiting parallel fifths, explanations Brahms rejected altogether. Yet the attempts by futurist musicians to expose the rule as a meaningless stricture were equally problematic from his perspective. Although the great composers of the past repeatedly appear to breach the rule, a refined logic—second nature, to be sure, as Adorno applies the phrase—usually motivates their choices. Largely because of the weakened pedagogical tradition, musicians had greater difficulty than before understanding that logic. Brahms's collection allows us a glimpse of him trying to grasp this second nature: parallel fifths that for the most part sounded irreproachable—logical, natural—to him, excerpted from music by composers he esteemed. And passages in his own music show that his study provided inspiration. At that late point in tonal

---

6. *History and Class Consciousness,* 207 and 234.

7. This title illustrates that position: Hans E. Wind [Kurt Blaukopf], *Die Endkrise der bürgerlichen Musik und die Rolle Arnold Schönbergs* (Vienna: Krystall-Verlag, 1935).

8. *Theory of the Novel,* 63–64.

9. "Music and New Music," in *Quasi una Fantasia: Essays on Modern Music,* trans. Rodney Livingstone (London: Verso, 1992), 251. Walter Benjamin also influenced Adorno's evolving understanding of "second nature." See Adorno, "The Idea of Natural History," trans. Bob Hullot-Kentor, *Telos* 60 (1984): 111–124.

music's history, as some composers threw off tradition's constraints and scholars such as Chrysander sought to understand nature as the foundation of certain musical practices, Brahms probed the underlying laws of contrapuntal conventions and their implications for his own creative work. But the villanella, which seemed to refer to musical practices partially based in first nature, confronted him with music of "foreign worlds" that defied that logic.

BRAHMS'S COLLECTION IN CONTEXT: THE EARLY PHASE OF WORK

In 1933, a much older Schenker transcribed Brahms's manuscript. The resulting publication included commentary in which he asserted that the composer at times anticipated his own theory of structural levels of voice-leading.[10] To support this claim, Schenker elucidated the means—making one voice cross another or introducing various manipulations and embellishments of the basic voice-leading—through which the composers in Brahms's collection had created only apparent consecutive fifths. And when he mentioned the manuscript in a book published two years later, he announced: "I was the first to make clear the relationship between strict counterpoint and free composition, within which the problem of parallel octaves and fifths is also solved."[11] In 1980, Paul Mast translated Schenker's monograph and added substantially to our understanding with further enlightening remarks and an admirable critical apparatus. Through careful research, Mast was able to surmise that Brahms had worked on the collection in at least two phases, one beginning in 1863 or 1864, when he seems to have entered the first examples, the other in the 1890s, when it is certain that he added many more. In approximate terms, pages 1–5 of Brahms's manuscript represent the early phase of work, pages 6–11 the later phase.[12]

Finally, in 1992, Laudon reconstructed one context for Brahms's interest in the topic: the polemical disputes in the middle of the century, and especially around 1860, concerning the validity of the rule. As in other controversies of the time, Austro-German musicians tended to split over the question into so-called classicist and futurist camps. August Wilhelm Ambros and Carl Friedrich Weitzmann, both sympathetic toward the second group, wrote treatises—the former in 1859, the latter in 1860 and 1861—advocating free or at least freer use of parallel fifths. Annotations in Brahms's manuscript confirm that he consulted Ambros's treatise both when he made the initial entries, probably as Mast argues in the mid-1860s, and again in the 1890s.[13]

Weitzmann took the more radical position of the two theorists. Although many attempts had been made to explain the rule on the grounds that parallel fifths are "contrary to nature," according to Weitzmann, "it appears to be based on opinion

---

10. Brahms, *Oktaven und Quinten u. a. aus dem Nachlass* (Vienna: Universal-Edition, 1933).

11. *Free Composition*, 1:57.

12. "Brahms's Study, *Octaven u. Quinten u. A.*: With Schenker's Commentary Translated," *Music Forum* 5 (1980): 159–166.

13. Ambros, *Zum Lehre vom Quinten-Verbote* (Leipzig: H. Matthes, 1859); Weitzmann, *Harmoniesystem* (Leipzig: C. F. Kahnt, 1860), and *Die neue Harmonielehre im Streit mit der alten, mit einer musikalischen Beilage: Albumblätter zur Emancipation der Quinten, Anthologie klassischer Quintenparallelen* (Leipzig: C. F. Kahnt, 1861. Brahms refers to Ambros on pages 2 and 8 in his manuscript. Mast, "Brahms's *Octaven u. Quinten*," 42–43, 104–105.

EXAMPLE 4.2.   Beethoven, Piano Sonata in C
major, Op. 53 / I, mm. 195–196

and prejudice, not on natural necessity or tenable rational arguments." He adduced
a passage from Beethoven's "Waldstein" Sonata (see ex. 4.2 and table 4.2, which
shows two additional sources) as he concluded defiantly: "the newer musical grammar can without hesitation annul that prohibition" (5).

Weitzmann alluded to the existence of organum as proof that successions of fifths
do not naturally offend the human ear (5); Ambros likewise began his treatise with
an extended discussion of that genre (1–5). Ambros made some good points as he
then cited various theoretical explanations from the Middle Ages to the nineteenth
century, while giving many examples of consecutive fifths from music by illustri-
ous composers. But he also made questionable or even crudely inaccurate assertions,
claiming for instance that from the rule's institution to his own time, musicians were
interested in whether successive fifths were visible rather than whether they were
audible (2). Ambros's comments on Renaissance vocal polyphony stand out as especially problematic. His examples include one passage by Dufay in which a di-

TABLE 4.2.   Some Frequently Cited Examples of Parallel Fifths

Example no.	Composer, work, and sources where cited
4.2	Beethoven, Piano Sonata in C major ("Waldstein"), Op. 53 / I, mm. 195–196 (Dommer, p. 319; Tappert, p. 85; Weitzmann, *Harmoniesystem*, p. 5)
4.5a	Mozart, *Don Giovanni*, act 2, no. 19, m. 61, also m. 80 (which I have cho-sen to use) (Brahms, examples 22, 90a and b; Tappert, p. 47; Weitzmann, example 2)
4.6	Gluck, *Armide*, act 2, scene 3, m. 81 (Ambros, p. 51; Brahms, examples 20 and 96; Dommer, p. 318; Tappert, p. 43; Weitzmann, example 1)
4.7a	Bach, Organ Toccata in D minor (BWV 565), mm. 7–9 (Ambros, p. 14; Brahms, example 35; Tappert, p. 41; Riemann, p. 725)
4.9a	Schubert, "In der Ferne," from *Schwanengesang*, D. 957, mm. 17–18 (Ambros, p. 21; Brahms, example 48a; Tappert, p. 97)
4.9b	Mendelssohn, *Midsummer Night's Dream*, no. 10, mm. 15–16 (Ambros, p. 41; Brahms, examples 16 and 98; Tappert, p. 98)

"Riemann" refers to his *Musik-Lexikon.* "Weitzmann" refers to *Die neue Harmonielehre.* "Brahms"
refers to Mast, "Brahms's *Octaven u. Quinten.*"

minished fifth moves to a perfect fifth and another in which a suspended sixth breaks up two fifths, along with a passage by Palestrina in which a tenth separates two twelfths. According to Ambros, that voice-leading strategy does not effectively mask the "bitter" sound of the consecutive twelfths. He seems to have been unable to adjust his hearing to the expectations of another time: his agenda was to show that composers never honestly followed the rule rather than to probe the aural ideal behind their choices. Even more controversial, Ambros asserts that making two voices cross to avoid consecutive fifths fixes the problem only "for the eye," quoting another passage from Palestrina's music (6–9). This treatise is evidence that Ambros had neither a good ear for nor a firm intellectual grasp of conventions of traditional counterpoint.

Like the division in Austro-German music worlds, the debate about parallel fifths lasted for decades, conducted in journals, monographs, and musical dictionaries, which of course expands the context Laudon established. More clearly than either Ambros or Weitzmann, these authors were trying—as was Brahms and as had various musicians in the past—to understand why some parallel fifths sounded acceptable and others did not. Tappert, a writer of journalistic criticism and Wagner apologist as well as a theorist and musicologist, contributed one of the most thorough treatments in 1869.[14] He went through various theoretical discussions, dwelling especially on Friedrich Marpurg's. This appears in a treatise that Brahms relied on heavily in his own counterpoint studies.[15] In a statement Tappert quoted (12), Marpurg concluded that since it is not possible to cover all the possibilities, "fine hearing and good power of judgment must come to the aid of the rules." This was Brahms's own attitude.

At one point Tappert rhetorically proposed "abolishing the fifth prohibition" and recounted a story about Beethoven (19). The composer asked Ferdinand Ries who had forbidden fifths. When Ries responded, "The rules; the theoretical textbooks of Fux, Marpurg, Kirnberger and all the others," Beethoven retorted, "Well, I allow them." Brahms would not have agreed with Beethoven's imperious attitude or with Tappert's admiring comment "That was a remark worthy of the titans!" We shall see that Brahms did not regard Beethoven's voice-leading as highly as he did the composer's treatment of theme-form relations. Brahms's position more resembled that of Bach, as Forkel represented it. "Everybody knows that there are cases in which [parallel perfect intervals] sound well," and Bach sometimes wrote these "so plainly that they offended every beginner in composition, but afterwards soon justified themselves." Forkel also reported Bach's fastidious questioning of consecutive intervals in middle voices that other musicians accepted without thinking.[16] Understanding how to apply the rule clearly required careful training and listening and a

14. Tappart, *Das Verbot der Quinten-Parallelen: Eine monographische Studie* (Leipzig: Heinrich Matthes, 1869). I quoted Tappert's review of two chamber pieces by Brahms in chapter 2. An entry in Heuberger's diary for 25 April 1887 makes it clear Brahms read the review and it gratified him. *Erinnerungen an Brahms,* 32.

15. *Handbuch bei dem Generalbasse und der Composition,* 3 vols. (Berlin: J. J. Schützens Wittwe, 1755–58). On Brahms's use of these volumes, see Virginia Hancock, *Brahms's Choral Compositions and His Library of Early Music* (Ann Arbor: UMI Research Press, 1983), 75.

great deal of experience. Still, Brahms—like Bach, Marpurg, and Tappert himself—believed it possible to grasp why some fifths sound fine and others do not.

In contrast to Ambros, Tappert viewed voice-crossing as a solution to potential fifths, quoting two of Bach's chorales but observing: "To be sure, this means is not convincing on piano-type instruments [*Klavieren*] and the organ" (22). And while he found the injunction against fifths "in its former version not in keeping with the times," he added that he did not want "to introduce anarchic conditions regarding successions of intervals" (25). From his personal collection of consecutive fifths Tappert selected a prodigious number that he separated into eight groups. Tappert covers most of the possible situations in which acceptable parallels occur, but some of his categories are vague and therefore overlap. Here are his categories of parallel fifths from *Das Verbot der Quinten-Parallele* (28):

1. "Circumstantial fifths," formed when a tenor substitutes for a soprano or vice versa
2. "Fifths not in a strict sense, returning regularly at the same position in the measure and beat," part of a sequential pattern of figuration or suspensions with other intervals between the fifths
3. "Fifths masked by pauses, delays, etc. but nevertheless to be considered faulty progression if lacking in unity" (explained thus on p. 38)
4. "Figuration fifths, arising through sequences of broken chords"
5. "Transitional fifths arising from anticipations, passing notes both accented and not, etc." (explained thus on p. 42)
6. "Developmental fifths," which come about through adhering to a pattern (often a written-out slow trill; explained on p. 61)
7. "Fifths justified because of tonal unity," that is, because they do not create a sense of disruption, including so-called Mozart fifths in which an augmented sixth chord resolves directly to an unadorned dominant
8. "Characteristic fifths," or the deliberate use of parallels for an expressive effect

Markings in Brahms's personal library show his attitude toward certain questions raised by these authors. For instance, in a counterpoint manual published in 1862, Heinrich Bellermann quotes and then rejects Ambros's statement that the crossing of the two voices in Palestrina's *Stabat mater* corrects the problem only "for the eye." In his copy, Brahms wrote "N[ota] B[ene]" next to Bellermann's rebuttal: "Fortunately, however, the human ear is equipped so that it can distinguish between the course of individual voices."[17]

Of particular value for understanding Brahms's views is his copy of Arrey von Dommer's *Musikalisches Lexicon,* published in 1865 (although he apparently did not

---

16. See Hans T. David and Arthur Mendel, eds., *The Bach Reader: A Life of Johann Sebastian Bach in Letters and Documents,* rev. ed. (New York: Norton, 1966), 319–320. Mast gives this citation in "Brahms's Octaven u. Quinten," 169, n. 12.

17. *Der Contrapunct oder Anleitung zur Stimmführung in der musikalischen Composition* (Berlin: Julius Springer, 1862), 67.

acquire it until 1879 or later).[18] The crucial entry for this topic is "Fortschreitung der Intervalle" (progression of intervals) and especially the section "Quintverbot" (fifth prohibition).[19] Using his own hearing as a guide, Dommer went through various factors that affect the sound of consecutive fifths: for example, whether the notes are in inner or outer voices. Like Bellermann, Dommer disagreed with Ambros's claim that (illusory) fifths produced by the crossing of two voices in Palestrina's motet do not differ from straightforward parallels. (See ex. 4.3a; ex. 4.3b gives Ambros's chordal reduction, which assumes the voice-crossing's irrelevance.) According to Dommer, like Tappert four years later, this voice-leading will not sound as consecutive fifths provided the two parts are written either for "singing voices or instruments with dissimilar timbres" (318). Brahms drew double vertical lines and again wrote "N[ota] B[ene]" to mark part of the discussion of voice-crossings. As we shall see, in his F Minor Clarinet Sonata he met the challenge of part-writing for the piano alone in which voice-crossings create unproblematic fifths.

Brahms also annotated a passage by Dommer saying that parallels matter "when they have true harmonic value rather than simply arising through the *coincidence of moving melodic voices*. If the latter is the case, then they are permitted without a doubt. The fifths in example 5c [Dommer's voice-leading, given as ex. 4.4a here] *definitely do not sound bad*" (318: the use of italics approximates the underlining in Brahms's copy; other instances of underlining will also be rendered in italic type). Like many other musicians, Dommer understood why certain fifths sound acceptable. Even the Viennese musician Selmar Bagge, who countered Weitzmann's polemic with one of his own and to this day has a reputation as a hidebound conservative, recognized that parallel fifths that arise this way are unproblematic.[20]

This particular voice-leading situation was personally relevant to Brahms during his first phase of work on the manuscript. As part of his collaborative counterpoint studies with Joachim, he had composed his A-flat Minor Organ Fugue in 1856. Joachim criticized the voice-leading in three passages, including one that featured this type of parallel fifths in two successive measures. When Brahms finally published a version of the fugue in 1864, he revised the other passages but not the parallel fifths: in neither measure did the second fifth, in Dommer's words, have "true harmonic value" (see ex. 4.4b).[21] A number of late nineteenth-century musicians, not just Brahms, understood the questions raised by consecutive fifths better than

18. Brahms asked Simrock to obtain a copy of the book in a letter of 5 October 1879. *Brahms Briefwechsel*, 10:130.

19. *Musikalisches Lexicon auf Grundlage des Lexicon's H. Ch. Koch's* (Heidelberg: J. C. B. Mohr, 1865). The entire entry runs from p. 314 to p. 324, with the discussion of consecutive fifths filling most of the space, 316–324.

20. "Die gekrönte Preisschrift von C. F. Weitzmann," *Deutsche Musik-Zeitung* I (1860): 233–235 and 241–243. On p. 234 he gives a number of examples of parallel fifths he finds acceptable, some of them surprisingly daring.

21. Brahms did not give the fugue an opus number. For a discussion of his revisions and Joachim's reaction to the first version, see David Brodbeck, "The Brahms-Joachim Counterpoint Exchange; or Robert, Clara, and 'the Best Harmony between Jos. and Joh.,'" in *Brahms Studies*, 1:52–54.

EXAMPLE 4.3a.   Palestrina, excerpt from *Stabat mater* as given by Ambros

fac   ut   te - cum   lu - ge - am.

Example 4–3a

EXAMPLE 4.3b.   Palestrina, excerpt from *Stabat mater* in Ambros's reduction

EXAMPLE 4.4a.   Example 5c in Arrey von Dommer, *Musikalisches Lexicon*, 318

EXAMPLE 4.4b.   Brahms, A-Flat Minor Organ Fugue (1864 version as published in the *Allgemeine Musikalische Zeitung*), mm. 56–58

Schenker later gave them credit for. Like Brahms, they used their ears, trained by listening to a particular repertory, as their ultimate guide.

BEAUTIFUL, CHARACTERISTIC, AND MERELY CHARACTERISTIC FIFTHS

In comments he entered during the later phase of work, Brahms produced his own six categories of parallels (see table 4.3). His efforts at categorization ended in frustration, for at the bottom of his list he wrote: "Where do the truly *bad* fifths and octaves remain, and where can they be found[?]" (113) The answer, although he did not offer it himself, was this: they could be found in music he did not like and therefore omitted. For what primarily distinguished his collection from Tappert's was the overall selection of repertory. Tappert included passages from Wagner and from composers who did not interest Brahms, such as the pianist-composers Stephen Heller and Carl Czerny. Despite his respect for Wagner as a composer, Brahms cited no music by the "New German School," and he collected far more examples from Bach and earlier composers. Virtually every composer he chose had had a sound, traditional musical education and therefore worked within an aural and conceptual framework like his own. By trying for the most part to learn from composers he already respected, he almost precluded voice-leading that would sound faulty to him.

The most interesting of Brahms's categories are the second—"beautiful, expressive, characteristic, *merely* characteristic"—and the third, "both [of the above] at the same time." Judging from the placement of Brahms's list in his manuscript (which I have tried to reproduce in table 4.3), the third seems to refer to the first category,

TABLE 4.3.   Categories of Parallel Fifths in Brahms's Manuscript, Bottom of Page 8

1. correct, good.	2. beautiful, expressive, characteristic
3. both at the same time.	*merely* characteristic,[a] in connection with these one should perhaps consider whether or not the same effect could be attained without them (Schubert)
4. careless	
5. bad, wrong.	6. questionable, needs further consideration

Mast, "Brahms's *Octaven u. Quinten*," 112–113. I have slightly changed the translation, and I have tried to approximate Brahms's placement of the categories in his manuscript, which is evident in the facsimile in Mast's article. A short vertical line connects "characteristic" with "*merely* characteristic [and so forth]," which is directly below it.

[a] Here Brahms inserted "as in bad progressions that result from consideration of the performer's convenience. (Beeth. Sonatas Op. 2 and 53." He added this at an angle and connected it with a line to "*merely* characteristic"; he then crossed out "and 53.")

EXAMPLE 4.5a.   Mozart, *Don Giovanni*, Act 2, No. 19, m. 80 (Brahms, MS p. 8; Mast, ex. 90b)

"correct, good," plus some facet of the second, either beautiful, expressive, or characteristic, but not "*merely* characteristic."

Brahms took particular pleasure in voice-leading in which an accented passing or neighboring tone creates one of the fifths. Consecutive fifths arise this way in more than half the passages he marked with an "a" (or, possibly, alpha), which Mast interprets to mean that Brahms "enthusiastically approved of" them.[22] Example 4.5a, from *Don Giovanni*, falls into the category of fifths that Brahms found correct and beautiful at the same time. Tappert placed the passage in his broad fifth category of "transitional fifths arising from anticipations, passing notes both accented and not, etc." Brahms reacted more subjectively, not only entering the special symbol but also reinforcing the point by writing "N. B. / Beautiful fifths," underscored with two lines, in the margin next to it.

This voice-leading no doubt pleased Brahms because in context the second, accented fifth is a dissonance. George Henschel quoted the composer as saying "I love dissonances very much, but on heavy beats, and then lightly and gently resolved!"[23] In the *Don Giovanni* passage, the treble C-sharp is dissonant, and Mozart treated it in Brahms's preferred manner. Brahms's other examples of this kind of fifths come from additional music by Mozart and from works by Schumann, Bach, Bizet, and (apparently) Mendelssohn.[24] The excerpt from *Carmen* that received his sign of approval—twice over—and an additional "*very good!*" features exactly the same voice-leading: the second, metrically stressed fifth is a dissonance, "lightly and gently resolved" (see ex. 4.5b). An elaborate set of conventions made such fifths dissonant in context, an effect he found as beautiful in Bizet's opera as in music by the four German composers.

---

22. Mast, "Brahms's *Octaven u. Quinten*": 168–171. The number is equivocal because Brahms connects two examples with a "vide," but marks only one with the sign. Most additional references to Mast's translation and commentary will be given in parentheses within the text. Sometimes, as in Mast's ex. 87 (here ex. 4.9c), Brahms uses parallel lines to indicate the parallel intervals. I have replicated Mast's practice of showing certain additional instances with bracketed lines, as in ex. 4.5a (Mast's ex. 90b), and of showing passages in which parallels are avoided through voice-crossings with bracketed broken lines, as in ex. 4.15c (Mast's ex. 120).

23. In conversation with Henschel; quoted in Kalbeck, *Brahms*, 3:85.

24. Mast, "Brahms's *Octaven u. Quinten*," 168–171. The Mendelssohn example does not have the sign next to it, but other evidence links it with the *Don Giovanni* excerpt, as Mast notes.

EXAMPLE 4.5b.   Bizet, *Carmen,* Act 1, No. 8, mm. 11–15 (Brahms, MS p. 6; Mast, ex. 69)

The examples Brahms refers to in parentheses, Beethoven piano sonatas and a Schubert song (see table 4.3), show that he understood "characteristic" fifths and octaves in a twofold sense: those that arise in idiomatic keyboard styles and those introduced for expressive purposes. In distinguishing between "characteristic" and "*merely* characteristic" uses, he brings into focus a question that underlies much commentary on parallel fifths, for example, regarding a famous passage from Gluck's opera *Armide:* does the expressive purpose justify voice-leading that otherwise would be regarded as faulty? (See table 4.2 and ex. 4.6.) Dommer quotes a theorist who referred to the action on stage—Armida's use of magic to put Rinaldo, the only knight who is resistant to her personal charm, into a sleep-like trance—to explain the fifths, but observes that no such justification expressed in a "poeticizing phrase" is called for. One of the fifths is "incidental, arising through melodic notes": C-natural, an embellishing note, sounds simultaneously with G, a harmonic note. In his copy of Dommer's *Lexicon,* Brahms wrote "(Marx)" next to the quotation from the unnamed theorist, but Ambros—and, undoubtedly, other musicians—also adduced the dramatic action to explain Gluck's voice-leading.[25] Brahms left no comments next to the *Armide* excerpt in his manuscript, which he entered in the first, and then recopied in the second, half. Schenker grouped it with others involving a single neighboring tone, and Tappert, working along similar lines to both Dommer and Schenker, placed it in his category of fifths arising from the coincidence of notes with and without harmonic significance. Citing Marx by name, Tappert (24–25) ridiculed his unnecessary extramusical explanation: these are characteristic but, obviously, not merely characteristic fifths.

A passage from Bach's D Minor Organ Toccata, which Brahms copied into his manuscript during the early phase of work, exemplifies his other subtype of characteristic fifths: those that come about through idiomatic writing for a keyboard instrument (see table 4.2 and ex. 4.7a). Ambros, after crassly reducing the right-hand part of a similar passage by Bach to parallel fifths (ex. 4.7c and d), referred to the toccata excerpt as "even more striking," while Tappert classified the parallels vaguely as "figuration fifths." More than six decades later, Schenker, in this instance as imprecise as Tappert, grouped the passage with others in which apparent fifths were "eliminated" through arpeggiation (153). But in 1887 Hugo Riemann had already

---

25. Marx discusses this passage in *Gluck und die Oper* (Berlin: O. Janke, 1863), 2:214–216. If this is Dommer's source, he did not quote Marx literally.

come up with a sophisticated interpretation (while also giving a "false" one) that anticipates remarks by Mast (172–173) nearly a century later. Riemann shows the root in the final statement of each triad moving to the third in the first statement of the following triad, creating a succession of alternating fifths and thirds (see ex. 4.7b).[26] This interpretation most likely represents how listeners attuned to fine points of voice-leading hear the parts proceeding. Like Gluck's fifths, these are not merely characteristic fifths. While they are manifestly both correct and character- istic, Brahms did not give either the Gluck or the Bach excerpt his sign of special approval.

Although few of the passages in his manuscript contained "truly bad fifths and octaves," he did indicate displeasure with some of his examples, as when in his list he designated the Schubert song and the Beethoven sonatas not just characteristic but "*merely* characteristic." Brahms did not use the "Waldstein" passage Weitzmann had quoted—thick chordal writing for piano apparently did not interest him—but instead took two, more linear passages with parallel octaves, along with two simi- lar passages from Beethoven's early C Major Sonata (Op. 2, No. 3). (See example 4.8 for one of the latter passages.) He did not care for any of the four excerpts he chose, for in addition to his comment in the list, he wrote "Claviersatz" (keyboard style) and "very unpleasant to me" and "not praiseworthy" next to them.[27]

Tappert defined characteristic fifths more narrowly than Brahms did, reserving his final category for passages in which composers deliberately aim for expressive qualities that violate conventional standards of beauty. Not only did he restrict his definition to one of Brahms's subcategories but also he limited it to instances the composer would in general have considered "merely characteristic." In introducing his final category, Tappert thus mentions the longstanding controversy as to whether it is acceptable to use "the faulty, ugly" for expressive purposes. The ex- cerpts by Mendelssohn and Schubert (given here as ex. 4.9a and 4.9b; see table 4.2) exemplify Tappert's understanding of characteristic fifths; the first pair are meant to suggest awkward rusticity, the other to emphasize a shocking phrase in Schubert's text. This is the song Brahms took exception to.

He entered both passages in the first half of his manuscript but recopied only the Mendelssohn in the second half. (He also did not recopy the passages from Bee- thoven's two C major piano sonatas.) While he recognized that the fifths in this song and another by Schubert were intentional, he speculated that they have an un- necessarily "weakening effect."[28] Yet he found exceedingly bold fifths that Bach in- troduced for text expression commendable (see ex. 4.9c), entering both his symbol of approval and "deliberate fifths" with a crossreference to the Schubert song and other pieces. As in Schubert's song, Bach's first pair of fifths moves from one root- position triad to another a half-step down at a meaningful point in the text: "vale

26. *Musik-Lexikon*, 3rd ed. (Leipzig: Max Hesse, 1887), 725, entry for "Parallelen."

27. Schenker explained Beethoven's compositional choices. Mast, "Brahms's *Octaven u. Quinten*," 158. Brahms later crossed out his criticism of the "Waldstein" passages in his list, which appears here as table 4.3.

28. Brahms offered a tentative recomposition of the passage by Schubert. This appears as ex. 38b in Mast, "Brahms's *Octaven u. Quinten*," 62. Schenker again defended Schubert's writing, 148–149.

EXAMPLE 4.6.   Gluck, *Armide,* Act 2,
Scene 3, m. 81 (Brahms, MS p. 2; Mast,
ex. 20)

EXAMPLE 4.7a.   Bach, D Minor Organ Toccata, BWV 565,
m. 8 (Brahms, MS p. 3; Mast, ex. 35)

EXAMPLE 4.7b.   Bach, D Minor Toccata excerpt in
"false" and "correct" reductions by Riemann

EXAMPLE 4.7c.   Bach, D Minor Harpsichord Concerto, BWV 1052 / I, mm.
130–132

EXAMPLE 4.7d.   Bach, excerpt from D Minor
Harpsichord Concerto in Ambros's reduction

EXAMPLE 4.8.   Beethoven, Piano Sonata in C Major, Op. 2, No. 3 / I, mm. 47–51 (Brahms, MS p. 1; Mast, ex. 5a)

EXAMPLE 4.9a.   Mendelssohn, *Midsummer Night's Dream,* No. 10, mm. 15–16 (Brahms, MS p. 9; Mast, ex. 9B)

EXAMPLE 4.9b.   Schubert, "In der Ferne," mm. 17–18, from *Schwanengesang* (Brahms, MS p. 4; Mast, ex. 48a)

EXAMPLE 4.9c.   Bach, *Gelobet seist du, Jesu Christ,* BWV 91, bass recitative, mm. 9–12 (Brahms, MS p. 7; Mast, ex. 87)

of tears." The fifths are startling and are not as easily explained as the others Brahms found beautiful, but the linear motion that follows the fifths serves to integrate the effect into the passage.[29] Brahms also did not convey the strong reservations about Scarlatti's "Claviersatz" that he did about Beethoven's: he must not have considered the Bach or Scarlatti examples to include *merely* characteristic fifths.

Brahms may well have believed that the contrapuntal training of Austro-German composers had weakened as early as the time of Beethoven and Schubert. Only about a fifth of his examples are by composers from Beethoven's generation or later, and a half-dozen of those come out of the French tradition he admired: thus he includes music by Méhul and Cherubini as well as Bizet. When he spoke with Heuberger in the 1896 conversation quoted at the beginning of this chapter, furthermore, he expressly indicated that he saw a decline already in Beethoven's music. "What, however, is much weaker in Beethoven, for example, than in Mozart and especially in Sebastian Bach is the use of dissonances. You don't find dissonances, true dissonances, used any longer in Beethoven as in Mozart. Just look at *Idomeneo!* . . . What splendid dissonances, what harmonies!!"[30] In contrapuntal matters Brahms usually sought inspiration in music by composers who preceded Beethoven, hence in part his interest in musicology.

BRAHMS AND THE VIERTELJAHRSSCHRIFT FÜR MUSIKWISSENSCHAFT

Musicology, one product of Liberalism's emphasis on scientific methods, sought to bring greater rigor to the study of music. As is well known, Brahms was on cordial terms with some of the most eminent early musicologists, and he himself prepared volumes for certain of the collected-works editions that began to appear. He edited, for example, Mozart's *Requiem* and two books of Couperin's *Pièces de Clavecin,* and he realized the figured bass of vocal duets and trios by Handel for Chrysander's complete edition. Along with Chrysander, two other prominent scholars with whom Brahms was friendly, Guido Adler and Phillip Spitta, collaborated on the *Vierteljahrsschrift,* the first musicological journal of any duration. A number of issues from the journal's ten-year run, 1885–94, survive in the composer's library (see table 4.1). Brahms's comments about Chrysander's article show he had misgivings about some of the pseudoscientific scholarship in this journal; moreover, as Virginia Hancock observes, at times he did not bother to cut all the pages in his copies.[31]

An exchange in his correspondence with Spitta offers more evidence of Brahms's attitude toward the *Vierteljahrsschrift.* In November 1888, Spitta casually suggested that Brahms look at an essay on Bach's *St. John Passion* in the most recent issue (see table 4.1). The composer replied that he did not always "burden" himself with

29. In the Bach edition Brahms used, Spitta placed a question mark next to the second pair of fifths. These fifths do not appear in the *Neue Bach Ausgabe.*

30. *Erinnerungen an Brahms,* 93. Brahms entered three passages from *Idomeneo* in the penultimate page of his manuscript, and gave one his sign of approval.

31. Hancock, *Brahms's Choral Compositions,* 84.

reading the journal but would seek out that article. Spitta, after noting that Brahms's comments "had somewhat depressed" him, made a dignified defense of the *Vierteljahrsschrift*. On the one hand, he and his colleagues did not aim their efforts at the same audience as that for musical newspapers; on the other hand, they did not have in mind merely "the other half-dozen music scholars in Europe." Spitta conceded: "Much in musicology, it is true, can hold only limited interest for a practical artist." But in his view, the very existence of the *Vierteljahrsschrift* was called into question if nothing in it had more general appeal.[32] As will become evident, although he expressed some disdain for the new field and the fledgling journal, Brahms took an intense interest in certain articles: musicology was indeed a source of renewal for him.

According to Adler, Brahms did belittle a particular contribution to the 1887 volume. In parenthetical comments in his memoirs, Adler noted that because of the one essay, Gustav Engel's "Eine mathematisch-harmonische Analyse des Don Giovanni von Mozart," he "was mocked by Brahms with the pointed remark, 'is that scholarship [or science: *Wissenschaft*]?'"[33] In the article (listed in table 4.1), Engel explored the question of whether Mozart's opera remains tonally unified if performed using just intonation. To this end, he calculated the discrepancies in the tuning of particular pitches that would accumulate in each number. Going through the entire opera in seventy pages of prose dense with mathematical symbols, he considered whether Mozart had compensated so that pitches had the same tuning at a number's end as at its beginning. Engel concluded that, with two exceptions, Mozart, miraculously, had done so throughout the opera (492). Odd as such an undertaking seems to us today, it was by no means eccentric at the time.

Engel may have assumed the superiority of just intonation because of its connection to the overtone series; other contributors to the *Vierteljahrsschrift* certainly made clear their bias in favor of this "natural" approach to intonation. Midcentury theorists such as Hauptmann had based their speculations on the pure perfect fifths and major thirds that occur in the overtone series, a position that received additional support later in the century from Helmholtz's work.[34] In contrast to Hauptmann, Helmholtz did not understand tonality itself to be a product of nature. Rather, he held that "the construction of scales and of harmonic tissue is a product of artistic invention, and by no means furnished by the natural formation or natural function of our ear, as it has been hitherto most generally asserted."[35] He recognized the tonal system to be second nature. Yet he wrote vigorously in favor of just intonation, even though tonality, as it had evolved, required tempered, if not necessarily equally tempered, intervals.

32. *Brahms Briefwechsel*, 16:83, 85–86; cited in part in Hancock, *Brahms's Choral Compositions,* 84.

33. *Wollen und Wirken: Aus dem Leben eines Musikhistorikers* (Vienna: Universal-Edition, 1935), 32. See also J. Murray Barbour, "Just Intonation Confuted," *Music and Letters* 19 (1938): 51

34. See the discussion of just intonation in the theories of Hauptmann and Helmholtz in Harrison, *Harmonic Function in Chromatic Music,* 236–237.

35. *On the Sensations of Tone as a Physiological Basis for the Theory of Music,* trans. Alexander J. Ellis (London: Longmans, Green, 1875), 568.

Not only did Helmholtz advocate just intonation, he also assumed just intonation when he tried to account for conventions of tonal music, basing his explanations of consonance and dissonance as well as the prohibition against successive perfect fifths on that assumption. He wrote that if, say, two voices proceed from the fifth between C and G to that between D and A, the (untempered) A will not belong to the same scale as the other pitches. Remarkably, he was not thinking within the framework of tempered pitches that is taken for granted in the tonal system that he was attempting to elucidate.[36] In another of the contradictions natural theories of music appear to be prone to, the overtone series was used to explain both the folk practice of singing in parallel perfect fifths and the injunction against the same consecutive intervals in cultivated practice. According to Chrysander, the overtone series was responsible for the supposedly natural tendency to sing in fifths, while according to Helmholtz, the same natural phenomenon caused cultivated musicians to ban parallel fifths.

Although Helmholtz's limited understanding of music led some of the most celebrated musicians of his own time to reject much of his work, musicologists were more receptive to his ideas, undoubtedly because they were trying to establish their field's scientific credentials. Articles and reviews in the *Vierteljahrsschrift* repeatedly demonstrate the marked resurgence of interest in just intonation at the time. Because of the topic's prominence, Brahms's friend Heinrich von Herzogenberg felt moved to contribute a short article on it for the final volume in 1894 (see table 4.1). Voicing a position similar to that of Adorno and many other twentieth-century musicians, Herzogenberg asserted: "only the pure major triad that underlies every harmonic system is a product of nature; further development into the conception of key, into a whole system, is the work of humans" (134). He finished by saying that he thought "the fine hearing of a well-educated musician [was] capable of more *inner connection with nature* than all theoretical doctrines" (emphasis added) (145). His conclusion came down on the side of musical talent and training rather than scientific reasoning and speculation. Like Helmholtz, Herzogenberg understood that music had more to do with culture than with nature, but in contrast to Helmholtz, he correctly observed the central place of temperament within that musical culture.

Brahms and other of his colleagues took a less evenhanded position on Helmholtz's work than Herzogenberg did. Kalbeck noted that the composer had an even greater loathing for scientific treatments of his art than for aesthetics: Brahms could not learn anything useful for his own work from either of them. According to his biographer, Brahms went so far as to call Helmholtz a "dreadful dilettante in musical matters."[37] In his personal copy of Dommer's *Lexicon,* the composer again showed his dislike of Helmholtz's musical theories by marking off a discussion critical of him and underlining a key phrase. Dommer praised Helmholtz for the contribution his work made to the understanding of timbre but added: "*no musician will agree* with his theory of the formation of consonant and dissonant intervals, har-

---

36. *On the Sensations of Tone,* 558.

37. *Brahms,* 1:279. See also the letter from Brahms of 13 July 1890 in Geiringer, "Brahms in Briefwechsel mit Mandyczewski," 343.

mony, etc.,"[38] a theory that he based, like his work on timbre, on interpreting the overtone series, a matter of first nature. The overemphasis on this kind of theory largely accounts for Brahms's ambivalence toward the *Vierteljahrsschrift*.

Writing to the composer during the summer of 1890, Mandyczewski described an encounter with Shohé Tanaka, author of an article in the *Vierteljahrsschrift* that discusses just intonation and related matters (see table 4.1). Tanaka owned one of the new, specially designed harmoniums that Helmholtz advocated, which allowed for distinctions between F-sharp and G-flat, G-sharp and A-flat, and the like. (The pianist and composer Hans von Bülow had already written a sarcastic article about Tanaka and the "purity" possible on his harmonium with the dateline of Christmas 1889.)[39] Mandyczewski, who played on the instrument for a quarter of an hour, relayed his reactions to Brahms:

> Pieces that don't modulate much can be rendered with acoustic purity. But that is all. The old feud between acousticians and musicians breaks out again over this instrument. Tanaka's G-sharp is acoustically pure, therefore lower than A-flat. For musicians, it is the other way around. Temperament is an unconditional necessity for musicians. Moreover, if a choir performed for me a chorale in the manner of Tanaka's harmonium, it would sing acoustically purely, to be sure, but musically incorrectly.[40]

(Temperament allows the enharmonic equivalence of G-sharp and A-flat within the tonal system. But the logic of that system includes the normative progression of G-sharp to A and A-flat to G and thus often motivates, say, string players to alter the tempered pitches, raising G-sharp and lowering A-flat.)

After acknowledging that instrumental music owed its "tremendous upswing" to temperament, Tanaka had concluded his 1890 article with a utopian statement about the future of just intonation. Regarding temperament, he noted: "one should not, however, forget that this system, if also convenient, corresponds to the laws of nature only in an imperfect manner and that a closer approximation to the latter in the course of humanity's progressive evolution is not ruled out" (90). Some twentieth-century composers would eventually work with the first nature of untempered intervals. But this possibility was, of course, anathema to Brahms, who found renewal within the second nature of temperament and tonality and of contrapuntal traditions, transmitted through repertory that he admired.

MUSICOLOGY AS INSPIRATION:
THE LATER PHASE OF WORK

When Heuberger visited Brahms in Ischl during the summer of 1892, the composer was more sanguine about musical training and the future of his art than he would be four years later. Indeed, he "beamed with joy" as he showed Heuberger

---

38. Entry for "Klang," 477.

39. *Hans von Bülow: Briefe und Schriften*, ed. Marie von Bülow, 2nd ed. (Leipzig: Breitkopf und Härtel, 1911), 9:252–254. See also Martin Vogel, *Die Lehre von den Tonbeziehungen* (Bonn: Verlag für Musikwissenschaft, 1975), 318. Vogel does not detect the sarcasm.

40. Letter to Brahms of 11 July 1890 in Geiringer, "Brahms in Briefwechsel mit Mandyczewski," 343.

the collected edition of Bizet's works he had recently received and extolled the French system of musical education, which at that point continued to foster technical finesse: "Yes, the French really still have schooling! In many places, it is true, Bizet attempts to abandon or extend the rule but always as someone who knows what is correct."[41] What Brahms means by schooling is surely not just teaching by the book but rather the transmission of a refined way of hearing and therefore composing music. At the same time, he is almost certainly referring to a specific "rule," the principles of voice-leading he was investigating in his manuscript. Bizet knew how "to abandon or extend the rule" in ways Brahms found praiseworthy, even beautiful, because he worked within a continuous, living tradition.

In part to make up for what he saw as deficiencies in his own musical education, Brahms, so to speak, became a musicologist. As Hancock demonstrates, his ongoing study of early music had a lifelong influence on his choral writing. His study of octaves and fifths, weighted heavily toward vocal polyphony, likewise had a traceable impact on his creative work, including his instrumental music. Felix Salzer and Carl Schachter observe parallel fifths that come about through embellishing notes in one of the Organ Preludes, which appeared posthumously as Op. 122. In Brahms's last published work for piano solo, the E-flat Rhapsody (Op. 119, No. 4), Laudon finds thick chords in contrary motion resembling those in the frequently cited excerpt from Beethoven's "Waldstein" Sonata.[42] But in his manuscript, Brahms showed little interest in voice-leading problems posed by chordal piano writing, preferring instead to focus on linear textures.

The literature on the manuscript has overlooked another, earlier Brahms piece connected to his contrapuntal studies. Writing to Brahms in 1878, the conductor Otto Dessoff pointed out a passage in his song *Todessehnen* (Op. 86, No. 6) "not because I disapprove, but rather only because I know your aversion toward fifths."[43] In response Brahms noted a similar succession of intervals in the next measure: "Of two sets of fifths in *Todessehnen* you cite only one. Ought you not to permit the first—as I have both?" (See ex. 4.10a and b.) Each time, the second fifth (between the voice and the piano left hand) is created by an accented passing note in the vocal part: in context, that note is harmonically superfluous, the fifth itself, a dissonance. As he wrote, "the fourth before the third [i.e., A before G-sharp in an E four-two chord in m. 26, G-sharp before F-sharp in a D four-two chord in m. 27] does not count and does not create bad parallel fifths."[44]

In his letter to Dessoff, Brahms also entered a related passage from a Mozart string quartet. (See ex. 4.10c and d; in this instance, the fifths are between the second violin and cello, the accented passing note in the cello and on the downbeat.) Although Brahms did not find the excerpt remarkable enough to include in his collection, Mozart had again composed both correct and beautiful fifths, more striking than the fifths in his own *Todessehnen*. That Dessoff could have considered the paral-

---

41. *Erinnerungen an Brahms,* 54.

42. *Counterpoint in Composition: The Study of Voice Leading* (New York: McGraw-Hill, 1969), 222; and Laudon, "The Debate about Consecutive Fifths," 60.

43. Letter of 7 July 1878, in *Brahms Briefwechsel,* 16:195.

44. Undated letter, in *Brahms Briefwechsel,* 16:199–201.

EXAMPLE 4.10a.   Brahms, mm. 26–27 from *Todessehnen,* from letter to Dessoff

EXAMPLE 4.10b.   Brahms, mm. 26–37 from score of *Todessehnen* (Op. 86, No. 6)

lels in Brahms's song potentially problematic suggests the decline in Austro-German music pedagogy. Many musicians had long recognized that such fifths were unobjectionable, but transmission of the rule's fine points had become spottier in the nineteenth century, hence Brahms's early decision to explore the questions himself.

The final phase of work on his manuscript must have begun after he received the Bizet edition in 1892 and before he wrote the 1894 letter to Mandyczewski that mentions Chrysander's article. He entered first one and then another excerpt from *Carmen.*[45] And annotations in the manuscript and patterns in the examples reveal the influence of the 1893 *Vierteljahrsschrift.* The extant copies in Brahms's library show he had read not only the article on Zacconi's treatise in the third issue but also an article from the first issue. While Brahms did not cut all the pages in the first issue, he did so for this article, in which Schwartz discusses the influence of Italian madrigalists on Hans Leo Haßler (see table 4.1). Most of Schwartz's Italian examples

45. These examples appear on manuscript pages 6 and 9.

EXAMPLE 4.10c.   Mozart, mm. 155–56 from K. 458 / IV, from letter to Dessoff

EXAMPLE 4.10d.   Mozart, mm. 155–56 from score of K. 458 / IV

come from madrigals by Marenzio, whose music he praises in the highest terms; others come from Andrea Gabrieli (14–15). Part of the discussion focuses on their approach to voice-leading, in particular their treatment of parallel or potentially parallel octaves and fifths.

Schwartz offers one example in which Marenzio follows the "requirements of strict counterpoint" (14), inserting a sixth created through a suspension between two perfect fifths (ex. 4.11a). Concerning other passages by both Marenzio and Gabrieli, he writes: "Such parallels are found even where the voices do not progress stepwise." In his examples (here ex. 4.11b and c), octaves or thirds break up parallel fifths, with skips to the fifths in one or both of the voices. (Ambros, it will be recalled, did not consider any of these strategies effective for masking the sound of parallel fifths.) Schwartz later observes: "With regard to parallel fifths and octaves the Italian rules hold for Haßler" (50) and gives several short examples (ex. 4.11d). In a footnote (15), he also quotes a short passage from a villanella (by Orazio Vecchi) and refers the reader to an article he wrote for the 1886 *Vierteljahrsschrift*. (See table 4.1; Schwartz briefly discusses the villanella in that earlier essay, citing the pas-

EXAMPLE 4.11a.   Excerpt from a madrigal
by Marenzio (*VfMw* 9 [1893]: 14)

EXAMPLE 4.11b.   Madrigal excerpts by Marenzio
and Gabrieli (*VfMw* 9 [1893]: 14)

EXAMPLE 4.11c.   Madrigal excerpts by Marenzio and Gabrieli
(*VfMw* 9 [1893]: 15)

EXAMPLE 4.11d.   Excerpts from Haßler (*VfMw* 9
[1893]: 50)

EXAMPLE 4.12a.   Haßler, *Lustgarten,* No. 36, mm. 10–13
(Brahms, MS p. 6; Mast, ex. 72)

sein Si - cher - heit   im fin - stern Wald ge - fun - den

sages by Nola [462] that Chrysander would later borrow, and alter, for his own
article.)

These elements from Schwartz's 1893 article—Marenzio, Haßler, the villanella,
and, indirectly, Gabrieli—show up in the second half of Brahms's manuscript. To
begin with, Brahms must have sought out passages in Haßler's *Lustgarten* in which
the voice-leading corresponds to Schwartz's examples. Although Brahms had long
known Haßler's music, in the manuscript he used only the four examples he entered on page 6 following the first excerpt from Bizet's *Carmen* (see table 4.4). And
he chose passages by Haßler that alternate fifths and octaves or perfect and imperfect consonances along the lines of Schwartz's examples. (See ex. 4.12a and b for
two of Brahms's Haßler selections.) While much in the *Vierteljahrsschrift,* as Spitta
expressed it, might hold "only limited interest for a practical artist," other articles
obviously did have something to offer Brahms.

From the 1890 *Vierteljahrsschrift* (see table 4.1), Brahms copied a villanella-like
piece by Jacobus Regnart from 1584, on the same sheet of paper on which he
copied the first of the four Haßler pieces; Schwartz had in fact cited this piece in
his 1893 article (32).[46] He then extracted passages from these two part-songs and
three others by Haßler and entered them on page 6 in his manuscript, making a
crossreference between the latter and a piece on page 5 by Giovanni Gabrieli, Andrea's uncle, which breaks up parallel perfect intervals in a similar manner. The articles in the 1893 *Vierteljahrsschrift* must have also given Brahms the idea of studying
villanelle by Marenzio, whose music he had encountered decades before in Carl von
Winterfeld's *Johannes Gabrieli und sein Zeitalter.*[47] In his manuscript, Brahms indicated
the source of the two Regnart excerpts, the 1890 *Vierteljahrsschrift,* and drew a large
brace that connected the Regnart and Marenzio examples on that page, noting
Chrysander's article in the 1893 *Vierteljahrsschrift* and observing: "folksong imitated."

46. See the description of Brahms's *Abschrift* in Hancock, *Brahms's Choral Compositions,* 23–24.
47. Carl Winterfeld, *Johannes Gabrieli und sein Zeitalter,* 3 vols. (Berlin: Schlesinger, 1834). According to Hancock, Brahms made a crossreference from a discussion of Marenzio in vol. 2 to a madrigal by
him that appears in score in vol. 3. *Brahms's Choral Compositions,* 97. Laudon errs when he cites Ambros's
Geschichte der Musik as a possible inspiration for Brahms's interest in Marenzio. "The Debate about Consecutive Fifths," 59.

TABLE 4.4. Aspects of Organization in the Second Half of Brahms's Manuscript

Page 6

Vogler, Catechismus (1625), "Jesus der ging den Berg hinein"	Bizet, *Carmen*, Act I, Nr. 8
Haßler, *Lustgarten Neuer Teutscher Gesang* (1601), Nr. 32	Haßler, *Lustgarten Neuer Teutscher Gesang* (1601), Nr. 35
Haßler, *Lustgarten Neuer Teutscher Gesang* (1601), Nr. 36	Haßler, *Lustgarten Neuer Teutscher Gesang* (1601), Nr. 5
Regnart, Tricinium, "Wer wirdet tröstet mich" [two excerpts]	
Marenzio, Villanelle a tre voci, Book I, No. 1	Marenzio, Villanelle a tre voci, Book I, No. 6
Marenzio, Villanelle a tre voci, Book I, No. 7	Marenzio, Villanelle a tre voci, Book I, No. 23
Marenzio, Villanelle a tre voci, Book I, No. 5	
Marenzio, Villanelle a tre voci, Book I, No. 13	

Page 7

Marenzio, *Villanelle a tre voci*, Book II, No. 5	Marenzio, *Villanelle a tre voci*, Book II, No. 11
Marenzio, *Villanelle a tre voci*, Book II, No. 14	Marenzio, *Villanelle a tre voci*, Book II, No. 18
Marenzio, *Villanelle a tre voci*, Book III, No. 1	Marenzio, *Villanelle a tre voci*, Book III, No. 9
	Bach, Cantata No. 91, *Gelobet seist du, Jesu Christ*, No. 4, Recitative

From page 8

Don Giovanni, No. 19, m. 61	Mendelssohn, *Variations sérieuses*, Var. 13
Don Giovanni, No. 19, m. 80	Mozart, A Minor Piano Sonata / II
	Beethoven, E Major Piano Sonata / I
	Chopin, Mazurka, Op. 30, No. 4

From page 9

Bach, G Major Organ Toccata	Mendelssohn, *Midsummer Night's Dream*
Bizet, *Carmen*, Act II, No. 12	Vivaldi-Bach, A Minor Organ Concerto / III

See Mast, "Brahms's *Octaven u. Quinten*," 72–103 and the facsimile of the manuscript. I have tried to approximate the placement of the excerpts on each page, but I have included neither Brahms's lists of additional passages nor his comments.

134

EXAMPLE 4.12b. Haßler, *Lustgarten,* No. 5,
mm. 13–15 (Brahms, MS p. 6; Mast, ex. 73)

Reading the 1893 *Vierteljahrsschrift* had thus reminded Brahms of another source for studying voice-leading as second nature, the music of Haßler.[48] But articles in both the 1890 and 1893 volumes also exposed him to different imitations, in villanelle and similar genres, of musical practices with an apparent basis in first nature. In his copy of Dommer's *Lexicon,* Brahms at some point marked off a related discussion in "Progression of Intervals." Dommer had written: "even today one can hear older and younger men or women and young girls who know nothing of the rules of harmony instinctively sing folk melodies in fifths because of the comfortable, natural voice range" (316). Later in the same entry, Brahms underlined a reference to "natural series of fifths in folk singing" (319).

In introducing the final category in his monograph, characteristic fifths, Tappert had observed that the use of such parallels "for purposes of expression is almost as old as the strict prohibition itself" and briefly discussed the villanella (95), the expressive purpose of which was clearly to evoke untutored—"natural"—singing. Perhaps the inadvertent singing in fifths that Zacconi and others likewise connected to the villanella intrigued Brahms because of his strong interest in folksong, especially relevant in the later phase of work, when he was also completing his *49 Deutsche Volkslieder* (WoO 33), settings that he published in 1894.[49] The practice possibly also interested him because of its very difference from his own practices: in this instance, unlike most of the rest of his manuscript, he was attempting to learn from music of a "foreign world."

Indeed, as the large number of excerpts from villanelle and related genres in Brahms's manuscript attest, the flagrant, characteristic breaking of the contrapuntal rule that marks these genres—which, unlike organum, postdate the rule—must have fascinated him. This aspect of his manuscript and in particular the twelve passages from Marenzio's villanelle on pages 6 and 7 has provoked little commentary, probably because, as the composer himself undoubtedly concluded, most of them

---

48. Mast writes that the Haßler examples "are in the light style of the villanella, but blatant parallels are not employed in them," "Brahms's *Octaven u. Quinten,*" 191.

49. On the context for his completing these settings, see Imogen Fellinger, "Brahms' beabsichtigte Streitschrift gegen Erk-Böhmes 'Deutscher Liederhort,'" in *Brahms-Kongress Wien 1983: Kongressbericht,* ed. Susanne Antonicek and Otto Biba (Tutzing: Schneider, 1988), 139–153.

cannot be explained by any extension of usual voice-leading rules. Schenker glibly and inaccurately connected the Marenzio excerpts "to an earlier, more elementary, kind of counterpoint, which still lacked the means to neutralize consecutive fifths."[50] Brahms's better knowledge of Marenzio's music and reputation must have led him to collect so many passages in the hope of understanding an underlying logic in the fifth progressions, possibly even in the hope of finding a use for them in his own music.[51]

We cannot know exactly when he annotated Dommer's *Lexicon,* but we can assume with reasonable security that he added the first passage from *Carmen* to his manuscript after 1892, probably in 1893 or 1894 when he entered the Haßler, Regnart, and Marenzio passages that follow. The latter excerpts look as if they were written at the same time; furthermore, the comments in his letter to Mandyczewski imply that Brahms had copied Marenzio's villanelle not long before he left Vienna for Ischl.[52]

Entering the examples on pages 6 and 7 initiated a sustained phase of work on the manuscript. On page 8, Brahms entered "classic" examples of parallel fifths from Beethoven's early E Major Piano Sonata and a famous mazurka by Chopin, and he recopied some he had cited earlier in the manuscript, from Gluck's *Armide* and Mozart's *Don Giovanni.*[53] In addition, he made a number of notes, evaluative markings, and crossreferences, and he began to enter his chosen passages, including those he recopied, in a more organized fashion. Table 4.4 shows that he aligned examples of "correct and beautiful" fifths from *Don Giovanni,* Mendelssohn's *Variations sérieuses,* and Mozart's A Minor Piano Sonata.[54] It also shows that he then entered other types of keyboard fifths below the excerpt from Mozart's sonata: characteristic fifths of one kind from Beethoven's sonata and of another kind from Chopin's pseudo-folk-style mazurka. Page 9 he devoted largely to characteristic fifths in the twofold sense in which he understood the concept, including examples from two Bach keyboard pieces and the famous excerpt from Mendelssohn's *Midsummer Night's Dream.* Indeed, the Bizet example on that page, unlike the first excerpt from *Carmen* on page 6, features exotic fifths that are perhaps "merely" characteristic fifths.[55] Most of the examples on pages 10 and 11 include voice-crossings or rests introduced to break up potential parallels. Reengagement with various

---

50. Mast, "Brahms's *Octaven u. Quinten,*" 148.

51. For a recent appreciative treatment of Marenzio's villanelle, see Ruth I. DeFord, "Marenzio and the *villanella alla romana,*" *Early Music* 27 (1999): 535–552.

52. The library of the Gesellschaft der Musikfreunde includes a handwritten score of Marenzio's villanelle, completed by Mandyczewski himself. Perhaps Brahms forgot this when he wrote to the musicologist about copying passages from the villanelle.

53. The Beethoven passage appears in Ambros, p. 20; Weitzmann, ex. 5; and Tappert, p. 85; the Chopin mazurka excerpt appears in Ambros, p. 22.

54. Ambros cites the passage from Mozart's A Minor Piano Sonata on p. 17. When Brahms recopied the *Don Giovanni* excerpt he added a related measure from the opera, as indicated in table 4.4.

55. Schenker's voice-leading explanation of the fifths is not convincing. See Mast, "Brahms's *Octaven u. Quinten,*" 156–157. Below the examples I have shown in table 4.4, Brahms entered a number of short passages from Scarlatti sonatas.

EXAMPLE 4.13.   Brahms, E-flat Clarinet Sonata, Op. 120 No. 2 / I, mm. 79–86

voice-leading situations represented in his manuscript left its mark on the part-writing in the F Minor and E-flat Major Clarinet Sonatas from the same summer of 1894.

DETAIL AS RENEWAL: ASPECTS OF VOICE-LEADING IN THE CLARINET SONATAS

In chapter 3, I discussed the linear style that Brahms introduced into the first movement of the F Minor Clarinet Sonata. In the same spirit, he used stems to delineate the voice-leading in the second movement's piano part. The textures in both clarinet sonatas in fact differ markedly from those in his other duo sonatas; the part-writing is both more transparent and more daring than before. So far, no one appears to have written about a number of passages that relate to his study of parallel fifths, even though his letter to Mandyczewski that summer demonstrates his renewed interest in it. To be sure, Jack Adrian pointed out three consecutive fifths in the development section of the first movement of the E-flat Major Clarinet Sonata, which he explained as "interposed between two different structural levels" and therefore excusable (see ex. 4.13).[56] But Adrian did not connect the fifths to

56. "The Ternary-Sonata Form," *Journal of Music Theory* 34 (1990): 66 and 69. The fifths occur between the piano left-hand part and the last note of the clarinet figuration in mm. 81, 83, and 86. Many notes intervene between the fifths.

EXAMPLE 4.14a.   Brahms, F Minor Clarinet
Sonata, Op. 120 No. 1 / II, mm. 1–2

Brahms's collection, nor did he mention related passages in that movement and other movements from both sonatas. With their spare and notably linear textures, these sonatas invited exposed application of the voice-leading manipulations discussed in the literature and represented in his manuscript.

From the beginning of the F Minor Clarinet Sonata's second movement, an Andante un poco adagio, Brahms creates unusual spatial/textural effects through his part-writing and use of register. Not only does he visually separate the piano part's voices but also he introduces bass-line anticipations of notes that reappear as inner-voice chordal tones in the following measure. Thus the low B-flat in m. 1 anticipates the right hand's B-flat in m. 2 (see ex. 4.14a). After the first formal section (mm. 1–23), each time Brahms brings back the opening measures he develops the texture through changes in figuration or voicing or both. In mm. 41–42, for instance, the opening measures return in E major (and then in C major four measures later) before the definitive tonic return in m. 49. The voices are placed more closely together than before, and the clarinet now plays the bass-note anticipation F-sharp (m. 41),

EXAMPLE 4.14b.   Brahms, F Minor Clarinet
Sonata, Op. 120 No. 1 / II, mm. 41–42

EXAMPLE 4.14c.   Brahms, F Minor Clarinet
Sonata, Op. 120 No. 1 / II, mm. 17–18

which is then transferred up an octave to the piano left hand (ex. 4.14b). While the
stems in the piano left hand create the semblance of parallel fifths, to the ear, the
C-sharp in m. 41 unmistakably moves not to the F-sharp in m. 42—the note transferred from the clarinet part—but rather to the C-sharp an octave higher.

In several measures in the piano part, Brahms comes up with similar voice-leading
that might have been expected to sound as parallel fifths yet does not do so. Consider, for instance, the fifths given to the piano right hand in m. 17 (ex. 4.14c): the
fact that one line of the piano treble is doubling the clarinet part at the octave makes
it utterly clear that the two piano voices do not proceed in parallel fifths. Even
when the treble line in the piano part moves from E-flat to A-flat in mm. 23–24
over a bass motion of A-flat to D-flat, the passage does not sound as parallel fifths
(ex. 4.14d). Taking up the implicit challenge made by musicians, including Tappert
and Dommer, who noted the need for human voices or dissimilar timbres to keep
parts distinct in such writing, Brahms managed to do so here just on the piano. For
one thing, he introduces eighth-note rests in the left hand: according to Tappert
(12), one of the "bones of contention" among music theorists was whether short
rests solve the problem of parallels. And, as I noted, rests preoccupied Brahms in
the final two pages of his manuscript, as did voice-crossings. In any case, the "real"

EXAMPLE 4.14d.   Brahms, F Minor Clarinet
Sonata, Op. 120 No. 1 / II, mm. 23–24

EXAMPLE 4.15a.   Brahms, E-flat Clarinet Sonata, Op. 120 No. 2 / II, mm.
7–18

voice-leading in the piano treble here is from E-flat to F: the A-flat sounds as an inner voice temporarily displaced up an octave.

The E-flat Clarinet Sonata's middle movement, an Allegro appassionato, seems to include blatant parallel fifths between the two hands of the piano part, E-flat over A-flat at the end of m. 11 moving to D-flat over G-flat in m. 12. But C is heard as the bass note throughout m. 11. Elsewhere (e.g., in mm. 14–15) there appear to be parallel fifths produced by contrary motion in the outer voices—D-flat over G-flat to B-flat over E-flat—another contested voice-leading situation.[57] (See ex. 4.15a for both of these passages.) The audible motion in the piano right hand, however, is from one B-flat to another an octave up, the intervening D-flat merely being fleeting arpeggiation. Interestingly, the apparent parallels occur where there is a significant textural change: flowing eighth-note arpeggiation becomes quarter-note block chords moving in a faster harmonic rhythm. These changes produce the kind of imbalance that makes the opening a theme rather than a melody,[58] that requires elaboration and thus justifies the motives and textures from the destabilizing measures (mm. 7–8, 15–16) becoming the basis of a new section (mm. 17–34).

57. See, for example, the discussion in Dommer, *Musikalisches Lexicon,* 317–319.

58. Schoenberg, *Fundamentals of Composition,* 102.

EXAMPLE 4.15b. Brahms, E-flat Clarinet Sonata, Op. 120 No. 2 / II, mm. 49–55

When the opening returns in m. 35, it is recomposed so as not to include the disruptive measures: it must close this time. The new version includes undeniable parallel fifths between the clarinet and piano left hand: F over B-flat to B-flat over E-flat (see ex. 4.15b). In this instance, the imitation of the clarinet part (from mm. 49–52) that begins on the upbeat to m. 53 in the piano right hand takes attention away from the parallel intervals, as does the fact that the left hand immediately subsumes the clarinet's B-flat into its figuration. Brahms entered an unlikely related example from a Victoria motet into the last page of his manuscript. In the Victoria passage (see ex. 4.15c), voice-crossings avert the problem of parallel fifths and oc-

EXAMPLE 4.15c. Victoria, *Ave Maria,* mm. 12–15 (Brahms, MS p. 11; Mast, ex. 120)

EXAMPLE 4.16a.   Brahms, E-flat Clarinet
Sonata, Op. 120 No. 2 / I, mm. 5–6

taves, and imitation in any case draws the ear to another line. An "a" next to the
example shows Brahms's enthusiastic approval of Victoria's voice-leading.

Although Brahms does not create oppositions as he did with the two harmonic
styles in the Clarinet Trio and the two textures in the F Minor Clarinet Sonata, in
these movements he has mixed idiomatic instrumental figuration with techniques
more closely associated with vocal writing: voice-crossings and, perhaps, imitation.
In the opening Allegro amabile from the E-flat Clarinet Sonata, he applies other
devices that are more linked to vocal than to instrumental writing: breaking up

EXAMPLE 4.16b.   Brahms, E-flat Clarinet Sonata, Op. 120 No. 2 / I, mm.
22–28

consecutive octaves with fifths or the reverse, interpolating sixths between two perfect fifths, and allowing a diminished fifth to move to a perfect fifth.

For example, at the beginning of the second phrase (mm. 5–6), the intervals between the piano treble and the clarinet line can be reduced to parallel fifths (see ex.
4.16a). But a number of features, beyond the fact that the piano treble constitutes a
middle voice, all mentioned in the traditional literature, make the voice-leading in
no respect problematic—at least for most nineteenth-century writers who considered the problem. For the first fifth in m. 5 is diminished, and the second fifth in
both mm. 5 and 6 has no harmonic significance and is, in any case, obscured by the
suspension, while the third fifth is likewise embellished by a lower neighbor note.

In the Allegro amabile's second thematic group, Brahms introduces parallel fifths
that are not as easily explained as either following or merely stretching traditional
voice-leading norms. Here the part-writing recalls what he had seen in Schwartz's
1893 article. This thematic group begins with a canon at the lower twelfth between
the clarinet and the piano bass line (mm. 22–27). Like any number of composers
before him, Brahms breaks up fifths—in this passage between the voices in canon—
with other intervals (see ex. 4.16b). He does so in some places (e.g., m. 23) by leap-
ing from a fifth to an octave, or vice versa, as Marenzio and Gabrieli had done in
the secular songs Schwartz cited. More strikingly, Brahms creates parallel fifths
through contrary motion between the piano treble and bass (mm. 23–24), a brief
instance of "characteristic" piano writing. In this case, the canon holds the listener's
attention and therefore mitigates any ill effects of parallel fifths that are not between
the voices in canon.

In the canon, Brahms made eclectic use of techniques that had appeared in
sixteenth- and seventeenth-century vocal music excerpted in the *Vierteljahrsschrift*.
But he found no application for Marenzio's villanelle. Judging from his comment
about "foreign worlds," Brahms could not fathom the apparent first nature paro-
died in the genre, which he came to know or to know better through reading the
journal. Nor did he accept the attempts at explaining voice-leading, either in the
villanella or in less peripheral repertory, through the appeals to nature that abounded
in the *Vierteljahrsschrift*. Still, his exposure to the journal clearly did stimulate his
creativity. The second thematic group of the E-flat Clarinet Sonata's Allegro amabile and the return of the opening in the same sonata's second movement, in particular, stand out for the ingenuity evident in the voice-leading.

The transparency of the part-writing visually exposes all of these real or averted
parallel fifths. But the sound is less bold than in many of the passages Brahms collected. All of the instances in his music I have cited are timid in comparison with
the passages from music by Mozart and Bizet and, especially, the cantata recitative
by Bach that Brahms admired. If Brahms did not become as daring as these composers, reading the articles by Schwartz and others and reconsidering the questions
that appear in the literature on parallel fifths nonetheless inspired him to experiment further with the limits of what he could accept as second nature. He had
effected his own, specifically nineteenth-century renewal of contrapuntal traditions.

CHAPTER 5

VOLKSCONCERTE AND CONCEPTS OF
GENRE IN BRAHMS'S VIENNA

During the winter of 1891, plans were underway in Vienna to present a series of modestly priced symphonic concerts during the following summer as part of a musical and theatrical exposition. For several years, journalists in the city had been calling for such *Volksconcerte*. One of them, Hofrat Johann von Wörz, had described Vienna as "musically starved," despite the city's many musical attractions, because the vast majority of the people had no opportunity to experience "the noblest products of pure music": that is to say, symphonies.[1] Contemporary critics often assumed that the symphony had peaked with the Viennese Classical composers and then gone into a discouraging decline. But they expressed considerable excitement about bringing the repertory of symphonic masterworks to a new audience.

In his diary, Heuberger noted Brahms's reaction to the concerts being planned for the summer exposition: "He laughed at the idea of organizing popular concerts [in Vienna]: [in Brahms's own words,] 'There is no audience for them here!' "[2] Heuberger, a composer and conductor, was also, like Wörz, a critic for a Liberal newspaper and an activist in the efforts to expand the audience for art music. Brahms, however—in this anecdote and elsewhere—showed that he was no meliorist in his later years. He appears not to have labored under any illusion that people were improving the world, or the occasional corollary that music might play a role in bettering it, or even that an unreached audience for the symphonic repertory existed in Vienna. While his skepticism may well resonate with attitudes some 115 years later, it set him apart from many musicians in his own time. For them, bringing concert music to the masses was as crucial as extending the vote to everyone—something that, of course, was also happening in incremental steps in Vienna around the turn of the century—and they viewed the symphonic repertory as central to their efforts.

Has any other musical genre ever been made to bear as much ideological freight as the symphony? One might well ask this question after reading about the various attempts to institute symphonic *Volksconcerte* and after extended immersion in com-

---

1. "*Volksconcerte* in Wien," *Wiener Sonn-und Montags Zeitung,* 2 June 1890. For Wörz, see Sandra McColl, *Music Criticism in Vienna, 1896–1897: Critically Moving Forms* (Oxford: Clarendon Press, 1996).

2. *Erinnerungen an Brahms,* 50, entry for 16 December 1891.

mentaries on the symphony from the late nineteenth and early twentieth centuries that invest the genre with a bewildering significance. Bekker summarized this critical tradition when he wrote in 1918: "according to the fundamental conditions of its essence the symphony is a matter of far-reaching general interest, the performance of a symphony tantamount to a musical assembly of the people [*Volksversammlung*]."[3] Bekker's conception of both the genre's content and its ideal audience had many precedents. Considerable evidence suggests that a number of observers in late nineteenth-century Vienna, in particular, shared inchoate versions of his views, despite a concert life utterly at odds with symphonic performance as *Volksversammlung*.

The widespread perception of deficiencies in Brahms's symphonies warrants examination in light of these ideas about the genre, couched in language that denied the realities of both politics and musical life in nineteenth-century Vienna. Critics often accused Brahms of composing chamber music for orchestra. Louis characterized his symphonies as having

> in content and its expression, a tender inwardness that brings the symphony closer to chamber music. Abandonment of that—in the highest sense of the word—popular, indeed democratic trait that distinguishes the Beethoven symphony in such an unparalleled way, and in its place, cultivation of an elegant aristocracy of taste that flatters the connoisseur.[4]

Even Kalbeck made much the same criticism of Brahms's symphonies in a conversation with Heuberger after a Viennese performance of the Fourth Symphony in January 1887:

> I had a strange conversation with Max Kalbeck about Brahms. K. said finally that B., despite his significance, is no master of the foremost rank, since execution prevails over power of invention. There is a lack of the great, noble popularity, the appealing to the common people [*Volk*], which, for example, distinguished Beethoven. "Symphonies must really be understandable to the *Volk*. Brahms's symphonies will never become that."[5]

Like Louis, Kalbeck invoked the image of "Beethoven the democrat." And he stressed the primacy of melodic invention and the common touch, both decisive factors in the meaning of the genre at the time, despite the fact that the *Volk* had virtually no access to symphonies in Vienna.

Bekker remarked on not only the imagined audience for the genre but also its content: "a matter of far-reaching general interest." The orchestral medium, the source of ideas about symphonic content, was as imbued with ideological import as the audience. Koch's well-known description in the late eighteenth century interpreted the orchestra iconically and in opposition to music with one performer on a part: "like the chorus in vocal music," the symphony expresses "the feelings of a whole multitude of people."[6] A similar view of the genre emerges in commentaries from

3. *Die Sinfonie*, 15.

4. *Die deutsche Musik der Gegenwart*, 153.

5. *Erinnerungen an Brahms*, 156, entry for 3 January 1887.

6. *Musikalisches Lexikon welches die theoretische und praktische Tonkunst, encyclopädisch bearbeitet, alle alten und neuen Kunstwörter erklärt, und die alten und neuen Instrumente beschrieben, enthält*, 2 vols. in 1 (1802; reprint, Hildesheim: Olms, 1964), col. 1386.

the late nineteenth century and beyond, but it has become even loftier. Bekker declared that in its "power to mold a community," the symphony was "in accord with the goals of religion" and suggested that the genre had assumed the role earlier assigned to masses, Passions, and oratorios.[7] Well into the twentieth century, the concept of the "monumental symphony" captured this attitude, often with special emphasis on the slow movement.

As recently as 1950, Bernhard Paumgartner wrote of the symphony's continuing significance, in the "post-war cultural confusion" of his own time, as "a monumental art performed by a multitude of players before a still greater multitude of listeners." Monumentality—sometimes interpreted as having to do with the sheer magnitude of a work but manifestly more complex than that—has clearer relevance to Bruckner's symphonies than to those of Brahms, as do other ideas that underlie Paumgartner's remarks. After separating genres into the communal and the purely private (the latter exemplified by the lullaby), he divided communal music into three basic categories, asserting that the various movements within the symphony show the imprint of all three. That is to say, he discerned traces of primordial social functions in each type of movement: of martial or ceremonial state music in the first, of dance music in the minuet or scherzo and also in the finale. And in the "emotional significance" of the slow movement he heard a residue of the sounds and spirit of music used in religious rites.[8] In Brahms's time, the aura that had developed around slow movements and the anticipated universality of symphonic content supported an expectation that the symphony could evoke a collective quasi-religious experience. This conception of the genre helps account for characteristics of Bruckner's symphonies such as the beginnings *ex nihilo,* adapted from Beethoven's Ninth, and the use of chorale textures and other topoi with sacred connotations,[9] topoi that appear much less frequently in Brahms.

The critical tradition that Bekker and Paumgartner summed up had evolved more or less simultaneously with the development of Liberal worldviews in the late eighteenth and nineteenth centuries. But Liberalism came increasingly under fire in the final decades of the nineteenth century with the advent of parties representing the interests of the newly and soon to be enfranchised. Despite the attendant efforts to restructure music life in Vienna and elsewhere, Adorno would later declare that Bekker's conception of the genre "always contained something ideological, since the humanity that formed facing a symphony . . . remained aesthetic and never extended into real social life."[10] The symphony's imagined connection to the common people became even more problematic toward the end of the century with the occasional attempts to realize the genre's utopian function. In their efforts to change the city's music life, activists encountered not only institutionalized elitism but also the frequent indifference of the *Volk* to symphonic concerts.

7. *Die Sinfonie,* 17–18.

8. "Das instrumentale Ensemble," in *Musica aeterna: Eine Darstellung des Musikschaffen aller Zeiten und Völker, unter besonderer Berücksichtigung des Musiklebens der Schweiz und desjenigen unserer Tage,* ed. Gottfried Schmid, 2 vols. (Zurich: Max S. Metz, 1950), 2:13–14.

9. On the latter, see Walter Wiora, "Über den religiösen Gehalt in Bruckners Symphonien," in *Religiöse Musik in nicht-liturgischen Werken von Beethoven bis Reger,* ed. Günther Massenkeil, Klaus Wolfgang Niemöller, and Walter Wiora (Regensburg: Gustav Bosse, 1978), 157–184.

10. *Einleitung in die Musiksoziologie,* 116.

Whether understood in the context of traditional Liberalism or of the revisionist political and social views of younger Liberals, Brahms's attitudes toward *Volksconcerte* and the symphony itself seem anomalous. In contrast to Bruckner, much of the time he did not strive for Beethovenian monumentality. Like his comment to Heuberger, Brahms's treatment of the genre "against the grain" suggests that he, for one, did not accept ideology of the symphony.[11] Was he a rare clear-headed realist? Did he perhaps recognize that the audience for his symphonies was in fact not the *Volk* but rather the small group of experts associated with chamber music and attuned to the refined logic of his musical arguments?

Because of the compositional choices by Brahms and other symphonists after Beethoven, critics considered the genre to have gone into a decline: the symphony and the slow movement—symphonic or not—had entered their late periods. Revitalizing both in new compositions that measured up to those of the past presented even greater problems than expanding the audience for the symphony, but the same essentialist ideas about genre informed perceptions of the challenges that composers faced.

CHAMBER MUSIC VERSUS SYMPHONY AND THE *ECHT SYMPHONISCH*

Until recently, most musicologists discounted the applicability of concepts of genre to the concert music that became the norm in the nineteenth century. Whereas in the past musical genres were defined by social functions and performance spaces, along with technical features related to those fundamental limiting factors, most "nontrivial" compositions from the nineteenth and twentieth centuries served one function, *Bildung,* and were conceived for one kind of space, the concert hall. Much of the criticism of Brahms's symphonies nonetheless followed from a framework of genre aesthetics based on a binary opposition between chamber music and symphonies. Ideas about the two genres inherited from the previous century took on heightened importance, even as the connections between those ideas and contemporary performance and compositional practices became increasingly tenuous.

Symphonic ideology did have a foundation in the material conditions mentioned by Paumgartner. Because a large group of players performs before an even larger group of listeners, a symphonic performance requires a sizable room. Beginning in the eighteenth century, writers concerned with questions of music aesthetics contrasted the traditional venues for symphony and chamber music: auditorium and chamber, respectively.[12] Drawing consequences from the basic difference between the performance spaces, critics opposed the audiences they associated with each, as

11. "Theses on the Philosophy of History," in *Illuminations: Walter Benjamin, Essays and Reflections,* ed. Hannah Arendt and trans. Harry Zohn (New York: Schocken Books, 1968), 257. "Composing against the grain" of a genre comes from Laurence Dreyfus, *Bach and the Patterns of Invention* (Cambridge, Mass.: Harvard University Press, 1996), 37.

12. Some writers continued to follow the old-fashioned tradition of opposing "chamber" to liturgical and theatrical styles, in which case they might be referring not to chamber style in the modern sense, but rather to symphonic style. See the entry by A. Tottmann for "Kammermusik," in *Allgemeine Encyclopädie der Wissenschaften und Künste,* vol. 32, ed. J. S. Ersch and J. G. Gruber (Leipzig: F. A. Brock-

well as the stylistic features the spaces and audiences entailed. An auditorium suggested a crowd (eventually, *the* crowd) and an acoustically determined need to compose in a plain and at the same time bold style. Performance in a chamber, on the other hand, implied a circumscribed audience and acoustics that permitted close attention to fine points, especially in the development of themes and motives.

By the late nineteenth century, both chamber music and symphonies received public performances in auditoriums, although usually small and large, respectively. Composers, moreover, had long since blurred the stylistic differences between the two genres. But the traditional distinctions of style continued to play a role in musical politics in the 1880s and beyond. In a standard encyclopedia published in 1885, the entry for "Kammermusik" summarized the assumed reciprocal effects of style, space, and audience. According to the anonymous author, chamber style, "conditioned by the allocation of chamber music for a narrow, consistently well-educated circle of listeners in a smaller room, is characterized by a more elaborate transformation and development of musical ideas, going into more detail."[13] In a similarly circular fashion, writers viewed the symphony as a more egalitarian genre by its nature, for the necessarily simpler but more colorful features of *echt symphonisch*—"truly symphonic"—style made the genre more accessible to the wider circles the performing venue already supposedly accommodated. These distinctions meant that musicians often placed the symphony on a higher level than chamber genres in the late nineteenth century, when breadth of appeal tended to triumph over esoteric refinements.

The response of one critic, Helm, to the premieres of Brahms's Clarinet Quintet and Bruckner's Eighth Symphony illustrates this valorization of the symphony. Both pieces received first performances in 1892, the former in January and the latter in December. While Helm welcomed the new addition to the repertory of chamber music, he took exception to another critic's assertion that the premiere had been "the most important musical event of the—whole year (!!)" In Helm's words, the year 1892

> still has long enough to go that who knows what beautiful and perhaps far more important music it will still bring us. Might not even Brahms himself surprise us in November or December with a new symphony? A genre that certainly stands a bit higher than even the most beautiful clarinet quintet.[14]

Resuming this argument in his review of Bruckner's symphony in December, Helm called Brahms's Clarinet Quintet "masterly" but then drew on topoi associated with the symphonic and chamber genres that diminished the significance of the quintet:

> What does even the most beautiful "chamber piece" mean—a genre that is effective only in a small space and therefore addresses itself to narrow circles—in comparison with a symphony like the latest by Bruckner, whose thrillingly all-powerful tonal language—

---

haus, 1882); quoted by Erich Reimer in his entry "Kammermusik," in *Handwörterbuch für musikalischen Terminologie*, ed. Hans Heinrich Eggebrecht (Wiesbaden: Franz Steiner, 1971), 11–12.

13. "Kammermusik," in *Brockhaus' Conversations-Lexikon: Allgemeine deutsche Real-Encyclopädie*, 13th ed., 16 vols. (Leipzig: F. A. Brockhaus, 1882–87), 10:53.

14. *Deutsche Zeitung,* 16 January 1892.

we experienced it joyfully in the Philharmonic concert—is capable of inspiring thousands upon thousands who have ears to hear and a heart to feel what is heard![15]

One must assume that Helm was trying to capture stylistic qualities rather than aim-
ing at an accurate representation of the available performing spaces: the large hall of
Vienna's Musikverein building, after all, seats only about 2,000 people.[16] Writing
many years later, he recalled the two 1892 premieres and invoked frequently used
fine-arts metaphors that likewise privilege the greater impact possible with orchestral
forces and truly symphonic style. "Even the finest, most successful pastel drawing—
with which a chamber-music piece by Brahms may perhaps be compared—can never
compete in immediate striking effect with a musical fresco in the boldest style."[17]

Discussions of the *echt symphonisch* and its popular appeal invariably hinged on
the nature of the themes and their development, both inextricably linked with the
composer's skill at orchestration. Bruckner's admirers often voiced approval of his
symphonic themes in language that conveys this conception of the genre. After a
performance of the Third Symphony, Speidel, for example, asserted that Bruckner
has "truly symphonic ideas, which were born in the orchestra and persist in the memory through their energetic vividness." Helm characterized the First Symphony's
opening in much the same way: "Who could forget even after one hearing the
sharply drawn, truly symphonic, and at the same time truly Brucknerian theme?"[18]
When Bekker later criticized the Romantic symphonists for having diminished the
"luminosity" of Beethoven's orchestra and "the power of its deployment," he also focused on questions of texture and melodic style. He wrote of "the tortuous unfolding of the thematic line and the complicated tissue of voices in Brahms, the aphoris-
tic kind of invention in Schumann, and—in comparison with Beethoven's powerful
brushwork—the effortlessly easy, almost trifling coloring in Mendelssohn."[19]

Widespread reservations about the Romantic symphonic repertory had opened
up opportunities for Bruckner's supporters, who promoted him as the new Beethoven. In an unusually long review of Bruckner's Seventh from 1887, the Berlin-
based critic Paul Marsop thus set Bruckner's achievements in relief against the supposed shortcomings of the Romantic symphony. Mendelssohn, whose *Lieder ohne
Worte* had become a recurring object of ridicule in criticism of the Romantic symphony, was the first (unnamed) foil for Bruckner. Using the familiar fine-arts imagery, Marsop asserted that if much in Bruckner seemed

> dashed off al fresco, the brush wielded by a powerful hand . . . these were neverthe-
> less forceful and emphatic strokes. Nothing of those ladylike, elegantly intertwined
> pencil arabesques, nothing of that *Lieder ohne Worte* texture, whose melodies, pallid as
> forget-me-nots, never flow freely from a full heart, but rather always pass through a

---

15. *Deutsche Zeitung*, 28 December 1892.

16. One recent source gives the number of seats as 2,087. Harald Goertz, *Österreichisches Musikhandbuch* (Vienna: Jugend und Volk, 1971), 151.

17. "Fünfzig Jahre Wiener Musikleben (1866–1916): Erinnerungen eines Musikkritikers," *Der
Merker* 8 (1917): 498.

18. *Fremden-Blatt*, 1 January 1891; *Deutsche Zeitung*, 17 December 1891.

19. *Die Sinfonie*, 44.

perfumed handkerchief. . . . No, everything is decisive, German, Beethovenian, in a word, *manly.*

Marsop admired the strong, un-Romantic quality of Bruckner's themes, Romantic revealingly coded here as "ladylike" in contrast to German, Beethovenian "manliness." But he also praised their fitness "for a consequential development, for a structure rising in a skillfully prepared *Steigerung* [intensification or climax]," an exciting and apparently requisite feature of the *echt symphonisch.*

Criticizing what he saw as the unsuitable melodic writing in most symphonies after Beethoven, Marsop drew attention in particular to Schumann's "most splendid" melodies that nevertheless remained ineffective as *symphonic* themes:

> For a theme that is itself beautiful or interesting in purely musical terms is still not a symphonic theme if it does not also have an outstandingly vivid character, if it does not appear immediately upon its first entrance in such a clearly defined shape to the listener that he, *even if he is only passably musical,* can follow it readily and without difficulty in its more remote transformations.[20]

The crux of the matter, it seems, was that even an uninitiated listener should be able to grasp a symphonic theme at once and recognize it in its subsequent guises.

Three quarters of a century later, Blume made a related point: in contrast to "the decay of formal construction" that he traces to the "emphatically lyric character" of most nineteenth-century music, "Bruckner's symphonies link up anew with Beethoven's thematic technique." For Blume, symphonic vividness derives from rhythmic qualities at the level of the motive as well as on the grandest possible scale. He notes how Bruckner develops "brisk, energy-laden motifs" into ever larger units, ultimately creating "the grandiose towering waves of intensification so characteristic of him." Unlike such composers as Schumann and Brahms, "Bruckner avoids the spinning of motifs into song-melody periods," which leads Blume to call him "the only genuine symphonist since Beethoven."[21] Even Adorno, who in 1934 admired Brahms's recasting of sonata form in the first movement of his Fourth Symphony, wrote later that the movement "could equally well have been composed as a piano quintet" because of the composer's partiality for chamber-music techniques of developing variation.[22] Like that of Schumann, Brahms's thematic style was rarely seen as adequate. He did not adhere consistently to the thematic ideal of the *echt symphonisch,* nor did he always organize his symphonies as a series of *Steigerungen:* he did not aim these works at the audience associated in stereotype with the genre.

VOLKSCONCERTE IN VIENNA

According to Bekker, a symphonist creates what can be read in the score and "at the same time an ideal image of the space and audience," an image that rarely cor-

---

20. "Anton Bruckner," *Berliner Tageblatt,* 10 August 1885; reprinted in *Kastner's Wiener Musikalische Zeitung* 3 (1887): 345–350, at 348. Emphasis added in final quotation.

21. *Classic and Romantic Music,* 143–144.

22. "Stravinsky," in *Quasi una Fantasia,* 166.

responded to concert conditions in Vienna.[23] Although to Wagner, Beethoven's symphonies seemed "to speak in large, vivid outlines to the people, to all of mankind,
in the spacious hall," the audience for them in Beethoven's Vienna had in general
been restricted, the hall not always spacious.[24] And to Helm, many decades later,
Bruckner's Eighth may have been "capable of inspiring thousands upon thousands."
Yet only two years before, Wörz had estimated that less than two-tenths of a percent
of the city's residents would ever hear an orchestral performance of a symphony.

Sociopolitical conditions in Vienna had not favored the growth of public concerts, linked elsewhere in Europe with the ascendancy of the middle classes: Austria remained organized along feudal-aristocratic lines later than other European
states. Stefan Kunze called it "almost paradoxical" that the glorious symphonic
repertory of Viennese Classicism is connected to a city with no concert hall reserved for orchestral performances and consequently no regular public concerts or
permanent symphonic orchestra until well into the nineteenth century.[25] Not only
was there a less substantial middle class in Austria than elsewhere before the second
half of the nineteenth century but also Metternich's police state would not have en-
couraged public gatherings of any kind. But, above all, public concerts flourished
later in Vienna than elsewhere because they were grounded in the capitalist system
that replaced feudalism and assisted the rise of the middle class, and these changes
took place more slowly in Austria than in other parts of Europe.[26]

The Vienna Philharmonic, it is true, had come into existence in 1842. Since the
Philharmonic players spent most of their working hours in the pit of the Hofoper,
however, this meant that the typical symphonic series featured only eight subscrip-
tion concerts a year. Expanding the audience for orchestral concerts meant founding and supporting a new orchestra. Beginning in the 1860s, musicians had made
periodic unsuccessful attempts to do so, with most observers blaming these groups'
failure on the lack of institutional or government funding.[27]

Toward the end of the 1880s, calls for reform of the city's musical life became
more insistent, largely no doubt because of the political climate in the city: rabble-
rousing politicians were using dangerous kinds of populist rhetoric to win the favor

23. *Die Sinfonie,* 13.

24. Richard Wagner, "Über die Anwendung der Musik auf das Drama" (1879), in *Gesammelte
Schriften und Dichtungen,* 3rd ed., 10 vols. (Leipzig, C. F. W. Siegel's Musikalienhandlung, 1897), 10:183.

25. *Die Sinfonie im 18. Jahrhundert: Von der Opernsinfonie zur Konzertsinfonie* (Laaber: Laaber-Verlag,
1993), 289. See also Friedrich C. Heller, "Die Zeit der Moderne," in *Von der Revolution 1848 zur Gegenwart,*
vol. 3 of *Musikgeschichte Österreichs,* ed. Rudolf Flotzinger and Gernot Gruber, 2nd ed. (Vienna: Böhlau
Verlag, 1995); and Ernst Kobau, *Die Wiener Symphoniker: Eine sozialgeschichtliche Studie* (Vienna: Böhlau Verlag, 1991).

26. N[achum] T. Gross, *The Industrial Revolution in the Habsburg Monarchy 1750–1914* (London:
Collins Clear-Type Press, 1972); and Kobau, *Die Wiener Symphoniker,* 15–16.

27. See, for example, Wörz, "*Volksconcerte* in Wien"; Wilhelm Frey, "Die Wiener Orchesterfrage,"
Neues Wiener Tagblatt, 1 and 11 February 1890; and a pamphlet by Albert Gutmann, *Volksconcerte in Wien:
Vorschläge zur Bildung eines Concertorchesters: Mittheilung an die Gesellschaft der Musikfreunde von ihrem Mitgliede Albert Gutmann* (Vienna: Verlag der kaiserl. und königl. Hofmusikalienhandlung Albert J. Gutmann, [1890]). Hanslick mentions an attempt in 1865 to institute a summer series of symphony concerts
in a semienclosed hall, "according to the Berlin model." Financial problems caused the enterprise to
founder quickly. *Geschichte des Concertwesens in Wien,* 2 vols. (Vienna: Wilhelm Braumüller, 1869), 1:410.

of the newly enfranchised lower middle class. Following a line of logic that may seem strange today, activists in Vienna's music worlds clearly believed that making the music enjoyed by the *Bildungsbürgertum* accessible to more of the populace would ease class tensions and help lower class Viennese rise above the circumstances of their birth and upbringing.

Ironically, given widespread attitudes toward the two genres, it proved easier to broaden the audience for chamber music than for the symphony. In 1849, seven years after the Philharmonic's inaugural season, the Hellmesberger String Quartet had begun to give public concerts—the first such Viennese group to do so on a regular basis since Beethoven's time. By the 1890s, in contrast to the situation with respect to orchestras, the city was home to many additional professional string quartets.[28] To reach more listeners, chamber ensembles could simply present their customary programs in larger halls or alternative spaces. When the Hellmesberger Quartet had moved its performances from the small to the large hall of the Musikverein building in the 1882–83 season, Helm deplored the decision as "dictated merely by business considerations." According to him, the larger hall had made the string quartets on the program sound "empty and shabby," in part because the players' efforts to cope with the hall's acoustics led them into stylistic improprieties. But when the group offered concerts in the same venue in 1890, with tickets set at "so-called *volksthümlich*"—that is, popular—prices, he muted his criticism, observing that "the idea of these classical *Volksconcerte* . . . corresponds so well to the democratic course of our time."[29] The times had changed, and so had the group's motivation for choosing the large hall.

Also in 1890, the violinist August Duesberg formed a string quartet that called itself the Erstes Wiener Volksquartett für Classische Musik (First Viennese People's Quartet for Classical Music). This group played concerts with what Helm called "a ridiculously low price" of admission.[30] In a pamphlet devoted to the quartet, Duesberg described the ensemble's goal as "the improvement of the people's music." He also appealed to the self-interest of the more privileged Viennese citizens: "If we endeavor to make music well known and liked by the people, to make it a necessity, it will be a diversion for the discontented and the revolutionary-minded from dark thoughts, a safeguard from their own souls."[31] In this sentence Duesberg, whose quartet was a favorite of the right-wing *völkisch* press, was playing on fears about the recently formed party on the left, that of the Austrian Socialists.

In Vienna as elsewhere, Socialists had organized their first May Day celebrations in 1889 and 1890. For the time being, Austrian Socialists focused their efforts on obtaining the vote for the working class and trying to alleviate the miserable living conditions that most of the populace endured, but after the turn of the century,

---

28. Professional string quartets formed in Vienna in the last two decades of the nineteenth century included those with Arnold Rosé, Rudolf Fitzner, and Carl Prill as first violinists and namesakes, along with the Wiener Damen-Streichquartett and the Erstes Wiener Volksquartett für Classische Musik, discussed later.

29. *Musikalisches Wochenblatt* 14 (1882): 388, and 22 (1891): 121.

30. *Musikalisches Wochenblatt* 22 (1891): 121.

31. *Ueber Hebung der Volksmusik in Hinsicht auf das "Erste Wiener Volksquartett für Classische Musik"* (Vienna: Lesk and Schwidernoch, [1892]), 3 and 23.

symphonic performances for the working class would become a priority for them, too.[32] Thus, like many younger Liberals, members of new parties on both the right and left considered *Volksconcerte* devoted to the classical repertory essential to the well-being of the "Volk." (This word had already acquired some of the rhetorical charge that the National Socialists would exploit with such devastating consequences several decades later.)

As various accounts attest, late nineteenth-century Vienna had long afforded its *Volk* many musical pleasures. A Gypsy band admired by Brahms himself performed regularly in the Prater. Singers and instrumentalists in various combinations, including the Schrammel Quartet—two violinists, a guitarist, and a clarinetist who performed on a now obsolete high-pitched G instrument—played in wine taverns. Military bands and popular orchestras like the reportedly fine one led by Eduard Strauss offered so-called promenade concerts in parks and refreshment rooms throughout the city. Many of these concerts were advertised as popular events, presumably because of both the low-priced tickets and the programs, which mixed lighter and more serious pieces, including at times individual symphonic movements.[33] In the early 1890s, furthermore, popular chamber performances became frequent occurrences. What Vienna continued to lack was reasonably priced concerts in which complete symphonies could be heard.

The Vienna Philharmonic presented one nonsubscription event per season, the "Nicolai Concert," which it billed as a popular concert, not because the price of admission warranted that label—apparently it did not[34]—but rather because of the choice of pieces. Typically, a program played by the Philharmonic followed a format familiar to us today: in the first half, an overture and concerto (or aria, transcription, serenade, or other nonsymphonic work), concluding in the second half with an entire symphony. For the Nicolai Concert of 1889, a program of assorted short pieces replaced the usual fare:

Schumann	Overture and Chorus for Large Orchestra
Mozart	Aria from *Le nozze di Figaro*
Beethoven	Minuet and Finale from String Quartet in C Major (Op. 59, No. 3) Lieder
Berlioz	"Ballet des sylphes" from *La damnation de Faust*
Haydn	Hunters' Chorus and Winter Chorus from *Die Jahreszeiten*[35]

Although the program was more consistently "classical" than what might be offered in a modern pops concert, Kalbeck accused the Philharmonic of engaging in a fu-

---

32. On the importance of music to the Austrian Social Democratic party and the tendency within the party to accept both the Liberal emphasis on *Bildung* and the centrality of the nineteenth-century middle-class repertory, see Johann Wilhelm Seidl, *Musik und Austromarxismus: Zur Musikrezeption der österreichischen Arbeiterbewegung im späten Kaiserreich und in der Ersten Republik* (Vienna: Böhlau Verlag, 1989).

33. Wörz, "*Volksconcerte* in Wien."

34. Indeed, Speidel remarked: "When the cost of admission for the best seats has been fixed so high that the daily bills for a middle-class family could be covered with it—where do the *Volk* sit then?" *Fremden-Blatt*, 7 March 1889.

35. For the programs played by the Vienna Philharmonic, see *Wiener Philharmoniker: 1842–1942*, 2 vols. in 1 (Vienna: n.p., 1942).

tile attempt "to flirt with the crowd's frivolous search for entertainment." He concluded his review by saying that "Beethoven's Ninth Symphony or some other big and difficult miracle of art would have proved more effective here than the seven numbers of a motley program that included orchestral music, choruses, arias, and lieder."[36] Like many other musicians and critics then, Kalbeck seems to have assumed the accessibility of such "difficult" but "effective" works as the Ninth: in 1889, he accepted ideology of the symphony.

Still, only a small fraction of the city's populace had the opportunity to hear symphonic performances, and the privileged few naturally came from the moneyed classes. According to an observer writing in 1888, "the Philharmonic concerts above all have a place among what is fashionable within our upper middle class; it is a mark of good breeding to be a subscriber."[37] Not all those who enjoyed the privilege of attending, moreover, appear to have treated the performances in general, and their concluding symphony in particular, with appropriate seriousness, to judge from the frequent complaints about frivolous behavior:

> One sees there, in addition to some truly competent listeners, many people who do not have the least taste for superior music; they go in order to be seen. An especially deplorable habit is the mass exodus made by the audience during the symphony that usually ends the program. An ever-increasing crowd pours out between movements to throw on their overcoats and get to their beloved midday meal.[38]

In short, the common people did not have access to the symphony, and those Viennese who did lacked the proper solemn focus.

The movement to bring the symphony to the *Volk* claimed its first victories in 1892. During the summer and fall, local entrepreneurs presented several series of concerts as part of the Musik- und Theater-Ausstellung that Heuberger and Brahms had discussed the previous winter, most of them orchestral performances by a pickup group formed for the occasion. Although only twenty-nine of the sixty-six concerts were designated "Populäre Concerte" because they offered somewhat lighter programs, general admission for all the concerts was set at a minimal level to make them easily affordable. At the opening of the Ausstellung, the critic Hirschfeld anticipated that the performances would "awaken enthusiasm for the elevated and beautiful in the widest circles of our population," and that the Ausstellung would find a way to "revive and strengthen musical feeling in the people."[39] At the end, an anonymous critic noted that attendance at the popular symphony concerts had indeed grown steadily: "a loyal and devoted core audience had formed and in the final concerts filled the large *Musikhalle* to the last seat."[40]

36. "Feuilleton. Musikalische Wohl- und Uebelthäter," *Die Presse,* 9 March 1889.

37. Anonymous (signed "x."), "Feuilleton. Unser Konzertpublikum," *Fremden-Blatt,* 25 November 1888.

38. Anonymous (signed "x."), "Feuilleton."

39. *Die Presse,* 7 May 1892. For Hirschfeld, see Leon Botstein, "Music and Its Public: Habits of Listening and the Crisis of Musical Modernism in Vienna, 1870–1914" (Ph.D. diss., Harvard University, 1985).

40. *Deutsche Kunst- und Musik-Zeitung* 19 (1892): 263.

In most of the Ausstellung performances, including one with Bruckner's Third as its symphonic culmination, the common, if controversial, practice of serving food and drink at popular concerts prevailed. Helm, by then both a Bruckner partisan and a critic for an anti-Liberal daily in Vienna and therefore manifestly biased, proclaimed the event a success with the people: "The usual exhibition meal 'with beer and meat' was being offered. But during the performance of this long and complicated work, which demands the most rapt attention and patience, the audience completely forgot about material pleasures and literally held its breath in order not to miss a single note."[41] Not surprisingly, he considered Brahms's First to have failed in the same setting: "That—apart from the grand finale—precisely this symphony with its ardor more directed inward is less suited for performance in a popular concert with beer and sausages goes without saying."[42] The final Ausstellung event surpassed the usual Philharmonic concert in the seriousness of its program: an overture by Gluck, Mozart's G Minor Symphony, and an aria by Weber in the first half, Beethoven's *Leonore* Overture No. 3 and the *Eroica* in the second. According to Helm, the symphonic conclusion again proved more important than refreshments, for at the beginning of the symphony the audience

immediately suspended its culinary pleasures and energetically hushed the serving waiters in order not to miss a note of Beethoven's sublime creation. . . . We speak at such length about this because with it the idea of popular symphony concerts so much disputed among us, indeed considered downright impossible in Vienna, celebrated the greatest triumph in the form described.[43]

Despite the evident success of many of the concerts, attempts to maintain the orchestra at the close of the Ausstellung ended in failure.

In a book about the Ausstellung published two years later in Germany, the musicologist Oskar Fleischer noted that the pride the organizers took in the symphony concerts

seems strange and startling in the German Empire, since in Berlin, for example, symphony concerts are, so to speak, daily bread. In Vienna, however, the symphonies of the Viennese Classical composers are exceptional features on concert programs; there are but few musicians who have heard all nine Beethoven symphonies in their life.[44]

While a potential audience for the symphony, obviously, was deprived in this state of affairs, most of Vienna's inhabitants do not appear to have felt any deprivation on this account: Brahms seems to have been partially correct. By 1897, even Kalbeck had come to share the composer's view, for he quipped that "nothing is more unpopular in Vienna than a popular concert." Responding to the latest efforts to inaugurate popular symphony concerts in the Musikverein building, Kalbeck observed that the endeavor had the advantages of "a serviceable orchestra, a capable

41. *Musikalisches Wochenblatt* 23 (1892): 477.
42. *Musikalisches Wochenblatt* 23 (1892): 516.
43. *Musikalisches Wochenblatt* 23 (1892): 516.
44. *Die Bedeutung der internationalen Musik- u. Theater-Ausstellung in Wien für Kunst u. Wissenschaft der Musik* (Leipzig: Internationale Verlags- und Kunstanstalt [A. Laurencic], [1894]), 64.

conductor, a splendid locale, and well-disposed critics: only the audience does not want to come."

Kalbeck explained that "popularity is not an attribute bestowed by decree from above, but rather a gift from below"; that something becomes popular only if it satisfies needs of the crowd: "Let us not deceive ourselves with fine figures of speech. Let us not cajole the people with illusions that are alien to them! The need to hear serious music is not universal in Vienna; in fact, it is as good as nonexistent." Viewing the situation more pragmatically—as he expressed it, from the perspective of eighteen years' experience in the city—than he had in 1889, Kalbeck noted the type of "popular" concert that thrived in the *Heuriger* of Vienna's outer districts. He wrote that to want to sacrifice its "modest charms" for the sake of "more noble pleasures or to despise it from the lofty standpoint of a higher morality would be not just a perverted, misplaced strictness, but also error and folly." For he found the advantages of Viennese musical life to lie precisely in "the connection with the *Volk,* the constant contact with the feelings that stir the souls of the masses, the reciprocal good terms between a natural art and an art of an elevated nature." These were qualities from which "even such sublime geniuses as Mozart, Beethoven, and Brahms, all three of whom came to Vienna as accomplished masters of their art, derived the richest rewards." Indeed, as we shall see, Brahms's exposure to the "natural art" of Gypsy musicians in Vienna and Budapest inspired the later chamber adagios that were found most successful by critics and audiences alike.

Kalbeck concluded by suggesting that the concert's organizer take his cues from Berlin's popular concerts, in which a complete symphony was placed between sets of lighter pieces. In Berlin, a custom had developed of ceasing to eat, smoke, and talk for the duration of the central symphony—similar to the show of respect that Helm had observed in popular performances of Bruckner and Beethoven—so that "the highest genre of instrumental music preserves its special aura." Listening to a symphony in these circumstances, "even the unmusical person improves his ear and begins to bring sense and order to the chaotic welter of tones."[45] Enlarging the audience for the genre had become a matter of incremental education rather than immediate understanding, and the symphonic experience itself had become a brief uplifting interlude amid mundane pursuits. But symphonic ideology would resurface after the turn of the century.

LIBERAL CONCEPTIONS OF THE
PUBLIC SPHERE AND IDEOLOGY
OF THE SYMPHONY

Not surprisingly, the *Eroica* occupied a pivotal position within the elaborate linguistic framework that conveyed both stylistic expectations of the symphony and utopian ideas about its function. For certain critics, the vital factor appears to have been neither technical innovations, such as the vastly expanded form of the first movement per se, nor even, directly, the connection to Napoleon. Of central sig-

---

45. *Neues Wiener Tagblatt,* 11 November 1897. I thank Sandra McColl for sending me a copy of this article.

nificance, rather, was the audience they considered Beethoven to have had in mind: no less than all of humanity. In composing his Third Symphony, Beethoven had washed away any traces of the *ancien régime* that still adhered to the genre. With the *Eroica,* according to Paumgartner, writing in 1950, Beethoven "determines the type for the century, indeed continuing to have an effect in our time." In his Third through Ninth symphonies, "the artist speaks . . . to humanity as earlier the rhapsodist, the orator, [spoke] to the people or at least to a multitude representing a broad cross-section of social strata as the 'public.' "[46]

By the late nineteenth century, "the people" and "the public" had become central to discussions of the genre, as had several related images: the symphony as public oration, a symphonic performance as a *Volksversammlung,* and the requisite style as "plain speaking." Almost seven decades before Paumgartner made his remarks about the *Eroica,* his father, the Viennese critic and prominent Wagnerite Hans Paumgartner, had used the same metaphor of symphonist as orator to criticize Brahms's symphonic writing. In 1882 he wrote: "Brahms lacks immediately gripping, breathtaking invention for the dithyramb that the symphony should be. It is as if the quiet, contemplative scholar had suddenly been dragged from his comfortable study to the speaker's platform of a *Volksversammlung.*"[47] Brahms remained ever the composer of chamber music, using subtle, scholarly reasoning rather than the populist rhetoric considered suitable for the symphony.

What Wagner himself had valued in Beethoven's symphonies, perhaps as prototype for his personal ideal of "endless melody," was a musical fabric in which every moment was compelling and meaningful.[48] Wagner described such a texture as "always enthralling through so vivid a movement that the listener cannot escape its impression, but rather, strained to extreme attention, must grant melodic significance to every harmonic note, indeed every rhythmic pause."[49] Like a masterful public speaker, the composer of such a "melody" *compels* the audience to listen.

Logically tied to the idea of a symphonic performance as a *Volksversammlung* is the conception of Beethoven's symphonic style as *oratio directa:* that is, plain speaking, a metaphor Hans von Wolzogen attributed to Wagner. Addressing the Viennese Academic Wagner Society shortly after Wagner's death, Wolzogen quoted from a conversation in which the composer had compared Beethoven's approach to the chamber and symphonic genres. In Wolzogen's account, Wagner said: "The same Beethoven, who in his quartets creates the greatest art, the most contemplative, cerebral work for only the most exclusive, artistically like-minded listeners, in his symphonies suddenly steps, fully popular, before the whole people. Then everything is *oratio directa!*"[50] Like many other musicians, Wagner assumed that audiences

---

46. "Das instrumentale Ensemble," 2:14.

47. *Wiener Zeitung,* 10 December 1882.

48. Thomas S. Grey, *Wagner's Musical Prose: Texts and Contexts* (New York: Cambridge University Press, 1995), 251–254; and Klaus Kropfinger, *Wagner and Beethoven: Richard Wagner's Reception of Beethoven,* trans. Peter Palmer (New York: Cambridge University Press, 1991), 103–110.

49. "Zukunftsmusik" (1860), in *Gesammelte Schriften,* 7:127.

50. *Erinnerungen an Richard Wagner: Ein Vortrag, gehalten am 13 April 1883 im Wissenschaftlichen Club zu Wien,* ed. Wiener Akademische Wagner-Verein [Viennese Academic Wagner Society] (Vienna: Verlag von Carl Konegan, 1883), 34.

for chamber music could take in the finely detailed arguments expected of that genre, but that symphonists must address the large and allegedly mixed audiences in auditoriums in an uncomplicated, forceful manner.

According to August Halm, symphonic style as the musical equivalent of "plain speaking" originated not with Wagner but rather von Bülow, an erstwhile member of his circle. In his book on Beethoven, Halm unpacked the image by contrasting what he called the decisive indicative mode of *oratio directa* with the "weakening, unstable" subjunctive of indirect speech (as this is rendered in the German language). Halm then interpreted the *oratio directa* of the symphony as speech that demands action from the listeners: what they have heard should continue to have an effect well after the experience.[51]

The politically tinged metaphors the various writers use do convey the impact of an expected style, a matter of constantly "enthralling" vividness, of striking themes and exciting intensifications: the emphatic pedal points, sequences, and crescendos considered idiomatic for the genre. But they also seem patently ideological. Consider the implications of a symphonist speaking to all of humanity, of a symphonic performance taking place before a *Volksversammlung* and stirring the people to action afterward. And I have repeatedly indicated that the contradiction between the metaphorical and real audiences was especially glaring in the context of late nineteenth-century Vienna, with its paltry eight performances a year before elite audiences. Why would ideas of genre have been framed in such illusory terms? As I implied earlier, the obfuscating linguistic framework has its source in fundamental assumptions of the Liberal worldview: a political outlook and ideas about music merge here as genre aesthetics.

Dahlhaus suggested that, at least through the eighteenth century, genres mediated between on the one hand stylistic proclivities of individual composers and on the other the requirements and expectations of the social classes that, in supporting musical production at a given time, determine the functions for music.[52] His formulation can be extended to the nineteenth century by considering possible symbolic functions of genres. Might not contemporary ideas about the symphony reflect how the supporting social strata at the time—along with the aristocracy, the educated middle and especially upper middle classes, the constituency of nineteenth-century Liberalism—chose to think of and therefore represent themselves and their world?

In a highly regarded monograph, Jürgen Habermas placed the idea of the public sphere near the center of Liberal philosophies. Through their collective and public exercise of reason, according to those ways of thinking, private citizens could limit the authority of the state, making it accountable to "public opinion." But newspapers and other organs of public opinion remained censored in Vienna later than elsewhere in Europe, from the defeat of Napoleon until well after the suppression of the midcentury rebellions. And when the Liberals finally came into

51. *Beethoven* (Berlin: Max Hesse, 1927), 55.
52. "Was ist eine musikalische Gattung?" *Neue Zeitschrift für Musik* 135 (1974): 622.

power in the late 1860s, the majority of the populace did not meet the requirements of property and education that most basically would have made them eligible to vote. Yet Liberalism held that the free enterprise system offered everyone the opportunity to become a member of the educated middle classes and thus gain the right to participate in the public sphere—as if education and property lay in reach for everyone. As Habermas noted, (ostensibly) achieving a "public engaged in rational-critical debate" did not mean the end of political domination, but rather the replacement of one form of domination, that under the feudal system, with another. He therefore concluded that the "bourgeois constitutional state, along with the public sphere as the central principle of its organization, was mere ideology."[53]

The public had been a key idea in aesthetics of the symphony almost from the beginning. It would go too far to impute a causal connection not only between the ascendancy of the middle classes and the development of public concerts in the modern sense but also between both of these and the rise of the symphony as an independent genre. For in documents concerning some of the earliest performances of symphonies as concert music, which occurred in courtly spaces, "public" retained its older meaning connected with sovereign rulers as representatives of their subjects, symphonies having a place in court events in which the ruler appeared in that public capacity. While virtually from its inception, the genre appears to have been associated with the public sphere, the meaning of that sphere changed early in the history of the symphony.[54]

Despite the meagerness of public performances (in the new sense) in Vienna, the metaphor of symphony as public oration (versus string quartet as conversation) was already current during Beethoven's lifetime;[55] as was Liberal vocabulary, well in advance of a political system that offered much support for Liberal tenets.[56] Half a century later, in 1869, Eduard Hanslick characterized the city's musical life as having progressed "from the patriarchal-aristocratic subjugation of art to its complete democratization."[57] Since their inception in 1842, the Philharmonic's concerts, it is true, had theoretically been open to anyone able to pay the price of admission. And he may have been distorting the situation from the perspective of Liberal privilege acquired only a few years before with the ratification of the new Constitution. Assessing Hanslick's comment in light of the actual state of affairs in Vienna, however, Ernst Kobau went so far as to call it "a grossly false assessment that . . . seems almost cynical."[58]

For many critics, the existence of a symphonic orchestra, like other aspects of the genre, had clear symbolic import. Bernhard Paumgartner, for example, stressed the significance of the move from aristocratic spaces to "the generally accessible,

53. *The Structural Transformation of the Public Sphere: An Inquiry into a Category of Bourgeois Society,* trans. Thomas Burger and Frederick Lawrence (Cambridge, Mass.: MIT Press, 1991), 125.

54. Kunze, *Die Sinfonie im 18. Jahrhundert,* 164.

55. Ludwig Finscher, "Symphonie," in *Die Musik in Geschichte und Gegenwart,* 2nd ed., ed. Finscher (Kassel: Bärenreiter, 1998), vol. 9, cols. 56–58.

56. Ernst Bruckmüller, *Sozialgeschichte Österreichs* (Vienna: Herold Verlag, 1985), 333–339.

57. *Geschichte des Concertwesens in Wien,* 1:xiii.

58. *Die Wiener Symphoniker,* 17.

large concert hall" and of "the new public as representatives of the *whole* people."[59] In the late nineteenth century, imagery associated with the symphony may even have fostered an illusory picture of "complete democratization" of Viennese musical life, just as the frequent misapprehension of Liberalism itself as democratic must have nurtured views that connected the genre to "the people." Both attitudes were based on misconceptions of the nature of representation, for clearly the ones representing others have greater power; an act of representation, even in an artistic event, is not neutral in this respect. In a pertinent *aperçu*, Stefan Zweig (1891–1943) looked back on the Vienna of his early childhood and recalled that members of Parliament elected by the well-to-do minority with the right to vote "truly and honestly believed that they were the spokesmen and representatives of 'the people.'"[60] A similar shortsightedness seems to have allowed symphonic performances before the select gatherings in the Musikverein building to be construed as metaphorical "assemblies of the people": the educated and propertied classes could somehow represent the *Volk* in public concert halls, as well as in Parliament.

NARRATIVES OF DECLINE AND THE CENTRALITY OF THE SLOW MOVEMENT

Ideas about genre may have helped perpetuate an unrealistically positive image of Liberal culture. But they also played a role in perceptions of decline, for writers who regarded Romanticism as signaling a falling-off of compositional aspirations and accomplishments often focused on specific genres. Ludwig Finscher notes that genres preserve "music-cultural memory," and the norms of those genres in turn are "derived from outstanding works."[61] By the late nineteenth century, Beethoven and the kinds of music of which he remained the undisputed master had attained a stature that cannot be exaggerated. Most aspects of the importance found in his oeuvre have long since entered accounts of nineteenth-century music history. For the most part, however, historians have overlooked the significance of his slow movements, as the culmination of a genre in its own right and thus a group of works that set standards only rarely met by subsequent composers. Like the symphony and string quartet, the Classical slow movement memorialized the imagined idealism of Beethoven's time.

Though recent music criticism and analysis have overwhelmingly favored first movements, by the second half of the nineteenth century, slow movements had achieved a central position in much writing on music.[62] Thus the following entry from a widely disseminated encyclopedia that appeared in 1886 makes a seemingly

---

59. "Das instrumentale Ensemble," 2:14. Habermas wrote about "representative publicity" (*repräsentative Öffentlichkeit*) as an effect of the movement toward universal suffrage in the nineteenth century, seen as necessary "to save the principle of publicity even against the tyranny of an unenlightened public opinion." *Transformation of the Public Sphere*, 137.

60. *The World of Yesterday: An Autobiography* (New York: Viking Press, 1943), 60.

61. "Werk und Gattung in der Musik als Träger kulturellen Gedächtnisses," in *Kultur und Gedächtnis*, ed. Jan Assmann and Tonio Hölscher (Frankfurt am Main: Suhrkamp, 1988), 300.

62. See my "Late-Nineteenth-Century Chamber Music and the Cult of the Classical Adagio," *19th-Century Music* 23 (1999): 33–61, and chapter 6 here.

unavoidable comparison between symphony and string quartet but also assumes as self-evident the cardinal importance of the slow movement:

> With respect to the suitable inner organization or musical character . . . Haydn's symphonies are distinguished from his quartets through broader disposition, larger ideas, harmonic splendor and fullness and a corresponding impetus toward the serious and sublime. And it was through this that he secured high status and decisive self-sufficiency for the symphony. At the same time with proper musical feeling he placed the center of gravity in the slow movement, in which all true symphonic composers, especially Mozart and Beethoven, have followed him.[63]

Predictably, the older Brahms seems to have rejected at least some facets of the slow movement's aura. In 1886, five years before Heuberger reported the composer's reaction to the planned *Volksconcerte,* he entered in his diary a piece of gossip that Brahms had passed on to him. Von Bülow had apparently requested that incense be burnt in the concert hall during a performance of the Adagio of Beethoven's Ninth Symphony "in order to heighten the mood." Brahms's reaction to his own story? He told Heuberger, "I really must find out if this is true."[64] (Keep in mind Brahms's attitude toward Catholicism.) According to the account by Bernhard Paumgartner that I quoted at the beginning, the symphonic slow movement recalls the sound and spirit of music used in religious ceremonies. The music itself created the atmosphere of sacred ritual.

Slow movements may well have been understood to express or even evoke religious experience before the late nineteenth century, but that conception of the genre was not much disseminated in print before then. The connection between slow movements and spirituality became evident when a "cult of Classicism" began to develop at midcentury, concomitantly with a rejection of Romanticism that was motivated in part by contemporary politics.[65] As one consequence of this polarized view of music history, writers who extolled Classicism at the expense of Romanticism had to interpret Beethoven's music as free of any Romantic tendencies. And critics who saw Bruckner as having renewed the great Beethovenian tradition also interpreted Brahms as continuing the lesser Romantic tradition. They considered this to be particularly detrimental to his symphonic slow movements.

In his recent monograph on Brahms's Second Symphony, Brinkmann observes that the inner movements of Romantic symphonies tend to be "character pieces of 'medium' dimensions and weight."[66] This sober assessment has many less neutral precedents. For example, in a 1941 article about Bruckner's adagios, the musicologist Walther Vetter devalued Schumann's symphonic slow movements as "charming character pieces rather than spiritual revelations"—the latter being exemplified,

---

63. Anonymous entry for "Symphonie" in *Brockhaus' Conversations-Lexikon,* 15:404.

64. *Erinnerungen an Brahms,* 155, entry for 14 November 1886.

65. See Ulrich Mahlert, *Fortschritt und Kunstlied: Späte Lieder Robert Schumanns im Licht der liedästhetischen Diskussion ab 1848* (Munich: E. Katzbichler, 1983), 8–29; Sanna Pederson, "Romantic Music under Siege in 1848," in *Music Theory in the Age of Romanticism,* ed. Ian Bent (New York: Cambridge University Press, 1996), 57–74; and my "*Volksconcerte* in Vienna and Late Nineteenth-Century Ideology of the Symphony," *Journal of the American Musicological Society* 50 (1997): 432–439.

66. *Late Idyll,* 144.

of course, by adagios of Beethoven and Bruckner.[67] More than a half-century after the fact, Vetter's comments echoed reactions to the first performances of Bruckner's Seventh Symphony in 1885. These remarks, for instance, had appeared at that time in a Munich newspaper: "No song without words inflated to an adagio, no elfin dance to a scherzo," followed by a seemingly inevitable comparison of Bruckner's Adagio and Scherzo to inner movements by Beethoven.[68] (Mendelssohn is again the obvious target.) Behind such observations lies not only a narrative of decline (and partial renewal) but also an aesthetic based on essentialist ideas of genre: for why must a symphonic slow movement not resemble a character piece? For those who accepted that aesthetic, the answer—and the view of Bekker and Paumgartner—would be that a character piece's lyricism and song-without-words texture are suitable for the self-expression associated with the solo piano, but a symphony must seem to express the sentiments of a group.

The solo piano had provided the natural vehicle for conveying Romantic subjectivity. Surveying the music of Schumann and Mendelssohn in 1845, Franz Brendel called the subject "completely self-focused" in *Kreisleriana* and saw the *Lieder ohne Worte* as the culmination of a trend toward "autonomous" melody: textures in which a single line expressed the sensibility of the solitary subject.[69] In the political turmoil of 1848 several years later, with many other musicians and critics, Brendel would reject both Romanticism and the social conditions in which it thrived. Wagner went so far as to castigate the piano itself, and, as we have already seen, Mendelssohn's *Lieder ohne Worte* became a pejorative catchword for musical Romanticism, most damning when applied to a symphony.[70] Beethoven inevitably provided a model in his sonatas and symphonies for the distinctions between the subjective and universal content required, respectively, by solo piano and orchestra.[71] And in discussions of the symphony, an inappropriate "Romantic" subjectivity was sometimes opposed to the ideal of "monumental" universality.

ROMANTIC VERSUS MONUMENTAL

This binary pair of attributes appears in contemporary reviews of Brahms's Third Symphony, the premiere of which Hans Richter conducted in Vienna in December 1883. Kalbeck wrote: "It would be interesting to know what stimulus from within or without we have to thank for [its] middle movements, which give the symphony a touch of Romanticism."[72] Several critics compared these middle movements and those in Brahms's First Symphony unfavorably with the opening allegros and finales of the same symphonies. Helm, for example, remarked on the oddness

---

67. "Das Adagio bei Anton Bruckner," *Deutsche Musikkultur* 5 (1940–41): 122.

68. Quoted in Göllerich, *Anton Bruckner,* vol. 4, pt. 3, 293.

69. "R. Schumann mit Rücksicht auf Mendelssohn-Bartholdy und die Entwicklung der modernen Musik," *Neue Zeitschrift für Musik* 22 (1845): 90 and 115.

70. Wagner, *Oper und Drama,* ed. Klaus Kropfinger (1852; reprint, Stuttgart: Reclam, 1984), 130–131. Wagner ridiculed the premise of songs *without words,* 264.

71. I provide a number of sources in "*Volksconcerte* in Vienna," especially at 432–434.

72. *Die Presse,* 5 December 1883.

of a situation in which "Brahms, who appears the most qualified disciple of Beethoven in the outer movements of his symphonies, remains decisively below his great
model in power and melodic concentration in the middle movements."[73] Dömpke,
in general a strong advocate for Brahms's music, likewise conveyed dissatisfaction
with those movements. About the Andante he wrote: "although not hard to grasp
and in part very expressive, [it] had not satisfied so purely and deeply as the first."
Responding directly to Richter's well-known reference to Brahms's Third as his
Eroica, Dömpke stressed that "the charming middle movements do not show the
slightest inner or outward resemblance to those of the *Eroica.*"[74]

After the second Viennese performance of Brahms's Third Symphony in 1885,
Dömpke again addressed the slow movement's content. This time he opposed
Schumann and Beethoven, quoting a witticism apparently current at that time: "in
Schumann's orchestra always just the one person is making music; in that of Bee-
thoven, all of humanity." He then asked rhetorically, "where do we place Brahms's
symphony with respect to these categories?" To this he responded:

> We today are too close to the increasing impact of Brahms's by no means completed
> work to be able yet to judge its level and position securely. This much, however, may
> already be said with assurance, that compared with Robert Schumann, Brahms rep-
> resents the more richly and thoroughly formed, the stronger, more universal nature
> showing the deeper affinity with Beethoven.

As in his earlier review, Dömpke saw Brahms as having more success in outer
movements:

> In the end, nevertheless, only single symphonic movements, like the finale of the Third,
> may be compared with Beethoven. In others, like the lovely Andante of the same
> work, an intense touch of Romanticism detracts from the monumental purity and
> solemnity that in analogous movements by Mozart and Beethoven fills the soul above
> all individual interest like eternal truths.[75]

On one side Dömpke aligns the names of Classical composers with the monumental and universal. On the other side he associates composers such as Schumann with
Romanticism and subjectivity, qualities considered inappropriate in the symphony.
His critique also suggests the inseparability of matters of symphonic content and
audience reception. Phrased in the lofty idealist language of the time, not only
should "all of humanity" seem to be making music but also the performance should
allow a group intuition of the Absolute. Dömpke wished to distance Brahms's symphonic slow movements from those of Schumann, in which the lone voice of the
pianist-composer could be heard, and to be able to position them more securely
with the "monumental purity" of similar movements by Beethoven and Mozart.

In an essay first published in 1934, Schering discussed the defining stylistic features of musical monumentality. He stressed the importance of a style suitable for
performance in a large space and consequently of clarity, simplicity, and extended

73. *Musikalisches Wochenblatt* 14 (1883): 654.
74. *Wiener Allgemeine Zeitung,* 5 December 1883.
75. *Wiener Allgemeine Zeitung,* 27 March 1885.

phrase-structures, together with the "predominance of simple but full harmonies and a certain splendor and power of sound." He also emphasized that composers should make audible the rules governing the disposition of their works: "The more sections and groups are sharply marked and a continuous constructive principle becomes perceptible, the greater the impact." In line with this last observation comes the heightened significance of techniques such as fugue, basso ostinato, and chains of sequences, which "because of their objective character are easily exploited for monumental effects."[76] Regarding the content of a monumental work—recalling traditional ideas about the symphony—"the personal, the subjective must disappear so the universal can come to light."[77]

In the Adagio assai of the *Eroica,* the work that, Dömpke accurately observes, the slow movement of Brahms's own Third Symphony in no way resembles, Beethoven creates an aura of monumentality through his particular renderings of some of the general stylistic attributes Schering notes. These include the etched melodies, full sound, and undeniable grandeur, all closely connected to the overriding funeral-march topos. Because of its "universal" significance, at least within the culture that gave rise to the musical signs for it—minor mode, dotted and double-dotted rhythms, slow tempo, and duple meter—the funeral-march type itself largely determined the monumentality of the movement's impact and affective content. Likewise contributing to the effect are the clearly delineated constructive principles that Schering finds vitally important, here those of variation and contrast, the latter provided by a thematic section in the major mode. Distinctly monumental in sound is the *Steigerung,* the sustained rise to a climax after that *maggiore,* in a lengthy passage that begins with a fugato and becomes increasingly impressive through other developmental devices such as modulating sequences. Schering cites the sequence for its "objective character," but a rising sequence set as a crescendo can also have a powerful impact. With respect to concerns of both audience reception and content, the sequence is well suited to the monumental symphony.

Early accounts such as Koch's must have formed a foundation for late nineteenth-century ideas about the symphony. Indeed, symphonic monumentality bears some resemblance to the late eighteenth-century aesthetic of the symphonic sublime.[78] New in the late nineteenth century is the emphasis on slow movements and the extension to those movements of certain stylistic expectations earlier reserved for opening allegros. For late eighteenth-century treatments of the symphony had linked the sublime, associated above all with first movements, to types of phrase-structure that create an impression of apparently limitless forward motion.[79] With reference

76. "Über den Begriff des Monumentalen in der Musik," *Jahrbuch der Musikbibliothek Peters für 1935* (Leipzig: C. F. Peters, 1936): 10, 11, and 12.

77. "Über den Begriff des Monumentalen in der Musik," 12.

78. See Dahlhaus's discussions of the symphonic sublime and symphonic monumentality in *Beethoven,* 67–80.

79. See Heinrich Christoph Koch, *Introductory Essay on Composition: The Mechanical Rules of Melody, Sections 3 and 4,* trans. Nancy Kovaleff Baker (New Haven: Yale University Press, 1983), 229–230. Baker translates Koch's word *erhabene* as "noble" rather than "sublime." For a discussion of the Adagio of Bruckner's Eighth and the aesthetics of the sublime, see Benjamin M. Korstvedt, *Anton Bruckner: Symphony No. 8* (New York: Cambridge University Press, 2000), 54–67.

to slow movements, as we shall see in chapter 6, "unendliche Melodie" conveys a related concept in the nineteenth century. In all movements of the late nineteenth-century symphony, techniques of intensification could serve the overlapping ideals of unending melody and monumentality.

While in no way critical of the Andante from Brahms's Third Symphony, Hanslick observed its brevity and the absence of any "real intensification or development." With apparent approval, he then mentioned a surprising aspect of the middle (the so-called second theme that begins in m. 41): "magical harmonies, sound effects that in alternating play recall lightly striking, variously tuned clocks."[80] These features, however—small size, subdued dynamics, eschewal of techniques of intensification, and Romantic harmonies and orchestration—precluded any consideration of the Andante as the monumental slow movement, the occasion for the communal event filling "the soul above all individual interest like eternal truths," that Dömpke wanted from Brahms.

After the first Viennese performance of Brahms's Fourth in January 1886, Dömpke did praise the *Steigerungen* in its slow movement: "Incidentally, we must point out the very beautiful symphonic intensification on which this Andante is constructed."[81] Although he may have conceived them as one overriding process, one *Steigerung*, the movement includes several intensifications, the most striking of which supports the modulation to the second theme (mm. 30–40). Still, he found that on the whole "the Andante seemed to us in comparison with the magnificent impetus of the outer movements not to touch deeply enough." The audience had responded more warmly to the Andante than the other movements, but Dömpke found the harmonic style antithetical to symphonic monumentality: "Precisely its remarkable perfume, its somewhat strangely seasoned harmonic language, which enchanted so many, for us stood in the way of a purer monumental effect." He was, of course, referring to the famous use of modal mixture in the Andante. Not only had Brahms blended scale steps from the parallel minor (E minor) with those of the primary major key (E major) but also he had borrowed the lowered second step that was historically linked to the Phrygian mode and was often introduced into minor-mode pieces.[82] Invoking the opposing term to "monumental," Dömpke criticized the harmonies as Romantic: "The movement stands in E major but, by allusion to the Phrygian church mode in E at the beginning, places the theme emphatically in C major or at least an apparent C major. Immediately thereafter following a fermata . . . the composer gives [the theme] . . . such a piquant [harmonic] admixture that we find ourselves here from the start on Romantic ground." While he admired Brahms's skill, Dömpke clearly regarded the harmonic style in the slow movement as excessively individual, especially when compared, inevitably, with Beethoven's sym-

---

80. Review reprinted in Hanslick, *Concerte, Componisten und Virtuosen der letzten fünfzehn Jahre: 1870–1885* (Berlin: Allgemeiner Verein für Deutsche Litteratur, 1886), 363.

81. For a discussion of the different application of intensifications in Bruckner's slow movements, see my "Formal Process as Spiritual Progress: The Symphonic Slow Movements," in *The Cambridge Companion to Bruckner*, ed. John Williamson (New York: Cambridge University Press, 2004), 186–200. All of the comments by Dömpke on Brahms's Fourth are from the *Wiener Allgemeine Zeitung*, 21 January 1886.

82. I discuss the harmonic language in the Fourth Symphony's Andante and an early examination by Riemann of it in "Plagal Harmony as Other."

phonies: "No one does such things so ingeniously and soberly as Brahms, no one does so for better reasons and with fuller awareness. Still, a harmonization like this perhaps belongs to those things that are a matter of personal taste, that are open to question now and then. In a symphony by Beethoven, nothing at all is open to question and never will be."

Like many other critics, Dömpke judged Brahms's slow movements according to purely aesthetic standards abstracted from three-quarters of a century's reception of Beethoven's achievements in that genre. For the quasi-religious experience he associated with the monumental symphony at best only remotely resembled contemporary descriptions of Viennese concert life. But the efforts by others in Vienna's music worlds to transform a symbolic into a concrete social function, a metaphorical into a more straightforward *Volksversammlung,* would eventually bear some fruit after the turn of the century.

IDEOLOGY OF THE SYMPHONY, MARXIST MUSIC HISTORY, AND BRAHMS'S LATENESS

When Brahms assumed in 1891 that there would be no audience for symphonic *Volksconcerte* in Vienna, he exaggerated the situation, as any number of anecdotes demonstrate. David Josef Bach, an important figure in the musical endeavors of the Austrian Social Democracy party, for example, recalled his first meeting with Schoenberg, which occurred at an outdoor military band concert in the early 1890s: "For most of us it was the only opportunity actually to hear a little music."[83] But this changed after the turn of the century. In 1905 Bach, by then a music critic for the party organ *Arbeiter-Zeitung,* helped organize the first Workers' Symphony Concerts (Arbeiter-Symphonie-Konzerte), possible now because Vienna had finally gained a second permanent orchestra in 1900.[84]

These concerts count as one of the signal achievements of the Austrian Social Democracy party.[85] They revived the symphonic ideology of the past; the compromises that Kalbeck, for one, had accepted in 1897 no longer seemed essential for the success of symphonic *Volksconcerte.* David Josef Bach maintained that although the inclusion of "so-called light music" had been considered necessary before, "to those starved for music a symphony by Beethoven was a greater attraction than even the most beautiful operetta music."[86] Hence under Bach's leadership the Workers' Symphony Concerts reverted to the format of the Philharmonic's concerts; indeed, the

---

83. "Aus der Jugendzeit," *Musikblätter des Anbruch* 6 (1924): 317.

84. This ensemble, overseen by a committee that included Kalbeck and Heuberger, would evolve into today's Wiener Symphoniker. I discuss some of the developments touched on here at greater length in "Musical Culture in Vienna at the Turn of the Twentieth Century," in *Schoenberg, Berg, and Webern: A Companion to the Second Viennese School,* ed. Bryan R. Simms (Westport, Conn.: Greenwood Press, 1999), 37–71.

85. For an alternative view, see Helmut Gruber, *Red Vienna: Experiment in Working-Class Culture 1919–1934* (New York: Oxford University Press, 1991), 96–102.

86. "Populäre Konzerte in Wien," *Musikbuch aus Österreich: Ein Jahrbuch der Musikpflege in Österreich und den bedeutendsten Musikstädten des Auslandes* 8 (1911): 27–28. Kobau notes that soon after the turn of the century, the Wiener Konzertverein, too, for the most part eliminated concerts with music in the "light" genres, *Die Wiener Symphoniker,* 21.

organizers went one step further in their purism and eliminated all program music. As Bach explained in 1923, they had begun with "symphonies that deliver nothing but their music, no program, no poetic explanation," because extramusical elements, usually a literary text, presuppose an understanding of their source and therefore a restricted audience with a certain type and level of education.[87] Bach's remarks cast a political light on the particular valorization of absolute music in Vienna (to be explored further in the epilogue).

On the occasion of the Beethoven sesquicentennial in 1920, Bach had offered another politically tinged interpretation of absolute music, in an article honoring a composer whose music speaks a "universally understandable language." Showing a Hegelian understanding of history, Bach wrote of representative individuals who appear "at decisive turning points,"with Beethoven emerging as such a world-historical figure at the end of the eighteenth century, "the beginning of the middle-class revolution."[88] By the time Bach made these remarks, the middle-class era, or long nineteenth century, had concluded decisively with World War I. Critics therefore assumed that the history of the era's music could be scanned as a whole. Bekker had in fact done this two years earlier in his sweeping overview of the symphony from Beethoven to Mahler, a survey of the genre that many Social Democrats, like many Liberals before them, considered the central musical type of the middle-class period. Articulating a perspective similar to that of Bach and other Socialist critics, including Paul Pisk and Hanns Eisler, Bekker attributed the unique distinction of Beethoven's symphonies to a brief historical moment in which it seemed possible to achieve the ideals of the French Revolution.[89] Beethoven had wished to communicate to the entire "human community" (16, 27), while symphonists before him had presupposed a restricted circle of listeners (15), and symphonists after him lost his universalizing impulse, directing their works to individual nations and social classes.

For Bekker, Brahms, along with his fellow Romantics Mendelssohn and Schumann, was thus a *bürgerlich* composer who wrote his symphonies with cultivated middle-class audiences in mind, whereas Schubert and Bruckner were specifically "Austrian" symphonists (36–43). Mahler's significance lay not only in his position as the third symphonist in the latter group but also in the hope his work offered for the future of music. Closing with the remark that "to us Mahler's total symphonic work, as the final, highest product of the Romantic worldview, is at once guarantor and foundation of a new idealism" (61), Bekker saw a reversal of the pat-

87. "Die Kunststelle," in *Kunst und Volk: Eine Festgabe der Kunststelle zur 1000. Theateraufführung,* ed. Bach (Vienna: Verlag Leopold Heidrich, 1923), 116, quoted in Seidl, *Musik und Austromarxismus,* 139. Bekker came to similar conclusions in *Die Sinfonie,* 46–49.

88. "Beethoven," *Arbeiter-Zeitung,* 16 December 1920.

89. A much shorter overview, similar in other respects to that of Bekker, forms part of an article by Pisk, "Zur Soziologie der Musik," *Der Kampf* 18 (1925): 184–187. *Der Kampf* was another organ of Austrian Social Democracy. Slightly later writings of this sort include Eisler, "Die Erbauer einer neuen Musikkultur" (1931), in *Musik und Politik: Schriften 1924–1948,* ed. Günter Mayer (Leipzig: VEB Deutscher Verlag für Musik, 1973), 140–167. See also Wind [Blaukopf], *Die Endkrise der bürgerlichen Musik,* 23–26. Although it does not directly address the symphony, Ernst Křenek's "Von der Würde der Abendländischen Musik" (1936) touches on related topics. This essay is reprinted in his *Zur Sprache gebracht: Essays über Musik* (Munich: Albert Langen and Georg Müller, 1958), 200–208.

tern of decline that had informed much late nineteenth-century commentary on the symphony.

In 1961, Adorno similarly observed that Mahler's monumentality "expresses his refusal to accept an intimacy that had . . . become the particular refuge of the most sophisticated composers such as Brahms," a monumentality "problematic in a society built on individualism."[90] Writing in this vein himself, Bekker had drawn on a by-now-familiar opposition, noting the Romantic symphonists' estrangement from the impulse to monumentality evident in Beethoven's symphonies. He dwelt on this above all in his treatment of Brahms, revisiting the perennial topos of Brahms as composer of chamber music, "a domain to which his symphonies also belong." Whereas certain inner movements of his symphonies count as chamber music pure and simple, in others Brahms attempts to "monumentalize" chamber music (40–41). Bekker's observations accord with reception of the symphonies over a century, extending to writers such as Schmidt and beyond.[91] The persistence of the ideas suggests that Brahms's apparent attitude toward the genre should be taken into account, even if no conclusions about his conscious intentions are possible.

It might be possible to analyze his symphonies more closely from a perspective conditioned by the aesthetic that emerges in the remarks of Bekker and other critics, which is based on essentialist yet at the same time coherent ideas. One could, for example, consider the form of a movement with respect to its organization, or nonorganization, around a series of *Steigerungen*—or overall *Steigerung*—instead of or in conjunction with considering its connection to a standard large-scale schema.[92] The inconsistency with which Brahms adhered to this and other expectations of symphonies manifestly frustrated many critics.

While the question of whether he deliberately composed against the grain of the genre cannot be answered, the perception that he did so—deliberately or not— underlies a prominent strand of Brahms reception. As Adorno observed, "no doubt in Brahms the private sphere displaces what one could call the real public character of music as the basis of expression." This observation is obviously more pertinent to his symphonies than his works in other genres. Adorno added: "But in his period the public character itself was socially no longer real, itself still more ideology, and it had something of that throughout the entire history of the middle class."[93] Once again, a sense of the lateness of Brahms's time comes through. Illusions about the efficacy of the public sphere had not been sustainable; the idealism of Beethoven's period had long sense faded. Bekker was right. Brahms did not compose for the audience that Beethoven had envisioned.[94]

---

90. Adorno, "Mahler," in *Quasi una Fantasia*, 89, translation modified slightly.

91. *Brahms und seine Zeit*, 89.

92. Ernst Kurth used this approach in *Bruckner*, 2 vols. (Berlin: Max Hesse, 1925).

93. *Einleitung in die Musiksoziologie*, 82.

94. Dahlhaus makes a similar point in *Nineteenth-Century Music*, 269.

CHAPTER 6

ADAGIOS IN BRAHMS'S LATE
CHAMBER MUSIC:
GENRE AESTHETICS AND
CULTURAL CRITIQUE

From a letter Brahms wrote to Clara Schumann in 1855, a comment on the Adagio espressivo of Robert Schumann's Symphony in C Major: "Only a German can compose such an adagio."[1]

From a letter von Bülow wrote in 1882 to his fiancée, Marie Schanzer, in remarks about Brahms: "I believe that the heart of no musician in the world . . . feels as deeply, has plunged itself so profoundly into the depths of his spirit as mine. Ah, his adagios! Religion!"[2]

From a multipart article Pohl wrote in 1890 on the history of chamber music: "We no longer have adagio profundity."[3]

From a 1939 fragment from Adorno's posthumously published monograph on Beethoven: "Beethoven's apparent asceticism towards subjective, spontaneous inspiration is precisely the way to elude reification. Beethoven, the master of positive negation: discard, that you may acquire. The shrinkage of the Beethovenian adagio is to be seen in this context. . . . Beethoven recognizes the incompatibility of the 'theme,' as a melody sufficient in itself, with the grand design. The mature Brahms had a very sensitive ear for this critical moment in Beethoven."[4]

By the late nineteenth century, adagios occasioned comments with far-reaching implications, with Schumann's adagio affirming the superiority of German culture for the young Brahms and von Bülow associating the adagios of the older Brahms with religion. (It was von Bülow who reportedly requested the burning of incense when he conducted the Adagio of Beethoven's Ninth four years later.) As a type, adagios could serve as a touchstone for the spiritual condition of the milieu in which they had been composed: toward the century's end, Pohl pessimistically linked deterioration in the adagio to a general falling-off. In music, the perceptions

---

1. *Clara Schuman-Johannes Brahms Briefe aus den Jahren 1853–1896,* ed. Berthold Litzmann, 2 vols. (Leipzig: Breitkopf und Härtel, 1927), 1:160, 8 December 1855.

2. *Hans von Bülow: Briefe und Schriften,* 6:176, 23 May 1882.

3. "Die Kammermusik der letzten drei Jahrhunderte," *Neue Zeitschrift für Musik* 86 (1890): 541.

4. *Beethoven,* 39–40.

of decline prominent in public discourse at the time often turned on matters of genre, and well before the *fin de siècle,* the adagio had become a point of reference in discussions of cultural questions.

Slow movements had not always occupied such a critical position. In practical terms, it was the increased valorization and more frequent performances of Beethoven's later string quartets, especially after midcentury, that accelerated the adagio's rise in status. Helm wrote of a "radical transformation in the public's attitude toward Beethoven," which he attributed in part to the failed revolutions in Europe.[5] In his words, "after the earthshaking political storms a certain fatigue and disillusionment set in, even in artistic matters, followed by a period of calm." Composers were uncertain of the direction in which (nonprogrammatic) instrumental music should go. In that time of retrenchment, the musical masterworks of the past gained in importance, a trend abetted by the many inexpensive scores that became available then. Helm also noted that instrumental technique had greatly improved in the second third of the nineteenth century, which finally made possible adequate performances of Beethoven's more difficult string quartets.[6] These events and tendencies fostered the creation of a canonic repertory of chamber music with his late quartets and adagios at the top, setting the standard for other composers.

In an 1868 survey of Robert Volkmann's music, Louis Ehlert noted the peripheral position of the post-Classical string quartet and the special difficulty of writing an adagio after Beethoven. About Volkmann's six quartets he observed that the "principal weakness lies in the slow movements. Volkmann cannot write an adagio in the strictest Beethovenian sense. But who can do so after Beethoven, except perhaps Schumann?" After asking whether even Schumann had been equal to this task, Ehlert turned to Mendelssohn, who, he concluded, "never wrote an adagio but only andantes. As strange as it may sound, there is an essential difference between the two." He then articulated what he saw as the specific technical challenge posed by an adagio: "The more slowly a theme is performed, the weightier, the more substantial and coherent, the more irreproachable and altogether better it must be. Post-Beethovenian themes do not bear such close scrutiny." Ehlert went on to explain his understanding of the contrasting expectations of an adagio and an andante:

> Just as we demand from tragedy different proportions, different actions, and a different scope than from comedy, so do we require of an adagio greater depth, grander proportions, and a broader outlook than of an andante. This, it must be said, does not call forth and resolve a conflict, but rather is simply a "Lied," an instrumental song.[7]

Because ideally it conveyed an atmosphere of intense significance, the adagio could become a symbol of artistic or spiritual quality or, by further extension, an expression of a national essence, as the opening quotation from the young Brahms

---

5. *Beethoven's Streichquartette,* 309.

6. *Beethoven's Streichquartette,* 317.

7. "Robert Volkmann: Ein Portrait," *Allgemeine Musikalische Zeitung* 56 (1868): 308–309. This journal has a complicated history. Volumes 1–50 appeared in 1798–1848, a second series in 1863–65, and a third series in 1866–81. In its third incarnation, the journal was briefly called "Leipziger Allgemeine Musikalische Zeitung." To simplify matters, I shall follow the practice of numbering the three series continuously and always referring to the journal by the simpler title.

suggests. In a history of chamber music that appeared in 1885, three decades after Brahms made his remark, Ludwig Nohl went so far as to assert that "nothing is more a product of the German way than [the] adagio." Evoking the cultural high point of Viennese Classicism, Nohl wrote of the "full awakening of inwardness" in the late eighteenth century, which had resulted in the adagio's coming "almost to seem richer than the entire rest of the [multimovement] form." Dwelling on the requisite soulfulness with a remark that "the complete mastery of musical technique could be evident and everything still seem empty," he again casually claimed a central European repertory as essentially German and made the stature of the adagio utterly clear. When a composer grasped the purpose established by Haydn and fulfilled by Mozart and Beethoven, "the adagio in German sonata forms belongs to that which is most beautiful not merely in music but in art altogether."[8]

For Nohl and other acolytes of Wagner, chamber music had peaked and in effect ended with Beethoven's late string quartets. Hence while he devoted considerable space in his *Evolution of Chamber Music* to the build-up toward the Classical climax, he treated chamber music by Schubert and Schumann together in one sentence. Mendelssohn merited only passing notice, and Brahms (along with any number of lesser known post-Classical composers) he ignored altogether.[9] Yet Ehlert, who otherwise had little in common with the Wagnerian or so-called futurist camp, also wrote about deterioration in the post-Classical string quartet, with particular attention to adagios after Beethoven.

Slow movements as such have received little attention in recent music criticism, but it appears that the adagio should hold a more important position in musicological accounts of late nineteenth-century intellectual history. In 1852, the cultural historian Wilhelm Riehl called the point in the previous century at which "we acquired an ear for the adagio" an "epoch-making" moment: before then, musicians had risked boring listeners with a "slow, mournfully serious musical work dying away in quiet passion."[10] By the late nineteenth century, audiences had long since learned to listen to adagios. Ehlert's remarks suggest, however, that because adagios posed severe demands with respect to the intertwining factors of expressive level and thematic integrity, they had become a challenge for composers. Evidence in letters and other documents makes it clear that Brahms recognized the problem. According to one frequently cited anecdote, after perusing a slow movement by Jenner, who would become his student, Brahms told him: "such a long adagio is the most difficult thing of all."[11]

Brahms's works display the different solutions he found as he moved his attention from one group of genres to another.[12] Adagios from his "first maturity" show

---

8. *Die geschichtliche Entwickelung der Kammermusik und ihre Bedeutung für den Musiker* (Braunschweig: Friedrich Vieweg und Söhne, 1885), 59.

9. *Die geschichtliche Entwickelung der Kammermusik,* 59. Nohl mentions Schubert and Schumann on p. 135 and the reception of Haydn by Schubert and Mendelssohn on p. 79.

10. "Das musikalische Ohr" (1852), in *Culturstudien aus drei Jahrhunderten* (Stuttgart: J. G. Cotta, 1859), 95–97.

11. *Brahms als Mensch,* 7.

12. See the appendix for a list of Brahms's slow movements with their tempo markings and years of completion.

the expansiveness and other Schubert-inspired features of that period in his career, while those in the C Minor String Quartet are in line with the drastic alterations in style produced by his struggles with that genre.[13] But the slow tempo of the adagio presented its own technical problems, of continuity and thematic coherence, as did the high standards that Beethoven established. After his first maturity, Brahms did not engage as consistently with the more difficult type of slow movement again until the late 1880s.

In the one adagio from the three chamber works first performed in the 1886–87 season, the Adagio affettuoso of the F Major Cello Sonata, Brahms used the subtleties of tonal/harmonic definition that are most noticeable in his later music to solve the crucial problem of melodic continuity. But, in a striking pattern, he turned to the resources of Gypsy performance practices in the late movements that bear the closest resemblance to Ehlert's description and at the same time best satisfied audience expectations of the adagio. Emulating the emotive low style of Gypsy instrumentalists allowed the older Brahms to compose in a more "expressive" manner that paradoxically also conveyed a more pronounced atmosphere of loftiness than did other approaches. In these adagios, he may appear to have appropriated the music of a subaltern culture. Taken into consideration along with the reticence toward melodic invention that Adorno noted, Brahms's introduction of this performance style into the high, and in some minds quintessentially German, type of the adagio raises complicated questions of meaning, of possible interpretation as an act at once of cultural critique and cultural appropriation. But it was, most basically, the transformation of what had been a tempo designation into a multifaceted genre that invites inquiry into Brahms's changing approaches and interpretation of his final adagios.

THE ADAGIO AS A GENRE

The importance of adagios in Austro-German music from the late nineteenth and early twentieth centuries should be self-evident, given their centrality in that repertory, which is even more obvious in the symphonies of Bruckner and Mahler than in Brahms's chamber music. Yet modern scholars have paid little attention to slow movements as such. Until recently, the few musicologists who treated this repertory rarely differentiated between andantes and adagios (as was also true of many nineteenth-century writers); often they did not even acknowledge distinctions between slow movements and fast types. Following customary practice, scholars instead focused their efforts on classifying slow movements according to formal patterns— ABA, sonata form with or without development, theme and variations, rondo—and creative deviations from these. Many late nineteenth-century musicians, however, clearly regarded such a movement less as an example of, say, a modified sonata form in the tempo of an adagio than as an adagio in a modified sonata form. In other words, the features that characterized adagios took precedence over considerations of form common to various movement types: the adagio had become an elevated genre unto itself.

13. Tovey uses "Brahms's first maturity" in reference to the works from the late 1850s through the mid-1860s, in "Brahms's Chamber Music," in *The Main Stream of Music and Other Essays,* 243.

Slow movements had been a far less privileged type in the late eighteenth century. In a frequently cited discussion of the symphony from that time, Johann Georg Sulzer assigned to the outer allegros the "expressions of grandeur, passion, and the sublime" considered suitable for the symphonic genre as a whole. According to Sulzer, the "andante or largo movement that comes in between the first and last allegro movements does not have so determined a character." This inner slow movement "is often of pleasant, pathetic, or sad expression," though still in "a style that is appropriate to the dignity of the symphony."[14] As Dahlhaus notes, other late eighteenth-century writers played the "sublime" symphonic allegro off against the "sentimental" (not necessarily symphonic) adagio, an opposition that could be made to work to the advantage of either movement type, depending on the critic's perspective.[15] Thus the "soul-stirring adagio" became a favorite topos in German novels of the period: in the words of Ruth E. Müller, "the aesthetic symbol of melancholy soliloquy and sentimentally excessive feelings of love."[16]

With the canonization of the Classical repertory, the slow movement—and especially the adagio—acquired loftier connotations for many listeners. In 1859, Marx ignored any earlier implications of mere sentimentality and linked the slow movement more narrowly with introspection, declaring that after the act of assertive creation manifested in a first movement, the composer retreats in the second to ask, "Who am I?"[17] Several nineteenth-century critics went even further, to view the Classical slow movement as offering the purest musical expression of intimations of transcendence. Thus Hector Berlioz wrote in 1862 of the "otherworldliness" of Beethoven's adagios:

> There are no human passions, no more earthly images, no innocent songs, no tender whispering there; there no sparks of wit flash, no humor bubbles over . . . he stands exalted above humankind and has forgotten it! Removed from the earthly sphere, he hovers alone and peaceful in the ether.[18]

(Ehlert, in contrast, emphasized conflict and resolution, attributes of many adagios but certainly not others, including that from Beethoven's Ninth.) In a related vein, Dvořák composed an "Andante religioso" for string quartet in 1870;[19] while Wagner's apostle Heinrich Porges asserted in 1872 that "almost every adagio by Beethoven"

14. *Aesthetics and the Art of Musical Composition in the German Enlightenment: Selected Writings of Johann Georg Sulzer and Heinrich Christoph Koch,* ed. Nancy Kovaleff Baker and Thomas Christensen (New York: Cambridge University Press, 1995), 107.

15. *The Idea of Absolute Music,* trans. Roger Lustig (Chicago: University of Chicago Press, 1989), 58–64.

16. *Erzählte Töne: Studien zur Musikästhetik im späten 18. Jahrhundert,* Beihefte zum Archiv für Musikwissenschaft 30 (Stuttgart: Steiner Verlag Wiesbaden, 1989), 52. I thank Jane Stevens for calling my attention to this monograph.

17. *Ludwig van Beethoven: Leben und Schaffen,* 2 vols. in 1 (1859; reprint, Hildesheim: Olms, 1979), 1:124.

18. Pohl cited Berlioz thus in "Die Kammermusik der letzten drei Jahrhunderte," 541, after having said that "no one has more beautifully conveyed the characteristic quality of the Beethovenian adagio than Berlioz." The passage Pohl quotes is from Berlioz, "Einige Worte über die Trio's und Sonaten von Beethoven," *Gesammelte Schriften,* trans. Richard Pohl, 4 vols. in 2 (Leipzig: Gustav Heinze, 1864), 1:72.

19. On this movement, see Hartmut Schick, *Studien zu Dvořáks Streichquartetten* (Laaber: Laaber-Verlag, 1990), 102–108.

could support Schopenhauer's claims about the "profound relationship between philosophy and music."[20] Drawing on the distinction between the sublime and the beautiful made by Schopenhauer (and others before him)—and with Hanslick's "musically beautiful" as a target—another Wagnerite, Arthur Seidl, in 1887 cited the Adagio of Beethoven's Ninth Symphony as his central example of the "musical sublime."[21]

As nineteenth-century writers indicated, the great Classical composers themselves had turned the slow movement from a humble into perhaps the highest movement type. Through what technical means did they accomplish this transformation? The logical first step in addressing this question is to probe the features that initially made slow movements seem a lesser type than first movements. Late eighteenth-century music theorists associated expressions of the serious and the sublime with certain kinds of melodic writing. Koch, for example, quoted Sulzer's distinction between the quality of expression in the outer allegros and inner slow movement of the symphony and then located "the most important external difference" between them in characteristic approaches to phrase-structure. In a slow movement, "melodic ideas are less extended and not so often compounded; thus more formal phrase-endings are used than in the allegro."[22]

But many later musicians took the opposite position, focusing on the *less confined* approach to phrase-structure in certain Classical adagios that had expanded the expressive range of slow movements and made them centrally important. After Wagner introduced the phrase *unendliche Melodie* in 1860, some musicians found that that concept conveyed their experience of the adagio: both as an emotional and spiritual revelation—the latter potentially equivalent to the former—and as a type whose forms were subordinate to a more fundamental melodic ideal.[23] Within the Germanic tradition, this conviction lasted well into the twentieth century. Ernst Kurth, for example, evinces little enthusiasm for most late eighteenth-century music, the symmetrical forms and frequent cadences of which he links to its secular orientation. But in a brief survey of the precursors of unending melody in 1923, he suggests that the melodic style of Classical music approaches endlessness "in some adagio movements of Haydn, Mozart, and Beethoven, thus, characteristically, where the expressive purpose rises above emphasis on sensuousness and earthly power into the spiritual."[24]

For Kurth, conceiving the adagio as a genre clearly supersedes traditional questions of form. In 1925 he made this explicit: the expressive impulse that had moti-

---

20. *Die Aufführung von Beethoven's Neunter Symphonie unter Richard Wagner in Bayreuth (22. Mai 1872)* (Leipzig: C. F. Kahnt, 1872), 19.

21. Arthur Schopenhauer, "Das ästhetische Wohlgefallen: Das Schöne und das Erhabene," in *Arthur Schopenhauer: Schriften über Musik*, ed. Karl Stabenow (Regensburg: Bosse, 1922), 77–89; and Arthur Seidl, *Vom Musikalisch-Erhabenen: Prolegomena zur Aesthetik der Tonkunst* (Leipzig: C. F. Kahnt Nachfolger, 1887).

22. *Introductory Essay on Composition,* 201. Johann Philipp Kirnberger had also noted that "short phrases are best suited for gentle, tender, agreeable, and particularly for fleeting, frivolous, and playful pieces. But long phrases are suited for emphatic and very serious sentiments, particularly for the expression of something quite pathetic." *The Art of Strict Musical Composition,* trans. David Beach and Jurgen Thym (New Haven: Yale University Press, 1982), 416.

23. Wagner, "Zukunftsmusik," in *Gesammelte Schriften,* 7:127.

24. *Romantische Harmonik und ihre Krise in Wagners "Tristan"* (2nd ed., 1923; reprint, Hildesheim: Olms, 1968), 448. The other forerunners included operatic recitative, instrumental cadenzas, and certain works

vated the quasi-unending melody of many Classical adagios also lay behind their idiosyncratic shapes, which "above all in later Beethoven do not allow exact derivation from any one of the fixed formal types. . . . Just as Classical composers, generally speaking, sought the greatest elevation above the earthly in the adagio, so also do their forms soar furthest beyond the fixed outlines there."[25] Beyond this oblique hint of a connection between Wagner's phrase techniques and the formal freedom of some Classical slow movements, Kurth offers no elucidation of what *unendliche Melodie* might mean in an adagio. These observations imply, however, that in the highest kind of adagios, melodic process often overrides points of structural articulation. Both on the level of the phrase and more extended formal levels, a freely unfolding melodic process should determine the overall shape, possibly by distorting "one of the fixed formal types."[26] Unlike the sonata allegro of first movements or the symmetrically grouped binary forms of the minuet/scherzo plus trio, no single form was ever associated with slow movements. In the adagios Kurth has in mind, the general concept of overcoming normative barriers through thematic generation may be more important than the particular norms of any one formal type.

The Cavatina (Adagio molto espressivo) from Beethoven's String Quartet in B-flat (Op. 130) illustrates such "proto-Wagnerian" techniques in a (late) Classical slow movement. Despite the prestige of the Cavatina, critics have tended toward excessive casualness in describing its melodic structure. Dahlhaus, for one, refers to the "first subject" as "an eight-bar 'period,' the simplicity and regularity of which is unaffected by a one-bar introduction and the repetition of the last bar" (see ex. 6.1a).[27] But is it really possible to divide mm. 2–9 into the symmetrical, cadentially articulated antecedent and consequent implied by "eight-bar period"? Beethoven almost consistently undercuts strong cadential progressions, even in m. 8, where the dominant chord moves to its first inversion before resolving in m. 9;[28] the composite line created by the intertwining of the two violins further ensures the melody's continuity.

And musicologists routinely write of a "second subject" (mm. 23 and following) in the Cavatina, even though this emerges from the preceding *Fortspinnung*. Since it enters at the moment of an "evaded" cadence ($V-I_6$),[29] moreover, most likely it gains the aural status of a separate theme only retrospectively, when it is repeated (mm. 32–39).[30] This second thematic statement does not quite finish, for the extraordinary *beklemmt* vision or memory interrupts it in m. 40. Daniel Chua characterizes

---

by Chopin. In these Kurth noted only technical features of *unendliche Melodie,* not its implications of music as revelation, 448–449.

25. *Bruckner,* 1:497.

26. "Theme" refers here to a discrete melodic unit, while "melody" refers more generally to the treble line of a large formal section or entire movement. "Thematic process" likewise refers to manipulation of the smaller unit, while "melodic process" refers to ongoing events in the treble line, which may encompass all of a movement.

27. *Beethoven,* 234.

28. Caplin calls this an "abandoned cadence" in *Classical Form,* 106–107.

29. Caplin, *Classical Form,* 101–106.

30. Furthermore, in a review of the book by Dahlhaus cited in n. 27, John Daverio suggests that this theme "promises to unfold as a variation of the opening idea, only to head off in another direction." See "Dahlhaus's Beethoven and the Esoteric Aesthetics of the Early Nineteenth Century," *Beethoven Forum* 2 (1993): 202.

EXAMPLE 6.1a.   Beethoven, B-flat String Quartet, Op. 130, Cavatina, mm. 1–9

this "excursion into a different world" as a "structural dislocation in which the centre does not connect up with the rest of the song."[31] For although this overt representation of emotional anguish—through melodic gestures borrowed from accompanied recitative—implies A-flat minor, it never cadences, nor does a dominant chord appear to indicate the impending return of the E-flat major opening theme. (See ex. 6.1b.) The expressive "dislocation" is undeniable. Beethoven's

31. *The "Galitizin" Quartets of Beethoven: Opp. 127, 132, 130* (Princeton, N.J.: Princeton University Press, 1995), 193.

EXAMPLE 6.1b.   Beethoven, B-flat String Quartet, Op. 130, Cavatina, mm. 47–50

choice of motivic/linear connections rather than a normatively clear harmonic articulation, however, does allow the sections to join smoothly in a "distinctly asymmetrical" adagio, as John Daverio puts it, that is "at once an affirmation and a denial of a simple ABA song form."[32] The irregularities of phrase-formation carry over into the large-scale shape; Kurth's observations about *unendliche Melodie* and formal liberties have a bearing on each other here. But which feature is prior to the other?

Kurth's twentieth-century idealization of the slow movement represents a late phase in a broader nineteenth-century cult of Classicism. The deepening of the adagio, for example, serves as a unifying topic in Helm's widely disseminated survey of Beethoven's string quartets, which appeared first in the *Musikalisches Wochenblatt* as a series that ran from 3 October 1873 through 21 September 1882. In the book version—in which Helm added an introductory discussion of Haydn and Mozart and an epilogue, "The String Quartet after Beethoven"—this concern emerged with even greater clarity, for the new chapters show an extraordinary focus on the adagio before and, especially, after Beethoven.[33] Regarding Beethoven himself, Helm writes that already in the first quartet of Op. 18 the slow movement "is longer than any quartet adagios by Mozart and many by Haydn" and calls it "a peculiarity of Beethoven to make the slow movement the crux of a composition" (10). Returning repeatedly to this topos, Helm spins a narrative of inevitability within Beethoven's spiritual/artistic development that culminates in the final slow movement, that of the F Major Quartet, Op. 135 (295). Although Beethoven marked his last slow movement "Lento assai, cantante et tranquillo," Helm calls it an "adagio." At least as Helm conceives it, the Classical adagio is a genre that could take

32. "Dahlhaus's Beethoven," 202.

33. A second edition of Helm's book appeared in 1910 and a third in 1921. Page references in the text are to the first edition.

precedence over literal instructions of tempo, as well as questions of both form and medium. Along similar lines, while current musicians would most likely refer to the opening movement of the C-sharp Minor Quartet, Op. 131, as a fugue, for Helm—here following Wagner himself—it is an adagio, which apparently only incidentally displays the characteristic opening moves and pervasive imitative texture of a fugue (223–224).[34] Once again a musician prioritizes concerns of tempo and melodic style over seemingly less significant generic or formal references. At several points, Helm draws slow movements outside the string quartet repertory into the discussion, grouping the variations of the E-flat Quartet, Op. 127, with the sonata-form Adagio sostenuto of the *Hammerclavier* Sonata, the Benedictus of the *Missa Solemnis,* and the double variations of the Ninth Symphony (163). All these movements presumably exemplify the late Beethoven adagio, for many Wagnerites the final stage in the development of the genre and of *unendliche Melodie* within it.

Regarding the Cavatina, Helm writes: "from the timid beginning to the softly fading final chord [it] constitutes a single unending melody in which there are no merely formal connecting links, no so-called passages; rather, everything appears without exception as most tenderly eloquent song" (124). This conviction—the view that every moment within an adagio had to be "song" (significant lyrical and motivic process)—also emerges in his description of the Adagio from the E-flat Quartet, Op. 74. Helm observes:

> Here there are no longer filling-out or transitional passages in the older sense, everything sings (or speaks) much more, every measure, every note. An opening and a secondary theme and then a middle section are quite graphically distinguishable. . . . But these themes fall into such long-breathed, broad periods, and their development is in so continuous a flow dominated by one impulse that no measure could be removed without damaging the sense of the whole. (127)

This adagio's "unending melody" comes about through the breadth and expressive coherence of its three themes and the rhetorically truncated restatements (mm. 102–113, 138–168) between them and at the end that guarantee continuous meaningfulness.

Already in 1866, Hermann Deiters had co-opted Wagner's phrase for a favorable review of the Andante, un poco Adagio of Brahms's F Minor Piano Quintet. Calling its first section (mm. 1–23) "really just one long, broadly elaborated period," Deiters admires the varied punctuation and contours of the four-bar phrases and the way the limited motivic material "expands in luxuriating gracefulness like an unending melody (here one could use this expression)."[35] He probably added the parenthetical comment to emphasize that he viewed this expansive yet symmetrically articulated section as a melody, for musicians had often questioned whether "unending melody" is melody at all.[36]

Even before Wagner provided a label in "Zukunftsmusik," critics complained about extended, supposedly obscure phrase-structures in Beethoven's late quartets and their

---

34. In 1854 Wagner wrote a programmatic interpretation of the C-sharp Minor Quartet, which he later incorporated into the centenary essay "Beethoven" of 1870, *Gesammelte Schriften,* 9:61–126.

35. *Allgemeine Musikalische Zeitung* 54 (1866): 142.

36. Thomas S. Grey, *Wagner's Musical Prose: Texts and Contexts* (New York: Cambridge University Press, 1995), 242–257.

deleterious effects on contemporary composers.[37] Thus, in 1853, an anonymous Viennese journalist, after praising the warmth and depth of feeling in the Adagio non troppo from Mendelssohn's E-flat String Quartet (Op. 44, No. 3), criticized the movement for lacking "any rhythmic articulation, any caesura in the melodic line." This he called a style "unfortunately quite popular with more recent composers, Beethoven having led the way in his final quartets."[38] Whether musicians approved of *unendliche Melodie* or not, the phrase had a resonant aptness with respect to slow movements in which "melody," broadly conceived, is most obviously the point.

EARLY SIGNS OF DECLINE: AN
ADAGIO BY VOLKMANN

As the Viennese journalist observed, Beethoven's late string quartets had already begun to have an impact on composers by 1853. In composing an adagio, it was no doubt easier to imitate outer features of Beethoven's late style, such as the lack of any "caesura in the melodic line," than create melodic material as compelling as that in his late adagios. In the 1868 study of Volkmann, Ehlert writes: "most motives that give the greatest pleasure" in an andante, the less difficult kind of slow movement, "would create an impression of openwork [*von durchbrochener Werk*] if we heard them in the tempo of an adagio."[39] The slower tempo makes the perception of a disturbing lapse in continuity more likely.

After discussing the problem of the post-Beethovenian adagio, Ehlert surveyed Volkmann's quartets, starting with his A Minor Quartet, Op. 9. He directed some of the strongest criticism in his overview at the Adagio of Op. 9 (composed in 1847, published in 1854), which, he noted accurately, "attempts to strike a deeper note" than the preceding Allegro "and move in the Beethovenian sphere of sentiment." Although he did not mention Volkmann's particular debt to the late quartets, this is indisputable. Volkmann replicates the keys in Beethoven's Op. 132 by placing the quartet as a whole in A minor and the Adagio in F major; more significant, he models the slow movement on the Op. 130 Cavatina. Like the Cavatina, Volkmann's Adagio opens and closes with a lovely, serene melody. Ehlert found fault not with this melody but rather with the movement's interior. In contrast to the Cavatina's brief "expressive dislocation," the center of Volkmann's Adagio consists of two extended episodes that at times simulate accompanied recitative. About the first episode, Ehlert wrote: "The first violin plays figuration with strong emotional import against the quiet progressions of the lower voices and expresses its excitement through an almost overly exaggerated mixture of the most varied note values." (See ex. 6.2.) This "breaks off with passionate abruptness in order to make way for a second episode that maintains the recitative character and leads rhapsodically back to the opening theme." His conclusion, that the Adagio "has many isolated fine points but does not cohere as a true whole," seems fair.[40]

---

37. Grey, *Wagner's Musical Prose*, 112–113. Although Wagner himself only belatedly came to appreciate Beethoven's last works, other composers did so much more quickly.

38. *Neue Wiener Musik-Zeitung* 2 (1853): 200.

39. "Volkmann," 309.

40. "Volkmann," 309.

EXAMPLE 6.2.   Volkmann, A Minor String Quartet, Op. 9, Adagio molto, mm. 52–58

Ehlert's critique of Volkmann's Adagio focused on the disjointed rhythms in the middle and an overall air of disunity. While he saw the problems in post-Beethovenian adagios as problems of melody, like other critics, he found it difficult to address the quality of a melody as such.[41] Twenty-five years later, the Adagio of Volkmann's Op. 9 prompted another discussion about melody, this time a private conversation between Brahms and his friend Billroth, which Billroth recorded immediately after the fact. For the most part, it should be noted, Billroth concurred with Hanslick's dislike of Beethoven's late music. In an 1888 letter to Hanslick, he writes that for him "the musically beautiful comes to an end" in the final quartets. Billroth did, however, refer to four of the late movements as "wonderfully beautiful," and three of these are adagios: the theme of the C Minor Piano Sonata's Arietta, Op. 111/II, the *Hammerclavier* Sonata's Adagio, and the Ninth's Adagio. (His other exception is the first movement of Op. 111.)[42]

After hearing a performance of Volkmann's quartet in 1892, Billroth reminded Brahms in a letter of an earlier conversation. Billroth had asserted the impossibility of defining "melody" and even less "why a melody is beautiful or not, rich or empty, boring or interesting," an opinion that Brahms by no means shared. Billroth wrote of his dissatisfaction with Volkmann's slow movement: "The Adagio, though made completely in the broad Beethovenian style, did not really please me, soon became boring. But why?" Brahms visited his friend three days later to explain "the signs of the 'beauty' of a melody."[43]

Sarabandes by Bach served as his exemplar of melodic beauty. In his explication, Brahms apparently ignored weaknesses in Volkmann's Adagio and chose instead to talk about the strengths of Bach's sarabandes, for the most part focusing on fine points in the voice-leading and treatment of cadences. He prefaced his musical analysis with a discussion of Goethe's short poem "Über allen Gipfeln." According to Billroth, Brahms analyzed this "in the most interesting way," speaking first about the poem's sustained mood and semantic integration and then about its many subtle technical details: "The beautiful cadences . . . the beautiful interruption of the meter . . . the beauty of the rhymes, the 'breath [*Hauch*]' that lies over the whole: *no word could be changed without destroying it.* The simplicity and conciseness of the whole. A beautiful adagio in the form of a poem."[44] Goethe's poem a beautiful adagio: utter perfection.

Brahms did not directly answer Billroth's question about melody. Like Ehlert, he spoke about coherence. Yet it is not difficult to point out some of the problems. For one, the basic theme in Volkmann's first episode is uninteresting, especially at the tempo of an adagio (see the viola and then the first violin in ex. 6.2); for another, the second episode includes too many portentous pauses, likewise difficult to make effective at that tempo. As when he studied the question of parallel fifths, Brahms

41. Ruth A. Solie pinpointed this problem more than two decades ago in her dissertation, "Metaphor and Model in the Analysis of Melody" (Ph.D. diss., University of Chicago, 1977).

42. Eduard Hanslick, *Aus meinem Leben,* 2 vols. (Berlin: Allgemeiner Verein für Deutsche Litteratur, 1894), 2:339–340, letter of 31 July 1888.

43. *Billroth-Brahms Briefwechsel,* 473–474, letter of 16 November 1893.

44. *Billroth-Brahms Briefwechsel,* 475–476, from notes dated 19 November 1893.

preferred to focus on what he admired, in this case, sarabandes by Bach and a poem by Goethe.

BRAHMS AND THE ADAGIO
BEFORE THE 1880s

The opinion Ehlert voiced about the difficulties of composing an adagio seems to have represented a new attitude. In his *Musikalisches Lexikon* of 1802, Koch had devoted a great deal of space to the effective *performance* of an adagio. But in the second edition, which appeared in 1865, thoroughly revised by Dommer, much of the emphasis had shifted to the successful *composition* of an adagio (which Koch had not addressed at all). Dommer thus observed: "For the slow tempo, much more than a quick, throws into bolder relief any feature that either in itself is not sufficiently meaningful or does not suit the overall character of the composition. Furthermore, a slow movement easily becomes exaggeratedly broad, ponderous, and, if there is not a satisfying richness of ideas, very boring."[45] His cautionary observation that every feature in an adagio had to be meaningful and expressively suitable foreshadows Helm's description shortly thereafter (in the series that began in 1873) of "unending melody" in Beethoven's later adagios. But elsewhere in the dictionary, Dommer stressed that because of the slower tempo composers should use simpler and less extended phrase-structures than in other movement types, since otherwise they would risk the incomprehension of audiences.[46] It appears that the demands on the composer of an adagio were many and sometimes contradictory.

Brahms came of age as a composer in the first decade or so after the middle of the century, during approximately the same years in which the melodic style in Beethoven's late music became a topic of controversy and the Classical adagio seems to have achieved cult status. The young Brahms's letters from the second half of the 1850s mention adagios with surprising frequency. On 27 June 1855 he reported to Clara Schumann that the night before, Joachim's quartet had played five string quartets by Haydn, which he called "amazingly fine and accomplished, with an abundance of beautiful and original ideas, especially in the splendid adagios, that is incredible."[47] In December of the same year, he praised an adagio by her husband (in the letter quoted at the beginning of this chapter). At the conclusion of a letter to Joachim of 11 July 1857, Brahms wrote that he was enclosing an organ concerto (assumed to be) by Wilhelm Friedemann Bach "because of the beautiful Adagio."[48] In January of the same year, he had sent the Adagio of his D Minor Piano Concerto to Joachim with this expression of self-doubt: "If only I could finally take pleasure in a successful adagio!"[49] When he mailed the slow movement of the A

---

45. Koch, *Musikalisches Lexikon*, "Adagio," cols. 62–66; and Dommer, *Musikalisches Lexicon*, "Adagio," 20–21. See also Gülke's observations about the effect of a slow tempo on the listener, which I cite in chapter 3, notes 41 and 42.

46. Dommer, *Musikalisches Lexicon*, "Sonate I (die moderne), 2 (Zweiter Satz)," 785.

47. *Schumann Brahms Briefe*, 1:118–119.

48. *Brahms Briefwechsel*, 5:183. According to the *Neue Bach Ausgabe*, the concerto was J. S. Bach's arrangement of a Vivaldi violin concerto with a slow movement marked "Largo e spiccato."

49. *Brahms Briefwechsel*, 5:166.

Major Serenade to Clara Schumann on 10 September 1859, Brahms sounded tentatively proud of his work: "I look forward to hearing from you at last about the adagio for the new serenade."[50]

At the time, musicians did not distinguish consistently between adagios and andantes in writing and, of course, also indicated gradations between the two in compositions: Andante moderato, Andante un poco Adagio, Poco Adagio, Adagio non troppo.[51] Brahms himself sometimes altered markings for tempo and expression. For example, in the autograph for the slow movement of Op. 34b, the two-piano version of what had been a string quintet and would become the F Minor Piano Quintet (the piece admired by Deiters), he changed "Andante" to "Andante, un poco Adagio."[52] Still, it does not seem inconsequential that all of the passages from his letters just cited refer to adagios. For he appears to have been struggling with the demands of this more challenging kind of slow movement during the same years in which he was grappling with orchestration and other aspects of musical craft.[53] Between the late 1850s and the mid-1860s, he produced significantly more adagios than andantes, a higher proportion than during any comparable period before the late 1880s (see the appendix)—and those from the later period tend not to be "such long adagios" as those from the earlier years.

For his three, very early piano sonatas, Brahms had composed andantes, before essaying adagios for his first published chamber work, the "confused" B Major Piano Trio, and the next instrumental pieces, the D Minor Piano Concerto and the two serenades.[54] The adagios in the D Minor Concerto and the D Major Serenade are a major advance on the technically immature Piano Trio; those in the A Major Serenade, A Major Piano Quartet, and Horn Trio sound not only mature but also distinctly different from each other.[55] Musicologists have stressed Brahms's innovative approach to large-scale form in these slightly later adagios, in particular his blending of formal signs associated with sonata procedures on the one hand and ternary form on the other.[56] (Brahms composed the Adagio of the D Minor Concerto

50. *Schumann Brahms Briefe*, 1:277.

51. According to Dommer's *Musikalisches Lexicon*, 785, "adagio" was often used to refer to any slow movement. On the other hand, certain critics—e.g., "H—l." in the *Neue Wiener Musik-Zeitung*, which lasted from 1852 to 1860—persistently referred to "adagios" as "andantes."

52. The autograph of the Sonata for Two Pianos in F Minor, Op. 34b, is in the Pierpont Morgan Library, New York (Cary 4).

53. On this period in Brahms's development, see Webster, "Schubert's Sonata Form and Brahms's First Maturity (II)."

54. After Brahms had recomposed the trio in 1889, he wrote to Clara Schumann that it was "no longer as confused as it had been earlier." *Schumann Brahms Briefe*, 2:393, letter of 3 September 1889.

55. Brahms wrote "January 1854" at the end of the B Major Piano Trio's autograph. Brahms sent a slow movement for the D Major Serenade, scored at the time as a nonet, to Joachim in September 1858. Although Joachim refers to it as an andante, it was probably the Adagio non troppo, *Brahms Briefwechsel*, 5:207. Brahms rescored the work for orchestra in 1859. I am writing only about the adagios from this period here. When musicians made a distinction between the two, an adagio was considered a greater compositional challenge than an andante. And I do not write about the Adagio of Op. 36, a set of variations with tempo changes, though a comparison with the variations of Op. 18 (Andante, ma moderato) is suggestive.

56. Elaine Sisman, "Brahms's Slow Movements: Reinventing the 'Closed' Forms," in Bozarth, *Brahms Studies*, 99.

EXAMPLE 6.3a.   Brahms, A Major Piano Quartet, Op. 26 / II, mm. 1–2

as a straightforward ternary form, the Adagio non troppo of the A Major Serenade as a textbook sonata-form movement.)

But the adagio, above all, demanded a certain type of melody, and the technical problems nineteenth-century musicians mentioned, when they chose to be explicit, concerned themes and phrase-structure. This emphasis on melody raises the question of whether the large-scale formal novelty of these adagios was an end in itself. Instead, an aesthetic specific to slow movements like the one I have described, centering on the constant transcending of both small- and large-scale formal barriers, may have more basically motivated Brahms's choices. For what fundamentally distinguishes these three adagios from the earlier ones is a qualitative difference in melodic style.

It is unlikely that the forms in the A Major Serenade, A Major Piano Quartet, and Horn Trio would even have been possible with the themes from the D Minor Piano Concerto and D Major Serenade. The themes in the later adagios, to begin with, may well strike listeners as less conventional, more arresting. Consider, for example, the opening of the Poco Adagio from the A Major Piano Quartet, in which a heterophonic haze of eighth-notes in the muted strings surrounds a gracefully arched, asymmetrically phrased melody in the piano (see ex. 6.3a).

In these later adagios, furthermore, individual thematic statements do not last as long. This contrasts with Brahms's earlier approach in the D Minor Concerto and D Major Serenade, where he fashioned very expansive themes or thematically homogeneous sections, with cadential overlaps at their boundaries.[57] Such long-breathed

---

57. The reduction in instrumental forces, from the large orchestra of the Concerto and the D Major Serenade to the small orchestra of the A Major Serenade and then the chamber ensembles of the A Major Piano Quartet and Horn Trio, may also have been a factor in the stylistic change.

EXAMPLE 6.3b. Brahms, A Major Piano Quartet, Op. 26 / II, mm. 9–14

melody in an adagio, however, poses problems for the listener, above all the difficulty that Dommer noted of apprehending music at a slow tempo. In the later adagios, a move toward smaller constructive units as well as more vivid melodic materials helps solve the problem, even though the overall impression is of a single, broad melody.[58]

Another strategy common to the adagios of the A Major Serenade, A Major Piano Quartet, and Horn Trio involved devising a seemingly subsidiary motive or theme

58. A remark made by a much older Brahms to Heuberger implies this ideal, as well as the related tendency to think of form in a slow movement as melody. *Erinnerungen an Brahms,* 23, entry for 21 November 1883.

that underlies or joins statements of apparently more important thematic materials and also unobtrusively establishes a particular tone. Thus in the A Major Piano Quartet, the eighth-note motion continues even after the cadence in m. 10 and subsequent codettas in mm. 10–13, undercutting the effects of those gestures of completion (see ex. 6.3b).[59] Throughout most of this Poco Adagio, the persistent eighth-note figure is an agent of both flux and continuity—at times a subterranean presence, at other times more in the foreground—lingering between thematic statements, then rising and falling within them. In all three movements, each recurrence of such accompanimental or transitional figures helps create a characteristic atmosphere and at the same time has the important formal function of keeping the melodic impulse in motion, resisting full-stop closure.

Through this sort of figuration, Brahms was able not only to meet the requirement that an adagio be continuously meaningful but also to extend a movement such as the A Major Piano Quartet's Poco Adagio to the sublime Schubertian lengths he preferred in this period. His priorities as a composer changed in the years that followed. While he gave most of his attention to large choral and orchestral works after 1865, in 1873 he finally managed to complete a pair of string quartets he was willing to have published.[60] The style of these quartets, in particular the first, contrasts starkly with that of the earlier chamber music. Gone are the lush sound and expansive forms of the past. Because the string quartet genre apparently induced extreme self-consciousness in him about every note, these works, even their slow movements, sound constricted, especially in comparison with the chamber music from before.[61] Forgoing picturesque figuration and extended transitions, Brahms relied instead on tight motivic connections to create an illusion of continuity throughout the Romanze, Poco Adagio of the C Minor String Quartet. Thus a transformed version of a cadential figure prominent in the first section (mm. 1–26) becomes the head-motive in the central section (see ex. 6.4).

In this adagio and two that followed it (those of the Second Symphony and G Major Violin Sonata, completed in the late 1870s), the general ideal of musical logic seems to have held more sway over Brahms's choices than an aesthetic specific to the adagio. Brahms would have greater success, at least according to reviewers, when he began to cultivate the adagio more intensively again in the late 1880s. But critics would see a renewal of the genre earlier in the decade in works composed by his emerging rival, Bruckner.

LATER DECLINE AND BRUCKNER'S RENEWAL

In Vienna, the Hellmesberger Quartet played a significant role in the enthusiasm for late Beethoven and chamber music in general that was apparent from midcentury on. The ensemble performed Beethoven's late quartets in its first series of public concerts in 1849–50, and already in its second season played two still unpub-

---

59. For codettas, see Caplin, *Classical Form*, 16.

60. According to the opus number and evidence in the letters, Brahms seems to have completed the two string quartets of Op. 51 by 1869. He completed revisions in 1873.

61. I discuss this in "Discourse and Allusion," 255–256.

EXAMPLE 6.4.   Brahms, C Minor String Quartet, Op. 51, No. 1 / II, mm. 24–28

lished masterpieces by Schubert, the C Major String Quintet and the G Major String Quartet. Throughout the 1850s, the group devoted special attention to Mendelssohn, as it did from the mid-1850s through the mid-1860s to Schumann. Brahms's works began to appear on its programs in the 1860s, with performances of them steadily increasing in the 1870s and 1880s.[62]

Between midcentury and the 1880s and even more thereafter, the sheer number of public chamber-music performances rose dramatically as new ensembles were formed. In 1890, Hirschfeld wrote that frequent and fine performances of the "accumulated classical treasures" in the city allowed music lovers to judge new works with confidence, "for the best that music, that chamber music, has achieved up to now provides a standard." Recently composed works indeed appeared on almost every program played by the Hellmesberger Quartet and after 1883 by its great local rival, the Rosé Quartet.[63] Hirschfeld noted, however, an inverse relationship between audiences' increased discernment and the quality of the new music: "the weaker artistic production becomes in our time, the stronger audiences' enjoyment and understanding become."[64]

When Wolf expressed a similar opinion in an 1884 review, he approached it indirectly, beginning with a seemingly enthusiastic observation about Vienna's chamber-music scene: "We are very pleasantly moved by the zealous cultivation of chamber music and the public's lively interest in this type of music." A hint of the sarcasm typical of much of his writing surfaced in the next sentence: "Oddly enough, even our contemporary composers are producing their most bearable music in this genre." After making it clear that in any case he considered it easier to compose for

62. The Musiksammlung of the Österreichische Nationalbibliothek has a compilation of the Hellmesberger Quartet's first 300 programs, from 4 November 1849 to 19 December 1889.

63. For the programs see *Das Rosé Quartett: Fünfzig Jahre Kammermusik in Wien. Sämtliche Programme von 1. Quartett am 22. Januar 1883 bis April 1932,* with an introduction by Julius Korngold (Vienna, n.p., n.y.). In chapter 5, I note some other quartets resident in Vienna.

64. *Die Presse,* 12 January 1892.

a string quartet than an orchestra, he reached his point: "Skillful play with techniques rather than the need to express a musical idea leads our modern composers to write chamber music." Comparing the adagios of recent chamber music to the inevitable Beethovenian model, Wolf found these movements to have suffered the most from the lack of inspiration, labeling them "insipid, affected, labored."[65]

For many musicians, the successful premiere of Bruckner's String Quintet on 8 January 1885 marked the renewal of chamber music and the adagio they had hoped for. In his review, Kalbeck did develop at some length the sarcastic trope of *Offenbarungsmusik*, of revelation as Bruckner's supposed compositional approach, suggesting that he transcribed the whisperings of both an angel and a devil. But "Offenbarungsmusik" has another, more obvious meaning: music that makes a profound effect, whose impact can be likened to that of divine revelation. Kalbeck turned to this part of the linguistic figure when he discussed the slow movement, taking an image from Dante's *Divine Comedy:* "If the three previously mentioned movements belong to the *Inferno,* the Adagio nevertheless comes directly from the *Paradiso.* Pure light issues forth, light in a thousand colors and nuances—the reflected splendor of an ecstatic vision right into seventh heaven."[66] With the sudden change in tone from sarcasm to wonder, compositional logic, the foundation of the Brahmsian aesthetic, temporarily ceased to be an issue. To me and probably many other listeners, the Adagio sounds the most coherent and clearly directed of the Quintet's four movements, but Kalbeck did not choose to discuss it in those terms. What he offered instead was a rapturous image; he held the Adagio to a different standard.

How does the Adagio communicate the "ecstatic vision" Kalbeck described? Certainly, Bruckner stresses the meaningfulness of each successive event by expanding transitional sections to Schubertian lengths, as well as other means, such as the *portato* chords played *ppp* (mm. 35–36) that prepare the entrance of the second theme. The first theme, the less chromatic of the two, does not play a direct role in the movement's crisis. But its head-motive and that of the second theme invert each other, and Bruckner invests this shared feature, like other instances of motivic relationship and transformation, with an air of significance. Consider the stretto in mm. 77–82 that comes after a partial restatement of the first theme (see ex. 6.5). The entrances of the first theme's head-motive rise in pitch and dynamics until the second theme reenters, pianissimo, in m. 83. In the climactic development that follows, sudden dynamic extremes underscore the increasing chromatic mutation and rhythmic diminution of motives from the second theme, as the music rises to a level of "expressiveness" that demystifies Kalbeck's description.

And the movement as a whole creates the requisite illusion of *unendliche Melodie.* In a review of a Viennese performance, Helm connected the expansive phrase-structure and the effect of spiritual revelation to—what else?—late Beethoven: "What a rapturously heartfelt outpouring of feeling, flowing forth in one truly 'unending'

65. *Hugo Wolfs musikalische Kritiken,* ed. Richard Batka and Heinrich Werner (Leipzig: Breitkopf und Härtel, 1911), 10; translation modified from *The Music Criticism of Hugo Wolf,* 10. Despite his futurist orientation, Wolf by no means rejected all post-Classical chamber music, for he praised string quartets by Schumann and Mendelssohn and even some chamber works by Brahms.

66. *Die Presse,* 28 January 1885.

EXAMPLE 6.5.   Bruckner, String Quintet, Adagio, mm. 77–84

stream! This Adagio has approximately the same effect as if it were a newly discovered piece from Beethoven's estate, originating in the master's final period and animated by his full inspiration."[67] From Helm's perspective, Bruckner had reversed chamber music's long decline and revived the great tradition that had seemed to end with Beethoven's death.

In a glowing review of the Quintet, the Viennese critic Emil von Hartmann expressed a dim outlook on the general state of chamber music: "To be sure, even in recent times much chamber music has been written, but how little of it after all is

67. *Deutsche Zeitung,* 8 April 1884.

worthy of having been written. And even that which is good only reminds us that the golden age of this musical genre lies far in the past."[68] Since the premiere of Bruckner's Quintet virtually coincided with the publication of Nohl's history of chamber music, reception of the two overlapped. In a passage no doubt aimed at Brahms, Nohl had written that German chamber music did not have the same stature as German dramatic and lyric music because no towering genius was composing in that genre. Hanslick retaliated in his review of the new work:

> We can help Mr. Nohl: let him look at Bruckner's Quintet. There he will find the pure Wagnerian style distilled on five instruments. . . . What Mr. Nohl so painfully missed is found, and a second edition of his "Evolution of Chamber Music" can make the final chapter glisten in that transfiguration, without which, to be sure, evolution and chamber music would remain only "illusion" [*Wahn*].[69]

Seidl took up the dispute in the *Musikalisches Wochenblatt*. Attacking Hanslick's critical approach and praising Nohl's book, Seidl asserted the value of having chamber music "for once, and if we are not mistaken for the first time altogether, treated as a whole"—a "whole," however, that omitted most of the nineteenth century. Despite his claim that Nohl's neglect of Brahms was "striking although explainable in the end," Seidl offered no explanation. Instead, he concluded that it was worth considering whether a renewal of chamber music might be expected from Bruckner: "one has only to take up the splendid Adagio of this wonderful Quintet to recognize from what depth of feeling, what original and inexhaustible source it was created."[70]

An incident five years later shows the continuing symbolic power of Bruckner's Quintet. According to a notice that appeared in the Viennese papers, the Hellmesberger Quartet decided to substitute the Quintet for Brahms's B-flat Sextet because of "popular demand." At the end of a review, Kalbeck noted the circumstances for the change in program for the upcoming concert. The Hellmesberger Quartet made the decision immediately after a notice went out that the Rosé (not the Hellmesberger) Quartet would be giving the first performance of a new Brahms piece, the G Major String Quintet. And Kalbeck called Bruckner's Quintet "that strange work, abounding in repulsive as well as alluring ideas, which some years ago gave rise to violent debates."[71]

UNENDING MELODY AND THE
ADAGIO AFFETTUOSO OF THE
F MAJOR CELLO SONATA

Brahms apparently decided to compose the work that would become his F Major Cello Sonata about two months after the premiere of Bruckner's String Quintet. According to Kalbeck, Robert Hausmann's masterful public performance of the E Minor Cello Sonata in Vienna on 3 March 1885 convinced him to write the sec-

---

68. *Musikalische Rundschau* 1 (1885): 8. The first issue, in which this article appeared, is dated 20 September.

69. *Entwickelung der Kammermusik*, 137; and concert review, *Neue Freie Presse*, 26 February 1885.

70. *Musikalisches Wochenblatt* 16 (1885): 327.

71. *Montags-Revue*, 1 December 1890.

ond sonata that Hausmann had requested some time before.[72] But a singular feature also connects the F Major Cello Sonata, which Brahms completed in the summer of 1886, with Bruckner's String Quintet. In both F major works, the adagio slow movement is in a major key a semitone above: G-flat in the quintet, F-sharp in the sonata. While Bruckner used this key relationship in two symphonies as well, Brahms used it only this once.[73]

Comments by Brahms recorded in various sources demonstrate his vehement re-action to the attention Bruckner started to receive in the winter of 1884–85. Schenker offers the most directly relevant anecdote. The Viennese musician Richard Robert told Schenker that, while walking with Brahms, he had ventured to praise the beauty of the Adagio from Bruckner's Quintet only to receive this acerbic response: "Just look beyond the eighth measure!"[74] The intensity of Brahms's feelings about Bruckner's sudden, belated success, along with the apparent timing of his decision to compose a second cello sonata and the technical connection between the works, suggests that Brahms may well have had Bruckner's Adagio in mind when he con-ceived his own Adagio affettuoso.

Kalbeck brought up another possible factor: the E Minor Cello Sonata's dis-carded slow movement, a work composed during his first maturity some two decades before. According to Kalbeck, Brahms removed the adagio "because he didn't want to overload the work," and he speculated that Brahms may have recomposed it as the Adagio affettuoso, for this "arouses the feeling it is the soul of the work, which now had to fashion for itself its body."[75] Although the published version of the E Minor Cello Sonata is lopsided, an extraordinarily long Allegro non troppo followed by two brief movements, it is difficult to envision a version of the Adagio affettu-oso that would have improved the balance. Still, Brahms did decide finally to dispense with the adagio—whatever it may have been: because the E Minor Cello Sonata's autograph disappeared, we know almost nothing for certain about the adagio.[76]

If Brahms did revive and rework the earlier slow movement as the Adagio affet-tuoso, he no doubt transposed it to fit within the new sonata's key and shortened it in line with the higher value he placed on conciseness after the mid-1860s. Evi-dence in the F Major Cello Sonata's autograph lends some support to a hypothesis not only that Brahms composed the work around the Adagio affettuoso in F-sharp major but also that this may derive from a movement in F major.[77] In other words,

72. *Brahms*, 4:33.

73. The Adagio of the Third Symphony, in D minor, is in E-flat major; the Adagio of the Eighth Symphony, in C minor, is in D-flat major.

74. "Erinnerungen an Brahms," *Der Kunstwart* 46 (May 1933): 481. Heuberger records another story in *Erinnerungen an Brahms*, 151–152, entry for 19 January 1885.

75. *Brahms*, 4:33.

76. His known habits as a composer support the hypothesis that he kept the adagio and found a new use for it many years later. Thus he based the first motet of Op. 74 on the early, unpublished *Missa canonica* and the G Major String Quintet's middle movement on two dances from a suppressed suite for solo piano.

77. Contrary to his usual habits, he separated the bifolio on which he entered the movement from the rest of the manuscript. For a late manuscript by Brahms, the autograph of the cello sonata contains an unusually large number of revisions. The second movement stands out as almost clean, and the one significant revision suggests that it may derive from a movement in F. See my "Brahms's Cello Sonata in F Major and Its Genesis," 148–152.

he may have composed the original slow movement for the E Minor Cello Sonata also in the key a semitone above the tonic: like the decision to compose a second cello sonata, the choice of the adagio's key may have been overdetermined.

Both Bruckner and Brahms emphasize semitonal voice-leading and internal key relationships a semitone apart: these movements thus replicate the basic key relationship in "organic" details (as do many other nineteenth-century compositions).[78] Bruckner's Adagio, for example, moves through C-flat major (mm. 23–34) to arrive at B-flat major, the second theme's key; and the central section of Brahms's Adagio affettuoso, a movement in F-sharp, is notated as F minor. In other respects, the two adagios are distinct from each other. Since Brahms had tightened up his treatment of transitional passages long before he composed the F Major Cello Sonata, he had precluded the expansiveness at such moments that help make Bruckner's Adagio—and in their own way, his own earlier adagios—so effective. As in a number of Bruckner's symphonic slow movements, the first theme of his Quintet's Adagio is of the solemn or devotional type noted frequently in the literature on him, which usually connects the type to similar themes in Beethoven, in particular the opening of the Ninth Symphony's Adagio.[79] Although Brahms composed themes of the same general type for the adagios of his early B Major Piano Trio and D Minor Piano Concerto, few of his later themes can be linked to it. In the F Major Cello Sonata, his choice of the adjective "affettuoso" (loving, tender) to qualify the tempo marking does not arouse expectations of a sacramental atmosphere.

The Adagio affettuoso is based throughout on imitative counterpoint, and Brahms uses this texture and his mastery of tonal/harmonic nuances to create, no less than Bruckner in his Adagio, an illusion of unending melody. I do not mention these various points of comparison to suggest that Brahms wrote the Adagio affettuoso primarily as a kind of compositional manifesto in response to Bruckner's Adagio. With other factors in the F Major Cello Sonata's genesis, however, his experience of Bruckner's Adagio may well have had an effect on his own movement's ultimate shape. For the Adagio affettuoso, in contrast to Bruckner's sprawling movement, offers a lucid and compact study of semitonal relationships in the service of melodic endlessness.

After an initial period (mm. 1–12), an apparent codetta becomes a brief transition that tentatively modulates to C-sharp major (mm. 12–16). Through the weakening effects of an imperfect cadence and the high registers of both cello and piano, the codetta that follows manages not to strengthen C-sharp major (mm. 16–19). In both codettas, Brahms emphasizes motion between a pair of semitone-related treble pitches, F-sharp and E-sharp, and the change in their relative stability effected through the modulation from F-sharp to C-sharp major. (See ex. 6.6a.) At other important

---

78. Other movements in both chamber works also feature these relationships. See my "Brahms's Cello Sonata in F Major and Its Genesis," 152–154, for a discussion of some of these features in the F Major Cello Sonata. Bruckner's first movement, it will be recalled, has famous semitonal shifts in the exposition and recapitulation, part of a pattern within the Quintet as a whole. Thus already in m. 1 of the first movement, Bruckner embellishes the F-major tonic with a D-flat triad, each of its pitches a semitone away from a pitch in the tonic triad, and the Scherzo is in D minor, and its Trio in E-flat major.

79. Wiora, "Über den religiösen Gehalt," 176.

EXAMPLE 6.6a.   Brahms, F Major Cello Sonata, Op. 99 / II, mm. 12–19

moments he draws attention to similar pairs of pitches and their changing status—in the central section to destabilize the notated key of F minor and thereby keep the melody from closing.

At the beginning of that section (m. 20), he inverts the C-sharp and E-sharp from the cadence in the previous measure and reinterprets them enharmonically, as shown in example 6.6b. Within the apparent new key of F minor, D-flat is unstable with respect to C, as the cello's motive in m. 20 already demonstrates. The ensuing passage is marked by a struggle between D-flat major, enharmonically the dominant of F-sharp major, and F minor, similarly represented by its dominant. At issue

EXAMPLE 6.6b.   Brahms, F Major Cello Sonata, Op. 99 / II, voice exchange in mm. 19–20

is whether the pitches D-flat and C represent scale degrees six and five in F minor or, in reverse order, the leading tone and tonic in D-flat major, an enharmonic dilemma that comes up repeatedly in Brahms's music, as we have seen.

Brahms organizes the first part of the new section around two roughly equivalent statements of a circular bass line (mm. 20–24, 24–28). The cello's plunging line in m. 24 places the semitone motion from D-flat to C in the bass. Although the resulting cadential six-four (in F minor) resolves quickly, the bass line's cycle has already begun again. Changes toward the end of the cycle and new, rhapsodic passage work in the piano make a second arrival on a cadential six-four (m. 28) more emphatic, but this resolves even less satisfactorily, and the key shifts back to D-flat major (mm. 30 and following). Despite the key signature, F minor has only tentatively been established through its dominant.

About this section Kalbeck commented: "One can no longer speak here of a melody; everything has become melody, even the middle voices and the bass, and they flow into each other in melancholy interpenetration."[80] In contrast to strategies in adagios from his first maturity—above all, the use of evocative accompanimental and transitional materials—here Brahms relies much more on degrees of tonal stability to create the effect of unending melody.

At the point where the D-flat/C conflict is resolved more or less definitively in favor of D-flat (m. 33), thematic fragments from the opening reappear in the bass line. Brahms now invokes the dominant-seventh/German-sixth equivalence. The prolonged D-flat seventh (mm. 37–39) could be a German-sixth chord in F minor—it follows a sequence (mm. 35–37) that ends on an F minor triad—but the broader harmonic setting (from m. 31) makes G-flat (F-sharp) the likelier key. Rather than concluding this section by resolving the D-flat seventh directly to F-sharp, Brahms has the seventh move deceptively (by semitone) to an apparent D seventh (prolonged in mm. 40–42), the German-sixth chord in the key of F-sharp. This leads finally, in the expected manner, to a cadential six-four in m. 43 and the return of the opening material.[81] At the beginning of the central section and leading out of it, as well as at every critical point within, semitonal relationships have kept the melody going. (The outer sections likewise use these relationships, although the periodic phrase-structure within them makes the effect less "unending.")

Brahms's audiences did not show the enthusiasm for the Adagio affettuoso or, for that matter, the F Major Cello Sonata as a whole that they initially did for the other two chamber works premiered during the same season. The first movement is idiosyncratic in a number of respects; perhaps its odd features did not prepare first-time listeners to be well disposed toward the slow movement. Or maybe the performers played the adagio too rapidly. Recent advocates of "authentic" Brahms performance practices have adopted the quicker tempos typical at the time. Yet several of the composer's close colleagues felt that his music was performed too fast, that its harmonic richness demanded slower tempos—and few Brahms movements

---

80. *Brahms,* 4:34–35.

81. Because the opening theme returns over a cadential six-four, no full cadence in F-sharp appears in the reprise until m. 63.

are harmonically richer than the Adagio affettuoso.[82] In any case, it made much less of an impact than did his late adagios in Gypsy style.

BRAHMS'S RENEWAL: THE ADAGIOS
IN GYPSY STYLE

In the chamber music completed between 1886 and 1894, Brahms indicated that six of the ten slow movements were to be performed at the tempo of an adagio (see the appendix). Of these, only three were notable successes in his lifetime: those of the D Minor Violin Sonata, G Major String Quintet, and Clarinet Quintet. In these adagios, but not the others, the composer drew on Gypsy style—or was it Hungarian style?[83] This distinction came up in a monograph from 1933 (among other things, the centennial of Brahms's birth) that the Hungarian musicologist Lajos Koch devoted to the composer's ties to Budapest and love of Gypsy music.

Describing Brahms's enthusiasm for Gypsy bands, which he had listened to in Vienna's Prater and on many visits to Budapest, Koch discusses the composer's appropriation of musical idioms he had heard repeatedly in both places. (Even before he moved to Vienna, Brahms had become well acquainted with the style through the music of Schubert and others and through his relationship with musicians such as Eduard Reményi.) Koch noted Brahms's early and continuing use of "Gypsy style" in a large number of pieces written between 1854 and 1880 for piano (two and four hands) and various chamber ensembles, compositions for the most part in quick tempos. In his later works, however, according to Koch, Brahms cultivated "Hungarian thematic style" in slow movements: "Just as, in the beginning, Brahms had been impressed by music in Gypsy style, now he absorbed Hungarian folk music's true, unadulterated essence and assimilated it into his chamber works."[84] What Brahms had listened to, both in Budapest and in the Prater, was presumably popular music composed largely by Hungarians and performed by Gypsies; certainly, he did not hear any of the "authentic Hungarian" folk music Bartók uncovered well before Koch wrote his essay. The link between the adagio's mystique and a national or ethnic essence had reappeared in (what should have been) an unlikely place. Because Koch moved his attention to slow movements, Brahms's style became pristinely Hungarian.

But why did Brahms's audiences find these three adagios so satisfying? For the response to them appears to have been overwhelmingly favorable, even when, in the case of the D Minor Violin Sonata, reactions to the other movements often were lukewarm. At the time, listeners customarily applauded after each movement that pleased them and if they were extremely enthusiastic made the performers re-

---

82. See, for example, Deiters, "Johannes Brahms II," in *Sammlung musikalischer Vorträge* 68, ed. Paul Graf Waldersee (Leipzig: Breitkopf und Härtel, 1898), 87.

83. The Andante con moto of Op. 87, a set of variations, is also in this style.

84. Wolfgang Ebert, "Brahms in Ungarn: Nach der Studie 'Brahms Magyarorságón' von Lajos Koch," in *Studien zur Musikwissenschaft: Beihefte der Denkmäler der Tonkunst in Österreich* (Tutzing: Schneider, 1986), 37:155. Ebert has translated from the Hungarian and provided some commentary on Koch's original essay.

peat the movement before letting them continue. Critics reported that audiences had demanded immediate repeat performances of all three adagios. One explanation for the positive reactions, that their exotic features delighted listeners, is weak, since reviews dwelt far less on that aspect than on the sense of profound emotion each adagio conveyed. Especially in his later years, Brahms avoided overt attempts at the expressive depth and scope that critics such as Ehlert considered essential to the genre. The fact that he allowed himself considerable expressive latitude in Gypsy style—and only in that style at this point—guaranteed the success of these adagios.

At the same time, Brahms appears to have emulated Beethoven's late adagios. Helm implied that the late adagios form a coherent group, an observation stylistic analysis supports. Thus Beethoven's focus on counterpoint in the last decade of his life is evident even in those lyrical movements, where his use of it furthers the illusion of *unendliche Melodie*. Another strategy, especially noticeable in the first thematic group (mm. 1–26) of the *Hammerclavier* Sonata's Adagio sostenuto, involves various kinds of repetition—overt or concealed, immediate or separated—of motives and longer thematic units to lengthen phrases asymmetrically. Also characteristic of the sound of Beethoven's late adagios is the prominence of the subdominant and related chords, as in the Cavatina's "second theme" (mm. 23–34).

Beethoven's evocation of accompanied recitative at the Cavatina's emotional crux sets it apart from the other adagios in Helm's group. Critics view that moment within a broader tendency in Beethoven's late instrumental music to call to mind the human voice and its capacity to suggest unmediated feeling.[85] Musicians have long noted, however, that accompanied recitative simulates affective immediacy more powerfully than other vocal types. As Sulzer observed already in the late eighteenth century, musical expression of strong emotions "in general becomes uneven and broken, which is absolutely contrary to the flowing nature of ordinary song," and therefore necessitates the style of accompanied recitative.[86] The rest of the Cavatina more closely approximates "ordinary song."

In general stylistic terms, the Adagio of the D Minor Violin Sonata resembles Beethoven's late adagios, and in particular the Cavatina, more than any other of Brahms's slow movements. Indeed, the Adagio features many of the same devices: contrapuntal cadences, marked presence of the subdominant, obsessive reiteration of motives, and imitation between overlapping phrases. In contrast to Beethoven in the Cavatina, Brahms uses Gypsy style at the two emotional high points (mm. 19–24, 51–62).[87] This style is intimately connected to improvisation—Brahms models the passages on a living performance practice—and although specifically instrumental, arguably can produce at least as strong a sense of emotional immediacy as accompanied recitative. He applies Gypsy style much as Beethoven uses recitative

85. See, for example, the chapter "Voice" in Joseph Kerman, *The Beethoven Quartets* (New York: Norton, 1966), 191–222.

86. Quoted in the entry for "Accompagnement" in Koch, *Musikalisches Lexikon*, 58.

87. In a review of the D Minor Violin Sonata, Pohl tersely connected the middle movements to the two parts of the Austro-Hungarian Empire: "Das Adagio ist transleithanisch, das Scherzo cisleithanisch empfunden." "Von der 26. Tonkünstler-Versammlung zu Wiesbaden: 27–30 Juni 1889 (Schluss)," *Musikalisches Wochenblatt* 19 (1889): 379.

in the Cavatina, and through strategies like those apparent in Beethoven's late adagios, largely avoids cadential stops as he draws out the Adagio's one theme in two statements.

Monothematicism, as in the D Minor Violin Sonata, or at least the unmistakable reappearance of opening motives in other themes—as in Bruckner's Quintet—apparently had a higher value in adagios than other movement types.[88] This must have been a consequence of the perceived problem of unity in an adagio Ehlert noted and of the related mode of conceptualizing an adagio as the generation of one melody representing a single inner experience. Regarding the Adagio of the D Minor Violin Sonata, Elisabeth von Herzogenberg wrote in a letter to Brahms: "in an adagio I prize continuity of sentiment above anything else."[89] About the similarly monothematic Adagio of his G Major String Quintet she wrote: "Middle sections with a contrasting character are always somewhat painful to me. Here one color is set off from another only in order to intensify the luminosity of each; the feeling flows to the end in the same grand pulses."[90]

In both adagios, the moments of pseudo-improvisation appear in transitional passages, thus creating a sense of urgency before each return to the theme's beginning. This is more striking in the G Major String Quintet's Adagio than in that of the D Minor Violin Sonata, for there are more such returns. The Quintet movement also features many more of the other special effects that mark a work as à l'hongrois: short subphrases, dotted rhythms, and, in m. 8, tremolos imitating the cimbalom.[91] In this Adagio, Brahms refers to the augmented seconds that appear between scale degrees three and four and six and seven in one version of the so-called Gypsy scale. These references keep the key inconclusive—it could be D minor or A minor—until the decisive move to the dominant of D minor in m. 51. The Adagio also simulates a Gypsy performance practice described in the extremely influential monograph on this music published under Liszt's name: a soloist emerges from the band to play an elaborate improvisation (e.g., in mm. 13–14 and 66–68).[92] Stylized improvisation accounts for the Adagio's unusual shape: five presentations in widely varying lengths of one open-ended theme, the fourth culminating in a dramatic prolonged dominant. Much of the movement's impact, moreover, derives from the inevitable return to the same beginning. Monothematicism, in sounding like an unavoidable fate here, allows the movement to project the tragic grandeur that Ehlert, for one, considered essential for an adagio's success.

The pseudo-extemporized passages push at the boundaries of chamber style, as to a much greater extent does the central section of the Clarinet Quintet's Adagio, with its sustained and unmistakable simulation of a Gypsy performance. Remark-

88. See, also, the motivically related themes in the Adagio of Dvořák's D Major String Quartet, which I discuss in "Chamber Music and the Classical Adagio": 56–57. Helm connects the Adagio's phrase-structure to late Beethoven in *Beethoven's Streichquartette*, 319.

89. *Brahms Briefwechsel*, 2:240.

90. *Brahms Briefwechsel*, 2:212.

91. Jonathan Bellman delineates a "lexicon" of Gypsy-Hungarian idioms in *The "Style Hongrois" in the Music of Western Europe* (Boston: Northeastern University Press, 1993), 93–130.

92. *Die Zigeuner und ihre Musik*, vol. 6 of *Gesammelte Schriften*, ed. and trans. L. Ramann (Leipzig: Breitkopf und Härtel, 1883), 288–289 and 294.

ably, among Brahms's later chamber compositions only the Clarinet Quintet's Adagio had an impact comparable to that of the Adagio from Bruckner's String Quintet, another work that likewise pushes at the limits of chamber style. And Brahms's movement succeeded as an adagio, not a gimmicky novelty piece, even though the source of inspiration for him, Gypsy style, lies outside the mainstream of possibilities for adagios.

As is true for many other adagios, formal theory, as it is usually applied, does not shed much light on the reasons for this movement's success. In the broadest terms, the movement falls into three large sections, of which the first (mm. 1–41) and third (mm. 87–127) are in three-quarter time and are in other respects, as well, virtually identical. (In the sort of overlap associated with Brahms's music, m. 87, which presents the opening motive over a dominant pedal, is both the last measure of the central section, in common time, and the first measure of the final section, which resumes three-quarter time in m. 88.) Each of these outer sections itself consists of four strains, the third of which contrasts with the other three, a typical shape for Hungarian *nóta* songs, a group of popular, as opposed to folk, tunes on which Gypsy performers improvised. As was readily audible to critics, moreover, Brahms uses the same head-motive (called *x* here) for the central and outer sections. (See ex. 6.7a and b for each opening strain.) The middle section's main body (mm. 52–73) likewise consists of four strains, over which Brahms composed elaborately decorative stylized improvisation.[93] But this crude description does not account even for many measures, especially in transitional passages, or for the movement's effectiveness, which has much less to do with formal matters per se than with Brahms's use of Gypsy style in the service of an adagio aesthetic.

Despite the place that composers such as Schubert and Liszt had developed for Gypsy style in concert music, it retained its otherness, which stemmed from its origins in popular music, its markedness against the German mainstream, and its status, above all in this movement, as a performance style.[94] In his 1802 *Lexikon,* Koch stressed the performance problems an adagio posed and deplored a common approach to handling them. According to Koch, one of the greatest mistakes was for the performer to try to sustain an adagio "through piling up of ornaments and variations of the melody, for in that way the real character of the piece is lost."[95] In the middle section of the Clarinet Quintet's Adagio, Brahms applies a performance style in which extravagant "piling up of ornaments and variations of the melody" were standard, but he controls the effect. It should be noted that in the climactic

---

93. Bálint Sárosi gives an example of such a *nóta,* along with a transcription of an improvised version by a clarinetist in a modern Gypsy band in *Folk Music: Hungarian Musical Idiom,* trans. Maria Steiner (Budapest: Corvina Press, 1986), 56–57.

94. Along similar lines, Bellman writes that the style's "gestures are immediately recognizable, whether because of specific Hungarian content or because they essentially contradict European musical conventions of the late eighteenth and nineteenth centuries." "The Hungarian Gypsies and the Poetics of Exclusion," in *The Exotic in Western Music,* ed. Jonathan Bellman (Boston: Northeastern University Press, 1998), 94.

95. *Musikalisches Lexikon,* col. 65.

passages of his String Quintet's Adagio, Bruckner likewise composes in heavy or-namentation (e.g., in mm. 107–110), as does Volkmann in his far less successful Op. 9 Adagio (e.g., in mm. 52–53).

Becoming as composer a Gypsy performer offered Brahms a repertory of ex-troverted musical topoi new to the adagio, in particular additional gestures of ex-temporized playing that give an appearance of freedom, both expressive and for-mal, otherwise not much in evidence in the adagios he composed after his first maturity. Brahms was surely conscious of the artifice involved in the "expressive-ness," even as he no doubt admired both the expressiveness and its artifice. In a re-lated vein, Daverio writes of Brahms's appropriation of Gypsy style in another work as "demonstrating that passion could be treated as a worthy object of the in-tellect," a remark that invites further elaboration.[96] On the one hand, few critics would attribute sincerity to Gypsy musicians' passion; genuine feeling does not seem to have been the point. Musical signifiers of passion were as stylized in their performances, as much objects to be manipulated, as their performance practices were stylized in Brahms's music. On the other hand, most critics would also ac-knowledge the effectiveness of the gestures of passion in both his music and theirs and of the gestures of spontaneous inspiration in his.

As already implied in connection with the G Major String Quintet, stylized im-provisation had an impact on the form of Brahms's adagios because it allowed him to take time, a great deal of time, in transitional passages, something that he tended to deny himself in the later adagios. In another context I mentioned that Brahms's reception of Schubert manifested itself in one masterpiece of his first maturity, the A Major Piano Quartet, in the (sublime) "effect of unbounded musical space, seem-ing to stretch into the beyond," especially in transitions. (I was referring in particu-lar to the finale.) In that chamber work, I asserted further, the "particular quality of the juxtaposed popular and sublime elements may represent the most profound Schubertian influence of all."[97] But in the Clarinet Quintet's Adagio, the popular and sublime elements come from one source, Gypsy style (which Brahms had learned in part from Schubert); they are indivisible rather than juxtaposed. Para-doxically, the taking of time in pseudo-improvised transitions—an emblem of pas-sion both central to the style and "popular" in its appeal to the point of potential vulgarity[98]—also accounts largely for the effect of elevation.

In commentary that more directly dismantles an apparent opposition, Daverio wrote with great insight of the connection between improvisation and developing variation.[99] Consider the climax of the Clarinet Quintet's Adagio, mm. 74–87, a passage that sounds transitional at the beginning and becomes transitional again at

96. *Crossing Paths: Schubert, Schumann, and Brahms* (New York: Oxford University Press, 2002), 241.

97. "Quartet No. 2 for Piano, Violin, Viola, and Cello in A Major, Opus 26," in *The Compleat Brahms: A Guide to the Musical Works of Johannes Brahms,* ed. Leon Botstein (New York: Norton, 1999), 121.

98. One has only to think of the emotionally manipulative use of rubato by popular performers of all kinds. In a related vein, Gypsies, their music, and their imagined lifestyle had become material for kitsch art in Brahms's time.

99. *Crossing Paths,* 226–227.

EXAMPLE 6.7a.   Brahms, Clarinet Quintet, Op. 115 / II, mm. 1–8

the end. Brahms twice presents (in mm. 74 and 75) a motive from the opening (called *y* here), followed each time by rhetorical "free" flourishes in the clarinet, before subjecting the motive to double diminution (m. 78), an intensification that leads to the movement's first key change.[100] While the clarinet, continuing the effect of pseudo-extemporization, moves dramatically and perilously from its high-

---

100. This motive figures prominently in an earlier transition (mm. 25–31).

EXAMPLE 6.7b.   Brahms, Clarinet Quintet, Op. 115 / II, mm. 52

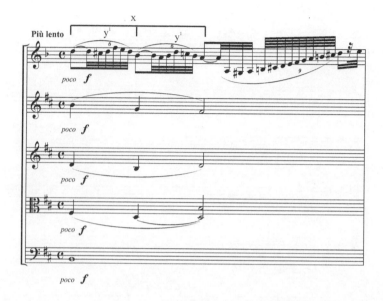

est to its lowest range, the cello plays *x* in a triply augmented version that incorporates another derivative of *y* (see ex. 6.7c). As Daverio suggests of Brahms's appropriation of Gypsy style in general, the motivic techniques in this passage are equally attributable to developing variation and simulated improvisation.[101]

Various writers have considered the chamber music with clarinet to be late works in a stronger sense than the preceding compositions, implying that Brahms had liberated himself from psychological constraints during his momentary retirement. Several superlatives certainly apply to the Clarinet Quintet. As a whole, it manifests the most thorough motivic integration of any multimovement work in his oeuvre. The Adagio, remarkably, in most performances, is the longest adagio of any Brahms had composed since the A Major Piano Quartet's Poco Adagio three decades before. Articulating yet another superlative, Specht marveled at the Adagio as a movement "masterly without willful mastery, where Brahms forgot himself and his striving after formal subtleties, and which for this reason belongs to the greatest of his creations."[102] In the Clarinet Quintet, Brahms found the means to compose "such a long adagio," which he had told Jenner was "the most difficult thing of all" only a few years before, because he "forgot himself," so to speak, in Gypsy style. The style provided the musical signs for appearing to forget oneself.

101. Dahlhaus writes similarly of the Cavatina, "the lyricism and the motivic working that seemed at first to be mutually exclusive prove to be in complete agreement." *Beethoven,* 237.

102. *Johannes Brahms,* 326.

EXAMPLE 6.7c.   Brahms, Clarinet Quintet, Op. 115 / II, mm. 74–81

Expressively, as well as motivically, the Clarinet Quintet is Brahms's most thoroughly integrated work. Together the movements convey one experience, an effect
underscored by the return of the first movement's opening motives in the coda of
the finale, a set of variations on a theme related to others in the quintet. The place
of the Adagio within the whole should therefore be considered. From that perspective, the display of uninhibited lamenting in the Adagio is a rare unequivocal
moment in a work otherwise altogether characteristic of Brahms in its introverted
mood and tendency toward blended affects. Borrowing from another musical culture permitted this unique performance of "raw" emotion.

Should we criticize his appropriation of a subaltern culture's music? Questions of appropriation and subaltern cultures are more complicated than they may appear initially, since Gypsies performed in the style only for non-Gypsies. The performance practices did not exist outside the dominant culture; Gypsies had other musics they played for themselves.[103] And the style consistently served commercial, even meretricious purposes, with performers modifying the style to suit their customers' tastes. In 1869, one observer went so far as to write: "In gypsy music the listener is the artist."[104] In his own Adagio, Brahms may be said to play the Gypsy, in that he clearly gives his audiences what they want.

Yet the movement is an adagio, not merely a simulacrum of a Gypsy performance, even in the central section, where he varies and develops motives that appear likewise in the outer and transitional sections, in a show of motivic connectedness that far surpasses that in Bruckner's Adagio. Does the sparseness of motivic material justify placing the Adagio with other late adagios by both Beethoven and Brahms in which Adorno observed "apparent asceticism towards subjective, spontaneous inspiration"? An easy affirmative response is not possible, since the outer sections' *nóta*-like song comes close to being "a melody sufficient in itself," and the very point of the transitional passages is to simulate "subjective, spontaneous inspiration." Perhaps Brahms, as German composer and Gypsy performer, was able to have it both ways in this Adagio, a movement that seems to have dissatisfied few listeners. Through motivic unity maintained even in pseudo-extemporized transitions that rival transitions in Bruckner's Adagio in their effectiveness and through the stance of significance built into borrowed gestures, Brahms created a "melody" spanning the entire movement that survived scrutiny at the tempo of an adagio. By thus renewing his artistic persona, he finally effected his own renewal of the genre.

103. Sárosi, *Gypsy Music,* trans. Fred Macnicol (Budapest: Corvina Press, 1978), 23–35.
104. Quoted in Sárosi, *Gypsy Music,* 245.

THE TWILIGHT OF LIBERALISM

In May 1890, Simrock sent Brahms a gift, Julius Langbehn's *Rembrandt als Erzieher* (Rembrandt as Teacher). This book, an early product of the new Germanism, had become a surprise hit, in part because its appearance more or less coincided with Wilhelm II's dismissal of Bismarck in March that year. In a letter to Simrock, the composer politely declined to read the book, well known for its despair about modern culture, its anti-Semitism, and its embracing of a dangerous irrationalism: "'Rembrandt' does not entice me." Although not with Brahms, Langbehn's book found an audience because the rapid pace of cultural change and accompanying feelings of malaise made German identity and community seem attractive notions to more people than before. Brahms had not rejected German nationalism altogether; indeed, he looked forward to reading a book that expressed an older type of it, Heinrich von Sybel's history of the Second Reich, which Laura von Beckerath had likewise sent him for his birthday.[1] And he repeatedly voiced his dissatisfaction with contemporary political and artistic trends in the last decade and a half of his life. But the blaming of convenient scapegoats and the unclear thinking evident in Langbehn's book could not appeal to members of Brahms's generation with his intellectual sophistication and general sense of decency—something that does come through, despite his many personal failings. The new trends did, however, expose flaws in the Liberal worldview.

VIENNESE LIBERALISM IN CRISIS AND THE VEREIN ZUR ABWEHR DES ANTISEMITISMUS

The ideology that Langbehn's book espoused only exaggerated the basic assumption of German cultural superiority that Austrian as well as German Liberals had

---

1. *Brahms Briefwechsel,* 12:24, from a letter dated 30 May 1890. On Langbehn and his book, see Fritz Stern, *The Politics of Cultural Despair: A Study in the Rise of the Germanic Ideology* (Berkeley: University of California Press, 1961), 97–182.

long made and added an overt, racial anti-Semitism. In the campaign for the March 1891 elections, the Liberal party itself capitulated and did not condemn anti-Semitism, as it had in the past.[2] Dismaying trends in Viennese politics led many Liberals to do some soul-searching. In June 1891, members of the city's *Bildungsbürgertum* formed the Verein zur Abwehr des Antisemitismus (Society to Combat Anti-Semitism); by 1895, the group had 4,520 members.[3] One founder was the Austrian writer Peter Rosegger, whose books both Brahms and Billroth admired but whom the anti-Semites claimed as one of their own because of ambiguous remarks that he had made in the mid-1880s and, we shall see, continued to make in the 1890s.[4] Other founding members included the geology professor and Liberal politician Sueß and the surgeons Nothnagel and Billroth, all three of whom had signed the open letter protesting Rector Maaßen's advocacy of a Czech elementary school in 1883. Some members of the new group also belonged to another organization with related political aims, the Österreichische Friedensgesellschaft (Austrian Pacifist Society), among them Rosegger and Brahms's friend Johann Strauß, the "Waltz King," whose third wife, Adele, was Jewish.[5] Another prominent friend of Brahms, Viktor Miller zu Aichholz (to whom, along with Aichholz's wife, Kalbeck would dedicate his biography of the composer), joined the Verein zur Abwehr des Antisemitismus in 1897.[6]

Brahms does not appear to have become a member and, as noted in chapter 1, was capable of referring crudely to Karl Goldmark's Jewishness as late, apparently, as 1893. But several sources record his vehement rejection of the new anti-Semitism that had become so powerful a feature of the contemporary political scene. About this there can be no question. Thus, in his diary, Heuberger quoted Brahms in 1890 on the Jew-baiting that was by then rampant in Vienna: "I can scarcely speak of it, it seems so deplorable to me. If the endless reinforcements of Galician Jews in Vienna were hindered, I would be in favor of it, but the rest is vileness."[7] (Many Liberal Jews in Vienna shared the composer's prejudice against the Galician Jews, who tended to resist the outward signs of assimilation and were seen as mired in "Bildungshass"—anti-intellectualism—and "orthodox obscurantism.")[8] Brahms's stubborn nationalism and his unambiguous stance regarding political anti-Semitism sum up the uncomfortable position that many Liberals found themselves in. Unable to relinquish their feelings that German culture surpassed all others, they also could not accept the twisted version of their prejudices promoted by radicals, who were gaining a majority. Viennese anti-Semitism had paradoxically become linked with both a politicized variety of Austrian Catholicism, whose leaders sometimes played the

---

2. Pulzer, *The Rise of Political Anti-Semitism,* 151.

3. Wistrich, *The Jews of Vienna,* 186–187.

4. See Herwig [Pichl], *Schönerer und die Entwicklung des Alldeutschtumes,* 4:556–558.

5. Brigitte Hamann, "Der Verein zur Abwehr des Antisemitismus," in *Die Macht der Bilder: Antisemitische Vorurteile und Mythen,* ed. Jüdisches Museum der Stadt Wien (Vienna: Picus Verlag, 1995), 253–263.

6. *Bericht der Dritten Generalversammlung des Vereines zur Abwehr des Antisemitismus* (Vienna: n. p., 1897), 14.

7. *Erinnerungen an Brahms,* 45, entry of 4 November 1890.

8. Wistrich, *Jews of Vienna,* 82–83.

German-nationalist card, and an extreme German nationalism that, shortly after Brahms's death in 1897, would include militant Protestantism as part of its program.[9]

In an early stage of planning, Rosegger apparently went so far as to propose that the new group call itself the Society to Combat Nationalism. Although Nothnagel opposed Rosegger's suggestion as unrealistic, he vehemently acknowledged the dangers of nationalism:

> We'll stick with anti-Semitism! This is a disease that can still be healed. The nationalistic malady is incurable and whoever succumbs to it is lost. The danger of this malady also lies in the fact that it is quite contagious. I hold nationalism to be the most dangerous sickness of humanity.[10]

Nothnagel had cured himself of this disease, just as Billroth had finally cured himself of anti-Semitism. (Already in 1889 Hans von Bülow had likewise declared himself cured—through the ministrations of the extreme anti-Semites in Germany—of "the *cholera morbus antisemiticus*.")[11] At the organization's second general meeting, Nothnagel gave a passionate speech about the history of anti-Semitism that culminated in a peroration against various types of discrimination. In his words, "there should be no room among us for racial differences as such: first a human being, then white, yellow, red, black; first a human being, then German, Slav, Semite, Romanic; first a human being, then Jew, Christian, and Muslim!"[12]

Commentary in Liberal newspapers also shows that there continued to be strong personal, if not party, resistance to the new political anti-Semitism and any remarks that might foster it. For even certain people with obvious good intentions, such as Rosegger, continued to be naïve about how their words might be construed. In an interview reported in the *Deutsche Zeitung* in 1893, Rosegger had incautiously observed: "Judaism has such an important impact on an economic orientation." A journalist, "Veritas," protested in the *Wiener Sonn- und Montags-Zeitung* a "dangerous sentence formulated as carelessly as it was unjustly," adding the withering phrase "as if Judaism teaches any economic orientation whatsoever as such." Since Roseg-

---

9. Andrew G. Whiteside, *The Socialism of Fools: Georg Ritter von Schönerer and Austrian Pan-Germanism* (Berkeley: University of California Press, 1975), 243–262.

10. This anecdote, which appears in several sources, can be traced to a talk given by Chaim Bloch, "Herzl's First Years of Struggle: Unknown Episodes and Personal Recollections," trans. Edward Jelenko, in *Herzl Year Book*, vol. 3: Herzl Centennial Issue, ed. Raphael Patai (New York: Herzl Press, 1960), 84. This talk is not annotated and contains at least one error, in that Bloch gives the inaugural year of the Viennese Verein zur Abwehr des Antisemitismus as 1888. The comments attributed to Nothnagel are consistent with other remarks ascribed to him.

11. According to Marie von Bülow, her husband, unmotivated by any evident outward occasion, made a public declaration upon his departure for America on 13 March 1889, "in consideration of the unsure validity of the pertinent return ticket." Quoting him in part, she wrote, "A decade earlier he had been 'stricken by the *cholera morbus antisemiticus*.'" According to him, he had later experienced "intermittent paroxysms," but the "involuntary homeopaths Liebermann v. Sonnenberg and Wilhelm Marr had effected temporary alleviation and the court preacher Doctor Adolf Stöcker, a complete cure." *Hans von Bülow: Briefe und Schriften*, 6:33. Cited in part with inaccurate documentation in Peter Gay, *Freud, Jews and Other Germans: Masters and Victims in Modernist Culture* (New York: Oxford University Press, 1978), 14–15.

12. Max Neuberger, *Hermann Nothnagel: Leben und Wirken eines deutschen Klinikers* (Vienna: Rikola Verlag, 1922), 442, n. 3.

ger's target had been capitalism, the journalist pointed out the Jewish ancestry of Ferdinand Lassalle and Karl Marx, the founders of German socialism.[13] "Veritas" did not note that a member of the Society to Combat Anti-Semitism had uttered the "dangerous sentence."

More organized resistance had come with the founding of the Society's own weekly newspaper, the *Freies Blatt,* which began publication in April 1892. For the most part, the *Freies Blatt* concerned itself with keeping track of and constantly countering what anti-Semites were writing in local journals and newspapers. Thus an entry under the heading "from anti-Semitic papers" in July 1892 noted remarks the prominent anti-Semitic writer Heinrich Pudor had made in the newspaper *Das zwanzigste Jahrhundert* (The Twentieth Century). Pudor had drawn attention to "the cast of Richard Wagner's face," asking whether "any feature, any cranny of Wagner's face is German or Teutonic." The anonymous observer in the *Freies Blatt* concluded ironically that Wagner's ancestry must ultimately be traceable to Galician Jewish roots: "In the end, no doubt, a Kohn from Pohrlitz was Wagner's forefather, and our Bruckner is the only great composer of purely German ancestry."[14] This response raises the question of whether Brahms's own ancestry had been seriously disputed, beyond the guilt by association that seems to have motivated the rhetorical references to him as Jewish cited in chapter 1.[15]

An obituary in the paper for Billroth, who died on 6 February 1894, affirmed that "the brilliant surgeon had completely freed himself from the erroneous views" apparent in his 1875 book—also discussed in chapter 1—which the newspaper characterized as written in "pre-anti-Semitic times."[16] This strange locution reflects a common perception that anti-Semitism before the "anti-Semitic movement" of the early 1880s did not count as such; the political and racial anti-Semitism that had arisen then was a new danger.

Despite the newspaper's high purpose and clear focus, the *Freies Blatt* did not flourish, for it aimed its efforts at the Liberal party's dwindling, well-to-do base: it preached to the converted. As Theodor Herzl, the future Zionist leader, expressed it in a letter to one of the Society's leaders, "the *Freies Blatt* is no newspaper, but a circular which does not circulate."[17] Documents from the 1890s reveal both Brahms and his friend Hanslick to have been as ineffectual as the Verein zur Abwehr des Antisemitismus and its newspaper, and Hanslick at times publicly as clumsy as Rosegger in an ever more unsettling situation.

HANSLICK AND THE CONTRADICTIONS
OF LIBERALISM

Hanslick did not produce any single writing that had as potently negative an impact as Billroth's 1875 book, nor were the changes in his outlook as dramatic. But

13. "Ein *Commisvoyageur* in Antisemitismus," *Wiener Sonn- und Montags-Zeitung,* 10 April 1893.
14. *Freies Blatt,* 24 July 1892, 8.
15. See also Daniel Beller-McKenna, "Revisiting the Rumor of Brahms's Jewish Descent," *American Brahms Society Newsletter* 19/2 (autumn 2001): 5–6.
16. *Freies Blatt,* 11 February 1894, 3.
17. Letter of 26 January 1893, cited in Bloch, "Herzl's First Years of Struggle," 80.

his reviews and other writings do give ample evidence of the Liberal bias toward German culture, while also demonstrating that he rejected new, extreme forms of that bias, such as attempts to purge German of words derived from other languages and replace them with Teutonic neologisms.[18] Thus in 1894 he wrote a "review" of one of the Duesberg Quartet's popular chamber concerts in which he neglected to mention the music played and focused instead on the "still greater service" that August Duesberg strove to perform through "purification of the German language." After noting substitutions such as "Tonspiel" for "Konzert" and "Vierspiel" for "Quartett," Hanslick remarked that the "leader of the 'Vierspiel' saw himself obliged nevertheless to call his program 'klassisch' and to enumerate 'Quartette' and 'Trios' in it."[19]

Hanslick showed sarcastic contempt for Duesberg's efforts in 1894. In a long letter to the *Neue Freie Presse* from 1891, which concerned related attempts in Germany, his tone was more earnest, his arguments more reasoned—and his personal bias more evident. Thus he made the patronizing remark that "such anxiety was suitable for the small 'interesting nationalities' that are creating a written language and literature for themselves for the first time." And he included this suspect sentence: "Music has its finest gift in being a universally understandable language, a cosmopolitan art." Today we recognize many musics and attempt to maintain a vigilant skepticism toward claims of universality—even Brahms acknowledged and tried to imagine "foreign worlds" of music. In this part of his letter, Hanslick was reacting to a nationalistically motivated "absurdity" in a Berlin newspaper, which had suggested "in utter seriousness" that German composers and publishers reject the centuries-old tradition of using Italian words in musical scores. He asserted "music's advantage of universal intelligibility," for which we should read the "advantage of universal intelligibility" of so-called absolute music, since he went on to discuss purely instrumental genres. In his words, "not only the sound of a given sonata or symphony but also the permanent record of it has been equally understandable to all nations up until now." He warned that if, in the present climate of "stubbornly accentuated nationalism," German publishers used their own language, publishers elsewhere would follow suit, and it would become impossible for German-speaking conductors to perform works from Hungary, Russia, Norway, Spain, and so on.[20]

The situation within the multinational, polyglot Habsburg Empire where Hanslick resided was obviously more acute than elsewhere in Europe. Conceptualizing music as a universal language would have had special meaning in the uniquely complicated Austro-Hungarian Empire, where antagonism between social classes, as well as nations, created an almost constant sense of crisis toward the century's end. In the first decades of the twentieth century, David Josef Bach still conceived absolute music as a universal language that could bridge class differences.

18. Schönerer's followers were prominent in these efforts in Austria.
19. *Fünf Jahre Musik* (Berlin: Allgemeiner Verein für Deutsche Litteratur, 1896), 286–287.
20. "Modernes im Zeitungs- und Theaterwesen (Ein Brief an die Herausgeber der 'Neuen freien Presse' in Wien) (1891)," reprinted in *Aus dem Tagebuche eines Musikers*, 92–100.

But the privileged position of purely instrumental tonal music derived most basically from the semblance of naturalness and logic it had acquired. Here the idea of absolute music shared common ground with Liberalism. Just as everyone was assumed to understand the language of tonal music, it appeared self-evident that a society founded on Liberal economic principles allowed everyone the opportunity to succeed: a natural logic seemed to operate here, too. That the Liberal outlook was merely second nature was already being exposed; the unmasking of absolute tonal music as second nature would occur somewhat later.

In Austria, Liberalism had briefly appeared to offer a solution to the imperial predicament: a strengthened central government that retained the traditional monarch and added a constitution ostensibly guaranteeing all citizens equal rights before the law. Political Liberalism did not hold sway for long in Austria because its own internal inconsistencies compromised it, but also because of the very belatedness of its development. Other aspects of the Liberal *Weltanschauung* developed earlier and deeper roots. These included faith in reason, education, and the primacy of German culture, beliefs that compensated for the common Liberal view that religion should be concerned with ethics and nothing else. In an 1894 memoir, Hanslick described his own religious upbringing in those terms: "The essence and foundation of religion should be only ethics; all faiths with the same moral principles were of equal worth. We became acquainted with the Biblical stories only from their amiable, tenderhearted, and poetic side, with the 'miracles' only as allegories."[21]

More clearly than many of his colleagues, Hanslick exemplified the contradictions of Liberalism. In 1883 Hanslick, along with Nothnagel, Billroth, Sueß, and others, had signed the open letter against establishing a Czech-language elementary school in Vienna. Yet he had grown up in Prague. Being a well-educated, middle-class person in Bohemia in the *Vormärz* period of Hanslick's youth had meant rejecting the Czech language in favor of German. He noted that although his father knew both languages, he spoke only German with his friends: "Naturally, since they always conversed about learned things, about art and politics." And he quoted a Prague native from a background like his own reacting to the Czech-nationalist movement that had developed after midcentury. In that person's words, " 'since one is nothing as an individual, one exaggerates one's race in order to feel vain about being part of it; that is nationalism.' " In an apparent non sequitur, Hanslick remarked on how surprised those living in *Vormärz* Prague would have been to see the splendid advances that Czech-language culture made in the second half of the century. Enumerating such "brilliant achievements" as a Czech theater, a Czech university, and a Czech academy of sciences, he also made it clear that these accomplishments had come about at the expense of friendly relations. Before midcentury, "Germans and Czechs got along peacefully, since the latter knew that anything they possessed in art and science, industry and even social graces derived from German culture."[22] Hanslick recognized Czech nationalism and certain forms of German nationalism, but he did not acknowledge nationalism in himself.

21. *Aus meinem Leben*, 1:6–7.
22. *Aus meinem Leben*, 1:15–17.

The mixture of good intentions, limited insight, and unwitting prejudice evident in Hanslick's memoir also emerges in his music reviews, in particular, those of his fellow Bohemian citizen Antonín Dvořák. Hanslick publicly championed Dvořák's music in 1879, when anti-Czech sentiment within the empire had already hardened. In his initial statement of support, Hanslick had refuted the "laughable suspicion" expressed in some Viennese quarters that efforts by the Czech-nationalist party had brought Dvořák into fashion. Naming the prominent *German* musicians in Berlin who had programmed Dvořák's works, he added: "Truly, no propaganda has been launched from Prague, and were such an attempt to be made—how far does Czech support go in the art world anyway?" Hanslick seems to have deplored the inequities. Yet, after extolling the many beauties of the Third Slavonic Rhapsody, which had just been performed in Vienna, he concluded: "To be sure, no one would want to maintain that Dvořák will necessarily develop into a second Beethoven. We still do not know if his abundant talent will also achieve full mastery in a variety of forms and soar out of the sphere of narrower national ideas to the heights of absolute universal art."[23] This statement begs the question of what "absolute universal art" is. Did Czech folk idioms, as a kind of external reference, make Dvořák's music less absolute or merely less universal, or both? Or did Hanslick simply consider the rhapsody a lesser kind of absolute music and therefore not "universal"?

Austro-German music served as the touchstone for universality in later reviews as well. In 1880, Hanslick observed with pleasure that the "national element" in Bedřich Smetana's E Minor String Quartet was "negligibly small, and consequently gathered that "in Czech music, the same as before, German is the 'customary language of the land.'"[24] Twelve years later, Hanslick wrote in a review of Dvořák's *Hussite* Overture: "this Slav knows his Beethoven more thoroughly than many a German."[25] And, after an 1893 performance of a string quartet, he noted approvingly that "the exclusively national character retreats more and more in the later Dvořák and appears only as a dialect, lightly coloring our universally understandable, fundamentally Beethovenian musical language."[26] Hanslick's reviews demonstrate both real enthusiasm for Dvořák's music—recall his description of the G Major Symphony cited in chapter 1—and condescension toward him as a Slav. None of his comments about Dvořák, however, approaches the callousness of Helm's parenthetic 1896 reference to the composer's F Minor Piano Trio as a work "that wishes to extend itself 'German-Classically' higher than it lies in the Slavic nature of the composer to do."[27] Unlike Helm, Hanslick at least meant well. All forms of German nationalism, in truth, were not the same.

In 1891, Hanslick described Italy as "the land of our modern musical culture's origin" and the practice of using Italian in a score as a tradition well worth preserving. But the musical language in which a composer couched "the sound of a given sonata or symphony" was self-evidently Austro-German for him. His con-

---

23. *Concerte, Componisten und Virtuosen der letzten fünfzehn Jahre*, 248 and 250.
24. *Concerte, Componisten und Virtuosen der letzten fünfzehn Jahre*, 285.
25. *Fünf Jahre Musik*, 190.
26. *Fünf Jahre Musik*, 236.
27. *Musikalisches Wochenblatt* 27 (1896): 456–457.

ception of absolute music as universally intelligible and at the same time necessarily German is of course patent ideology, part of a system of beliefs that served to buttress a status quo of inequality, but also an increasingly fragile equilibrium in the empire.

TRACES OF BRAHMS'S POLITICAL OUTLOOK IN THE 1890s

Did Brahms modify his political views as the level of public discourse deteriorated? Entries in Heuberger's diary certainly convey the sad situation that Viennese Liberals found themselves in by the mid-1890s. In remarks dated 16 May 1895, Heuberger described Brahms's fury the previous evening because of Lueger's mayoral victory:

> The master was completely horrified about the fact that the anti-Semites had gotten the upper hand in the official positions of the city of Vienna and that Lueger had become vice-mayor and would soon be mayor: "Didn't I tell you already years ago that it would happen? You and all the others, too, laughed at me then. Now it's come to pass and with it the clerical economic system. If there were an 'Anti-Clerical Party'— that would make sense! But anti-Semitism is insanity!"[28]

Although Brahms made a disparaging comment about socialism—the Christian Socials' "clerical economic system"—in passing, Lueger's anti-Semitism above all inspired the expression of outrage recorded by Heuberger.

The same evening, Brahms recounted to Heuberger "amusing details" about a benefit concert that a friend and colleague, the Italian mezzo-soprano Alice Barbi, had sung the day before, 14 May 1895. The profits were supposed to have been divided equally between the residents of the Slovenian city Laibach (Ljubljana), recently devastated by an earthquake, and the building of a Catholic chapel in Vienna. Barbi had "originally wanted to sing for the poor of Vienna and was already annoyed about being approached with the chapel. Laibach was fine with her." After the concert, women from the sponsoring committee informed Barbi that the half previously designated for Laibach would instead be donated to the Ursuline and Carmelite orders of nuns: thus the committee would give all the profits to Catholic charities. Heuberger's conclusion—Brahms or Barbi had probably already articulated it—was that Countess Windischgrätz, the wife of the Conservative aristocrat who led the central government's tenuous Conservative/Liberal coalition, had not let Barbi sing for the poor of Vienna "because it would have been to the Liberals' advantage."[29] This convoluted anecdote again shows the strength of the public perception of the musicians around Brahms as Liberals, and of their view of themselves as such. The story also demonstrates their helplessness, at least in this incident, to do what they saw as right, to practice (small acts of) charity toward the city's many indigent and otherwise suffering people, because of the ugly political situation.

Some Viennese Liberals, among them Sueß, responded to their party's crisis in the 1890s by embracing Social Democracy as the inevitable next step in the evolu-

28. *Erinnerungen an Brahms,* 82. Franz Josef II refused to certify Lueger's election for the time being.
29. *Erinnerungen an Brahms,* 82.

tion of Austria's sociopolitical system. Already in the fall of 1891, an article in the *Wiener Sonn- und Montags-Zeitung* praised Sueß as "one of the few in the [Liberal] party who knows to resign himself to the socialist direction in which the tendency of our time moves." While "dogmatic Liberalism" held that with feudalism's end, "the highest level of perfection had been achieved," according to the anonymous journalist, Sueß saw Liberalism as "only a transitional step in the development toward something better."[30] By "Liberalism" the journalist meant "capitalism," which Social Democratic doctrine did view as merely an intermediate stage between feudalism and the socialism of the future.

In most respects, Brahms's own perspective seems to have remained that of a "dogmatic" Liberal. An overlooked small collection in the Viennese Stadt- und Landesbibliothek's Handschriftensammlung offers further evidence for the composer's habits as a member of the city's upper middle-class elite. Brahms's valued final housekeeper, Celestine Truxa, had the foresight to retrieve sixteen items, with dates from 1891 through 1896, that the composer had discarded: invitations, membership cards, receipts for contributions to charitable organizations, and a printed acknowledgment of having received a piece of mail:

1. Invitation from the mayor of Vienna to a reception at City Hall on 6 January 1892
2. Invitation from the mayor of Vienna to a reception at City Hall on 3 January 1891
3. Invitation from the mayor of Vienna to a reception at City Hall on 9 January 1894
4. Membership card for the Wiener Asyl-Verein für Obdachlose for 1896: ten florins
5. Membership card for the Deutscher Schulverein for 1893: one florin
6. Membership card for the Protestanten-Verein for 1894: one florin
7. Membership card for the Protestanten-Verein for 1893: 100 florins
8. Membership card for the Tonkünstler-Verein for the 1892–93 season
9. Membership card for the Tonkünstler-Verein for the 1893–94 season
10. Membership card for the Tonkünstler-Verein for the 1894–95 season
11. Membership card for the Tonkünstler-Verein for the 1895–96 season
12. Honorary invitation as a member of the Board of Directors for the Gesellschaft der Musikfreunde to the Concordia-Ball on 2 February 1891
13. Honorary invitation from the Evangelische Vereinigungen in Wien to a "social evening" on 28 February 1893
14. Receipt for a member's contribution to the Rudolfiner-Verein for 1892: twenty-five florins
15. Printed acknowledgement from Brahms of having received a piece of mail (his "Correspondenz-Karte")

30. "Fragmente der Woche (Professor Sueß gegen den orthodoxen Liberalismus)," *Wiener Sonn- und Montags-Zeitung,* 9 November 1891.

16. Letter of 1 February 1895 from the Directorate of the Leipzig Gewandhaus Concerts to accompany an honorarium of 2000 Marks for his participation in the fifteenth concert of the season

Some of the salvaged materials offer little to a historian. We already know, for example, that Brahms belonged to the Viennese Tonkünstler-Verein from its founding in the mid-1880s. And the invitation to the Concordia Ball (as honorary president of the Tonkünstler-Verein), hosted by a society for journalists and other writers, and the three invitations from Vienna's mayor to a yearly City Hall reception merely confirm his high status in the city. Several items, however, have more than passing interest because of the connections between the various groups and other Viennese organizations and individuals.

One receipt (item 4), for instance, shows that Brahms contributed to an organization for the city's homeless. Further research into the records of the group, the Wiener Asyl-Verein für Obdachlose (Viennese Shelter Society), establishes that he made a similar donation every year for more than two decades.[31] While none of his closest friends and colleagues contributed to this group, his final physician, Freud's collaborator and fellow Jew Josef Breuer, did so each year, as did Vienna's most significant Jewish organization, the Israelitische Cultus-Gemeinde (Jewish Religious Community), munificently. In 1852 the Cultus-Gemeinde had been "authorized as the sole agency for supervising the cultic, religious-educational, and charitable needs of Viennese Jews."[32] Within the Jewish community, this group reflected Liberal demographics and practices in Vienna as a whole. The organization's leadership consisted of wealthy Jews such as bankers and lawyers who still professed their religion but otherwise supported assimilation with the German-speaking Bürgertum. The Cultus-Gemeinde also mirrored broader Liberal trends in its undemocratic structure: a Jew was required to pay a substantial tax in order to vote on the group's policy decisions.[33] Most of the Cultus-Gemeinde's undertakings were aimed at Vienna's Jews, but the records for the Wiener Asyl-Verein für Obdachlose make it clear that the group's charitable activities extended to the needy in the larger Viennese community.

Another receipt acknowledges Brahms's donation in 1892 as a member of the Rudolfiner-Verein (named after the late Crown Prince Rudolf) toward the hospital that Billroth was building. Additional research into this group's records likewise shows that Brahms gave a generous sum every year from its founding in 1881 through 1897, when he died. Though less generously than Brahms, Breuer also contributed, as did another Jewish physician, Victor Adler, a seminal figure in the

31. I looked first at the *Jahresbericht des unter dem Protectorate Ihrer Majestät der Kaiserin Elisabeth stehenden Asylvereins für Obdachlose in Wien "Erstes Asyl für Obdachlose, Blattgasse" pro 1896* (Vienna: Im Selbstverlage des Vereines, 1897). I then looked at other yearly reports and established that he contributed every year, beginning, at the latest, in 1882.

32. Wistrich, *The Jews of Vienna,* 88–89.

33. Wistrich, *The Jews of Vienna,* 88–91. Indeed, Wistrich notes that "in an age of growing democratization in Austrian politics . . . the Jewish community remained more oligarchical in its internal tax and voting structure than the wider community," 91.

Austrian Socialist party and, before that, a member of the anti-Liberal circle around Schönerer until the latter espoused racial anti-Semitism in 1883.[34] The yearly reports, which include information about the patients, show that the hospital was indeed ecumenical, for the patients identified their religions as variously Catholic, Protestant, Jewish, and even Muslim.[35]

Two of the most intriguing receipts date from 1893. That year Brahms gave one florin to the Deutscher Schulverein (German School Society), an organization with a checkered history. Founded in 1880 by the group around Schönerer—Adler, Heinrich Friedjung, and others—the Schulverein supported German-language schools in the empire's outer regions to help German-speaking residents who wanted to maintain their heritage and to make it easier for their children to continue speaking German.[36] After Schönerer left the group in 1886 because it refused to eject Jews, the Schulverein's financial situation deteriorated, to the point that it sent out a public appeal in December 1892, occasioning taunts by the *Deutsches Volksblatt*.[37] Brahms thus made his (minimal) contribution at a meaningful time.

The significance of the generous sum, 100 florins, that he gave, also in 1893, to the Protestanten-Verein, which was raising funds to build a chapel, is harder to determine.[38] Beginning with Kalbeck, who referred to the composer as a "heretic," Brahms's biographers have usually regarded him as having been an unobservant Christian in his adult years, to have become a Liberal like Hanslick in this respect. On the one hand, we do know that Brahms felt only contempt for the revitalized Catholicism promulgated by the Christian Socials in the 1890s. Moreover, an open letter from a self-identified Protestant in the *Deutsches Volksblatt* of 9 November 1892 stressed the connection between Liberalism and Protestantism in Austria. Writing disapprovingly that "most of the Protestant newspapers swim in Jewish Liberal waters," the author also noted many Protestants' belief that they had "only the Liberals to thank for the Evangelicals' having finally in 1861 received equal

34. For an account of Adler, see McGrath, *Dionysian Art and Populist Politics,* especially 208–237.

35. *Erster Jahres-Bericht (Vereinsjahr 1881) des unter dem Protectorate Seiner kaiserlichen und königlichen Hoheit des durchlauchtigsten Erzherzogs und Kronprinzen Rudolf stehenden Rudolfiner-Vereins zur Erbauung und Erhaltung eines Pavilion-Krankenhauses behufs Heranbildung von Pflegerinnen für Kranke und Verwundete in Wien nebst dem Protocolle der Generalversammlung des Vereines vom 12. Februar 1882* (Vienna: Im Selbstverlage des Rudolfiner-Vereins, 1882). I looked at this report and those for subsequent years through 1897.

36. An account of the organization, its goals, and its history—including the crisis associated with Schönerer's departure—appears in Dr. August Ritter von Wotawa, *Der Deutsche Schulverein 1880–1905: Ein Gedenkschrift im Auftrage der Vereinsleitung* (Vienna: Verlag des Deutschen Schulvereins, 1905).

37. "An das deutsche Volk in Oesterreich!" appeared in the *Mitteilungen des Deutschen Schulvereines* no. 45 (December 1892): 1–2. A notice, "Vom Deutschen Schulvereine" appeared in the evening edition of the *Deutsches Volksblatt,* 14 November 1892. The anonymous author asked rhetorically why the director, Dr. Moriz Weitlof, had not turned "directly to the Jews and their companions, the Liberals," in his appeal. A report of a similar response by another anti-Semitic but non-Viennese organ, the *Grazer Tagblatt,* appears in "Der Deutsche Schulverein u. die verschämten Antisemiten," *Freies Blatt,* 20 November 1892.

38. C[arl] Neuß and Dr. Johann Kaiser, *Chronik der Wiener evangelischen Gemeinde Augsburger Bekenntnisses vom Zeitpunkte ihrer Entstehung bis auf die Gegenwart* (Vienna: Theodor Daberkow's Verlag, 1904), 85, reports on this as a goal of the "newly founded 'Protestantenverein.'" The authors note that by 1894 the organization had collected 3,000 florins for this purpose, 93.

rights in Austria."[39] Perhaps Brahms's generosity stemmed in part from a perception that Austrian Protestantism provided a bulwark against the threat that the Christian Socials posed to Liberalism in Vienna. On the other hand, the aging Brahms may simply have felt an inclination to return to the religion of his childhood.

Certainly, his pride in German culture requires a nuanced reading that considers all of the evidence and possibilities. Although Brahms's friendship with Widmann foundered temporarily because of the latter's criticism of the new kaiser, Wilhelm II, in the summer of 1888, the composer manifestly drew the line at certain forms of German nationalism. By the winter of 1894–95, Brahms was repeating witticisms at the expense of the German kaiser. Wilhelm II had had the audacity to have "Sang an Aegir," a composition—trivial at best—addressed to the Norse god of the sea, published under his name as the text's author and the music's composer, arranged for thirteen different instruments or ensembles.[40] (The jokes, unfortunately, do not translate from German into English.)[41]

How then are we to interpret Brahms's continuing admiration for Bismarck? For an entry in Heuberger's diary for 2 May 1895, immediately before the entry that recorded Brahms's story about Alice Barbi and his outrage at Lueger's electoral victory, makes this clear. The composer spoke with great warmth about a recently published collection of speeches by the former chancellor: "And most of them extempore. Perhaps a sentence polished here or there, but on the whole improvised. An enormous intellect! And eighty years old!"[42] Despite his expression of enthusiasm for Bismarck's oratorical skill into old age, Brahms, who habitually wrote comments in his books, made no marks in his copy of the speeches (though he did add sentences from them to a collection of quotations that he had begun as a young man).[43] By 1895, his chauvinism may have dwindled to insistently repeated expressions of allegiance to the ousted Iron Chancellor.

Indeed, Brahms owned a book by Otto Gildemeister, published in Germany in 1896, that included the essay "Der Kampf gegen die Fremdwörter" (The Struggle against Foreign Words), which Gildemeister had written in 1886.[44] In contrast to Brahms's copy of Bismarck's speeches, his copy of Gildemeister's carefully reasoned essay contains many annotations. The author went meticulously through subtle differences in meaning, considering distinctions between words of foreign extraction that had long since entered the German language and the German words with

39. "Protestanten und Juden," *Deutsches Volksblatt,* 9 November 1892. Both the person who wrote the letter quoted in the article and the author of the article itself are anonymous.

40. Recent research, furthermore, suggests that Wilhelm II wrote neither the text nor the music.

41. *Erinnerungen an Brahms,* 165. He also alluded to one of the jokes in a letter to Simrock of 30 November 1894. *Brahms Briefwechsel,* 12:157.

42. *Erinnerungen an Brahms,* 82.

43. *Des jungen Kreislers Schatzkästlein: Aussprüche von Dichtern, Philosophen und Künstlern,* ed. Carl Krebs (Berlin: Deutsche Brahms-Gesellschaft, 1909). The Handschriftensammlung of the Wiener Stadt- und Landesbibliothek holds the original manuscript (Ia 79562). A perusal of the manuscript indicates that a number of items were omitted from the published version and also makes clear, through changes in handwriting and ink, where Brahms began making entries again toward the end of his life.

44. *Essays* (Berlin: Verlag von Wilhelm Hertz, 1896), 211–243.

which the purifiers wished to replace them. Brahms's many markings imply that he, like Hanslick, recognized the caricature that pride in German culture had become in many quarters.

And it pleased Brahms to an extraordinary degree when the French Academy admitted him as a foreign member in 1896. He told Heuberger:

> I wished to write a letter of thanks in French, but my French is not exemplary. Even Hanslick did not trust himself to write a letter to the Academy. So I simply wrote a letter in German to the Academy, probably the first they ever received. I thanked them very much and excused myself, that I had not wanted to write in bad French to the guardians and masters of the French language![45]

This anecdote and the 1892 story recounted at the beginning of chapter 4, which revealed his respect for musical education in France, show that his attitude toward that country was not what it had been in 1871. In that year he had composed the *Triumphlied,* a bombastic display of patriotism (which most Brahms scholars prefer to forget) to celebrate the German victory in the Franco-Prussian War.[46] To a limited extent he does seem to have been able to change with the times.

QUESTIONS OF NATIONALISM IN MUSIC: KALBECK AND BRAHMS

In reaction to radical German nationalism and the other kinds of nationalism that had developed in the empire, some Viennese began to promote a consciously pluralistic conception of Austrian culture in the 1890s. Because the Secessionist movement in the fine arts advocated just such a view, "a form of art that would weld together all of the characteristics of our multitude of constituent peoples into a new and proud unity," it began to receive government support toward the decade's end.[47] Around the turn of the century, certain members of the city's music world, younger than Brahms or Hanslick, voiced similar ideas about Austrian instrumental music. Indeed, they located the source of its quality in the empire's very mixture of ethnic groups. Thus, at several points in the Brahms biography, Kalbeck took pains to emphasize the multifarious sources of Viennese music. For instance, in the second volume, which appeared in 1906, he declared: "It should not be forgotten that Viennese music, like the Viennese people, is a mixed product. The foreign tribes on Austria's borders, who for centuries stood through war and peace in close two-way communication with the Germans, brought with them musical elements capable of splendid fusion." And he went on to note the distinct musical contributions of the Italians, the Slavs, and the Hungarians.[48]

45. *Erinnerungen an Brahms,* 101, entry for 24 March 1896.

46. For an exception, see Daniel Beller-McKenna, *Brahms and the German Spirit* (Cambridge, Mass.: Harvard University Press, 2004).

47. Zuckerkandl, *My Life and History,* 142–143; quoted by Schorske in "Gustav Klimt: Painting and the Crisis of the Liberal Ego," in *Fin-de-Siècle Vienna,* 237.

48. *Brahms,* 2:8.

The same year (1906), Guido Adler made a related point in an unsigned report of a speech he had given at Vienna University to celebrate the 150th anniversary of Mozart's birth. In the article, which he wrote for the *Neue Freie Presse,* Adler asserted that it was possible to recognize Austrian culture most clearly in "that art that is bound to no specific language": purely instrumental music with no program or other text attached to it. And in a climactic piece of rhetoric, he imagined Viennese Classical music as a model for the conduct of Austria's internal affairs. "As the customs of the Austrian peoples are interwoven in musical works by Classical composers, as the motivic material is taken from the national stores, which the artists . . . develop into Classical structures, so may statecraft join the particularities of the various peoples into a higher unity."[49] For Kalbeck and Adler, the idea of a specifically Austrian style in instrumental music had taken hold: as an image of the empire's pluralistic richness, its intertwined ethnic identities brought further together but not effaced.

Already in an 1890 review of Brahms's G Major String Quintet, Kalbeck had focused on its references to Vienna's sounds. He wrote that no other Brahms work "with the possible exception of the first set of *Liebeslieder* Waltzes more clearly draws attention to its place of origin through the local accents peculiar to it" than this quintet. According to Kalbeck, even more than the finale, which evoked a Gypsy/Hungarian czardas, the opening Allegro's second theme, the Adagio, and the third movement's Trio show such traces. Kalbeck considered these "local accents" to be "characteristic of the composer, even more characteristic of his place of residence, in which German humor, Slavic melancholy, and Hungarian high spirits flow into each other unobserved."[50] (When he revised his comments for the biography, Kalbeck remembered to include the Italians' contribution to the ethnic mixture.)[51]

Other musicians also liked to try their hand at detecting vestiges of "ethnic" styles in Brahms's music. Joachim, for example, heard the Trio in the Clarinet Trio's third movement as resembling an Austrian *Ländler,* and that in the corresponding movement of the Clarinet Quintet as "Slavically tinged."[52] Comments of this sort are rarely reliable—what one person heard as Hungarian, another called Slavic.[53] The significance of all such idioms was that they stand out from German "universality," something more easily tolerated in music by Brahms than by a Slav such as

---

49. *Neue Freie Presse,* 27 January 1906. Although the article is not signed, according to Edward R. Reilly, the autograph demonstrates that Adler wrote it. I consulted an unpublished list by the late Dr. Reilly, "The Papers of Guido Adler at the University of Georgia: A Provisional Inventory," 12–13, which Dr. Reilly kindly allowed me to see.

50. *Montags-Revue,* 1 December 1890.

51. *Brahms,* 4:210. He also remembered to include the Waltzes, Op. 39, as another exception.

52. Letter to Clara Schumann of 25 November 1891 in *Briefe von und an Joseph Joachim,* ed. Johannes Joachim and Andreas Moser, vol. 3 (Berlin: Julius Bard, 1913), 403.

53. Helm noted the Hungarian sound in the G Major String Quintet's finale but heard late Beethoven as the "godfather" of the Adagio. *Deutsche Zeitung,* 29 November 1890. Hanslick likewise heard the "slightly Hungarian coloration" of the finale, but referred to the Adagio as "perhaps Slavically tinged." *Neue Freie Presse,* 1891; reprinted in *Aus dem Tagebuche eines Musikers,* 318. Most critics, as noted in chapter 6, hear the Adagio as influenced by Gypsy/Hungarian style.

Dvořák. It is probably safest to conclude with Kalbeck that traces of these "local accents" in the G Major String Quintet—and in the Clarinet Quintet and Trio—make the work seem more "Viennese," more Schubertian than *Reichsdeutsch*. At times the sound of these late chamber works from 1890 and 1891 caused Brahms to be received as—possibly because he had become—more Viennese than many born and bred in the city.

BRAHMS, CULTURAL DESPAIR, AND MUSIC AS SECOND NATURE

As the story about his publisher and Langbehn's book illustrates, Brahms rejected certain expressions of cultural despair common in the 1890s. A number of anecdotes indicate, however, that he felt no similar inhibitions about voicing his discouragement about music's future. In the summer of 1896, he expressed such fears to Mahler, in a conversation that Mahler relayed to Specht.[54] And in December 1896 he criticized the conclusion of Strauss's *Also sprach Zarathustra:* "B major and C major at the same time! I would have had nothing against it if something had happened in each key that no longer left out the other, so that this combination had come about as if inevitably on its own."[55]

Taken together, these anecdotes suggest that Brahms worried about both the neglect of teachable disciplines such as counterpoint and figured bass and the decline in the less easily grasped quality of "thinking logically in music." The imitation of his own style by Alexander Zemlinsky and other young composers at the turn of the century and beyond would not have alleviated his concern for the future of music.[56] Even a critic as conservative as Walter Niemann saw the problems in such misguided shows of respect. In 1913 he wrote: "Perhaps no style is outwardly so personally marked and outwardly so easily but also so fruitlessly—and slavishly—copied as that of Brahms, no disciple is placed so narrowly in a circle with his master as the 'Brahmsian.'"[57] Already in 1909, Louis regretted that he and others in his generation had not been open to learning from Brahms. Louis attributed this lack of receptiveness to youths' tendency to underestimate the value of technique but also to divisions in the music world at the time. Like Niemann in this regard, Louis deplored academic musicians' appropriation of Brahms after his death, a theme that continued in various sources from the twentieth century's first four decades.[58]

Thus, unable to accept any other compositional approach, Schenker in 1912 and again in 1935, shortly before his death, called Brahms, in a famous phrase, "the last

54. *Johannes Brahms,* 353.

55. *Erinnerungen an Brahms,* 118, entry for 15 December 1896.

56. Walter Frisch, "The 'Brahms Fog': On Analyzing Brahms Influences at the Fin de Siècle," in *Brahms and His World,* ed. Frisch (Princeton, N.J.: Princeton University Press, 1990), 81–99.

57. *Die Musik der Gegenwart und der letzten Vergangenheit bis zu den Romantikern, Klassizisten und Neudeutschen* (Stuttgart: Schuster und Loeffler, 1913), 48.

58. *Die deutsche Musik,* 156–157.

master" of German music.[59] Bekker may have had Schenker, with others, in mind when he chastised Brahms's disciples for their "intolerance" in 1933, an attitude that he attributed to "a deep love for a disappearing beautiful world."[60] Agreeing with Schenker in one respect, Bekker asserted: "Brahms is definitely the last of his line, and the more the temporal distance from him grows, the clearer this knowledge becomes" (57). Certainly, the eeriness today of listening, for instance, to works by Brahms's younger colleague Robert Fuchs composed in the 1920s but stylistically consistent with music from the mid–nineteenth century suggests the futility of trying to hold on to the past.

As a classicist composer in the late nineteenth century, Brahms worked within an aging musical tradition; he cultivated a second nature that could not easily be made expressive again. In his time, the "complex of signification" that was captured in stylistic and formal conventions of the common-practice period had become, more than ever before, in Lukács's words, "rigid and strange"—hence the proliferation of academic art.[61] Brahms's responses to the historical circumstances in which he worked took various forms. On the one hand, his implicit recognition that he was working toward the end of a music- and social-historical era and of the limitations that came with this may account for his frequent eschewal of conspicuously public gestures in his symphonies. On the other hand, he clearly modeled his attitude toward the theme–form problem on Beethoven without falling into the trap of classicist imitation. Brahms, furthermore, appears to have had a more open mind to possible sources of renewal than many of his contemporaries, as well as his early twentieth-century epigones. Thus his interest in sixteenth- and seventeenth-century vocal music discussed in issues of the *Vierteljahrsschrift für Musikwissenschaft* and his eclectic use of what he learned from that music in his own instrumental music goes well beyond the usual manifestations of historicism. Along similar lines, he permitted himself to apply the vulgarities of Gypsy style to the most elevated of all so-called German musical types, the adagio.

The semblance of freedom that Gypsy style gave to his final adagios temporarily addressed a recurring theme in criticism of his music, the perception that despite his consummate technical mastery, his music was weak in content and expression. Making a play on Nietzsche's famous phrase, Specht wrote in 1912 of the "melancholy of potency" he heard in Brahms's compositions, speculating that the music would have been "stronger, more freely flowing, more unforgettable" if he had been less intent on utter perfection.[62] In some of the late music, above all the opening movement of the D Minor Violin Sonata, Brahms does dwell on the artifice. But his manipulation of technique and the very level of the artifice produce their own eloquence and, in any case, self-reflexive mannerism is only one manifestation

59. *Beethoven's Ninth Symphony: A Portrayal of Its Musical Content, with Running Commentary on Performance and Literature As Well*, trans. John Rothgeb (New Haven: Yale University Press, 1992), dedication page; and *Free Composition*, 1:94.

60. "Brahms," *Anbruch* 15 (1933): 56, 57. Bekker later notes that Brahms "reclusively displays that great world's image before night comes over it," 58.

61. *Theory of the Novel*, 64, translation modified.

62. "Zum Brahms-Problem," *Der Merker* 3 (1912): 44.

of his music's lateness and his compositional virtuosity. His mastery of craft also allowed the moments of expressive complexity that evoke Freud's Vienna, as well as the sense of estrangement that comes through in the Clarinet Trio's opening Allegro and the unearthly harmonic beauty in the outer sections of the Clarinet Quintet's third movement. "Melancholy of potency" does not capture the affective qualities of those passages or indeed of, for example, the Clarinet Quintet in its entirety. Contrary to Specht's observation, the ostensible futility of Brahms's complete technical command did not determine the quality of expression. Rather, through his command of musical logic, his ability to find meaning in aging conventions, Brahms was able to write music that often sounds both of its time and at odds with it. Beyond the pleasures afforded by its compositional sophistication and its sheer sonorous beauty, the music may be said to express the melancholy of someone who was part of a culture that could not last much longer, a middle-aged person aware of lateness.

BRAHMS'S MULTIMOVEMENT WORKS: DATES OF COMPLETION AND TEMPO DESIGNATIONS FOR THE SLOW MOVEMENTS

Piano Sonata in C Major, Op. 1	Andante	1853[1]
Piano Sonata in F-sharp Minor, Op. 2	Andante con espressione	1852
Piano Sonata in F Minor, Op. 5	Andante; Andante molto	1853
Piano Trio in B Major, Op. 8	Adagio non troppo	1854
Serenade in D Major, Op. 11	Adagio non troppo	1858
Piano Concerto in D Minor, Op. 15	Adagio	1857
Serenade in A Major, Op. 16	Adagio non troppo	1859
String Sextet in B-flat Major, Op. 18	Andante, ma moderato	1860
Piano Quartet in G Minor, Op. 25	Andante con moto	1861
Piano Quartet in A Major, Op. 26	Poco Adagio	1861
Piano Quintet in F Minor, Op. 34	Andante, un poco Adagio	1864
String Sextet in G Major, Op. 36	Adagio	1865
Cello Sonata in E Minor, Op. 38[2]		1865
Horn Trio in E-flat Major, Op. 40	Adagio mesto	1865
String Quartet in C Minor, Op. 51, No. 1	[Romanze] Poco Adagio	1873[3]
String Quartet in A Minor, Op. 51, No. 2	Andante moderato	1873[4]
Piano Quartet in C Minor, Op. 60	Andante	1874
String Quartet in B-flat Major, Op. 67	Andante	1875
Symphony in C Minor, Op. 68	Andante sostenuto	1876
Symphony in D Major, Op. 73	Adagio non troppo	1877
Violin Concerto, Op. 77	Adagio	1878
Violin Sonata in G Major, Op. 78	Adagio	1879
Piano Concerto in B-flat Major, Op. 83	Andante	1881
Piano Trio in C Major, Op. 87	Andante con moto	1882

1. The years in which the works were completed, rather than published, are given. Brahms kept a handwritten inventory for the works through Op. 79; his letters provide information on the others. See Alfred Orel, "Ein eigenhändiges Werkverzeichnis von Johannes Brahms: Ein wichtiger Beitrag zur Brahmsforschung," *Die Musik* 29 (1936–37): 529–541.

2. As discussed in chapters 2 and 6, Brahms removed the slow movement from Op. 38 before publication. Another three-movement work, Op. 120, No. 2, concludes with variations marked Andante con moto but does not have an internal slow movement.

3. According to Brahms, he finished the string quartets, Op. 51, "for the second time" in 1873; most likely he had completed an earlier version by 1869. See Orel, "Ein eigenhändiges Werkverzeichnis," 538.

String Quintet in F Major, Op. 88	Grave ed appassionato	1882
Symphony in F Major, Op. 90	Andante	1883
Symphony in E Minor, Op. 98	Andante moderato	1885
Cello Sonata in F Major, Op. 99	Adagio affettuoso	1886
Violin Sonata in A Major, Op. 100	Andante tranquillo	1886
Piano Trio in C Minor, Op. 101	Andante grazioso	1886
Double Concerto in A Minor, Op. 102	Andante	1887
Violin Sonata in D Minor, Op. 108	Adagio	1888
Piano Trio in B Major, Op. 8 (revised)	Adagio	1889
String Quintet in G Major, Op. 111	Adagio	1890
Clarinet Trio in A Minor, Op. 114	Adagio	1891
Clarinet Quintet in B Minor, Op. 115	Adagio	1891
Clarinet Sonata in F Minor, Op. 120, No. 1	Andante un poco Adagio	1894
Clarinet Sonata in E-flat Major, Op. 120, No. 2[5]		1894

4. See note 3.
5. See note 2.

BIBLIOGRAPHY

Published Correspondence

Billroth und Brahms im Briefwechsel. Edited by Otto Gottlieb-Billroth. Berlin: Urban und Schwarzenberg, 1935.

Briefe von und an Joseph Joachim. Edited by Johannes Joachim and Andreas Moser. Vol. 3: 1869–1907. Berlin: Julius Bard, 1913.

Clara Schumann-Johannes Brahms Briefe aus den Jahren 1853–1896. Edited by Berthold Litzmann. 2 vols. Leipzig: Breitkopf und Härtel, 1927.

Geiringer, Karl. "Johannes Brahms in Briefwechsel mit Eusebius Mandyczewski." *Zeitschrift für Musikwissenschaft* 15 (1933): 337–370.

Hans von Bülow: Briefe und Schriften. Edited by Marie von Bülow. 2nd ed. Vols. 6–9. Leipzig: Breitkopf und Härtel, 1907–11.

Johannes Brahms Briefwechsel. Berlin: Deutsche Brahms-Gesellschaft, 1907–20. 16 vols.

> Vols. 1–2. *Johannes Brahms im Briefwechsel mit Heinrich und Elisabeth von Herzogenberg.* Edited by Max Kalbeck. 1907.
>
> Vols. 5–6. *Johannes Brahms im Briefwechsel mit Joseph Joachim.* Edited by Andreas Moser. 1908.
>
> Vols. 9–12. *Johannes Brahms Briefe an P. J. und Fritz Simrock* (vols. 9–10). *Johannes Brahms Briefe an Fritz Simrock* (vols. 11–12). Edited by Max Kalbeck. 1917–19.
>
> Vol. 16. *Johannes Brahms im Briefwechsel mit Philipp Spitta und Otto Dessoff.* Edited by Carl Krebs. 1920.

Johannes Brahms und die Familie von Beckerath mit unveröffentlichten Brahmsbriefen und den Bildern und Skizzen von Willy von Beckerath. Edited by Kurt Stephenson. Hamburg: Christians Verlag, 1979.

Books, Articles, and Dissertations

Adler, Guido. *Wollen und Wirken: Aus dem Leben eines Musikhistorikers.* Vienna: Universal-Edition, 1935.

Adorno, Theodor Wiesengrund. *Aesthetic Theory.* Translated by Robert Hullot-Kentor. Minneapolis: University of Minnesota Press, 1997.

———. *Beethoven: The Philosophy of Music.* Edited by Rolf Tiedemann. Translated by Edmund Jephcott. Stanford: Stanford University Press, 1998.

———. *Einleitung in die Musiksoziologie: Zwölf theoretische Vorlesungen.* Frankfurt am Main: Suhrkamp Verlag, 1973.

————. *Essays on Music.* Edited by Richard Leppert. Translated by Susan H. Gillespie. Berkeley: University of California Press, 2002.

————. "The Idea of Natural History." Translated by Bob Hullot-Kentor. *Telos* 60 (1984): 111–124.

————. *Musikalische Schriften I–III: Klangfiguren (I), Quasi una fantasia (II), Musikalische Schriften (III).* Vol. 16 of *Gesammelte Schriften.* Frankfurt am Main: Suhrkamp Verlag, 1978.

————. *Musikalische Schriften V.* Edited by Rolf Tiedemann and Klaus Schultz. Vol. 18 of *Gesammelte Schriften.* Frankfurt am Main: Suhrkamp Verlag, 1984.

————. "On the Final Scene of *Faust.*" In *Notes to Literature,* edited by Rolf Tiedemann and translated by Shierry Weber Nicholsen, 1:111–120. New York: Columbia University Press, 1991.

————. "On the Score of *Parsifal.*" Translated by Anthony Barone. *Music and Letters* 76 (1995): 384–397.

————. *Philosophie der neuen Musik.* Frankfurt am Main: Suhrkamp Verlag, 1976.

————. *Quasi una Fantasia: Essays on Modern Music.* Translated by Rodney Livingstone. London: Verso, 1992.

Adrian, Jack. "The Ternary-Sonata Form." *Journal of Music Theory* 34 (1990): 57–80.

Agawu, Kofi. "Ambiguity in Tonal Music: A Preliminary Study." In *Theory, Analysis and Meaning in Music,* edited by Anthony Pople, 86–107. Cambridge: Cambridge University Press, 1994.

Aldwell, Edward, and Carl Schachter. *Harmony and Voice Leading.* 2nd ed. Fort Worth: Harcourt Brace Jovanovich, 1989.

Althusser, Louis. "Contradiction and Overdetermination: Notes for an Investigation." In *For Marx,* translated by Ben Brewster, 87–128. New York: Verso, 1996.

Ambros, August Wilhelm. *Zum Lehre vom Quinten-Verbote.* Leipzig: H. Matthes, 1859.

Bach, David Josef. "Aus der Jugendzeit." *Musikblätter des Anbruch* 6 (1924): 317–320.

————. "Populäre Konzerte in Wien." *Musikbuch aus Österreich: Ein Jahrbuch der Musikpflege in Österreich und den bedeutendsten Musikstädten des Auslandes* 8 (1911): 27–35.

Bahr, Hermann. *Austriaca.* Berlin: S. Fischer Verlag, 1911.

————. *Essays.* Leipzig: Insel-Verlag, 1912.

Ballantine, Christopher. *Music and Its Social Meanings.* New York: Gordon and Breach, 1984.

Barbour, J. Murray. "Just Intonation Confuted." *Music and Letters* 19 (1938): 48–60.

Barone, Anthony Edward. "Richard Wagner's *Parsifal* and the Hermeneutics of Late Style." Ph.D. diss., Columbia University, 1996.

Bauer, Wilhelm. *Die öffentliche Meinung und ihre geschichtlichen Grundlagen.* Tübingen: Mohr, 1914.

Bekker, Paul. "Brahms." *Anbruch* 15 (1933): 56–58.

————. *Die Sinfonie von Beethoven bis Mahler.* Berlin: Schuster und Loeffler, 1918.

Beller, Steven. *Vienna and the Jews 1867–1938: A Cultural History.* New York: Cambridge University Press, 1989.

————, ed. *Rethinking Vienna 1900.* New York: Berghahn Books, 2001.

Bellermann, Heinrich. *Der Contrapunct oder Anleitung zur Stimmführung in der musikalischen Composition.* Berlin: Julius Springer, 1862.

Beller-McKenna, Daniel. *Brahms and the German Spirit.* Cambridge, Mass.: Harvard University Press, 2004.

————. "Revisiting the Rumor of Brahms's Jewish Descent." *American Brahms Society Newsletter* 19/2 (autumn 2001): 5–6.

————. "The Rise and Fall of Brahms the German." *Journal of Musicological Research* 20 (2001): 87–210.

Bellman, Jonathan. "The Hungarian Gypsies and the Poetics of Exclusion." In *The Exotic in Western Music,* edited by Jonathan Bellman, 74–103. Boston: Northeastern University Press, 1998.

———. *The "Style Hongrois" in the Music of Western Europe.* Boston: Northeastern University Press, 1993.

Benjamin, Walter. *Illuminations: Walter Benjamin, Essays and Reflections.* Edited by Hannah Arendt and translated by Harry Zohn. New York: Schocken Books, 1968.

Biba, Otto. *Johannes Brahms in Wien.* Vienna: Gesellschaft der Musikfreunde, 1983.

Billroth, Theodor. *Prof. Dr. Th. Billroth's Antwort auf die Adresse des Lesevereins der deutschen Studenten Wien's.* Vienna: Carl Gerold, 1875.

———. *Über das Lehren und Lernen der medicinischen Wissenschaften an den Universitäten der deutschen Nation nebst allgemeinen Bemerkungen über Universitäten: Eine culturhistorische Studie.* Vienna: C. Gerold's Sohn, 1876.

Blackbourn, David. *The Long Nineteenth Century: A History of Germany, 1780–1918.* New York: Oxford University Press, 1998.

Bloch, Chaim. "Herzl's First Years of Struggle: Unknown Episodes and Personal Recollections." Translated by Edward Jelenko. In *Herzl Year Book,* vol. 3, Herzl Centennial Issue, edited by Raphael Patai, 77–90. New York: Herzl Press, 1960.

Blume, Friedrich. *Classic and Romantic Music: A Comprehensive Survey.* Translated by M. D. Herter Norton. New York: Norton, 1970.

Botstein, Leon. "Brahms and Nineteenth-Century Painting." *19th-Century Music* 14 (1990): 154–168.

———. "Music and Its Public: Habits of Listening and the Crisis of Musical Modernism in Vienna, 1870–1914." 2 vols. Ph.D. diss., Harvard University, 1985.

Botstein, Leon, and Linda Weintraub, eds. *Pre-modern Art of Vienna 1848–1898.* Annandale-on-Hudson, N.Y.: Edith C. Blum Institute, 1987.

Boyer, John W. *Culture and Political Crisis in Vienna: Christian Socialism in Power, 1897–1918.* Chicago: University of Chicago Press, 1995.

———. *Political Radicalism in Late Imperial Vienna: Origins of the Christian Social Movement, 1848–1897.* Chicago: University of Chicago Press, 1981.

Bozarth, George S., ed. *Brahms Studies: Analytical and Historical Perspectives.* Oxford: Clarendon Press, 1990.

Brahms, Johannes. *Des jungen Kreislers Schatzkästlein: Aussprüche von Dichtern, Philosophen und Künstlern.* Edited by Carl Krebs. Berlin: Deutsche Brahms-Gesellschaft, 1909.

———. *Oktaven und Quinten u. A.* Edited and with a commentary by Heinrich Schenker. Vienna: Universal-Edition, 1933.

Breuer, Josef, and Sigmund Freud. *Studies in Hysteria.* Translated by A. A. Brill. Boston: Beacon Press, 1937.

Brinckmann, A[lbert] E[rich]. *Spätwerke grosser Meister.* Frankfurt am Main: Frankfurter Verlags-Anstalt A.-G., 1925.

Brinkmann, Reinhold. *Late Idyll: the Second Symphony of Johannes Brahms.* Translated by Peter Palmer. Cambridge, Mass.: Harvard University Press, 1995.

Broch, Hermann. *Hugo von Hofmannsthal and His Time: The European Imagination, 1860–1920.* Edited and translated by Michael P. Steinberg. Chicago: University of Chicago Press, 1984.

———. "The Style of the Mythical Age." Introduction to *On the Iliad,* by Rachel Bespaloff, translated by Mary McCarthy, 7–33. Bollingen Series 9. Washington, D.C.: Pantheon Books, 1947.

Brockhaus' Conversations-Lexikon: Allgemeine deutsche Real-Encyclopädie. 13th ed. 16 vols. Leipzig: F. A. Brockhaus, 1882–87.

Brodbeck, David, ed. *Brahms Studies.* Vol. 1. Lincoln: University of Nebraska Press, 1994.

Bruckmüller, Ernst. *Sozialgeschichte Österreichs.* Vienna: Herold Verlag, 1985.

Burkholder, J. Peter. "Museum Pieces: The Historicist Mainstream in Music of the Last Hundred Years." *Journal of Musicology* 2 (1983): 115–134.

Cammarota, Lionello. *Gian Domenico del Giovane da Nola: I documenti biografici e l'attività presso la SS. Annunziata con l'opera completa.* 2 vols. Rome: Edizioni de Santis, 1973.

Caplin, William E. *Classical Form: A Theory of Formal Functions for the Instrumental Music of Haydn, Mozart, and Beethoven.* New York: Oxford University Press, 1998.

Charmatz, Richard. *Deutsch-österreichische Politik: Studien über den Liberalismus und über die auswärtige Politik Österreichs.* Leipzig: von Duncker und Humblot, 1907.

Chua, Daniel K. L. *The "Galitizin" Quartets of Beethoven: Opp. 127, 132, 130.* Princeton, N.J.: Princeton University Press, 1995.

Dahlhaus, Carl. "Brahms und die Idee der Kammermusik." In *Brahms-Studien,* vol. 1, edited by Constantin Floros, 45–57. Hamburg: Karl Dieter Wagner, 1974.

———. *The Idea of Absolute Music.* Translated by Roger Lustig. Chicago: University of Chicago Press, 1989.

———. *Ludwig van Beethoven: Approaches to His Music.* Translated by Mary Whittall. Oxford: Clarendon Press, 1991.

———. "Musikkritik als Sprachkritik: Musikalische Logik." In *Klassische und romantische Musikästhetik,* 278–290. Laaber: Laaber-Verlag, 1988.

———. *Die Musiktheorie im 18. und 19. Jahrhundert,* part 1, *Grundzüge einer Systematik.* Vol. 10, *Geschichte der Musiktheorie.* Darmstadt: Wissenschaftliche Buchgesellschaft, 1984.

———. *Nineteenth-Century Music.* Translated by J. Bradford Robinson. Berkeley: University of California Press, 1989.

———. "Was ist eine musikalische Gattung?" *Neue Zeitschrift für Musik* 135 (1974): 620–625.

Daverio, John. *Crossing Paths: Schubert, Schumann, and Brahms.* New York: Oxford University Press, 2002.

———. "Dahlhaus's Beethoven and the Esoteric Aesthetics of the Early Nineteenth Century." *Beethoven Forum* 2 (1993): 189–204.

David, Hans T., and Arthur Mendel, eds. *The Bach Reader: A Life of Johann Sebastian Bach in Letters and Documents.* Rev. ed. New York: Norton, 1966.

DeFord, Ruth I. "Marenzio and the *villanella alla romana.*" *Early Music* 27 (1999): 535–552.

Deiters, Hermann. "Johannes Brahms II." In *Sammlung musikalischer Vorträge* 68, edited by Paul Graf Waldersee, 75–112. Leipzig: Breitkopf und Härtel, 1898.

Dommer, Arrey von, ed. *Musikalisches Lexicon auf Grundlage des Lexicon's H. Ch. Koch's.* Heidelberg: J. C. B. Mohr, 1865.

Dreyfus, Laurence. *Bach and the Patterns of Invention.* Cambridge, Mass.: Harvard University Press, 1996.

Duesberg, August. *Ueber Hebung der Volksmusik in Hinsicht auf das "Erste Wiener Volksquartett für Classische Musik."* Vienna: Lesk und Schwidernoch, [1892].

Ebert, Wolfgang. "Brahms in Ungarn: Nach der Studie 'Brahms Magyarorságón' von Lajos Koch." *Studien zur Musikwissenschaft: Beihefte der Denkmäler der Tonkunst in Österreich* 37 (1986): 103–164.

Eder, Karl. *Der Liberalismus in Altösterreich: Geisteshaltung, Politik und Kultur.* Vienna: Verlag Herold, 1955.

Eggebrecht, Hans Heinrich. *Musikalisches Denken: Aufsätze zur Theorie und Ästhetik der Musik.* Wilhelmshaven: Heinrichshofen, 1977.

Eisler, Hanns. "Die Erbauer einer neuen Musikkultur." In *Musik und Politik: Schriften 1924–1948,* edited by Günter Mayer, 140–167. Leipzig: VEB Deutscher Verlag für Musik, 1973.

Federhofer, Hellmut. "Der Manierismus-Begriff in der Musikgeschichte." *Archiv für Begriffsgeschichte* 17 (1973): 206–220.

Fellinger, Imogen. "Brahms' beabsichtigte Streitschrift gegen Erk-Böhmes 'Deutscher Liederhort.'" In *Brahms-Kongress Wien 1983: Kongressbericht*, edited by Susanne Antonicek and Otto Biba, 139–153. Tutzing: Schneider, 1988.

Fellinger, Richard. *Klänge um Brahms: Erinnerungen.* Berlin: Deutsche Brahms-Gesellschaft, 1933.

Finscher, Ludwig. "Symphonie." In *Die Musik in Geschichte und Gegenwart*, edited by Ludwig Finscher. 2nd ed. Vol. 9, cols. 56–58. Kassel: Bärenreiter, 1998.

———. "Werk und Gattung in der Musik als Träger kulturellen Gedächtnisses." In *Kultur und Gedächtnis*, edited by Jan Assmann and Tonio Hölscher, 293–310. Frankfurt am Main: Suhrkamp, 1988.

Fleischer, Oskar. *Die Bedeutung der internationalen Musik- u. Theater-Ausstellung in Wien für Kunst u. Wissenschaft der Musik.* Universal-Bibliothek für Musik-Litteratur 6–7. Leipzig: Internationale Verlags- und Kunstanstalt (A. Laurencic), [1894].

Floros, Constantin. *Brahms und Bruckner: Studien zur musikalischen Exegetik.* Wiesbaden: Breitkopf und Härtel, 1980.

Flotzinger, Rudolf, and Gernot Gruber. *Von der Revolution 1848 zur Gegenwart.* Vol. 3, *Musikgeschichte Österreichs.* 2nd ed. Vienna: Böhlau Verlag, 1991.

Forkel, Johann Nikolaus. *Allgemeine Geschichte der Musik.* Vol. 1. Leipzig: Schwickert, 1788.

Foster, Peter. "Brahms, Schenker and the Rules of Composition: Compositional and Theoretical Problems in the Clarinet Works." Ph.D. diss., University of Reading, 1994.

Franz, Georg. *Liberalismus: Die deutschliberale Bewegung in der habsburgischen Monarchie.* Munich: Verlag Georg D. W. Callwey, 1955.

Freud, Sigmund. *On the Interpretation of Dreams.* Translated by Joyce Crick. New York: Oxford University Press, 1999.

Frisch, Walter. "Brahms and Schubring: Musical Criticism and Politics at Mid-Century." *Nineteenth-Century Music* 7 (1984): 271–281.

———. *Brahms and the Principle of Developing Variation.* Berkeley: University of California Press, 1984.

———, ed. *Brahms and His World.* Princeton: Princeton University Press, 1990.

Fuchs, Robert. *Geistige Strömungen in Österreich: 1867–1918.* Vienna: Globus-Verlag, 1949.

Gay, Peter. *Freud, Jews and Other Germans: Masters and Victims in Modernist Culture.* New York: Oxford University Press, 1978.

Geiringer, Karl. *Brahms: His Life and Work.* 3rd ed. New York: Da Capo Press, 1981.

Gerhard, Anselm. "'Ein kühn hingeworfenes Räthselwort': Das Klavierstück WoO 60 und die Voraussetzungen von Beethovens 'Spätstil.'" *Musiktheorie* 12 (1992): 217–234.

Gildemeister, Otto. *Essays.* Berlin: Verlag von Wilhelm Hertz, 1896.

Gilliam, Bryan. "The Two Versions of Bruckner's Eighth Symphony." *19th-Century Music* 16 (1992): 59–69.

Goertz, Harald. *Österreichisches Musikhandbuch.* Vienna: Jugend und Volk, 1971.

Goldmark, Karl. *Notes from the Life of a Viennese Composer.* Translated by Alice Goldmark Brandeis. New York: Boni, 1927.

Göllerich, August. *Anton Bruckner: Ein Lebens- und Schaffens-bild.* 4 vols. in 9. Vols. 2–4, edited by Max Auer. 1922–37; reprint, Regensburg: Gustav Bosse Verlag, 1974.

Grasberger, Franz, ed. *Anton Bruckner in Wien: Eine kritische Studie zu seiner Persönlichkeit.* Vol. 2, *Anton Bruckner: Dokumente und Studien.* Graz: Akademischer Druck- u. Verlagsanstalt, 1980.

Graybill, Roger C. "Harmonic Circularity in Brahms's F Major Cello Sonata: An Alternative to Schenker's Reading in *Free Composition.*" *Music Theory Spectrum* 10 (1988): 43–55.

Grey, Thomas S. *Wagner's Musical Prose: Texts and Contexts.* New York: Cambridge University Press, 1995.

Gross, N[achum] T. *The Industrial Revolution in the Habsburg Monarchy 1750–1914.* London: Collins Clear-Type Press, 1972.

Gruber, Helmut. *Red Vienna: Experiment in Working-Class Culture 1919–1934.* New York: Oxford University Press, 1991.

Gülke, Peter. *Brahms–Bruckner: Zwei Studien.* Kassel: Bärenreiter, 1989.

———. "Introduktion als Widerspruch im System: Zur Dialektik von Thema und Prozessualität bei Beethoven." *Beiträge zur Musikwissenschaft* 14 (1969): 5–40.

———. "Kantabilität und thematische Abhandlung: Ein Beethovensches Problem und seine Lösungen in den Jahren 1806–1808." *Beiträge zur Musikwissenschaft* 15 (1970): 252–273.

Gutmann, Albert. *Volksconcerte in Wien: Vorschläge zur Bildung eines Concertorchesters: Mittheilung an die Gesellschaft der Musikfreunde von ihrem Mitgliede Albert Gutmann.* Vienna: Verlag der kaiserl. und königl. Hofmusikalienhandlung Albert J. Gutmann, [1890].

Haar, James. "Classicism and Mannerism in 16th-Century Music." *International Review of the Aesthetics and Sociology of Music* 25 (1994): 5–18.

Habermas, Jürgen. *The Structural Transformation of the Public Sphere: An Inquiry into a Category of Bourgeois Society.* Translated by Thomas Burger and Frederick Lawrence. Cambridge, Mass.: MIT Press, 1991.

Halm, August. *Beethoven.* Berlin: Max Hesse, 1927.

———. *Von Zwei Kulturen der Musik.* Munich: G. Müller, 1913.

Hamann, Brigitte. "Der Verein zur Abwehr des Antisemitismus." In *Die Macht der Bilder: Antisemitische Vorurteile und Mythen,* edited by the Jüdisches Museum der Stadt Wien, 253–263. Vienna: Picus Verlag, 1995.

Hamann, Richard. *Gründerzeit.* Edited by Jost Hermand. Munich: Nymphenburger, 1971.

Hancock, Virginia. *Brahms's Choral Compositions and His Library of Early Music.* Ann Arbor: UMI Research Press, 1983.

Hanslick, Eduard. *Am Ende des Jahrhunderts.* Berlin: Allgemeiner Verein für Deutsche Litteratur, 1899.

———. *Aus dem Tagebuche eines Musikers.* Berlin: Allgemeiner Verein für Deutsche Litteratur, 1892.

———. *Aus meinem Leben.* 2 vols. Berlin: Allgemeiner Verein für Deutsche Litteratur, 1894.

———. *Aus neuer und neuester Zeit.* Berlin: Allgemeiner Verein für Deutsche Litteratur, 1900.

———. *Concerte, Componisten und Virtuosen der letzten fünfzehn Jahre: 1870–1885.* Berlin: Allgemeiner Verein für Deutsche Litteratur, 1886.

———. *Fünf Jahre Musik (1891–1895).* Berlin: Allgemeiner Verein für Deutsche Litteratur, 1896.

———. *Geschichte des Concertwesens in Wien.* 2 vols. Vienna: Wilhelm Braumüller, 1869.

———. *Vom Musikalisch-Schönen: Ein Beitrag zur Revision der Ästhetik der Tonkunst.* 8th ed. Leipzig: Johann Ambrosius Barth, 1891.

Hansen, Matthias. *Anton Bruckner.* Leipzig: Philipp Reclam jun., 1987.

Harrison, Daniel. *Harmonic Function in Chromatic Music: A Renewed Dualist Theory and an Account of Its Precedents.* Chicago: University of Chicago Press, 1994.

Harten, Uwe, ed. *Anton Bruckner: Ein Handbuch.* Salzburg: Residenz Verlag, 1996.

Hauptmann, Moritz. *Die Natur der Harmonik und der Metrik: Zur Theorie der Musik.* Leipzig: Breitkopf und Härtel, 1853.

Held, Julius S. "Commentary." *Art Journal* 46 (1987): 127–133.

Heller, Friedrich C. "Die Zeit der Moderne." In *Von der Revolution 1848 zur Gegenwart,* vol. 3, *Musikgeschichte Österreichs,* edited by Rudolf Flotzinger and Gernot Gruber, 2nd ed., 91–172. Vienna: Böhlau Verlag, 1995.

Helm, Theodor. *Beethoven's Streichquartette: Versuch einer technischen Analyse dieser Werke im Zusammenhange mit ihrem geistigen Gehalt.* Leipzig: C. F. W. Siegel's Musikalienhandlung, 1885.

———. "Fünfzig Jahre Wiener Musikleben (1866–1916): Erinnerungen eines Musikkritikers." *Der Merker* 6–11 (1915–20).

Helmholtz, Hermann von. *On the Sensations of Tone as a Physiological Basis for the Theory of Music.* Translated by Alexander J. Ellis. London: Longmans, Green, 1875.

Henschel, George. *Personal Recollections of Johannes Brahms: Some of His Letters to and Pages from a Journal Kept by George Henschel.* Boston: Richard G. Badget, 1907.

Hepokoski, James. "The Dahlhaus Project and Its Extra-musicological Sources." *19th-Century Music* 14 (1991): 221–246.

Herwig [Eduard Pichl]. *Georg Schönerer und die Entwicklung des Alldeutschtumes in der Ostmark: Ein Lebensbild.* 4 vols. 1912–23; reprint, Oldenburg: Gerhard Stalling, 1938.

Heuberger, Richard. *Erinnerungen an Johannes Brahms: Tagebuchnotizen aus den Jahren 1875 bis 1897.* Edited by Kurt Hofmann. 2nd ed. Tutzing: Hans Schneider, 1976.

Hofmann, Kurt. *Die Bibliothek von Johannes Brahms: Bücher- und Musikalienverzeichnis.* Schriftenreihe zur Musik. Hamburg: Karl Dieter Wagner Verlag, 1974.

Hruby, Carl. *Meine Erinnerungen an Anton Bruckner.* Vienna: Friedrich Schalk's Verlag, 1901.

Jameson, Fredric. *Late Marxism: Adorno, or, The Persistence of the Dialectic.* London: Verso, 1990.

Jenner, Gustav. *Johannes Brahms als Mensch, Lehrer und Künstler: Studien und Erlebnisse.* Marburg in Hessen: N. C. Elevert, 1905.

Jordan, Roland, and Emma Kafalenos. "The Double Trajectory: Ambiguity in Brahms and Henry James." *19th-Century Music* 13 (1989): 129–144.

Judson, Pieter M. *Exclusive Revolutionaries: Liberal Politics, Social Experience, and National Identity in the Austrian Empire, 1848–1918.* Ann Arbor: University of Michigan Press, 1996.

Kalbeck, Max. *Johannes Brahms.* 4 vols. Vol. 1, 4th ed., 1921. Vol. 2, 3rd ed., 1921. Vol. 3, 2nd ed., 1912–13. Vol. 4, 2nd ed., 1915. Reprint, Tutzing: Hans Schneider, 1976.

Kann, Robert A. *The Multinational Empire.* 2 vols. New York: Columbia University Press, 1950.

Kannonier, Reinhard. *Zwischen Beethoven und Eisler: Zur Arbeitermusikbewegung in Österreich.* Vienna: Europaverlag, 1981.

Karnes, Kevin C. "Another Look at Critical Partisanship in the Viennese *fin de siècle:* Schenker's Reviews of Brahms's Vocal Music, 1891–92." *19th-Century Music* 26 (2002): 73–93.

Keiler, Allan. "Melody and Motive in Schenker's Earliest Writings." In *Critica musica: Essays in Honor of Paul Brainard,* edited by John Knowles, 169–191. Amsterdam: Gordon and Breach, 1996.

Kerman, Joseph. *The Beethoven Quartets.* New York: Norton, 1966.

Kirnberger, Johann Philipp. *The Art of Strict Musical Composition.* Translated by David Beach and Jurgen Thym. New Haven: Yale University Press, 1982.

Knauth, Paul. *Goethes Sprache und Stil im Alter.* Leipzig: Eduard Avenarius, 1898.

Kneif, Tibor. "Brahms—Ein bürgerlicher Künstler." In *Johannes Brahms: Leben und Werk,* edited by Christiane Jacobsen, 9–13. Wiesbaden: Breitkopf und Härtel, 1983.

Knepler, Georg. "Brahms historische und ästhetische Bedeutung." In *Johannes Brahms, oder, die Relativierung der 'absoluten' Musik,"* edited by Hanns-Werner Heister, 37–80. Hamburg: von Bockel Verlag, 1997.

Kobau, Ernst. *Die Wiener Symphoniker: Eine sozialgeschichtliche Studie.* Vienna: Böhlau Verlag, 1991.

Koch, Heinrich Christoph. *Introductory Essay on Composition: The Mechanical Rules of Melody, Sections 3 and 4.* Translated by Nancy Kovaleff Baker. New Haven: Yale University Press, 1983.

————. *Musikalisches Lexikon welches die theoretische und praktische Tonkunst, encyclopädisch bearbeitet, alle alten und neuen Kunstwörter erklärt, und die alten und neuen Instrumente beschrieben, enthält.* 2 vols. in 1. 1802; reprint, Hildesheim: Olms, 1964.

————. *Versuch einer Anleitung zur Composition.* Vol. 2. Leipzig: Adam Friedrich Böhme, 1787.

Köhler, Louis. *Johannes Brahms und seine Stellung in der Musikgeschichte.* Hannover: Verlag von Arnold Simon, 1880.

Kohlschmidt, Werner. "Die Problematik der Spätzeitlichkeit." In *Spätzeiten und Spätzeitlichkeit: Vorträge, gehalten auf dem II. Internationalen Germanistenkongreß 1960 in Kopenhagen,* edited by Werner Kohlschmidt, 16–26. Bern: Francke Verlag, 1962.

Korngold, Julius, ed. *Das Rosé Quartett: Fünfzig Jahre Kammermusik in Wien. Sämtliche Programme von 1. Quartett am 22. Januar 1883 bis April 1932.* Vienna: n.p., n.y.

Korstvedt, Benjamin M. *Anton Bruckner: Symphony No. 8.* New York: Cambridge University Press, 2000.

Koselleck, Reinhart, ed. *Bildungsbürgertum im 19. Jahrhundert.* Industrielle Welt 41. Stuttgart: Klett-Cotta, 1990.

Knauth, Paul. *Goethes Sprache und Stil im Alter.* Leipzig: Eduard Avenarius, 1898.

Křenek, Ernst. *Music Here and Now.* Translated by Barthold Fles. New York: Norton, 1939.

————. "Von der Würde der Abendländischen Musik" (1936). In *Zur Sprache gebracht: Essays über Musik,* 200–208. Munich: Albert Langen and Georg Müller, 1958.

Kropfinger, Klaus. *Wagner and Beethoven: Richard Wagner's Reception of Beethoven.* Translated by Peter Palmer. New York: Cambridge University Press, 1991.

Kross, Siegfried. *Johannes Brahms: Versuch einer kritischen Dokumentar-Biographie.* 2 vols. Bonn: Bouvier Verlag, 1997.

Kunze, Stefan. *Die Sinfonie im 18. Jahrhundert: Von der Opernsinfonie zur Konzertsinfonie.* Vol. 1. *Handbuch der musikalischen Gattungen.* Laaber: Laaber-Verlag, 1993.

Kurth, Ernst. *Bruckner.* 2 vols. Berlin: Max Hesse, 1925.

————. *Romantische Harmonik und ihre Krise in Wagners "Tristan."* 2nd ed. 1923; reprint, Hildesheim: Olms, 1968.

Laudon, Robert T. "The Debate about Consecutive Fifths: A Context for Brahms's Manuscript 'Oktaven und Quinten.'" *Music and Letters* 73 (1992): 48–61.

Leibnitz, Thomas. *Die Brüder Schalk und Anton Bruckner dargestellt an den Nachlaßbeständen der Musiksammlung der Österreichischen Nationalbibliothek.* Tutzing: Hans Schneider, 1988.

Lissa, Zofia. *Aufsätze zur Musikästhetik: Eine Auswahl.* Berlin: Henschelverlag, 1969.

Liszt, Franz. *Die Zigeuner und ihre Musik.* Vol. 6 of *Gesammelte Schriften.* Edited and translated by L. Ramann. Leipzig: Breitkopf und Härtel, 1883.

Louis, Rudolf. *Anton Bruckner.* Munich: George Müller, 1905.

————. *Die deutsche Musik der Gegenwart.* Munich: Georg Müller, 1909.

Luft, David. *Eros and Inwardness in Vienna.* Chicago: University of Chicago Press, 2003.

Lukács, Georg. *Die Grablegung des alten Deutschland: Essays zur deutschen Literatur des 19. Jahrhunderts.* Neuwied: Rowohlt, 1967.

————. *History and Class Consciousness: Studies in Marxist Dialectics.* Translated by Rodney Livingstone. London: Merlin Press, 1971.

————. *Die Theorie des Romans: Ein geschichtsphilosophischer Versuch über die Formen der großen Epik.* Munich: Deutscher Taschenbuch Verlag, 1994.

————. *The Theory of the Novel: A Historico-Philosophical Essay on the Forms of Great Epic Literature.* Translated by Anna Bostock. Cambridge, Mass.: MIT Press, 1971.

MacDonald, Malcolm. *Brahms.* New York: Schirmer Books, 1990.

Mahlert, Ulrich. *Fortschritt und Kunstlied: Späte Lieder Robert Schumann im Licht der liedästhetischen Diskussion ab 1848.* Munich: E. Katzbichler, 1983.

Marpurg, Friedrich Wilhelm. *Handbuch bei dem Generalbasse und der Composition.* 3 vols. Berlin: J. J. Schützens Wittwe, 1755–58.

Marx, Adolf Bernhard. *Gluck und die Oper.* 2 vols. Berlin: O. Janke, 1863.

———. *Ludwig van Beethoven: Leben und Schaffen.* 2 vols. in 1. 1859; reprint, Hildesheim: Olms, 1979.

Mason, Daniel Gregory. *The Chamber Music of Brahms.* New York: Macmillan, 1933.

Mast, Paul. "Brahms's Study, *Octaven u. Quinten u. A.:* With Schenker's Commentary Translated." *Music Forum* 5 (1980): 1–196.

McColl, Sandra. "A Model German." *Musical Times* 138 (March 1997): 7–12.

———. *Music Criticism in Vienna, 1896–1897: Critically Moving Forms.* Oxford: Clarendon Press, 1996.

McGrath, William J. *Dionysian Art and Populist Politics in Austria.* New Haven: Yale University Press, 1974.

Mersmann, Hans. "Alterswerke der Kunst." In *Lebensraum der Musik: Aufsätze–Ansprachen,* 118–122. Rodenkirchen: P. J. Tonger Musikverlag, 1964.

———. *Deutsche Romantik.* Vol. 3 of *Die Kammermusik.* Leipzig: Breitkopf und Härtel, 1930.

Mitis, Oskar von. *Das Leben des Kronprinzen Rudolf mit Briefen und Schriften aus dessen Nachlass.* Edited by Adam Wandruszka. Vienna: Herold, 1971.

Mitschka, Arno. "Der Sonatensatz in den Werken von Johannes Brahms." Inaugural-diss., Johannes-Gutenberg-Universität zu Mainz, 1961.

Müller, Ruth E. *Erzählte Töne: Studien zur Musikästhetik im späten 18. Jahrhundert.* Beihefte zum Archiv für Musikwissenschaft 30. Stuttgart: Steiner Verlag Wiesbaden, 1989.

Musgrave, Michael. *A Brahms Reader.* New Haven: Yale University Press, 2000.

———. *The Music of Brahms.* Oxford: Clarendon Press, 1994.

Nautz, Jürgen, and Richard Vahrenkamp, eds. *Die Wiener Jahrhundertwende: Einflüsse, Umwelt, Wirkungen.* Vienna: Böhlau Verlag, 1993.

Nelson, Thomas K. "Brahms's Fantasies: In Accorde with Max Klinger." *American Brahms Society Newsletter* 18/1 (spring 2000): 1–5, and 18/2 (fall 2000): 4–7.

Neuberger, Max. *Hermann Nothnagel: Leben und Wirken eines deutschen Klinikers.* Vienna: Rikola Verlag, 1922.

Neuß, C[arl], and Dr. Johann Kaiser. *Chronik der Wiener evangelischen Gemeinde Augsburger Bekenntnisses vom Zeitpunkte ihrer Entstehung bis auf die Gegenwart.* Vienna: Theodor Daberkow's Verlag, 1904.

Nicholsen, Shierry Weber. *Exact Imagination, Late Work: On Adorno's Aesthetics.* Cambridge, Mass.: MIT Press, 1997.

Niemann, Walter. *Brahms.* Berlin: Schuster und Loeffler, 1920.

———. *Die Musik der Gegenwart und der letzten Vergangenheit bis zu den Romantikern, Klassizisten und Neudeutschen.* Stuttgart: Schuster und Loeffler, 1913.

Niemöller, Klaus Wolfgang. "Spätstilaspekte." In *Festschrift Arno Forchert zum 60. Geburtstag am 29. Dezember 1985,* edited by Gerhard Allroggen and Detlef Altenburg, 175–183. Kassel: Bärenreiter, 1986.

Nohl, Ludwig. *Die geschichtliche Entwickelung der Kammermusik und ihre Bedeutung für den Musiker.* Braunschweig: Friedrich Vieweg und Söhne, 1885.

Notley, Margaret. "Brahms as Liberal: Genre, Style, and Politics in Late Nineteenth-Century Vienna." *19th-Century Music* 17 (1993): 107–123.

———. "Bruckner and Viennese Wagnerism." In *Bruckner Studies,* edited by Paul Hawkshaw and Timothy L. Jackson, 54–71. New York: Cambridge University Press, 1997.

———. "Discourse and Allusion: The Chamber Music of Brahms." In *Nineteenth-Century Chamber Music,* edited by Stephen E. Hefling, 242–286. New York: Schirmer Books, 1998.

————. "Formal Process as Spiritual Progress: The Symphonic Slow Movements." In *The Cambridge Companion to Bruckner,* edited by John Williamson, 186–200. New York: Cambridge University Press, 2004.

————. "Late-Nineteenth-Century Chamber Music and the Cult of the Classical Adagio." *19th-Century Music* 23 (1999): 33–61.

————. "Musical Culture in Vienna at the Turn of the Twentieth Century." In *Schoenberg, Berg, and Webern: A Companion to the Second Viennese School,* edited by Bryan R. Simms, 37–71. Westport, Conn.: Greenwood Press, 1999.

————. "Plagal Harmony as Other: Asymmetrical Dualism in Instrumental Music by Brahms." *Journal of Musicology* 22 (2005): 90–130.

————. "Quartet No. 2 for Piano, Violin, Viola, and Cello in A Major, Opus 26." In *The Compleat Brahms: A Guide to the Musical Works of Johannes Brahms,* edited by Leon Botstein, 119–121. New York: Norton, 1999.

————. "*Volksconcerte* in Vienna and Late Nineteenth-Century Ideology of the Symphony." *Journal of the American Musicological Society* 50 (1997): 421–454.

Nowak, Leopold. "Form und Rhythmus im ersten Satz des Streichquintetts von Anton Bruckner." In *Festschrift Hans Engel zum siebzigsten Geburtstag,* edited by Horst Heussner, 260–273. Kassel: Bärenreiter, 1964.

Orel, Alfred. "Ein eigenhändiges Werkverzeichnis von Johannes Brahms: Ein wichtiger Beitrag zur Brahmsforschung." *Die Musik* 29 (1936–37): 529–541.

Paddison, Max. *Adorno's Aesthetics of Music.* New York: Cambridge University Press, 1993.

Paumgartner, Bernhard. "Das instrumentale Ensemble." In *Musica aeterna: Eine Darstellung des Musikschaffen aller Zeiten und Völker, unter besonderer Berücksichtigung des Musiklebens der Schweiz und desjenigen unserer Tage,* edited by Gottfried Schmid, 2 vols., 2:11–118. Zurich: Max S. Metz, 1950.

Paupié, Kurt. *Handbuch der österreichischen Pressegeschichte 1848–1959.* 2 vols. Vienna: Wilhelm Braumüller, 1960.

Pederson, Sanna. "Romantic Music under Siege in 1848." In *Music Theory in the Age of Romanticism,* edited by Ian Bent, 57–74. New York: Cambridge University Press, 1996.

Perger, Richard von, and Robert Hirschfeld. *Geschichte der k. k. Gesellschaft der Wien.* 2 vols. Vienna: Adolf Holzhausen, 1912.

Pinter, Charlotte. "Ludwig Speidel als Musikkritiker." 3 vols. Ph.D. diss., University of Vienna, 1949.

Pisk, Paul A. "Zur Soziologie der Musik." *Der Kampf* 18 (1925): 184–187.

Porges, Heinrich. *Die Aufführung von Beethoven's Neunter Symphonie unter Richard Wagner in Bayreuth (22. Mai 1872).* Leipzig: C. F. Kahnt, 1872.

Prosl, Robert Maria. *Die Hellmesberger: Hundert Jahre aus dem Leben einer Wiener Musikerfamilie.* Vienna: Gerlach und Wiedling, 1947.

Pulzer, Peter. *The Rise of Political Anti-Semitism in Germany and Austria.* Rev. ed. Cambridge, Mass.: Harvard University Press, 1988.

Rehberg, Willi. "Brahms-Erinnerungen." *Der Weihergarten: Beilage zu Melos* (July/October 1933): 25–26.

Reich, Willi. *Alban Berg: Mit Bergs eigenen Schriften und Beiträgen von Theodor Wiesengrund-Adorno und Ernst Křenek.* Vienna: H. Reichner, 1957.

Reimer, Erich. "Kammermusik." In *Handwörterbuch für musikalischen Terminologie,* edited by Hans Heinrich Eggebrecht. Wiesbaden: Franz Steiner, 1971.

Reiter, Elisabeth. *Sonatensatz in der späten Kammermusik von Brahms: Einheit und Zusammenhang in variativen Verfahren.* Tutzing: Hans Schneider, 2000.

Riehl, W[ilhelm] H[einrich]. *Culturstudien aus drei Jahrhunderten.* Stuttgart: J. G. Cotta, 1859.

Riemann, Hugo. *Musik-Lexikon.* 3rd ed. Leipzig: Max Hesse, 1887.

———. *Präludien und Studien: Gesammelte Aufsätze zur Aesthetik, Theorie und Geschichte der Musik.* 2 vols. in 3. Wiesbaden: Kraus Reprint, 1976.

Rosand, David. "Editor's Statement: Style and the Aging Artist." *Art Journal* 46 (1987): 91–93.

Rosen, Charles. *Sonata Forms.* Rev. ed. New York: Norton, 1988.

Said, Edward. "Thoughts on Late Style." *London Review of Books,* 5 August 2004, 3–7.

Salzer, Felix, and Carl Schachter. *Counterpoint in Composition: The Study of Voice Leading.* New York: McGraw-Hill, 1969.

Sárosi, Bálint. *Folk Music: Hungarian Musical Idiom.* Translated by Maria Steiner. Budapest: Corvina Press, 1986.

———. *Gypsy Music.* Translated by Fred Macnicol. Budapest: Corvina Press, 1978.

Schapiro, Meyer. *Theory and Philosophy of Art: Style, Artist, and Society.* New York: Braziller, 1994.

Schenker, Heinrich. *Beethoven's Ninth Symphony: A Portrayal of Its Musical Content, with Running Commentary on Performance and Literature as Well.* Translated by John Rothgeb. New Haven: Yale University Press, 1992.

———. "Erinnerungen an Brahms." *Der Kunstwart* 46 (May 1933): 475–482.

———. *Free Composition (Der freie Satz): Volume 3 of New Musical Theories and Fantasies.* Translated and edited by Ernst Oster. 2 vols. New York: Longman, 1979.

———. *Heinrich Schenker als Essayist und Kritiker: Gesammelte Aufsätze, Rezensionen und kleinere Berichte aus den Jahren 1891–1901.* Edited by Hellmut Federhofer. Hildesheim: Olms, 1990.

Schering, Arnold. "Brahms und seine Stellung in der Musikgeschichte des 19. Jahrhunderts." *Jahrbuch der Musikbibliothek Peters für 1932,* 9–22. Leipzig: C. F. Peters, 1933.

———. "Über den Begriff des Monumentalen in der Musik." *Jahrbuch der Musikbibliothek Peters für 1935,* 9–24. Leipzig: C. F. Peters, 1936.

Schick, Hartmut. *Studien zu Dvořáks Streichquartetten.* Laaber: Laaber-Verlag, 1990.

Schilling, Ulrike. *Philipp Spitta: Leben und Wirken im Spiegel seiner Briefwechsel: Mit einem Inventar des Nachlasses und einer Bibliographie der gedruckten Werke.* Kassel: Bärenreiter, 1994.

Schmalfeldt, Janet. "Form as the Process of Becoming: The Beethoven-Hegelian Tradition and the 'Tempest' Sonata." *Beethoven Forum* 4 (1995): 37–71.

Schmidt, Christian Martin. *Johannes Brahms und seine Zeit.* 2nd ed. Laaber: Laaber-Verlag, 1998.

Schoenberg, Arnold. *Fundamentals of Composition.* Edited by Gerald Strang and Leonard Stein. London: Faber and Faber, 1970.

———. *The Musical Idea and the Logic, Technique, and Art of Its Presentation.* Edited and translated and with a commentary by Patricia Carpenter and Severine Neff. New York: Columbia University Press, 1995.

———. "The Orchestral Variations, Op. 31: A Radio Talk." *Score* 26 (July 1960): 27–40.

———. *Style and Idea: Selected Writings of Arnold Schoenberg.* Edited by Leonard Stein and translated by Leo Black. Berkeley: University of California Press, 1984.

———. "Vortrag, zu halten in Frankfurt am Main am 12. II. 1933." Translated by Thomas McGeary. *Journal of the Arnold Schoenberg Institute* 15/2 (November 1992): 22–90.

Schopenhauer, Arthur. "Das ästhetische Wohlgefallen: Das Schöne und das Erhabene." In *Arthur Schopenhauer: Schriften über Musik,* edited by Karl Stabenow, 77–89. Regensburg: Bosse, 1922.

Schorske, Carl E. *Fin-de-Siècle Vienna: Politics and Culture.* New York: Vintage Books, 1981.

———. *Thinking with History: Explorations in the Passage to Modernism.* Princeton, N.J.: Princeton University Press, 1998.

Schreiber, Ulrich. "Kunst als spätzeitliche Selbstobjektivation des Menschen: Carlo Gesualdo und das Problem anachronistischer Spätwerk." *Hifi Stereophonie: Musik-Musikwiedergabe* 14/5 (1975): 470, 472, 474–475.

Seidl, Arthur. *Vom Musikalisch-Erhabenen: Prolegomena zur Aesthetik der Tonkunst.* Leipzig: C. F. Kahnt Nachfolger, 1887.

Seidl, Johann Wilhelm. *Musik und Austromarxismus: Zur Musikrezeption der österreichischen Arbeiterbewegung im späten Kaiserreich und in der Ersten Republik.* Vienna: Böhlau Verlag, 1989.

Shreffler, Anne C. "Berlin Walls: Dahlhaus, Knepler, and Ideologies of Music History." *Journal of Musicology* 20 (2003): 498–525.

Simmel, Georg. *Goethe.* Leipzig: von Klinkhardt und Biermann, 1913.

Smith, Peter H. "Brahms and the Neapolitan Complex: Flat-II, Flat-VI, and Their Multiple Functions in the First Movement of the F-Minor Clarinet Sonata." In *Brahms Studies,* edited by David Brodbeck, 2:169–208. Lincoln: University of Nebraska Press, 1998.

———. "Brahms and the Shifting Barline: Metric Displacement and Formal Process in the Trios with Wind Instruments." In *Brahms Studies,* edited by David Brodbeck, 3:191–230. Lincoln: University of Nebraska Press, 2001.

———. "Brahms and Subject/Answer Rhetoric." *Music Analysis* 20 (2001): 193–236.

———."Liquidation, Augmentation, and Brahms's Recapitulatory Overlaps," *19th-Century Music* 17 (1994): 237–261.

Solie, Ruth A. "The Living Work: Organicism and Musical Analysis." *19th-Century Music* 4 (1980): 147–156.

———. "Metaphor and Model in the Analysis of Melody." Ph.D. diss., University of Chicago, 1977.

Solomon, Maynard. *Beethoven.* 2nd ed. New York: Schirmer Books, 1998.

———. *Beethoven Essays.* Cambridge, Mass.: Harvard University Press, 1988.

Specht, Richard. *Johannes Brahms.* Translated by Eric Blom. New York: Dutton, 1930.

Stern, Fritz. *The Politics of Cultural Despair: A Study in the Rise of the Germanic Ideology.* Berkeley: University of California Press, 1961.

Sturke, August. *Der Stil in Johannes Brahms' Werken: Eine stilkritische Untersuchung seiner Klavier-, Kammermusik-, Chor- und Orchesterwerke.* Würzburg: Konrad Triltsch, 1932.

Subotnik, Rose Rosengard. *Developing Variations: Style and Ideology in Western Music.* Minneapolis: University of Minnesota Press, 1991.

Sulzer, Johann Georg, and Heinrich Christoph Koch. *Aesthetics and the Art of Musical Composition in the German Enlightenment: Selected Writings of Johann Georg Sulzer and Heinrich Christoph Koch.* Edited by Nancy Kovaleff Baker and Thomas Christensen. New York: Cambridge University Press, 1995.

Tappert, Wilhelm. *Das Verbot der Quinten-Parallelen: Eine monographische Studie.* Leipzig: Heinrich Matthes, 1869.

Tietze, Hans. "Earliest and Latest Works of Great Artists." *Gazette des Beaux-Arts* 26 (1944): 273–284.

Tovey, Donald Francis. *The Main Stream of Music and Other Essays.* Cleveland: Meridian Books, 1959.

Urbantschitsch, Viktor. "Die Entwicklung der Sonatenform bei Brahms." *Studien zur Musikwissenschaft* 14 (1927): 265–285.

Valjavec, Fritz. *Der Josephinismus: Zur geistigen Entwicklung Österreichs im 18. und 19. Jahrhundert.* Brno: R. M. Rohrer, 1944.

Vetter, Walther. "Das Adagio bei Anton Bruckner." *Deutsche Musikkultur* 5 (1940–1): 121–132.

Vogel, [Adolf] Bernhard. *Johannes Brahms: Sein Lebensgang und eine Würdigung seiner Werke.* Leipzig: Max Hesse's Verlag, 1888.

Vogel, Martin, ed. *Beiträge zur Musiktheorie des 19. Jahrhunderts.* Regensburg: Gustav Bosse Verlag, 1966.

————. *Die Lehre von den Tonbeziehungen.* Bonn: Verlag für Musikwissenschaft, 1975.

Wagner, Cosima. *Cosima Wagner's Diaries.* Edited by Martin Gregor-Dellin and Dietrich Mack. Translated by Geoffrey Skelton. 2 vols. New York: Harcourt, Brace, Jovanovich, 1978–80.

Wagner, Manfred. *Bruckner: Leben-Werke-Dokumente.* Mainz: Schott, 1983.

Wagner, Richard. *Gesammelte Schriften und Dichtungen.* 3rd ed. 10 vols. Leipzig: C. F. W. Siegel, 1897.

————. *Oper und Drama.* Edited by Klaus Kropfinger. Stuttgart: Reclam, 1984.

Weber, Max. *The Rational and Social Foundations of Music.* Translated and edited by Don Martindale, Johannes Rieder, and Gertrude Neuwirth. Carbondale, Ill.: Southern Illinois University Press, 1958.

————. *Die rationalen und soziologischen Grundlagen der Musik.* 2nd ed. Munich: Drei Masken Verlag, 1924.

Weber, William. "A Myth of Musical Vienna." In *International Musicological Society: Report of the Twelfth Congress, Berkeley, 1977,* edited by Daniel Heartz and Bonnie Wade, 314–315. Kassel: Bärenreiter, 1981.

Webster, James. "Schubert's Sonata Form and Brahms's First Maturity (II)." *19th-Century Music* 3 (1979): 52–71.

Weitzmann, Carl Friedrich. *Harmoniesystem.* Leipzig: C. F. Kahnt, 1860.

————. *Die neue Harmonielehre im Streit mit der alten, mit einer musikalischen Beilage: Albumblätter zur Emancipation der Quinten, Anthologie klassischer Quintenparallelen.* Leipzig: C. F. Kahnt, 1861.

Whiteside, Andrew G. *The Socialism of Fools: Georg Ritter von Schönerer and Austrian Pan-Germanism.* Berkeley: University of California Press, 1975.

Wiener Philharmoniker: 1842–1942. 2 vols. in 1. Vienna: n.p., 1942.

Wind, Hans E. [Kurt Blaukopf]. *Die Endkrise der bürgerlichen Musik und die Rolle Arnold Schönbergs.* Vienna: Krystall-Verlag, 1935.

Winterfeld, Carl. *Johannes Gabrieli und sein Zeitalter.* 3 vols. Berlin: Schlesinger, 1834.

Wiora, Walter. "Über den religiösen Gehalt in Bruckners Symphonien." In *Religiöse Musik in nicht-liturgischen Werken von Beethoven bis Reger,* edited by Günther Massenkeil, Klaus Wolfgang Niemöller, and Walter Wiora, 157–184. Regensburg: Gustav Bosse, 1978.

Wistrich, Robert S. *The Jews of Vienna in the Age of Franz Joseph.* New York: Oxford University Press, 1989.

Wolf, Hugo. *Hugo Wolfs musikalische Kritiken im Auftrage des Wiener Akademischen Wagner-Vereins.* Edited by Richard Batka and Heinrich Werner. Leipzig: Breitkopf und Härtel, 1911.

————. *The Music Criticism of Hugo Wolf.* Edited and translated by Henry Pleasants. New York: Holmes and Meier, 1979.

Wolzogen, Hans von. *Erinnerungen an Richard Wagner: Ein Vortrag, gehalten am 13 April 1883 im wissenschaftlichen Club zu Wien.* Edited by the Wiener Akademischer Wagner-Verein [Viennese Academic Wagner Society]. Vienna: Verlag von Carl Konegan, 1883.

Wotawa, Dr. August Ritter von. *Der Deutsche Schulverein 1880–1905: Ein Gedenkschrift im Auftrage der Vereinsleitung.* Vienna: Verlag des Deutschen Schulvereins, 1905.

Zöllner, Erich, ed. *Öffentliche Meinung in der Geschichte Österreichs.* Vienna: Österreichischer Bundesverlag, 1979.

Zuckerkandl, Berta Szeps. *My Life and History.* Translated by John Sommerfield. New York: Knopf, 1939.

Zweig, Stefan. *The World of Yesterday: An Autobiography.* New York: Viking Press, 1943.

Autograph Materials Cited

Gesellschaft der Musikfreunde, Vienna: Johannes Brahms

Abschriften. Copies of vocal pieces by Hans Leo Hassler, Jacob Regnart, and Christoph
    Demant.
Autograph score of Cello Sonata in F Major.
Autograph score of Clarinet Quintet.
Octaven u. Quinten u. A.
Sketches for Clarinet Sonata in F Minor.
Undated letter to William Kupfer.

Handschriftensammlung, Wiener Stadt- und Landesbibliothek, Vienna

Celestine Truxa Collection
Johannes Brahms, "Schöne Gedanken über Musik. Heft II: Schatzkästlein des jungen
    Kreisler." Ia 79562

Pierpont Morgan Library, New York: Johannes Brahms

Autograph score of Two-Piano Sonata in F Minor. Cary 4.
Autograph score of Clarinet Sonata in F Minor. Robert Owen Lehmann Collection, on
    deposit.

Reports by Viennese Organizations

Jahresberichte

Asylverein für Obdachlose in Wien
Rudolfiner-Verein
Verein zur Abwehr des Antisemitismus
Wiener Akademischer Richard Wagner-Verein
Wiener Konzertverein

Mitteilungen

Deutscher Schulverein

Nineteenth- and Early Twentieth-Century Newspapers and Journals Cited

Allgemeine Musikalische Zeitung
Arbeiter-Zeitung
Deutsche Kunst- und Musik-Zeitung
Deutsche Musik-Zeitung
Deutsches Volksblatt
Deutsche Worte
Deutsche Zeitung
Freies Blatt
Fremden-Blatt
Illustrirtes Wiener Extrablatt

Der Kampf: Sozialdemokratische Monatsschrift
Kastner's Wiener Musikalische Zeitung
Der Merker
Montags-Revue
Musikalische Rundschau
Musikalisches Wochenblatt
Neue Freie Presse
Neue Zeitschrift für Musik
Neue Wiener Musik-Zeitung
Neues Wiener Tagblatt
Ostdeutsche Rundschau
Pester Lloyd
Die Presse
Sonn- und Montags-Zeitung
Unverfälschte Deutsche Worte
Vierteljahrsschrift für Musikwissenschaft
Wiener Abendpost
Wiener Tagblatt
Wiener Allgemeine Zeitung
Wiener Sonn- und Montags Zeitung
Wiener Zeitung

INDEX

Printed in the USA/Agawam, MA
March 18, 2015

10805.003